HINDU TRIBES AND CASTES AS REPRESENTED IN BENARAS

HINDU TRIBES AND CASTES AS REPRESENTED IN BENARAS

WITH ILLUSTRATIONS

M. A. SHERRING

GYAN

Published by

Gyan Publishing House
5, Ansari Road
Daryaganj, New Delhi-110002
Phone: 011-47034999, 9811692060
E-mail: books@gyanbooks.com

Distribution Network
gyanbooks.com
India, USA, Canada, UK, Australia, France

ISBN : 978-81-212-3481-8 (PB)
First Published, London, 1872

2nd Impression 2020

Printed at: Gyan Press, Delhi.

Hindu Tribes and Castes As Represented in Benaras
Author: M. A. Sherring

HINDU

TRIBES AND CASTES,

AS REPRESENTED IN

BENARES.

BY THE

Rev. M. A. SHERRING, M.A., LL.B., Lond.;

AUTHOR OF "THE SACRED CITY OF THE HINDUS," &c., &c.

"Homo sum; humani nihil a me alienum puto."

WITH ILLUSTRATIONS.

CALCUTTA:
THACKER, SPINK & CO.,

BOMBAY:
THACKER, VINING & CO.

LONDON:
TRUBNER AND Co.

1872.

PREFACE.

THIS work is of a practical character, and professes to be a description of the actual circumstances of the castes and tribes, of which it treats. No one can be more alive to the difficulty of the task he has undertaken than the writer himself. Although he has striven to make the work as complete as possible, he is deeply conscious of the imperfectness of his achievement. It has appeared to him strange that hitherto no one has attempted to give in English a consecutive and detailed account of the castes of India. The author has endeavoured to present an outline of them as existing in Benares, the religious and social metropolis of India, in the hope that other persons in various parts of the country will investigate the subject and add their quota to the enterprise until it be completed.

Undoubtedly, Benares is a very favourable spot for the commencement of a work of this nature. First or last, representatives from all the tribes of India come up to the sacred city. Perhaps no city in the world draws to itself such a motley assemblage of tribes and tongues. Much information, more or less trustworthy, has thus been collected in Benares respecting races whose haunts are in remote regions of India. Nevertheless, the dissertations in this work relating to them must be regarded as simply tentative. Many persons who have made certain castes and races their special study would doubtless wish for fuller statements about them than have been given here. Those who have published their views will find their writings referred to; so that the reader may, if he chooses, investigate them more thoroughly. Such as have not made public their researches, are earnestly requested to do so without delay. It should be borne in mind that the object of the author has been to gather together in one all the Hindu families with which he was acquainted. A critic, living in other parts of the land, would very likely be able to show the incompleteness of his performance; and indeed in Benares itself, in spite of his vigilance, it is not improbable that some castes, where the aggregate number is so great, have escaped his notice.

To his numerous native friends, the author makes the observation, that they must not imagine that because he has described their peculiar institution of caste in some of its divisions and ramifications, he has done so out of admiration or even respect for it. He feels for it neither the one nor the other; but regards it as a monstrous engine of pride, dissension, and shame, which could only have been invented in an utterly diseased condition of human society. Moreover, his intense conviction is, that, next to the universal prevalence of the Christian faith, the greatest boon to India would be the absolute and complete renunciation of caste. The author has pourtrayed the institution as a phase of humanity, and because he considers that every aspect of human society, even the most distorted and ugly, should be fairly represented and fully understood.

"Homo sum; humani nihil a me alienum puto."

CONTENTS.

LIST OF ILLUSTRATIONS.

HINDU

TRIBES AND CASTES.

INTRODUCTION.

WHILE Brahmanical families in early times preserved, with great and unremitting care, the purity of their race, nevertheless, it is plain, from the statements of Manu, that many new tribes were continually being created by the intercourse of Brahmans with women of other castes. For instance, a son of a Brahman married to a woman of the Vaisya caste, was called Ambashtha, or Vaidya; and a Brahman's son of a Sudra wife was called Nishâda, and also Pârasava (*a*). The same origin is assigned by the Dharmâ Purâna to the Varajîvî, or astrologer (*b*); and by the Tantra, to the Brahme-sudra (*c*). From the marriage of a Brahman with a Kshatriya woman, according to the same Purâna, have sprung the Kumbhakâra, or potter, and Tantravâya, or weaver (*d*); and from a Brahman husband and Vaisya wife, the Kansakâra, or brazier, and the Sankhakâra, or worker in shells (*e*). Again, Manu states, that the male progeny of Brahman husbands and Kshatriya wives occupied a rank between the two, and were termed Mûrdhâbhishikta, Mâhishya, and Karana, or Kayastha (*f*). These were not illicit connexions, but connexions of marriage, recognized as such by all classes, and regarded as honourable and right. The only difference between them and marriages of Brahmans with Brahman women was, that the children of the latter marriages continued in the same caste as both their parents, and therefore possessed, socially and legally, far greater privileges than children of the other marriages.

A Brahman could be married to women taken from all four of the prime castes,—that is to say, he might have, for example, four wives, the first taken from the Brahmanical caste, the second from the Kshatriya caste, the third from the Vaisya caste, the fourth from the Sudra caste (*g*). The sons of these wives inherited differently. The son of the Brahmani wife received four parts out of ten of the inheritance; the son of the Kshatriya wife, three; the son of the Vaisya wife, two; and the son of the Sudra, one (*h*). But it is specially added, in regard to the son of a Sudra woman and Brahman father, he could inherit nothing unless his mother had been *lawfully married* to his father; and the same observation is

(*a*) Manu, Chap. X., 8.

(*b*) Colebrooke's Essays, p. 272.

(*c*) *Ibid.*

(*d*) *Ibid.*

(*e*) Colebrooke's Essays, p. 272.

(*f*) Manu, Chap. X., 6.

(*g*) Manu, Chap. IX., 149.

(*h*) *Ibid*, 153.

made likewise respecting the son of a Sudra woman and a Kshatriya or Vaisya father (*a*). This relationship subsisting between husband and wife of two different, not to say widely separated, castes, was not held to be disgraceful or worthy of denunciation. On the contrary, while it was less dignified for a Brahman to marry a woman of a lower caste than a woman of his own, yet marriage in the one case was just as legal as marriage in the other.

But it was not the peculiar privilege of the Brahman to solicit the hand of a woman of another caste. The same privilege was enjoyed by members of all the higher castes in regard to castes beneath them. Indeed, apparently, there was no such rigid restriction in those early ages on intermarriages like that which exists among the castes at the present day. It was considered to be improper for men of the superior castes to take their first wives from any caste except their own; but their other wives might be taken from the lower castes with propriety. It is explicitly stated by Manu, that a Vaisya man might take a Vaisya, and also a Sudra, woman, to be his wives; and a Kshatriya man might take a Kshatriya, a Vaisya, and a Sudra woman, for his wives (*b*). From the union of a Kshatriya husband with a Sudra sprang the Ugra, the Nâpita, or barber, and the Maudaka, or confectioner (*c*). The Tambuli, or betel seller, and the Tanlika, were, says the Dharmâ Purâna, the fruit of the union of Vaisya men with Sudra women (*d*).

Moreover, many castes have originated from the marriage of men with women of castes higher than their own. Some of these connexions are spoken of with strong disapprobation; nevertheless, they were permitted, and the law gave them its protection. The Sûta came from a Kshatriya husband and Brahmani wife; and the Mâgadha and Vaidiha, from the union of a Vaisya with a Brahmani (*e*). From a Sudra father and Brahmani mother, the Chandâla was born. The Kshatri or Kshatta sprang from a Sudra and Kshatriya woman; the Ayogava from a Sudra and a Vaisya woman; the Karmakâra, or smith, and Dâsa, or sailor, from the union of Sudras with Kshatriya women (*f*). "The Jâtimâlâ," says Mr. Colebrooke, "expressly states the number of forty-two mixed classes, springing from the intercourse of a man of inferior with a woman of superior class" (*g*).

Other castes were formed by the marriage of members of the four castes with members of the irregular castes. The offspring of a Brahman and an Ugra woman was an Avrita; of a Brahman and an Ambastha woman, an Abhîra; and of a Brahman and an Ayogava woman, a Dhigvana (*h*). The Pukkasa caste came from the son of a Sudra woman and a Nishâda husband; and the Kukkutaka caste, from the son of a Nishâda woman by a Sudra husband (*i*).

New castes were created likewise by the intermarriage of the irregular castes. It is manifest that these latter tribes soon fell into the habits of their progenitors, and not only

(*a*) Manu, Chap. IX., 155.
(*b*) Manu, Chap. III., 13.
(*c*) Colebrooke's Essays, p. 273.
(*d*) *Ibid.*
(*e*) Manu, Chap. X., 11.
(*f*) Colebrooke's Essays, p. 274.
(*g*) *Ibid*, 274, 275.
(*h*) Manu, Chap. X., 15.
(*i*) *Ibid*, 18.

established themselves in separate castes, but endeavoured to keep such castes pure by removing from their midst the issue of marriages between themselves and women of other castes, or between the members of one irregular caste and the members of other irregular castes. Hence a further sub-division of tribes. The son of a Kshatri man and an Ugra woman became a Swapâka; and the son of a Vaidiha man and an Ambastha woman became a Vena (*a*). Again, from the union of a Vaidiha with an Ayogava woman, came the Maitrîyaka caste; of a Nishâda with an Ayogava woman, the Mârgava, or Dâsa, called also, says Manu, Kaivarta, by people dwelling in Arya-varta; of a Nishâda with a Vaidiha woman, the Kârâvera; of a Vaidiha with a Kârâvera woman, the Andhra; of a Vaidiha with a Nishâda woman, the Mîda; of a Chandâla with a Vaidiha woman, the Pândusopâkâ; of a Nishâda with a Vaidiha woman, the Ahindika; of a Chandâla with a Pukkasa woman, the Sopâka; of a Chandâla with a Nishâda woman, the Antyâvasâyin; and of a Dasya, one of the aboriginal tribes, with an Ayogava woman, the Sairindhra (*b*).

Many castes were also created by persons driven from their own tribes through the infraction or non-performance of caste rules. Sons born of Brahman parents, failing to perform the assigned ceremonies on being invested with the Brahmanical cord, or in any other way breaking the rules of their order, became outcasts, were debarred from the privilege of the *gayatri*, and were styled Vrâtyas. From them sprang castes designated Bhûrjakantaka, Avantya, Vâtadhâna, Pushpadha, and Saikha (*c*). Similarly, outcasts from the Kshatriya tribe founded the following castes: Jhalla, Malla, Nichhivi, Nata, Karana, Khasa, and Drâvira (*d*). From outcasts of the Vaisya tribe sprang the Sudhanwan, Chârya, Kârusha, Vijanman, Maitra, and Sâtwata castes (*e*).

Inattention to religious duties, or neglect of Brahmans, was evidently, in those days of punctilious ceremonies and priestly domination, sufficient reason for expulsion from caste. No fewer than twelve castes are stated by Manu to owe their origin to persons ejected from the Kshatriya tribe alone, for the reasons just given. They are as follows: Paundraka, Udra, Drâvira, Kâmboja, Yavana, Saka, Pârada, Pahlava, Chîna, Kirâta, Derada, and Khasa (*f*).

Had the creation of new castes continued to be made in succeeding ages with the same ease and rapidity as they were in these earlier times, it is plain that the caste system would have destroyed itself, in two ways,—first, by the multiplication of new castes throughout the land, and, secondly, by the intermarriages of all the castes. The increased strictures imposed upon the castes, especially upon the primary ones, and the prohibition of irregular marriages,—that is, of marriages of members of one caste with members of another,—gave in later years strength and vitality to a system which otherwise must soon have become extinguished. At what epoch this fundamental change in its constitution was made, is not known, but it is a question worthy of thorough investigation.

(*a*) Manu, Chap. X., 19.
(*b*) *Ibid*, 32—39.
(*c*) *Ibid*, 20, 21.
(*d*) Manu, Chap. X., 22.
(*e*) *Ibid*, 23.
(*f*) *Ibid*, 43, 44.

The clear and explicit statements of Manu are decisive on the causes of the multiplication of castes in his day. Indeed, it is evident that some of the lowest castes, perhaps many, were in part derived from the highest. The Chandâla, for instance, although held in abomination by all the tribes, simply because his Sudra father was fortunate enough to marry a Brahman woman, was in reality half a Brahman. The Ugra, too, who is depicted as a man of ferocious bearing, cruel and mean, was nevertheless half a Kshatriya, but, in public estimation, belonged to a debased tribe. If the existing low-caste races of India are, for the most part, as some suppose, the descendants and representatives of degraded castes created as above described, it must then in fairness be acknowledged, that many of them are more or less tinctured with either Brahmanical, Kshatriya, or Vaisya blood.

This, however, very inadequately exhibits the whole case. The Nishâda was the son of a Brahman and a Sudra; and the Vaidiha, the son of a Vaisya and a Brahmani. The son of a Nishâda married to a Vaidiha woman founded a new caste, as already stated, namely the Kârâvera, a low, ignominious tribe, whose occupation was to handle and trade in leather (*a*); yet, as to blood, he was one half a Brahman, one quarter a Vaisya, and one quarter a Sudra. Again, the son of a Nishâda father and Chandâla mother was one half a Brahman and the other half a Sudra. His caste of Antyâvasayin had for its occupation the burning of dead bodies, and was held in the utmost abhorrence, "contemned even by the contemptible" (*b*). The following is a list of inferior castes, with their pedigrees and occupations, derived entirely from Manu (*c*):

PEDIGREE OF INFERIOR CASTES.

Name.	Pedigree.	Proportion of Brahman, Kshatriya, Vaisya, and Sudra blood.	Occupation, Residence, &c.	
Ambastha ...	Brahman father ... Vaisya mother ...	Half Brahman ... Half Vaisya ...	Physician.	
Nishâd ...	Brahman father ... Sudra mother ...	Half Brahman ... Half Sudra ...	Fisherman.	
Ugra ...	Kshatriya father ... Sudra mother ...	Half Kshatriya ... Half Sudra ...	Fierce and cruel. Hunts animals that dwell in holes.	
Mâgadha ...	Vaisya father ... Kshatriya mother ...	Half Vaisya ... Half Kshatriya ...	Travelling Merchant	Not permitted to perform rites in honor of his forefathers.
Súta ...	Kshatriya father ... Brahman mother ...	Half Kshatriya ... Half Brahman ...	Horse trainer, and carrier ...	Ditto ditto.
Vaidiha ...	Vaisya father ... Brahman mother ...	Half Vaisya ... Half Brahman ...	Attends on Women ...	Ditto ditto.
Ayogava ...	Sudra father ... Vaisya mother ...	Half Sudra ... Half Vaisya ...	Carpenter ...	Ditto. Most degraded of mortals.

(*a*) Manu, Chap. X., 36.
(*b*) *Ibid*, 39.
(*c*) Manu, Chap. X., 8—51.

Name.	Pedigree.	Proportion of Brahman, Kshatriya, Vaisya, and Sudra blood.	Occupation, Residence, &c.
Kshatri	Sudra father Kshatriya mother	Half Sudra Half Kshatriya	Hunts animals that live in holes; Not permitted to perform rites in honor of his forefathers. Most degraded of mortals.
Chandâla	Sudra father Brahman mother	Half Sudra Half Brahman	Ditto ditto.
Avrita	Brahman father Ugra mother	Half Brahman. One quarter Kshatriya. One quarter Sudra.	
Abhîra	Brahman father Ambastha mother	Three quarters Brahman. One quarter Vaisya.	
Dhigvana	Brahman father Ayogava mother	Half Brahman One quarter Vaisya One quarter Sudra	Seller of Leather.
Pukkasa	Nishâda father Sudra mother	One quarter Brahman Three quarters Sudra	Hunts animals that live in holes.
Kukkutaka	Sudra father Nishâda mother	Three quarters Sudra. One quarter Brahman.	
Swapâka	Ugra father Khatrî mother	Half Kshatriya Half Sudra	Must live outside the village or town.
Vena	Vaidiha father Ambastha mother	Half Brahman Half Vaisya	Musician.
Maitrîyaka	Vaidiha father Ayogava mother	Half Brahman One quarter Vaisya One quarter Sudra	Sounds a bell at dawn.
Mârgava or Dâsa	Nishâda father Ayogava mother	Half Sudra One quarter Brahman One quarter Vaisya	Boatman.
Sairindhra	Dasya father Ayogava mother	Half Dasya. One quarter Vaisya. One quarter Sudra.	
Kârâvera	Nishâda father Vaidiha mother	Half Brahman One quarter Vaisya One quarter Sudra	Leather trader.
Andhra	Vaidiha father Kârâvara mother	Half Brahman Three-eighths Vaisya One-eighth Sudra	Hunts wild animals.; Must live outside the village or town.
Mîda	Vaidiha father Nishâda mother	Half Brahman One quarter Vaisya One quarter Sudra	Ditto; Ditto.
Pândusopâka	Chandâla father Vaidiha mother	Half Brahman One quarter Vaisya One quarter Sudra	Works in cane and reeds.
Sopâka	Chandâla father Pukkasa mother	Three-eighths Brahman Five-eighths Sudra	Executes punishment on criminals; A sinful wretch.
Ahindika	Nishâda father Vaidiha mother	Half Brahman One quarter Vaisya One quarter Sudra	Jailor.
Antyâvasâyin	Chandâla father Nishâda mother	Half Brahman Half Sudra	Assists in burning the dead; Held in the greatest contempt by all classes.
Chunchu	...	...	Hunts wild animals.
Madgu	...	...	Ditto.

In addition to the above, there were evidently many other castes of an inferior order. Manu mentions five tribes of outcast Brahmans (*a*); seventeen of outcast Kshatriyas (*b*); six of outcast Vaisyas (*c*). Three castes of Brahmanical rank, on the mother's side, and three others of Kshatriya or Vaisya rank, on the same side, produced by intermarriages with women of their own tribes a great number of mean and degraded races (*d*). The same six castes by marrying into other castes, superior to themselves in rank, originated fifteen new castes; and by marrying into others of a lower rank, fifteen more (*e*).

Altogether, Manu gives the names of a considerable number of degraded castes. But in reality he does much more than this, in supplying us with a key to the entire caste system, in its development from the four primitive castes. Given the four chief castes, he shows how from them new castes may be made in an unending series; and furnishes elaborate illustrations of the method pursued in his day. His statements are in accordance with human nature, and with the usages of other races. Nothing is plainer than that, practically, in Manu's time, Hindus of the superior castes commonly intermarried with the inferior castes. Undoubtedly, the children of these intermarriages had a stain upon them; but this circumstance imposed little apparent check on the intermarriages themselves. Although there is considerable discrepancy in the accounts of Manu and other Hindu writers respecting these matters, nevertheless, if the words of Manu are worthy of credit, it is proved, beyond all dispute, that, in the epoch in which he lived, inferior castes were created on an extensive scale.

Taking it for granted, that existing castes in India are in the main representatives of ancient castes, it is manifest that, if there be any truth in the statements of Manu, they are, with few exceptions, like their ante-types, of a very mixed character. The exceptions are the Brahmanical, Kshatriya, and perhaps some of the Vaisya castes. All other castes are of mixed blood. This includes, of course, the Sudras, who, at the present time, consist of a multitude of castes; and in the age of Manu, although reckoned as now among the four original castes, were, in comparison with the first three, regarded as mean and disreputable.

It is a question not yet settled, whether the primitive castes were three or four in number. It is strongly contended by some persons that the Sudras are not at all of Aryan origin, and it is pretty certain that the Vaisyas were once an agricultural race. On this subject, the remarks of Dr. John Muir on a paper, by Dr. H. Kern, Professor of Sanskrit in the University of Leyden, entitled "Indische Theorieën over the Standenverdeeling (Indian Theories on the Division into Castes)," read before the Dutch Royal Academy of Science, in the Literary Department, are of considerable interest. "In this dissertation Dr. Kern combats the idea, that the caste system arose during the Vedic era, since it was already regarded as an institution as old as the sun and moon by the author of the

(*a*) Manu, Chap. X., 21.
(*b*) *Ibid*, 22, 44.
(*c*) *Ibid*, 23.
(*d*) Manu, Chap. X., 29.
(*e*) *Ibid*, 31.

Purusha Sûkta; so that it is indifferent to the solution of the question whether that well-known hymn is one of the most recent in the Rik-sanhitâ or not. At the same time, Dr. Kern observes that there is nothing to show whether all the legal prescriptions relating to caste were at that time in force, or even theoretically known or not. Professor Kern also points to the fourfold division of classes as being found in the Zendavesta (in this he had been preceded by Professor Haug, at least in so far as the recognition of three classes goes); and concludes from this, as well as from the evidence of the Purusha Sûkta, that the fourfold caste-division is more ancient than the old extant Indian sources. It is to be hoped that these views of Professor Kern will attract the attention of other Zend and Sanskrit scholars, and be thoroughly discussed. 'Truth like a torch, the more it's shook, it shines'" (*a*).

Whether the Sudras were Aryans, or aboriginal inhabitants of India, or tribes produced by the union of the one with the other, is of little practical moment. They were at an early period placed in a class by themselves, and received the fourth or last degree of rank, yet at a considerable distance from the three superior castes. Even though it be admitted that at the outset they were not Aryans, still, from their extensive intermarriages with the three Aryan castes, they have become so far aryanized that, in some instances, as already shown, they have gained more than they have lost, and certain tribes now designated as Sudras are in reality more Brahmans and Kshatriyas than anything else. In short, they have become as much absorbed in other races as the Celtic tribes of England have become absorbed in the Anglo-Saxon race; and their own separate individuality, if they ever had any, has completely vanished.

On the other hand, it is plain that not a few of the aboriginal tribes of India retiring into the fastnesses of the country as the Aryan races advanced, maintained their distinctiveness for many ages, and still maintain it. Other aboriginal tribes intermingled with their conquerors to such an extent that it is impossible to draw a line of demarcation between them. All that can be affirmed respecting them is, that they either belong to some of the many ramifications of the great Sudra caste, or to castes of a lower grade still.

The only castes, therefore, that have, for the most part, preserved their purity of blood, are the Brahmans, Kshatriyas, and perhaps some of the Vaisyas. I say for the most part, because, in former days, an intruder might, under certain circumstances, enter one or other of the privileged castes. Many Brahmans, Kshatriyas, or Vaisyas, may have become outcast, or may have married women of inferior castes, so that their offspring, of necessity, were cut off from their own tribes. In this manner, members of these castes, or children partly sprung from them, may have been merged in the lower castes. But none of the lower castes could easily enter the upper, which are consequently, as just remarked, comparatively pure-blooded castes. All the rest are of impure or mixed blood. I use the word 'comparatively' as simply distinguishing the three higher from all the remaining castes, for stringent as the laws of caste have been, yet even these three have

(*a*) Trübner's Literary Record, for June 1871, p. 188.

not been able to preserve themselves from an occasional taint. The least affected have been the Brahmans; and the most, the Vaisyas. The infanticide practised by Rajpoots has been a fruitful cause of the intermingling of low caste blood with their own. Failing to secure wives for their sons, on account of the great paucity of girls in their own tribes, they have, for many generations, contracted alliances with girls of low castes, especially the Râj Bhars, who, having been purchased or carried off from their families, have been transformed into Râjpûtanîs, or wives of Râjpoots.

We thus arrive at the conclusion, that existing Hindu castes are of two kinds: first, those of comparatively pure blood, Brahmans, Kshatriyas, and perhaps some of the Vaisyas; secondly, those of impure or mixed blood, embracing all the castes not included in the first division. The first have maintained their individuality from ancient times to the present. The rest have not done so; but have intermarried with the higher castes, with one another, and with conquered aboriginal races.

Unlike the superior castes, the mixed castes have, in the lapse of time, not only changed their names, but, probably, to some extent, their occupation likewise; and, therefore, it is hardly possible, except in rare cases, to trace them to their origin. There is one peculiarity observable in all the castes in modern days, not to be found in any one of them in primitive ages. The facility for intermarriages has given place to rigid exclusiveness, so that it is now absolutely impossible for the pure castes to intermarry with the mixed, or for the mixed to intermarry with one another. No one ever hears of a Brahman marrying a Vaisya, much less a Sudra; or of a Kshatriya marrying a Vaisya; or of a Vaisya marrying a Sudra; or even of one Sudra caste intermarrying with another Sudra caste; yet all such intermarriages were permitted in early Hindu times. But the peculiarity becomes more striking still when we look into the constitution of the separate castes. Each caste contains usually several, sometimes many, sub-divisions or sub-castes. For example, the Kayasth, or writer caste, in the North-Western Provinces, has twelve sub-divisions. These cannot eat rice together, nor can they intermarry except with the first of the twelve. Again, the Barhai or carpenter caste has seven sub-castes, which are so distinct from one another that they hold no direct social intercourse with each other, either by marriage, or by eating or smoking together. I am unable to afford any information either respecting the causes of the cessation of intermarriages between the castes, or respecting the epoch or epochs when it occurred; nor am I aware that Hindu writings throw any important light on this phenomenon.

It is worthy of note that, in adhering to certain important caste rules and distinctions, many of the lower castes are much more rigid than the higher castes. The Barhai caste, just referred to, is an instance in point. Its sub-divisions cannot intermarry. Yet Brahmans of the same tribe, in all its clans and sub-divisions, commonly intermarry; and Rajpoots, not merely of one tribe, but of many, frequently intermarry, and come to each other's festivals. The Chamâr, or leather-dealer, is many degrees lower in the social scale than the Barhai; nevertheless, all the seven clans which compose that caste are every whit as stringent and exclusive on the subject of marriage as the separate clans of the Barhai caste. It is hard to account for this strange spirit of exclusiveness among the lower castes, not found, to the same extent, among the higher. Perhaps it arose originally from their servile imitation of the social rigidity of the upper castes. Being more ignorant and less intelligent, they have copied their masters so closely and pertinaciously that at last they have gone beyond them. But this is mere conjecture.

How it came to pass that castes became split up into a number of sub-divisions, each cherishing a spirit of iron exclusiveness in regard to the rest, is a question much more easy of solution than that just started; and has already been, to some extent, discussed. Many of these sub-divisional distinctions are territorial, and were occasioned by the dispersion of a caste, which thenceforward became known by appellations superadded to its own, denoting the towns, cities, or districts, in which its scattered members resided. In this manner the caste separated into clans, each of which managed its own affairs, held *panchayats* or councils, and maintained a distinct and independent existence. As these clans were not amenable to one another or to the caste itself considered as a federal whole, gradually they became jealous of each other's rights, and at length, impelled by the national habit of exclusiveness, abandoned one another reciprocally, and assumed to themselves absolutely all the functions and prerogatives of castes.

It is common to speak of the castes of India in their relation to the Hindu religion; and in that light they may very properly be regarded. Yet they sustain another highly important relation. Ethnologically they are so many tribes and clans, with separate histories and customs. The members of a caste are, doubtless, united together by peculiar sacred and social ties. In addition, they bear a tribal relation to one another of great significance. Each caste, in virtue of its distinctiveness, and of its holding no marriage connexion with other castes, either in its neighbourhood or elsewhere, is in fact a tribe governed by laws of the most imperious character. The races of men, whether in ancient or modern times, have seldom, in any country, been divided into separate tribes and clans by such sharply-defined boundaries, over which it is impossible for one to pass to another, as we find separating the various castes of India. Indeed, so absolute and tyrannical is this spirit of exclusiveness, that the castes are taught to believe that there is a natural distinction subsisting between them which utterly forbids their union. In many cases, as already observed, the sub-divisions of the same caste hold no intercourse with one another, and do not intermarry. These I have frequently termed clans, for the reason that they profess to belong to one and the same caste and tribe, and in all likelihood actually sprang from one source, yet being practically distinct tribes. Nevertheless, I have thought it better to speak of them as clans and sub-divisions rather than as separate tribes.

It will thus be understood why, in designating many of the castes, I have frequently employed the word 'tribe,' and not the word 'caste'; and have preferred the use of ethnological terms to a term which is used only very partially in an ethnological sense, and is associated with other and different questions.

PART I.

THE BRAHMANICAL TRIBES.

CHAPTER I.

THE BRAHMAN IN RELATION TO THE PAST, THE PRESENT, AND THE FUTURE.

THE Brahman occupies the highest rank among Hindus for at least three reasons. The first is his assumed sanctity. By the people generally he is regarded as a pure, stainless, twice-born being, divine as well as human, worthy of unbounded admiration and worship. He is the priest of the Hindu religion, directing the ceremonies performed at the temples, sacred wells, sacred tanks, sacred rivers, and at all other hallowed places throughout the land. He is present to sanction, and give effect to, the great social festivals of his countrymen, held at marriages, at births of sons, and at deaths. He casts the horoscope, tells the lucky days, gives spiritual counsel, whispers *mantras* or mysterious words, executes magical incantations and charms, and is at once household god, family priest, and general preceptor and guide, in behalf of the many millions of Hindus residing in the vast country lying between the Himalayas and Cape Comorin.

The second reason of the Brahman's superiority is, that for many ages, perhaps from the outset of his career, when with other Aryans he first entered the plains of India, he has been intellectually in advance of the rest of the Hindu race. Endowed with an extremely subtle, rather than with a powerful, mind,—which by long habit, perpetuated from age to age, and from family to family, he has trained to the utmost keenness,—dogmatic, self-willed, pertinacious, and supremely arrogant and vain, he has in turn encountered and beaten the intellects of all the other tribes, and has attained the position of a victor, with whom it is considered to be hopeless infatuation to contend.

The third reason is a consequence of the second. The Brahman is not merely a thinking, but also a reading, man. He possesses, and perhaps reads, the holy canon—Vedas, Shástras, and Puránas. He has been the author of Hindu literature; he has interpreted its secrets to his countrymen; he has sharpened his own understanding by its instrumentality, but has withheld it from them.

Other reasons might easily be adduced to account for the Brahman's elevation above all other Hindu tribes. But these are some of the most important, and will suffice. Light of complexion, his forehead ample, his countenance of striking significance, his lips thin, and mouth expressive, his eyes quick and sharp, his fingers long, his carriage noble and almost sublime, the true Brahman, uncontaminated by European influence and manners, with his intense self-consciousness, with the proud conviction of superiority depicted in every muscle of his face, and manifest in every movement of his body, is a wonderful specimen of humanity walking on God's earth.

Yet the Brahman has lived his day. His prestige is rapidly on the decline, and is only maintained at its ancient pitch in remote villages and in the fastnesses of superstition in great cities. Here, as of old, it envelopes him like a glory. But the further he removes from such places, the more dim becomes the glory, until it fades away altogether. Education and other influences are treating the Brahman roughly. Yet the fault is his own. He has had a better start, by reason of his great natural endowments, than any Hindu of the castes below him; but he has neglected his opportunities. I fear he has been too proud, too self-satisfied, to avail himself of them. Some of his race, not many, have, however, done so, and have succeeded. But in proportion to their numbers and importance, the Brahmans, especially the pandits, or those Brahmans who are regarded as men of learning, not merely by other castes, but also by the members of their own, have not applied themselves to the acquisition of the knowledge imparted in the colleges and schools established by the English in India to an equal degree with some of the castes inferior to them.

Education, in the European sense, is fast stripping the Brahman of his divine assumptions, and reducing him to the condition of ordinary humanity. But to this condition he does not wish to come. Were he, in the spirit of true philosophy, to submit calmly to the changes which are coming over the land, and endeavour to turn them to his own advantage, he might still occupy the highest position intellectually among all Hindu tribes, as he has done so long and so persistently. But his belief in Brahmanism, in the systems, and habits, and traditions of his ancestors prevents him from exercising a wise judgment in the matter. He claims, in virtue of his caste, special honour and attention. Should he condescend to receive or impart instruction in his own dearly cherished sacred literature, in the educational establishments organized by the Government or missionaries in the country, he must be granted exceptional privileges. From a kindly, though perhaps injurious, consideration for his sensitiveness, such exceptional privileges he, for the most part, obtains. Similarly, in other concerns, he likes to regard himself as needing special arrangements for meeting his special circumstances. And it must be confessed he is very often successful in attaining his wishes, not only with Europeans, but also with Hindus, for they both desire to pay him respect, for the sake of what he is, and of the brilliant associations connected with his tribe. Yet it is certain that he is thereby left behind in the great race of improvement which the Hindus have commenced.

Sometimes—and the instances are not infrequent, and indeed in certain parts of the country are numerous—the Brahman is content to stand on a level with others, and casts in his lot with them. At once he proves his equality with the best of them, and often his superiority. He is quick in the acquisition of knowledge; he makes a sharp accountant; he is a clever diplomatist, an acute lawyer, a subtle, if not profound, judge, an accomplished professor, an effective writer. He need never be ashamed of his abilities, or ask special favours for himself. He is by nature mentally strong; and might, if he chose, be in the future the leader of public thought in India as he has been in the past.

But he is not prepared for such a social revolution, and is consequently unconsciously giving place rapidly to others far below him in caste-rank, and who, in former times, were of little or no consideration at all, but who are now already tripping him up and passing on to the front. The Kayasth, or writer caste, and the Vaisya, or trading caste, are seizing the golden opportunities that education, civilization, and a thousand favourable circumstances are, in these days, placing within the reach of the natives of India, and are striving with conspicuous success to make the best use of them. It is not too much to affirm, that in regard to the part they are taking in the development and growth of the nation, and in promoting its prosperity, they are even at the present time of more account than the Brahmans, blindly treading the old well-worn tracks, which, from the infatuation of obstinacy and folly, they seem unwilling and unable to abandon.

CHAPTER II.

GENEALOGY OF THE BRAHMANICAL TRIBES, AND THE CLASSIFICATION OF THEIR ORDERS ACCORDING TO THEIR OBSERVANCE OF THE VEDIC RITUALS—HONORARY TITLES—DIVISIONS INTO CLANS—SIX SPECIAL DUTIES—RELIGIOUS CEREMONIES OF THE BRAHMANS—THE NAKSHATRAS.

Section 1.—Genealogy of the Brahmanical Tribes.

THE Brahmans of all tribes, according to Hindu writings and traditions, are originally descended from seven Rishis, or sages, held by Hindus universally in profound veneration as semi-deities of great sanctity and wisdom. These, as given by the Nirnai Sindhu, and also by the Dharmâ Sindhu, are as follows:—

1. Bhrigu.
2. Angirâh.
3. Atrî.
4. Viswâmitra.
5. Kasyap.
6. Vashisht.
7. Agastîh.

Each of these Rishis stands at the head of a great division, the various members of which are further sub-divided into sections, termed *gotras* or classes. These *gotras* are found more or less in all the twelve tribes. Many, but not all, of the original *gotras* are as follows:—

Gotras descended from Bhrigu Rishi.

1. Vatsa.
2. Bida.
3. Arshtikhena.
4. Yaska.
5. Mitryu.
6. Shunak.
7. Bainya.

Gotras descended from Angirâh Rishi.

1. Gautam.
2. Bharaddwâj.
3. Kewal Angiras.

Gotras descended from Atrî Rishi.

1. Atre.
2. Bâdbhutak.
3 Garishthîra.
4. Mudhgala.

Gotras descended from Viswâmitra Rishi.

1. Kaushika.
2. Lohit.
3. Raukhshak.
4. Kâmkâyana.
5. Aja.
6. Katab.
7. Dhananjya.
8. Agamarkhan.
9. Pûran.
10. Indrakaushika.

Gotras descended from Kasyap Rishi.

1. Nidruba.
2. Kasyap.
3. Sândila.
4. Rebha.
5. Langâkhshi.

Gotras descended from Vashisht Rishi.

1. Vashisht.
2. Kundin.
3. Upamanyu.
4. Parâshara.
5. Jâtukaraniya.

Gotras descended from Agastîh Rishi.

1. Idhamabâhar.
2. Somabâhar.
3. Sambhabâhar.
4. Yagyabâhar.

From these seven *gotras*, other *gotras* have been derived, which are now looked upon as of superior degree, and equal to them in rank. For instance, each of the three *gotras*, descended from Angirâh Rishi, stands at the head of a family of *gotras*, as follows:—

Gotras descended from Gautam.

1. Apâs.
2. Shard-dwân.
3. Kaumand.
4. Dîrgtamâ.
5. Anthanâ.
6. Renu Pâlî.
7. Râhû Gana.
8. Som Râj.
9. Bâma Deo.
10. Brihaddakâya.

Gotras descended from Bharaddwâj.

1. Bharaddwâjî.
2. Garg.
3. Rikhsha.
4. Kapili.

Gotras descended from Kewal Angiras.

1. Harita.
2. Nâmangiras.
3. Ambarîkha.
4. Dhauwana.

The original *gotras*, with many others that have sprung from them, are found more or less in all the Brahmanical tribes. When, and how, they became scattered, is, for the most part, unknown. Yet, as the Brahmans have been exceedingly careful in the preservation of the purity of their blood, it is, I conceive, extremely probable, that the same *gotras*, in different tribes and branches of tribes, have a common ancestral *gotra* from which they are descended. But they have become distinct races, which, if belonging to separate tribes, do not now intermingle. Indeed, the members of the same *gotra*, of the same tribe, cannot now intermarry; and marriages among Brahmans are always between different *gotras*, which, however, must belong to the same tribe. Were a man and woman of the same *gotra* to marry, their union would be regarded as concubinage, and not marriage; and their children would be considered illegitimate. Moreover, both they and their children would be unable to present the *pinda* or sacred offering to their ancestors, which every sincere Hindu esteems it his duty and privilege to make ; and if they ventured to present it, the offering, in Hindu belief, would be rejected.

Section II.—Classification of the Gotras or Orders according to their Observance of the Vedic Rituals.

In their ceremonies the Brahmans follow the rituals or instructions of one or other of the four Vedas. Five of the principal *gotras* observe the Sâm Veda; five others, the Rig Veda; five others, the Yajur Veda; and five, the Atharvan Veda, as follows :—

Gotras.	
Kasyap Kâsyap Vatsa Sândila Dhananjya	Follow the Sâm Veda.

Gotras.	
Bhârgau Sânkrita Garg (or Chândra) Bhrigu Saunak	Follow the Rig Veda.

Gotras.	
Bharaddwâj Bhâraddwâj Angirâh Gautam Upamanyu	Follow the Yajur Veda.

Gotras.	
Kaushika Gritakaushika Mudhgala Gâlawa Vashisht	Follow the Atharvan Veda.

The rest of the Brahmans, of all *gotras*, follow the Yajur Veda.

Section III.—Honorary Titles ; Divisions into Clans ; Six Special Duties.

While there is no manner of doubt that the Brahmans were originally more closely united than they are at present, and probably consisted of only one tribe, there is no historical record among Hindus of the periods and circumstances of their development into ten tribes. Their traditions, however, may be regarded as tolerably safe guides on such matters. These all agree in pointing to a period when the Brahmans were one people. Moreover, in the age of Manu, as is manifest from his Institutes, they were as yet undivided. He gives no intimation of separate tribes existing among them. The division into ten is, I suspect, comparatively modern.

Great and important distinctions subsist between the various tribes of Brahmans. Some are given to learning; some to agriculture; some to politics; some to trade. The Mahratta Brahman is a very different being from the Bengali, while the Kanoujiya differs from both. I am only imperfectly acquainted with this branch of the subject. Mr. Campbell's recent work on the Ethnology of India might have contained more information upon it. In his remarks on the Brahmans he loses sight of their great tribal distinctions.

Besides the divisions of Brahmans into tribes and *gotras*, they are still further classified according to certain honorary designations or titles. For instance, a Dube, or Do-Veda, is a descendant of one who prefessed to have read two Vedas; a Tiwâri, corrupted from Trivedi, of one who had read three Vedas; a Chaube, of one who had read all four Vedas. Dikshit (initiated), Misr (probably from Misra, mixed), Pânde, Shukul, Awasthi, Upadhya, Bâjpeî, Pâtakh, are, with those first mentioned, some of the more prominent of such titles.

After this comes the name of the clan, or family, which is frequently derived from a village or district. The clan will have perhaps two or more branches, each of which has its own appellation. In addition, as every Brahman wears the sacred cord, he is further designated according to the number of knots tied at the ends. He may be Triprawa, Pânchprawa, or Sâtprawa, a Brahman with a three-knotted, five-knotted, or seven-knotted cord, and so on. A Brahman, therefore, would be fully described somewhat as follows: His name, say, is Sambhu Nârâyana; and he is a Triprawa Brahman of the Apastambh branch of the Dharmpûrâ clan, of the Misr rank, of the Kausik gotra, of the Sarjupârî division, of the Kânkubja tribe of Gaur Brahmans.

A Brahman has to perform six kinds of duties, as follows:—

1. To study the Vedas.
2. To teach the Vedas.
3. To offer sacrifices.
4. To cause others to sacrifice,—that is, to perform the offices of a priesthood.
5. To receive alms.
6. To give alms.

Only those Brahmans that perform all these six duties are reckoned perfectly orthodox. Some perform three of them,—namely, the first, third, and fifth,—and omit the other three ; yet they suffer in rank in consequence. Hence, Brahmans are divided into two kinds, the Shat-karmas and the Tri-karmas, or those who perform the six duties and those who perform the three only. The Bhûinhâr Brahmans, for instance, are Tri-karmas, and merely pay heed to three duties. Their position as Brahmans, however, is well known to be depreciated thereby. This subject, in regard to the Bhûinhârs, will be alluded to again.

Section IV.—Religious Ceremonies of the Brahmans.

The customs and ceremonies of the Brahmans, at certain periods of life, and on special occasions, are very peculiar, differing in many respects from those observed by other castes. They are divided into a number of *sanskârs*, or *karamas,—i. e.*, ceremonies.

First Karam.—Garbhâdhân. This is performed when a Brahmani, or wife of a Brahman, indulges the hope of offspring. The Brahman and his wife worship Ganesh, the god of wisdom; the Nakshatras, or twenty-seven divisions of the zodiac, under one or other of which every child is supposed to be born; the twenty-eight Yogas, and other deities. It has eight divisions as follows:

1. Punyâh-vâchan. A Brahman comes and sprinkles water over husband and wife, and repeats a *mantra*, or charm.
2. Mâtrikâ-pûjan. They both perform *pûja*, or worship certain idols, and also make a rude figure called *mâtrika*, representing a woman, on walls and other places.
3. Basardhârâ. They draw eight lines with clarified butter on walls; and also perform *pûjâ.*
4. Nândi-shrâddh. They worship their ancestors; place Kusha grass in four different places; and feed Brahmans.
5. They perform the burnt sacrifice of the Hom.
6. A silver plantain is presented as a *dân*, or gift, to Brahmans.
7. Godbhâran. The things which have been presented in sacrifice are placed in the lap of the woman.
8. A feast is given to Brahmans.

Second Karam.—Punsawan. This consists of ceremonies performed in the fourth month, which are the first five, or Punyâh-vâchan, Mâtrikâ-pûjan, Basardhârâ, Nândi-shrâddh, and the Hom, noticed above. In addition, the juice of the Soma plant is mixed with the jatâ, or hanging-roots, of the Bar tree, ground to a powder, and applied to the woman's nose. The hair of the woman is bound up in the fashion called *beuri;* and the name of the neighbouring river is pronounced.

Third Karam.—Simanto-Nâyana. Performed in the seventh or eight month. The first five ceremonies of the first karam are observed. Taking the twin-fruit of the Bar tree (or two individual fruits united together), three stalks of Kusha grass, and a porcupine's quill, they part the woman's hair at the proper place of division, or *mang*, and while *mantras* are being recited, and women are singing, a vessel full of water is placed on her thigh.

Fourth Karam.—Jâtkaram. This takes place at the birth of the child. The five ceremonies are performed. Clarified butter and honey are given to the infant, being first poured into a silver vessel through a golden ring ; and charms are breathed into its ear, to preserve it from evil spirits, and from the innumerable ills to which this flesh is heir. Five Brahmans are summoned to read *mantras* on five sides of the house. The spot is sanctified by *mantras;* and *mantras* sanctify the infant, over whom the Brahmans say Ashmâ-bhatwâ. Fire is placed before the door, and the Hom sacrifice is burnt together with yellow mustard and rice. During the first six days, the mother is attended by a chamain, or wife of a chamâr, and only eats food called chauâni, made of sugar, clarified butter, and spices. After the sixth day, she begins to partake of cooked food. For twelve days, singing and music are more or less kept up at the house, and friends come and go, offering their congratulations, and bringing with them nicely prepared *pawn;* but during this period, however, the mother is permitted to touch no one. On the twelfth day, friends bring various kinds of presents, and the woman having bathed, the restriction as to touching is removed. If a boy is born in the nineteenth Nakshatra called *mûl*, the woman is not clean till the twenty-seventh day, and is consequently unable, during the interval, to touch any one. The process by which the father, in such case, is suffered to see his child for the first time is very curious. On this day melted clarified butter is brought in a brass vessel, and the child being placed upon his shoulder in such manner as to cast a reflection of itself upon the butter, the father looks in and beholds the reflected image. After this the child is placed in a *barma-sup*, or winnowing basket, and is brought outside of the house as far as the eaves. The woman then worships the goddess Bhawâni, by offering chauâni placed on seven cakes. This custom prevails in all the castes. There is a certain condition of this Nakshatra, happily rare, on the occurrence of which, should a child be born, its father is prohibited from beholding it for the space of twelve years.

Fifth Karam.—Nâma-karan. This is the ceremony of naming the child, which is performed twelve days after its birth. The five special ceremonies, already repeatedly referred to, are practised, and the name is given.

Sixth Karam.—Nishkarman. Performed when the child is four months old. The five ceremonies are observed. Ganesh is worshipped, and the infant is brought out to behold the sun and moon.

Seventh Karam.—Anaprâshanna. Performed in the case of a girl, five months after birth; and in the case of a boy, six months. After worshipping fire on a lucky day, the child is made, for the first time, to eat the various kinds of food eaten by Hindus.

Janangânth. This ceremony is performed when the child is one year old, when the parents worship Ashtachiranjana,—that is, eight deities. These are Ashwathamâ, Raja Bali, Veda Vyâs, Hanumân, Bibhishan, Kripâchârya, Parasrâm, Mârdandî and Chhasti (goddesses). The reflected face of the child is exhibited in melted butter.

Eighth Karam.—Chûrâkaran. Performed when the child is between one and three years of age. Turning the child with its face to the east, *kusha* grass is placed in the hair, which is anointed with cow-dung. Having done this three times successively, *mantras* or charms are then said, and the boy's hair is cut, or rather shaved, with a razor.

Karanbeda. When the child is between three and five years of age, its two ears are pierced. The worship of Ganesh forms part of the ceremony.

Ninth Karam.—Upnayana. This is the important ceremony connected with the initiation of the child, between his fifth and eighth year, into the mysteries of Brahmanism, by decorating him with the Janeo, or sacred thread. The first four rites of the second Karam,—namely, Punyâh-vâchan, Mâtrikâ-pûjan, Basardhârâ, and Nândi-shrâddh,—having been observed, the child and its father both make atonement for any sins which they may have committed, which partly consists of bestowing presents of money and other things to Brahmans. They then give *baran*, or money and nuts, to ten Brahmans for repeating *gayatris*, or sacred texts, a thousand times. Thereupon, the boy's head is shaved; after which eight boys and the child's mother eat food together, and ten Brahmans are presented with money, nuts, and sacred threads. The boy is now covered with a veil, called Antrapat, while Sanskrit sentences are read, and fire is placed upon an altar. The child's head is then adorned with a *mâlâ*, or wreath, and he is made to sit on the altar. The Kardhani, or rope of muj, a kind of grass, is bound round his waist three times, and as many knots are tied in it as correspond to the number of years of his life. The *langauti*, or long cloth worn by Brahmans and by other Hindus, is placed upon him, and a deerskin, called *Krishnâ-jin*, is wrapt about his shoulders, and a rod torn from the Palâs tree is put in his hand. While charms are being uttered the sacred cord is thrown over his shoulder, and the *gayatri*, or sacred text, is breathed into his ear together with Madhyân Sandhia. The sacrifice of the Hom is performed, and the young disciple is taught certain duties, some of which are the following,—not to sleep on a bed, not to tell a lie, to purify himself with water, not to play with boys, to beg alms, and so forth. Finally, the parents give *dakshina*, or presents, to the Brahmans, and the ceremony terminates.

Tenth, Eleventh, Twelfth, and Thirteenth Karmas.—These four ceremonies are the reading of the Vedas by the young Brahman. The first consists of the general study of the four Vedas ; the second, of the Rig Veda ; the third, of the Yajur Veda ; and the fourth, of the Sâm Veda.

Fourteenth Karam.—Samâbartan. The young Brahman having been occupied for some time in reading with his teacher asks his permission to visit his home.

Fifteenth Karam.—Gaudam. A ceremony at which cows are given to Brahmans.

Bâgdân. A ceremony preceding marriage. The father of a Brahmani girl visits the youth and proposes his daughter to him in marriage, and, at the same time, makes various presents to him.

Sixteenth Karam.—Byâh. The ceremony of marriage, which has fourteen divisions and gradations, as follows:

1. Bâgdân. The bride's father proceeds to the house of the bridegroom, and after worshipping him and making presents of money, cloth, and other things, utters these words, 'I will give my daughter to thee.' In some cases the bridegroom himself goes to the house of the bride.

2. Simantinî-pûjan. The bridegroom, accompanied by all the members of his family, goes to the bride's house; whereupon both bride and bridegroom are worshipped; first the bride's party worships the bridegroom, and then the bridegroom's party worships the bride.

3. Hardî-uthânâ. Hardî or haldî, a yellow pigment, and oil, having been sent from the bride's house to the bridegroom, are rubbed upon his body: he then bathes: after which the ceremonies of Ganesh-pûjan (worship of Ganesh),

Punyâh-vâchan, Mâtrikâ-pûjan, Basardhârâ-pûjan, and Nândi-shrâddh, before mentioned, are performed.

4. Barât. Marriage procession. The bridegroom and his friends go in state to the house of the bride.

5. Madhu-parakh. Kusha grass being placed on a wooden seat the bridegroom is made to sit upon it. Thereupon, honey, curds, and sweetmeats are given him to eat, and various presents are placed before him.

6. Agnîsthâpan. Fire is placed upon an altar, and *mantras*, or sacred texts, are recited.

7. Antrapat. A veil is put over the bride and bridegroom, and Sanskrit verses are read.

8. Kanyadân. The names of three deceased ancestors having been uttered the bride's father gives his daughter, together with presents of money and other things, to the bridegroom.

9. Hom. Fire is placed on the altar, and *lâwâ*, a kind of parched grain, is presented by the bridegroom's brother to both bride and bridegroom, and a portion is thrown upon the altar.

10. Sapt-padî. The bride and bridegroom having first placed their feet on the *lâwâ* on the altar, walk together round the Marwâ, or place where the rite is performed.

11. Sendhûrdharnâ. The bridegroom having put *sendhûr*, a red pigment, into the parting of the bride's hair, five married women, called *sohâgins*, step forward and perform the same operation.

12. Gaudam. Money equal to the price of a cow is given to the family priest, or purohit.

13. Brâhman-bhojan. Brahmans are fed, and money is given to them.

14. Badhu-pravesh. The bridegroom is placed for four days in the house of the bride, after which she is taken home to his house, and the goddess Lakshmi is worshipped.

In addition to the sixteen *karmas* now noticed, there are also elaborate ceremonies performed on the death of a Brahman, forming, in the estimation of some persons, a seventeenth *karam*. These ceremonies are as follows:—

Ceremonies performed on the death of a Brahman.

1. Kshhour. The head of the man who takes the principal part in these ceremonies is shaved.

2. Utkrânt Srâddh. Offerings called *pinda* (*a*) are made in the name of the deceased.

3. Uthâpan. The body is placed upon a bier in order to be borne upon men's shoulders to the bank of a stream—in Benares, to the Ganges—for cremation.

4. Shavâlankâr. The body is wrapped in cloth.

5. Bisrâm Srâddh. While being carried to the place of burning, the bearers put the body down in the road, and take rest; a *pinda* is then offered in the name of the deceased.

6. Dahan-Srâddh. On arriving at the place where the body is to be burnt, a *pinda* is again offered.

7. Chitâ-rachnâ. The wood is placed in proper order for burning the body.

8. Agni-sthâpan. An altar is erected, on which, while sacred texts are repeated, fire is put.

9. The body is then placed on the wood, clarified butter or a piece of gold is put into its mouth, and wood is heaped upon it all round. When these preparations have been concluded, the man whose duty it is to fire the pile first walks round it three times, beginning from the left side. He then applies the torch to the wood, in the direction of the head, if the deceased be a male, and in that of the feet, if a female. All present must remain until the head has burst open, when the person officiating fills a pitcher with water and walks three times round the fire, on each occasion making a small hole in the vessel with a stone, which being completed, he places the stone upon the ground, and walking backwards lets fall the pitcher upon it. This is called kapâl-kriyâ. He then takes up the stones, which he makes use of again in another ceremony.

10. Asthisan-chain-srâddh. A *pinda* is offered in the name of the deceased.

11. Nagna-prachhâdan-srâddh. A *pinda* also is offered, because the body remains naked while being consumed.

12. Pâthai. A *pinda* is given likewise, in order that the soul of the deceased may go to its place of rest.

13. Kravyâd-mukh-srâddh. A *pinda* is presented in the name of the fire.

14. The stone which has been retained is then smeared with cow-dung mixed with sacred ashes and *aulâ*, a fruit; after which a handful of water, together with *til* (*b*) seed, is thrown upon the stone.

(*a*) The *pinda* is made of cooked rice worked up into a ball with clarified butter, honey, sugar, and *til* seed.

(*b*) The *til* is a small seed from which oil is expressed.

15. Mashân-bâshi-srâddh. A *pinda* is offered for the proprietor of the ground on which the cremation has taken place, that he may not be injured by the spirit of the departed.

16. Bali-pinda-srâddh. Three *pindas* are offered in behalf of the deceased; a handful of water with *til* is cast on the chitâ or burning pile; and the pile is thrown down by abundance of water being poured upon it.

All who have taken part in the ceremony of burning are unclean for ten days, during which time they may not touch any one.

17. For ten days *pindas* are offered, one on each of the even days, and two on the odd days.

On the tenth day all shave their heads, and become again ceremonially clean.

18. Brikhosarg. A bull receives the mark of Siva upon its rump, and is offered in the name of the deceased.

19. Adya-srâddh. A *pinda* is offered on the eleventh day.

20. Khorsi. This *pinda* is also offered on the same day.

21. Ashya or bed, a horse, a cow, and other things are given to the Mahâbrahman, or priest who has officiated in some of these ceremonies.

22. Sapindi. A *pinda* is offered on the twelfth day.

23. Sudh-srâddh. A *pinda* is offered on the thirteenth day. The spirit of the deceased is supposed to have hovered about the spot, where the body was burnt, for twelve days; but on the thirteenth takes its departure to another sphere. Brahmans are fed, and all the ceremonies are at an end.

The above ceremonies are not merely performed on the death of a Brahman, but are also, for the most part, observed on the death of any other Hindu.

Section V.—The Nakshatras.

The Nakshatras are regarded by Hindu astrologers as heavenly bodies which have great influence on mankind, not only at the time of their birth, but during the whole course of their life on earth. They are also said to constitute the twelve signs of the zodiac, two and-a-quarter Nakshatras forming one sign. Again, they are spoken of as quasi-deities, whose favour needs to be propitiated, and whose frown is fatal to health and life. There is no question that the Nakshatras are a source of infinite terror to Hindus of all castes, and of vast emolument to the Brahmans. They are consulted at births and marriages, and in all times of difficulty, of sickness, and of anxiety. Journies are commenced under their direction; and according to their decision, days and events become lucky or unlucky. The consultation of the Nakshatras is a part of the Hindu's life, and is as important in his eyes as the institution of caste or the worship of the gods.

The Nakshatras are twenty-seven in number. In the following list it will be observed that the word '*shânti*' is affixed to several names. It means 'rest,' or 'quiet,' and shows that the ill-natured deity, to whom it refers, requires a ceremony of pacification to be performed in the event of a child being born at the time of her appearance in the heavens, in order that calamities and dangers which she threatens to send upon the child, or its parents, or other relatives, or on its friends, or on its caste, may be averted. Wherever the word '*shânti*' is added, the particular danger, and the object of it, are likewise stated.

The Twenty-seven Nakshatras.

1. Ashwani—Shânti. Danger is threatened to the parents of the child.
2. Bharanî.
3. Kritikâ.
4. Rohinî.
5. Mrigâshirâ.
6. Argrâ.
7. Punarvasû.
8. Pushya—Shânti. Danger is threatened to parents and other relatives.
9. Ashlesâ or Ashya-lekhâ—Shânti. Out of sixty hours, during which she is dominant, only the last four are fraught with danger. If a child be born in the last of these, evil may happen to its father; if in the third, to its mother; if in the second, to itself; and if in the first, to its parents, to its brother, to its caste, and to wealth, if it has any.
10. Maghâ—Shânti. Danger is threatened to parents and other relatives.
11. Purvâphâlguni.
12. Uttarâphâlguni.
13. Hasta.
14. Chitrâ—Shânti. Danger is threatened to parents, and to the men of the same *gotra* or branch of families.
15. Swâti.
16. Vishâkâ—Shânti. Danger is threatened to the younger child of the father's brother, if a daughter; and if a son, the danger will pass to the younger sister of his wife.
17. Anurâdhâ.
18. Jieshthâ—Shânti. The sixty hours of its dominance are dangerous, as follows: the first six, to the maternal grandmother of the child; the second six, to its mother's father; the third six, to its mother's brother; the fourth six, to its mother; the fifth six, to the child itself; the sixth six, to all the members of the same *gotra;* the seventh six, to its own family; the eighth six, to its brother; the ninth six, to its father-in-law; the tenth six, to all its relatives.

19. Mûl—Shânti. If a child is born during the first fifty-six hours of her dominance, danger impends over the entire family; if in the fifty-seventh, danger threatens the father only; if in the fifty-eighth, the mother only; if in the fifty-ninth, itself. The last hour, or the sixtieth, is devoid of danger, but, nevertheless, requires *Shânti*.

20. Purvâshârâ.
21. Uttarâshârâ.
22. Sravan.
23. Dhanishta—Shânti. Danger is threatened both to its father and itself.
24. Shatatâraka.
25. Purvâbhâdrâpadâ.
26. Uttarâbhâdrâpadâ.
27. Revatî—Shânti. Danger is threatened both to its parents and itself.

CHAPTER III.

TEN PRINCIPAL BRAHMANICAL TRIBES. SUPPLEMENTARY TRIBES. THE FIVE GAUR TRIBES OF NORTHERN INDIA. THE KANYAKUBJA BRAHMANS. FIRST SUB-TRIBE—THE KANOUJIYA BRAHMANS PROPER. GOTRAS. CLANS. KANOUJIYA BRAHMANS OF BENGAL—VARENDRA, RARHIYA, PASHCHATIYA, AND DAKSHINATIYA.

THE Brahmans of India are classed under two great divisions, named Gaur and Drâvira, each of which consists of five tribes. These are mostly separated by geographical boundaries. Speaking somewhat generally, the Gaur tribes are found in Northern India, and the Drâvira tribes in the Deccan or Southern India. The river Nirbuddha in Central India is commonly regarded as a rough geographical line of demarcation between the Gaurs and Drâviras. Yet there is an important distinction between them which ought to be always borne in mind, that the former are of greater antiquity than the latter, the Southern Brahmans having in fact originally migrated from the tribes in the North. In addition to the ten well-known principal tribes, there are several supplementary tribes, which, although not usually reckoned amongst them, are doubtless of Brahmanical origin.

DIVISIONS OF BRAHMANS.

The Gaur, or Northern Division, consisting of Five Tribes.

I. Kânyakubja or Kanoujiya.
II. Sâraswat.
III. Gaur.
IV. Maithila.
V. Utkala.

The Drâvira, or Southern Division, consisting of Five Tribes.

I. Mahârâshtra.
II. Tailanga.
III. Drâvira.
IV. Karnâta.
V. Gurjar.

Supplementary Tribes.

I. Mâthur, or Mathurâ ke Chaube.
II. Mâgadh, or Sâkâdwîpî.
III. The Mâḷwâ Brahmans.
IV. The Kurmâchalî Brahmans.
V. The Naipâlî Brahmans.
VI. The Kâshmîrî Brahmans.
VII. The Sapt-Shatî Brahmans.
VIII. The Shenevi Brahmans.
IX. The Palashe Brahmans.
X. The Sengardaro Brahmans.
XI. The Sankâhâr Brahmans.
XII. The Thatiya Brahmans.
XIII. The Ahwâsî or Haiwâsî Tribe.
XIV. The Byâs Tribe.
XV. The Bilwâr Tribe.
XVI. The Lrikhîshwar Tribe.
XVII. The Agâchî Brahmans.
XVIII. The Bâgariyâ or Parchuniyâ Brahmans.
XIX. The Unwâriyâ Brahmans.
XX. The Golâpurab Brahmans.
XXI. The Lyâriyâ Tribe.
XXII. The Nâde Tribe.
XXIII. The Myâle Brahmans.
XXIV. The Dasâdwîpî Tribe.
XXV. The Dehrâ-dûn Brahmans.

The Kânyakubja Brahmans belong to the old Kingdom of Kanouj, and are found dispersed over a large portion of the North-Western Provinces, as far as Benares, where they are very numerous, especially that branch of them known as Sarwaria or Sarjupârî, which is scattered over the country from the northern bank of the Sarju, on the confines of Oudh, its original home, to Benares, and beyond. The Sâraswat Brahmans are in the north-west of India; the Gaurs are found in the vicinity of Delhi, and in Bengal; the Maithilas inhabit the northern part of Behar; and the Utkalas have their home in Orissa. The five Drâvira tribes may be separated, like the five Gaurs, by geographical boundaries. The Mahârâshtras belong to the Mahratta country; the Tailangas, to Telingânâ; the Drâviras, to the Tamil-speaking districts; the Karnâtas, to the Carnatic; and the Gurjars, to Gujerat. Of the subordinate or supplementary tribes, the Mâthurs are found in the city of Mathura and its neighbourhood; the Sâkâdwîpîs, in the old Magadh country; the Mâlwâ Brahmans, in Mâlwâ; the Kurmâchalîs, in Kumaon; the Naipâlis, in Nepal; the Kâshmîrîs, in Cashmere; the Sapt-Shati Brahmans, in Bengal; the Shenevi Brahmans, in the Mahratta country; the Palashe Brahmans in Southern India. The remainder are found in various places, chiefly in Northern India, and are of little weight or importance. I am not aware that any of them have representatives in Benares; which circumstance is sufficient to prove their insignificance. They are given here in order that the list may be as complete as possible. Probably most of them are Brahmans who have degraded from the original stock.

It is important to observe, as a distinguishing caste-characteristic of all these tribes, that, although some of them may partake of cooked food together, yet they do not intermarry. The five Gaur tribes are entirely distinct from one another, both in regard to marriage and eating food; and are likewise, in these respects, distinct from the five tribes of Southern Brahmans. Yet the five Drâviras are not quite so exclusive in their relations to one another. None of them intermarry; nevertheless, four out of the five can eat together. These are the Mahârâshtra, the Tailanga, the Drâvira, and the Karnâta. None of them, however, eats with the Gurjar tribe, owing to certain peculiarities in this tribe not found in the rest. The supplementary tribes keep themselves aloof from one another and from all other tribes.

Some of the great seats of Hinduism and Brahmanical learning, Benares especially, are always more or less frequented by representatives from these tribes. It is not my intention, however, to attempt to furnish a complete detailed account of all of them. Having undertaken to give, as far as possible, a full statement respecting the castes of Benares, I shall consider that my obligation in regard to the Brahmanical castes will be fulfilled by a description of the great Kânyakubja tribe indigenous to the Benares city and province. Information concerning the remaining tribes, I shall supply, so far as I am able, and as inquiry may bear fruit.

THE FIVE GAUR TRIBES OF NORTHERN INDIA.

THE Gaur Brahmans, as already stated, embrace the five great indigenous tribes found in Northern India, from Orissa and Eastern Bengal through Behar, the North-West Provinces, Oudh, Rohilkhand, to the extreme west of the Panjab, and extending southwards as far as the Nirbuddha in Central India. The word 'Gaur' properly applies to Bengal, especially the central portion. How it has come to pass that the term is employed as a designation of the entire race of Northern Brahmans, is difficult thoroughly to understand. While it has this general use, it is also of limited application, and is the appellation of one of the five tribes. Whether the general use arose from the particular, or the particular from the general, is by no means clear. History and tradition afford no satisfactory solution. The local Gaurs are found in two places separated by a wide interval,—namely, the vicinity of Delhi, and Bengal. Common tradition points to Bengal as their original seat; but as we know that the eastern part of the country was occupied by the Brahmans at a period subsequently to their immigration into the western provinces, this is manifestly erroneous. As Hariana, Hastinâpûr, and the neighbouring country formed one of the earliest seat of the Brahmans in India, it is not improbable that the modern Gaurs of that quarter, together with those in Bengal and elsewhere, who have branched off from them, are their lineal descendants. The antiquity of these primitive Gaurs, combined with their wandering character, may have gradually given rise to the custom of designating the Brahmans generally over a wide extent of country as Gaurs, and so may have been adopted as a term applicable to all the tribes within its bounds. But the subject is involved in mystery and uncertainty. It will be further discussed in the section on the Gaur Brahmans Proper.

FIRST TRIBE OF GAUR BRAHMANS:—KANYAKUBJA OR KANOUJIYA.

This tribe of Gaur Brahmans occupies the extensive tract of country lying between Behar and the western part of the Doab. It consists of five great divisions, as follows :—

Divisions of the Kanoujiya Tribe.

I. Kanoujiya Proper.
II. Sarjupâria or Sarwaria.
III. Jijhotiya.
IV. Sanâdhiya.
V. Kanoujiya Brahmans of Bengal.

The last division has four branches:—

1. Vârendra.
2. Rârhiya.
3. Pashchâtiya.
4. Dakshinâtiya Vaidik.

The Brahmans of the first division inhabit the country of the old kingdom of Kanouj, and are also found more or less in other parts of the North-Western Provinces, between the limits already stated. They are the Kanoujiya Brahmans Proper. The other divisions have sprung from them, and, in some places, exist side by side with them. In Benares and its neighbourhood, the Kanoujiyas Proper are numerous; but the Sarjupâris are more so. The Bhûînhârs, of whom many, though not all, belong to the Sarjupâria division, are a large and influential body in all that province. Of the four divisions, the Kanoujiyas Proper are highest in rank. Being more scrupulous in regard to ceremonial observances than the other three, they occupy in relation to them the position of Kulin Brahmans,—that is, Brahmans of a purer race. They also keep themselves, on this account, somewhat distinct from them, especially in the matter of marriage; for while they permit their sons to contract alliances with their daughters, they do not suffer their daughters to wed their sons. They do not drink spirits, yet they will eat meat offered in sacrifice. But they will eat nothing made of flour by a Halwai, or Hindu confectioner, which, however, the Sarjupâri Brahmans will do. Nor will they eat *puris*,—sweet cakes made with *ghi*, or clarified butter,—manufactured by a stranger not of their own caste; but the Sarjupâris have no scruple on this point likewise.

FIRST SUB-TRIBE.

Section I.—The Kanoujiya Brahmans Proper.

The particular boundaries of this family are the Districts of Shâhjehânpûr, and a portion of Pilibhît, to the north-west; the Districts of Kânpûr, and part of Fathpûr, to the north; the District of Banda, to the west; of Hamîrpûr, to the south; and part of Etawah, to the south-west. The Kanoujiyas, says Mr. W. C. Plowden, in the General Report of the Census of the North-West Provinces, for the year 1865, Vol. I, p. 81, "are not found in any number above Etawah; in fact, in the Meerut Division they are not known, and in Rohilkhand they number little more than one thousand; a small colony of nine hundred and ninety-eight existing in Morâdabâd, and sixteen persons of the same sub-division being recorded as residents of Bijnour."

The Kanoujiyas Proper have professedly six branches, or *gotras*, which are called Khatkul, or six families; but in reality they reckon six and-a-half, which are practically seven. They are the following:

Gotras of the Kanoujiya Brahmans Proper.

Gautam.	Kâsyap.
Sândil.	Kâshtip.
Bhâraddwâj.	Garg.
Upmân.	

Each of these *Gotras* is a class by itself, comprising one or more families or clans designated by certain honorary titlès, as Misr, Shukul, and so forth.

CLANS AND TITULAR RANK CONNECTED WITH THESE GOTRAS.

Clans of the Gautam Gotra, bearing the title of Awasthî.

First Clan, First Branch	Mâdhû.
„ Second ditto	Parbhâkar.
„ Third ditto	Devâkar.
„ Fourth ditto	Chandrâkar.
Second Clan	Khenchar.
Third ditto	Belaurâ.
Fourth ditto	Mawaiya.
Fifth ditto	Bare.

Clans of the Sândil Gotra, bearing the title of Misr.

First Clan	Ankin.
Second ditto, First Branch	Baije Gânw.
„ Second ditto	Mânj Gânw.
„ Third ditto	Sothiaun.
„ Fourth ditto	Badarka.
Third Clan	Gopînâthî.
Fourth ditto	Parsukh.
Fifth ditto	Durgâpûr.

Clans of the Sândil Gotra, bearing the title of Dîkshit.

First Clan, First Branch ... ... Anter.
„ Second ditto ... ... Hans Râm ke Asâmî.
„ Third ditto ... ... Jâgeshwar ke Asâmî.
Second Clan, First Branch ... ... Parasarî.
„ Second ditto ... ... Bhainsai.
Third Clan ... ... Gârumau.

Clans of the Bhâraddwâj Gotra, bearing the title of Shukul.

First Clan, First Branch ... ... Bâlâ.
„ Second ditto ... ... Chhange.
Second Clan, First Branch ... ... Bhaudatt.
„ Second ditto ... ... Devâkar.
Third Clan ... ... Harî.
Fourth ditto, First Branch ... ... Durgá Dás.
„ Second ditto ... ... Bhainsai.
Fifth Clan, First Branch ... ... Pâtan.
„ Second ditto ... ... Nawaiyin.
Sixth Clan ... ... Dhani.
Seventh ditto ... ... Tari.

(This is properly the principal Clan, from which the others are said to have been derived. For some unexplained reason, it is now the seventh on the list.)

Eighth Clan ... ... Bigahpûr.
Ninth ditto ... ... Gûdarpûr.

Clans of the Bhâraddwâj Gotra, bearing the title of Trivedî.

First Clan, First Branch ... ... Mandan.
„ Second ditto ... ... Jethî.
„ Third ditto ... ... Lahurî.
Second Clan ... ... Soch.

Clans of the Bhâraddwâj Gotra, bearing the title of Pânde.

First Clan ... ... Gegâson.
Second ditto ... ... Khor.
Third ditto ... ... Amrâ.
Fourth ditto ... ... Nagwâ.
Fifth ditto ... ... Kushâ.
Sixth ditto ... ... Pachwâr.

Clans of the Upmân Gotra, bearing the title of Pâthakh.

First Clan ... ... Mauraun.
Second ditto ... ... Chhitupûrî.
Third ditto ... ... Jânâpûrî.
Fourth ditto ... ... Serhupûrî.

Clans of the Upmân Gotra, bearing the title of Dûbe.

First Clan ... ... Gharwâns.
Second ditto ... ... Kesarmou.
Third ditto ... ... Jarâjmou.
Fourth ditto ... ... Naurâtampûr.
Fifth ditto ... ... Matîkarhâ.
Sixth ditto ... ... Surâjpûr.
Seventh ditto ... ... Khewaliya.
Eighth ditto ... ... Unaiyân.
Ninth ditto ... ... Patnahá.

Clan of the Kâsyap Gotra, bearing the title of Trivedi.

One Clan ... ... Hari.

Clan of the Kâsyap Gotra, bearing the title of Tiwâri.

First Clan, First Branch ... ... Damâ.
" Second ditto ... ... Gopâl.
" Third ditto ... ... Gobardhan.
" Fourth ditto ... ... Châtu.
Second Clan ... ... Harbasipûr.
Third ditto ... ... Janghîrâbâd.
Fourth ditto ... ... Umrî.
Fifth ditto ... ... Sakhrej.
Sixth ditto ... ... Benaura.
Seventh ditto ... ... Sâmpe.
Eighth ditto ... ... Ghâg.

Clans of the Kâshtip Gotra, bearing the title of Bâjpei.

First Clan, First Branch ... ... Khâlewâle.
" Second ditto ... ... Ûnchewâlî.
Second Clan ... ... Mathurâ.
Third ditto ... ... Kâshî Rám.
Fourth ditto ... ... Chandanpûr.

Clan of the Garg Gotra, bearing the title of Chaubi.

One Clan ... ... Gargaiya.

Section II.—Kanoujiya Brahmans of Bengal.

Although some of the Brahmans of Bengal are descended from the Gaurs Proper, yet the great majority are the posterity of Brahmans from Kanouj. These Brahmans, says Mr. Colebrooke, in his essay on the 'Enumeration of Indian Classes,' originally published in the Asiatic Researches, "are descended from five priests, invited from Kânyakubja, by Adiswara, king of Gaura, who is said to have reigned about nine hundred years after Christ. These were Bhatta Nârâyana, of the family of Sândila, a son of Kasyapa; Daksha, also a descendant of Kasyapa; Vedagarva, of the family of Vatsa; Chandra, of the family of Saverna, a son of Kasyapa; and Sri Hersha, a descendant of Bhâradwâja. From these ancestors have branched no fewer than a hundred and fifty-six families, of which the precedence was fixed by Ballâla Sena, who reigned in the eleventh century of the Christian era. One hundred of these families settled in Vârendra; and fifty-six in Rârâ. They are now dispersed throughout Bengal, but retain the family distinctions fixed by Ballâla Sena. They are denominated from the families to which their five progenitors belonged, and are still considered as Kânyakubja Brahmans. At the period when these priests were invited by the king of Gaura, some Sâraswat Brahmans, and a few Vaidikas, resided in Bengal. Of the Brahmans of Sâraswat, none are now found in Bengal; but five families of Vaidikas are extant, and are admitted to intermarry with the Brahmans of Rârâ."

"Among the Brahmans of Vârendra, eight families have pre-eminence; and eight hold the second rank:

1.—Varendra Brahmans.

Eight Kûlîn.

1. Maitra.	5. Lahari.
2. Bhîma or Kâlî.	6. Bhaduri.
3. Rudra Vâgîsi.	7. Sâdhu Vâgîsi.
4. Sangamini or Sandyâl.	8. Bhadara.

The last was admitted by election of the other seven.

Eight Sudra Srotriya.

Eighty-four Kashta Srotriya.

The names of these ninety-two families seldom occur in common intercourse.

Among those of Rârâ, six hold the first rank.

2.—Rarhiya Brahmans.

Six Kûlin.

1. Mukhuti, vulgarly, Mukhurjee.	4. Ghoshâla.
2. Ganguli.	5. Bandyagati, vulgarly, Banerjee.
3. Kânjelata.	6. Châtati, vulgarly, Chaturjee.

Fifty Srotriya.

The names of these fifty families seldom occur in common intercourse.

"The distinctive appellations of the several families are borne by those of the first rank; but in most of the other families they are disused; and *serman*, or *sermâ*, the addition common to the whole tribe of Brahmans, is assumed. For this practice, the priests of Bengal are censured by the Brahmans of Mithila and other countries, where that title is only used on important occasions, and in religious ceremonies" (*a*). Vârendra is north of the Ganges, in the District of Râjshahy; and Rârâ is the country to the west of the Bhagirathi river.

3.—Pashchatiya Vaidik.

4.—Dakshinatiya Vaidik.

(*a*) Colebrooke's Essays, pp. 277, 278.

CHAPTER IV.

THE SARJUPARIA OR SARWARIA BRAHMANS, OR SECOND SUB-TRIBE OF KANOUJIYA BRAHMANS—THE SAWALAKHI BRAHMANS—THE MAHA-BRAHMAN, OR ACHARJA—THE GANGA-PUTRA, OR SON OF THE GANGES—THE GAYAWAL—THE PRYAGWAL—THE OJHA—THE BHANRERIYA.

SECOND SUB-TRIBE.

The Sarjuparia, or Sarwaria, Brahmans.

Section I.—The Sarwaria Brahmans Proper.

This name is given to the descendants of those Brahmans who originally occupied the country beyond the Sarju river, in the kingdom of Oudh, and were, tradition reports, emigrants from Kanouj. They are now a very numerous branch of the great Kanoujiya tribe of Brahmans, and are found from Bahraich in Oudh, and the borders of Nepal, throughout the provinces of Benares and Allahabad, as far south and west as Bundelkhand, including the northern portion of that territory. The word Sarwaria is a corruption of Sarjupâria, which comes from *Sarju*, the river of that name, and *pâr*, the other side. Socially, the Sarjupâri Brahmans are not considered of equal rank with the Kanoujiya Brahmans Proper, although they themselves naturally do not admit the inferiority. One tradition states, that Sarjupârî Brahmans were degraded from their position as Kanoujiya Brahmans on account of their receiving alms, whereupon Râmâ Chandra took them under his protection, and gave them possessions on the other side of the Sarju. Another tradition, more gratifying to the Sarjupâris themselves, is, that they were specially invited from Kanouj by Râma, on the completion of the war with Ceylon.

The Sarwarias are very numerous in the Gorakhpûr district, where, according to Buchanan, they are divided into nineteen clans. This statement, however, needs confirmation. With the means at his command for making elaborate inquiries and researches, it is much to be regretted that this diligent and patient investigator was not more careful in verifying, systematizing, and digesting the vast information he acquired on every subject.

The Sarjupâris acknowledge sixteen sub-divisions or *gotras*, of which three are in the first rank, and thirteen in the second. They are as follows:—

Principal Gotras of the Sarjupâria Brahmans.

1. Garg.
2. Gautam.
3. Sândil.

Brahmans of these *gotras*, in their relation to Brahmans of the remaining *gotras*, are regarded as Kûlîns.

Inferior Gotras of the Sarjupâria Brahmans.

1. Bhâraddwâj.
2. Vashisth.
3. Vatsa.
4. Kasyap.
5. Kâsyap.
6. Kausik.
7. Chandrâyan.
8. Sâvaranya.
9. Parâsar.
10. Pulasta.
11. Vrigu.
12. Atri.
13. Angirâ.

(Kâsyap *gotra* is, by some, considered separate from the Kasyap *gotra*. Kâs-syap was the son of Kasyap.)

The list of the thirteen inferior *gotras* is apt to vary to some extent, though most of the names here given will be found in every list. I shall not enumerate all the separate clans of each of these *gotras;* but shall content myself with furnishing one or more of some of them.

Clans and Titular Rank of the Sarwaria Brahmans.

Clan of the Garg Gotra, bearing the title of Pânde : Itiyâ.
Clan of the Gautam Gotra, bearing the title of Dûbe : Kanchaniya.
Clan of the Sândil Gotra, bearing the title of Pânde : Triphala.

Clan of the Sândil Gotra, bearing the title of Tiwâri : Pindî.
Clan of the Bhâraddwâj Gotra, bearing the title of Dûbe : Brihadgrâm.
Clan of the Vatsa Gotra, bearing the title of Misr : Paiyâsî.
Clan of the Vatsa Gotra, bearing the title of Dûbe : Samadârî.
Clan of the Kasyap Gotra, bearing the title of Misr : Rârhî.
Clan of the Kâsyap Gotra, bearing the title of Pânde : Mâlâ.
Clan of the Kausik Gotra, bearing the title of Misr : Dharmpûrâ.
Clan of the Chandrâyan Gotra, bearing the title of Pânde : Chapâlâ.
Clan of the Sâvaranya Gotra, bearing the title of Pânde : Itârî.
Clan of the Sâvaranya Gotra, bearing the title of Pânde : Jurwa.
Clans of the Parâsar Gotra, bearing the title of Pânde :

1. Lohandî.
2. Bâmpûrâ.
3. Biroura.
4. Sîlâsam Dhamoulî.

The following is a list of some other clans with their titles, the *gotras* of which I am unacquainted with :—

Clans.	*Gotras.*	*Titles.*
Adharj	... ...	Pânde.
Ashtâr Kapâl	... ...	do.
Bishtoulî	... ...	do.
Lahasarî	... ...	do.
Madharhia	... ...	do.
Agastiya	... ...	do.
Machiaun	... ...	do.
Luhdî	... ...	do.
Ad-cholâ	... ...	do.
Chârpânîhâ	... ...	do.
Parsiya	... ...	do.
Bhurhariya	... ...	do.
Chândâ	... ...	Shukul.
Bihrâ	... ...	do.
Kanjay	... ...	do.
Mâmkhor	... ...	do.
Bheru-bakrua	... ...	do.
Sat	... ...	do.
Unchahariya	... ...	do.
Newârî	... ...	do.
Muther	... ...	Chaube.
Naipûrâ	... ...	do.
Sirjam	... ...	Tiwâri.

Clans.	*Gotras.*	*Titles.*
Suhagaura	... ...	Tiwâri.
Dhaturâ	... ...	do.
Hannâ	... ...	do.
Dihimâ	... ...	do.
Mujaunâ	... ...	do.
Biduâ	... ...	do.
Gurouli	... ...	do.
Trigonait	... ...	do.
Khuria	... ...	Upâdhiya.
Bhabhaya	... ...	Misr.
Pîyâsî	... ...	do.
Mârjani	... ...	do.
Panrahâ	... ...	do.
Shaunrejî	... ...	do.
Bharsî	... ...	do.
Pîparâ	... ...	do.
Karelî	... ...	Ojhâ.
Nipania	... ...	do.
Parwâ	... ...	Dûbe.
Tilaurâ	... ...	do.

The Brahmans of the two remaining Sections of this Chapter, while placed here in association with the Sarjupârî sub-tribe, are, strictly speaking, only partially connected with them, and are much inferior in rank to the pure Sarjupâris.

Section II.—The Sawalakhi Brahmans.

The story of these Brahmans is strange enough. A certain Raja, it is said, wishing to give a great feast to Brahmans, invited a lac and a quarter, or one hundred and twenty-five thousand, to his palace. His servants, however, being unable to collect so large a number, gathered together a multitude of people of all castes, and decorating them with the sacred cord, made them look like Brahmans. The Raja, thinking them all of the genuine twice-born caste, washed their feet, fed them, and gave them alms. They and their descendants have been from this time regarded as Brahmans. Another account is, that the Raja wishing to perform an important sacrifice requiring the presence of a lac and a quarter of Brahmans, assembled a crowd of people from all quarters, without distinction of rank or caste, and, bestowing upon them the sacred thread, employed them at the sacrifice; from which time they have held the distinction of Brahmans. Tradition is not uniform respecting the name of this singular eclectic Raja. Some accounts speak of him as a Raja of Rewah, or Raja Ram Baghel, or Raja Ram simply, of Mâdhu Garh. He is also represented to have been the famous Ram Chandra; or Manick Chand, brother of Jai Chand of Kanouj; or one of the Sarnait Rajas. It is manifest, therefore, that it is difficult to trace the origin of the tale. The exact date of the circumstance is professed to be given by Munshi Kishori Lal, in his essay on caste, who, with true Hindu instinct, makes light of historic puzzles. He states that it occurred in the year 1563 of our era, during the reign of Akbar.

Although the truth or falsity of this wholesale manufacture of Brahmans from a promiscuous assemblage of persons of inferior castes be enveloped in mystery, yet there is no question that it is commonly believed, not merely by ignorant and unthinking people, but also by intelligent natives of education and learning. Many of the existing Brahmanical castes in Benares and its neighbourhood belong to the Sawalakhî class. Indeed this class is comprehensive and elastic, and readily recognizes all those Brahmans who have lost their family traditions and can give no satisfactory account of their predecessors. The Sawalakhis, on certain conditions, especially by the payment of money, have been permitted to unite themselves by marriage with the Sarwarias, and are now for the most part included among them. The Gayâwâls, Pryâgwâls, Gangâ-putras, Mahâ-Brahmans, and other Brahmans engaged in special sacrificial ceremonies, of whom I shall presently give a more detailed account, are, in these parts, chiefly Sawalakhis. All of this class are considered to be inferior Brahmans; and the titles which they assume, such as Misr, Dûbe, Pânde, Tiwâri, and so forth, are held in much less esteem than are the same titles when worn by other Brahmans.

The number of separate clans of the Sawalakhi Brahmans is very large. The following list represents a few of them ranged according to their honorific titles:—

Clans: Dûbe.

1. Beluâ Saurî.
2. Chillu-pâr.
3. Shiva-man.
4. Sakawî-Bhârgu.
5. Matîâre.
6. Khirauhâ.
7. Rupauhuli.
8. Kothrâ.
9. Karaundâ.

Clans: Upâdhia.

1. Kewet-bansî.
2. Tusuwâ.
3. Tirphala.

Clans: Tiwari.

1. Khairî.
2. Tigunâit.

Clans: Misr.

1. Mârjani.
2. Suara-tânr.
3. Parharahâ.

Clans: Dikshît.

(Unknown.)

Clan: Pânde.

1. Barbas.

Clans: Awasthi.

(Unknown.)

Clans: Pâthakh.

(Unknown.)

Section III.—Other Clans.

There are several classes of Brahmans of subordinate rank engaged in the performance of special and peculiar ceremonies and services which, in the estimation of Hindus, are of great importance. These classes, as already stated, are, in the Benares Province, generally regarded as belonging to the Sawalakhî Brahmans. Why Brahmans of a higher grade do not in that part of the country undertake such duties, is not apparent. One reason, prominently brought forward by the natives themselves, is, that the superior Brahmans are far too sacred to engage in such services, which, however, it is alleged, are the proper vocation of men of an inferior grade. Thus it comes to pass, that the high Brahmans look down upon, despise, and almost loathe the lower Brahmans, and will hold no intercourse with them. The former, in no case whatever, will receive a present of money on the banks of the Ganges, or of any other stream, and would consider themselves as having committed a gross sin were they to do so; while the latter will readily do so. Again, while the inferior Brahmans are always anxious to receive presents and offerings, some duties, more or less connected with their religion, are performed by the superior Brahmans without emolument or reward from those who are the objects of them; which is quite consistent with the circumstance that they perform many other duties for which payment is rigidly exacted. For instance, the teachers of the Vedas and Shastras, as a rule, receive nothing from their pupils; on the contrary, often contribute towards their support. But if those same teachers were invited to a marriage festival, or were requested to cast the horoscope of a child, or to determine the lucky day for entering on a new enterprise, they would expect to be remunerated for the same. In the matter of teaching the sacred books, while they are not paid by their scholars, not a few are amply supported by Hindus of wealth and rank in their neighbourhood, who regard it as a very meritorious act to appropriate their money in this manner. It is notorious that Brahmans of all ranks do not scruple to receive gratuities on great public occasions—as the marriage of a

Raja, or the visit of a wealthy native coming on pilgrimage to Benares—merely as Brahmans, without having discharged any duties whatever, and do not hesitate to attend the great man's Brahmanical dinner in thousands. Moreover, many members of the sacred caste wander about the country as professional beggars, levying their black-mail on all the subordinate castes. Stalwart men, of splendid physique, daubing themselves with ashes and paint, and streaking their foreheads, arms, and chests with the symbolical marks of Vishnu or Shiva, are not ashamed to beg from house to house, and from village to village, and to threaten with their anger, and even with their curse, the obsequious and superstitious natives.

1. The *Mahâ-Brahman*, or great Brahman, called also *Mahâ-pâtra*, is employed by Hindus in times of mourning and on the death of their relatives. The day after a Hindu dies, an earthen vessel, called *ghant*, is filled with water, and is hung upon a tree by a cord, and replenished night and morning. Every evening a small lamp, or *chirâgh*, is lit, and placed over the mouth of the vessel. These operations are performed by the person who has applied the torch to the funeral pile. The vessel, having been previously consecrated by the Mahâ-Brahman, has a small hole drilled into its bottom, from which the water issues in drops. The object of the water is to appease the thirst of the departed spirit; and of the lamp, to shed light upon it during the darkness of the night. The Mahâ-Brahman is present on the first day, and recites *mantras*, or certain sacred texts, for the well-being of the deceased. After a prescribed number of days, he appears again, breaks the vessel, and demands his customary reward, consisting of the clothes, horses, palanquins, and all other personal effects of the departed one, as well as food and money. When a Brahman dies, the vessel hangs up for ten days before being broken; for a Kshatriya it hangs up twelve days; for a Vaisya, fifteen; and for a Sudra, one month. This was the old custom; but in these degenerate days, all share alike, and the vessel is suspended ten days for everybody.

Although the title of Mahâ-Brahman is given to the Brahman officiating on these occasions, yet he is by no means regarded as great, as the prefix *mahâ* would imply, for, in the estimation of the entire caste, he occupies a very mean position. It is in fact a contemptuous epithet. No other Brahman will touch a Mahâ-Brahman. Should he by chance do so, he must bathe, and wash his clothes.

The Mahâ-Brahman is the same as the Achârj of Bombay and other parts of Western India.

2. *Gangâ-putra*, or son of the Ganges, is a term applied to the Brahman who presides over the religious ceremonies performed on the banks of the river Ganges at Benares or elsewhere. He is also found at sacred wells, tanks, and other pools of water in its neighbourhood, to which devotees resort. He likewise directs pilgrims to the temples, or other places, to which they may desire to go. They do nothing without first taking counsel of him, and receiving his instructions. On arriving at the hallowed stream he takes a little water, and pours it into their hands, in which also he deposits a few dry blades of the *kusha* grass, and repeats the proper *mantras*, or Sanskrit texts. They then bathe in the river; on completing which ceremony, the Gangâ-putra gives each a small quantity of *chandan*, or powdered sandal-wood, which they apply to their foreheads on a spot perpendicular to the ridge of the nose. Thereupon, the pilgrims present him with their offerings, and proceed to their quarters; but should they wish beforehand to visit some of the celebrated temples, and to pay their devotions there, he accompanies them thither, although this is the special duty of the Bhanreriya, another class of inferior Brahmans. At Benares the number of Gangâ-putras is very large. The *ghats*, or stairs leading down to the river, are apportioned out to them, and they watch over their several boundaries with much jealousy. Moreover, they lay claim to the entire bank between high and low water-mark, which, seeing that the difference is upwards of fifty feet, is considerable. As a class, they are notorious for coarseness of manners, licentiousness, and rapacity. Yet the tens of thousands of pilgrims, who every year visit Benares, are almost entirely at their mercy. Many of these come from remote parts of India, and not a few are of the female sex. Most of them arrive tired and worn out by travel, yet full of joy at the thought of having at length reached the sacred city. Unsuspectingly, they entrust themselves to the sons of the Ganges, who with all their wickedness at home have a reputation abroad for sanctity. These enfold them within their toils, fleece them of their money, and otherwise behave towards them in a shameless manner, while the poor pilgrims, being generally utter strangers, having no means of redress, patiently submit to maltreatment and ignominy. It would be well if the Government authorities exercised control not only over the Gangâ-putras, but also over all the priests of the temples in Benares, so as to secure their good behaviour and the comfort of pilgrims and other worshippers.

The Gangâ-putras are separated from all other Brahmans, and are regarded as of an inferior grade. They can intermarry, however, with *pandâs*, or temple-priests.

3. The *Gayâwâl* is an agent of the priests of Gayâ. He collects pilgrims in Benares and its neighbourhood, with whom he proceeds to Gayâ, a famous place of pilgrimage in the province of Behar. He also receives money and other presents intended for the priests and temples of that city. The Gayâwâls are abundant in Behar, where they are divided into fourteen *gotras*, or clans, which are precisely of the same name as those of the Sâkâdwîpî or Magadh Brahmans. The *Pryâgwâl* is an agent performing the same duties in behalf of the priests and temples of Pryâg, or Allahabad. Emissaries from *Jagannáth*, and from other well-known sacred spots frequented by Hindu pilgrims, also reside in Benares, and look after the interests of their sacred religious fraternities. Like the Gangâ-putras and Mahâ-Brahmans, they are all of inferior Brahmanical caste, and only intermarry amongst themselves.

4. The *Ojhâ* is a person who is supposed to have especial jurisdiction over *bhûts* and *prets*,—that is, imps and goblins,—in the existence and evil influence of which, most Hindus, particularly the uneducated, place implicit credence. When a Hindu falls sick, it is customary to send for the Ojhâ Brahman, that he may exorcize the foul spirit. On arriving at the house the Ojhâ seats himself on the ground, and places in front of him a small quantity of barley, the grains of which he counts. He then meditates. After a reasonable time he announces his decision, to the effect, that the *bhût*, or imp, which has seized and entered into the sick person, is a *bhût* attached to the family of a deceased father-in-law, or uncle, or anybody else whom his fancy may hit upon, or is a strange and unknown *bhût* that seized him at a certain place while travelling, or is some other still, which his powers of invention enable him to account for. Thereupon, the Ojhâ orders some cloves to be brought, which, after reciting several texts in the way of charms or incantations, are folded in a cloth, and tied to the bedstead on which the invalid is lying. On this the latter is instructed to declare what *bhût* is within him. This he does by stating, "I am the *bhût* of my father-in-law, or uncle, or of a certain house, or tree, or hill," according as he has been directed. Then the Ojhâ suggests that a sheep, or goat, or other animal, should be sacrificed; that the *hom*, or burnt-offering, should be made; and that presents should be given to the Brahmans. This terminates the ceremony of exorcism, and the intruding *bhût* should then in decency withdraw, and the patient recover. Fortunately for the Ojhâ, his fee and perquisites do not depend on this latter contingency.

Formerly, the Ojhâ was always a Brahman: but his profession has become so profitable that sharp, clever, shrewd men in all the Hindu castes have taken to it, and find employment proportioned, it may be, to the skill they display in the exorcising process.

5. The *Bhanreriya* is a man of considerable influence in Benares, although in reality holding a very low position among Brahmans. He is by profession a prognosticator of coming events; and it needs scarcely be added that, in a large city like Benares, penetrated through and through with superstition, his services are much in request from the highest Hindu to the lowest. To this lucrative occupation he adds another. The multitudes of pilgrims who are constantly visiting the sacred city from all parts of India every month of the year, require a great many guides to direct them to those interesting places in the city, the famous wells, and tanks, and temples, and ghats,—to which it is usual for pilgrims to go and there pay their devotions,—and to initiate them into the duties to be performed at each spot. The Bhanreriyas discharge the functions of guides to such persons, and are well paid for their pains, especially as they do not scruple to take various kinds of presents, which more respectable Brahmans would reject with indignation. The god Saturn, or Sanîchar, is mostly worshipped by these people. As Saturday is the day sacred to this deity, on which he receives special adoration, it is customary for the Bhanreriyas to receive presents of oil on this day in honour of the god.

The Bhanreriya is also called Bhaddalî, from following the tenets of Bhaddal. Many of the clan are found at Rudrpûr, in the Gorakhpûr district; and the village has consequently received the appellation of Bhaddalpûr, or town inhabited by Bhaddalîs. It is said, and is commonly believed in that neighbourhood, that Bhaddalpûr is the birth-place of the race. The clan is likewise spoken of by the terms Dakaut and Joshî.

CHAPTER V.

THE BHUINHAR BRAHMANS—THE KINWARS—THE BEMWARS—THE SAKARWARS—THE DUNWARS—THE KASTWARS—HISTORICAL SKETCHES OF THE FAMILIES OF THE MAHARAJA OF BENARES, THE LATE RAJA SIR DEO NARAIN SINGH BAHADUR, AND OF BABU FUTTEH NARAIN SINGH.

THE BHUINHAR BRAHMANS.

Section I.

THESE Brahmans belong chiefly, though not exclusively, to the Sarwaria branch of the Kanoujiya tribe. They are found in large numbers in the city of Benares, and in the district and province of the same name, and even as far as the northern part of Behar.

Some doubt has been thrown on the purity of their blood as Brahmans. It has been said that they are Kshatriya or Rajpoot Brahmans; or are partly Rajpoots and partly of other castes; or are a race of bastard Brahmans. I have been unable to obtain any trustworthy evidence for such assertions. Nevertheless, there is no question that they do not occupy a high rank and position among the Brahmanical races. The reasons for this I conceive to be three-fold:—

1. The Bhûinhârs are addicted to agriculture, a pursuit considered to be beneath the dignity of pure, orthodox Brahmans. The word is partly derived from *bhûin* or *bhûmi*—land.

2. They have accepted and adopted in their chief families the secular titles of Raja, Maharaja, and so forth, distinctions which high Brahmans altogether eschew. Hence, such Bhûinhârs have in a sense degraded from their position of Brahmans to that of Rajpoots, whose honorific title of Singh they commonly affix to their names. The Maharaja of Benares, who is the acknowledged head of the Bhûinhâr Brahmans in that city, is styled Maharaja Ishwaree

Narain Singh. The title of Singh is borne by all the members, near and remote, of the Maharaja's family.

3. The Bhûînhârs only perform one-half of the prescribed Brahmanical duties. They give alms, but do not receive them; they offer sacrifices to their idols, but do not perform the duties and offices of a priesthood; they read the sacred writings, but do not teach them.

Sir Henry Elliot says:—"We perhaps have some indications of the true origin of Bhûînhâr in the names of Gargabhûmi and Vatsabhûmi, who are mentioned in the Harivansa as Kshatriya Brahmans, descendants of Kasiya princes. Their name of Bhûmi, and residence at Kâsî (Benares), are much in favour of this view; moreover, there are to this day Garga and Vatsa Gots, or Gotras, amongst the Sarwaria Brahmans" (*a*).

It is quite true, as before remarked, that this tribe is numerous in Benares and its neighbourhood, though not as descendants of Kasiya princes. The Maharaja of Benares is undoubtedly a Bhûînhâr; but his family dates only from the first-half of the preceding century. There is no evidence to show that in olden times princes of Benares were ever Bhûînhârs.

By the people of the country of other castes, among whom they dwell, they are called indiscriminately Bhûînhârs, Gautams, and Thâkurs. The term Brahman is not, I believe, applied to them in common conversation, as it is to other Brahmans; but this is no valid argument against their right to the title. The Bhûînhârs call themselves Brahmans; have the *gotras*, titles, and family names of Brahmans; practise, for the most part, the usages of Brahmans, and, in default of proper evidence to the contrary, must be regarded as Brahmans.

While the Gautams of Benares are called Bhûînhârs, they are so simply from the accident of the Bhûînhârs there mostly belonging to the Gautam *gotra*. There are other *gotras* of Bhûînhârs besides the Gautam. Moreover, although the Bhûînhârs are chiefly connected with the Sarwaria branch of the Kânkubja tribe of Brahmans, yet some of them are allied to the Kanoujiya Brahmans Proper. For instance, the Bâbûs of Champur in the Chaprah district are Bhûînhârs of this latter sub-tribe. The name of their clan is Eksariya; of their *gotra*, Parâsar; and of their title, Dîkshit. They have three Pravaras,—namely, Shakti, Vasisht, and Parâsar. They originally followed the Sâma Veda of the Kauthumiya Sâkhâ, or branch; but as there were no Brahmans in that part of the country learned in the Sâma Veda to perform for them the offices of the priesthood, they embraced the Yajur Veda of the Madhyan-deva Sâkhâ.

(*a*) Elliot's Supplemental Glossary, Vol. I, p. 21.

In the face of the peculiar Brahmanical terminology and nomenclature in use among the Bhûînhârs, which differ *in toto cœlo* from those employed by all other castes, of their Brahmanical habits and customs, and of their claim to be regarded as Brahmans, the statement of Mr. Campbell in his recent work on the Ethnology of India (page 66), that "there seems to be no doubt that this class is formed by an intermixture of Brahmins with some inferior caste," is untenable. He assigns no reason for such an observation further than that "they live in strong and pugnacious brotherhoods, and are in character much more like Rajpoots than Brahmins."

The opinion of Mr. Beames, in his edition of Sir H. Elliot's Supplemental Glossary on the physical characteristics of the Bhûînhârs, is true and worth recording: "They are a fine manly race, with the delicate Aryan type of feature in full perfection, yet," he adds, "their character is bold and overbearing, and decidedly inclined to be turbulent,"—a strong expression, which it would not be easy to substantiate or justify.

The following is a list of some of the clans, *gotras*, and titles of the Bhûînhâr Brahmans:—

Clans.	*Gotras.*	*Titles.*
Eksadiya.	Garg.	Misr.
Sankarwâr.	Gautam.	Dîkshit.
Kinwâr.	Sândil.	Upâdhiya.
Bemwâr.	Kâsyap.	Pânde.
Dunwâr.	Bhâraddwâj.	Tiwâri.
Chaudhari.	Vatsa.	Pâthakh.
Kulhâ.		Bharsî-Misr.
Pipra.		
Jaithariya.		
Rausadiya.		
Kastwâr.		

The most important of these clans in Benares is the Bipra branch of the Gautam *gotra*, of the Misr rank, to which belong the Maharaja of Benares together with the noble families connected with him, and the family of the late Raja Sir Deo Narain Singh and of his son Raja Sambhu Narain Singh. It is of the Kauthumiya Sâkhâ, or branch, of Brahmans, following the ritual of the Sâma Veda. It has three Praviras (distinguished by the number of knots in the Brahmanical cord)—the Gautam, Angiras, and Autathiya. The clan intermarries with the Bhûînhârs of the Madhyandiva Sâkhâ, or branch, of Brahmans, observing the ritual of the Yajur Veda. It is traditionally allied to the Sarjupârî Brahmans of the village of Madhubani, beyond the Gogra, who, strange to say, are Shat Karmas,—that is, perform the *six* duties enjoined on Brahmans. This relationship seems to show that the Bhûînhâr Brahmans, who now observe only three of the Brahmanical obligations, were once orthodox, and observed the entire six.

The Maharajah of Bettiah is a Bhûînhâr of the Jaithariya clan of the Kâsyap *gotra*, of the Madhyandana Sâkhâ, observing the ritual of the Yajur Veda. The Raja of Sheohâr, the Râjkumâr Babu of Mâdhoban, and several small landholders of Champâran, are of the same caste (*a*). The Chaudhari clan of the Bhâraddwâj *gotra*, with the title of Pânde, is of the Madhyandana Sâkhâ, which follows the Yajur Veda. And the Kolhas are of the Kâsyap *gotra*, of the Madhyandana Sâkhâ, which also practises the ceremonies of the Yajur Veda.

Section II.—Bhûînhâr Tribes of the Ghazipûr District.

1. The Kinwâr Bhûînhârs have three great divisions, called after their ancestors; these are—

1. Râjdhar.
2. Makund.
3. Pithour Rai.

The Kinwâr Bhûînhârs are related to the Kinwâr Rajpoots. A branch of the Bhûînhârs in the Ghazipûr District became Mahomedans, and settled in the village of Barah and the surrounding territory, in the Zamanîah *pargannah*. The village has a population of upwards of five thousand persons. The Makund clan are more wealthy than the Râjdhar; but are not so high in rank.

2. The Bemwâr Bhûînhârs have fourteen villages in the Narhî *pargannah* of the Ghazipûr district, some of which are very large. They are said to have originally come from Bempûr, and to be descended from Dawan Rai, from whom they can trace their pedigree to themselves through thirty generations. The chief village of the Bemwârs is Narhî, in which are five thousand three hundred inhabitants. They are a very prosperous and loyal people.

3. The Sakarwâr Bhûînhârs are related to the Sakarwâr Rajpoots, as is shown in the account of the latter tribe. In the Ghazipûr district they are, remarks Dr. Oldham, "generally rich, and have retained the greater part of their

(*a*) Elliot's Supplemental Glossary, Mr. Beames' Note, Vol. I, p. 23.

hereditary property." These people "occupy a very fertile tract of lowland country."

4. The Dunwâr Bhûînhârs state that they came from the neighbourhood of Fathpûr-Sikrî, and are descended from a Brahman named Duna Chârgiya. Branches of the family settled, at various times, in the Azimgarh, Benares, and Ghazipûr districts. Jhain Bhat colonized a part of the Zamanîah *pargannah* of the latter district, where his posterity still flourishes. They are, says Dr. Oldham, "frugal and industrious." He adds, "the ancestor of Dunwârs of two or three villages was in the military service of the emperor; and received from him for his valour the title of 'Khan,' which is borne to the present day by all his descendants."

5. The Kastwâr Bhûînhârs occupy about twenty-six villages in the Mahomadabâd *pargannah* of the Ghazipûr district. They profess to have inhabited that territory for ages past, and to be the descendants of the few Brahmans who originally were located among the aboriginal population. Respecting this circumstance, Dr. Oldham makes the following important and suggestive observation: "they may be regarded as a link which connects the Hindu occupation of the Gupta era with the Hindu occupation of the district in modern times" (*a*).

The relationship undoubtedly subsisting between the Bhûînhâr Brahmans and Bhûînhâr Rajpoots is exceedingly interesting. Dr. Oldham throws some light on this subject in his account of the Bhûînhârs inhabiting the Ghazipûr district. He remarks, that "there are numerous sub-divisions, or tribes, of the Bhûînhârs, and these are generally, if not always, called by the name of some of the recognized Rajpoot clans, or races. Thus we have Kinwâr, Gautam, and Kausik Bhûînhârs, as also Kinwâr, Gautam, and Kausik Rajpoots; but there are many Rajpoot tribes which have no representative among the Bhûînhârs. Whether any connexion exists between the Rajpoot and Bhûînhâr tribes of the same name, is an obscure point; but, in this district, the Bhûînhâr and corresponding Rajpoot tribes sometimes name the same city or country as the first home of their race; and, in one case, a Bhûînhâr and a Rajpoot tribe both claim descent from a common ancestor, and each admits that the pretensions of the other are well-founded" (*b*).

The Bhûînhârs "are congregated," says Sir H. Elliot, "chiefly in Deogânw of Azimgarh; in Gorakhpûr; in Doabeh and Saidpûr Bhitrî, of Ghazipûr; and

(*a*) For further information on these tribes, see Dr. W. Oldham's Historical and Statistical Memoir of the Ghazipûr District, pp. 67—70.

(*b*) Memoir of the Ghazipûr District, p. 43.

in Majhâwar, Mehwârî, Sheopûr, Narwan, Kol Asta, Dhûs and Kaswar of Benares; also in Majhowa, Simrânw, and Mehsî of Champâran, in Behâr." To which Mr. Beames adds, "this caste is widely spread all over Northern Behar, Benares, and Gorakhpûr; and less frequent in Southern Behar" (*a*). In Allahabad, there are upwards of a thousand Gautam Brahmans, and in Banda more than three thousand, meaning, I suppose, Bhûînhârs. In Gorakhpûr, there are thirty thousand; in Azimgarh, forty-six thousand; in Jaunpûr, three thousand; in Mirzapûr, four thousand; and in Benares, twenty-one thousand. The last census returns, from which these numbers are taken, are, I fear, not very trustworthy, and can only be regarded as giving the truth approximately. For instance, in the Benares district the Bhûînhârs are, in all probability, not fewer than fifty or sixty thousand in number. In Benares, Ghazipûr, Gorakhpûr, Bhâgalpûr, and probably elsewhere, Bhûînhâr Rajpoots are found as well as Bhûînhâr Brahmans. The Raja of Tamkohî is at the head of the Bhûînhâr Rajpoots.

Section III.

As the Bhûînhârs are the most prominent personages amongst the natives of Benares, I purpose giving here a brief account of several of their distinguished families. The first will be that of the Maharaja of Benares.

HIS HIGHNESS ISHWAREE NARAIN SINGH BAHADUR, MAHARAJA OF BENARES.

This nobleman is the recognized head of the native community of the city and district of Benares, and, in virtue of such position, exerts a great influence upon all classes of the people. In ordinary times, this influence operates calmly and secretly, yet its incidence is felt in every direction. Its recognition and acknowledgment have become a part of the instinctive consciousness of the Hindus of the city and neighbourhood; and they never question its weight or authority. But it is in times of strife and stir that this occult power exhibits its real energy. Then the people look to the Maharaja as to their natural leader, and place themselves at his disposal. His word comes to them with far greater force than the command of any other person, be he who or what he may. Such authority is not peculiar to the Maharaja of Benares, for it is possessed by many nobles in India, and is frequently wielded too by them much more than he cares to wield it. It differs altogether from that of an English nobleman among his tenantry. It is like that which the nobility of England held in their hands in

(*a*) Supplemental Glossary, Vol. I, pp. 22, 23.

the age of feudalism—is like that of the Campbells, and MacCulloms, and Grahams, in Scotland, two hundred years ago.

The family of the Benares prince is not old; compared with the great families of Udaipûr and Joudhpûr, is but of yesterday. Little is known about the ancient Rajas of Benares, save that there were such men. They have passed away, and scarcely a name survives. In the beginning of the last century, when the Sircar, or territory, of Benares, came into the possession of the Nawab of Oudh, who governed it in subordination to his Suzerain, the Mogul Emperor, Mîr Rûstam Shâh was appointed as deputy, or lieutenant, to direct its affairs, and to act as ruler in behalf of the Nawab. There was then living at Gangâpûr, a village eight miles from Benares, a small zemindar, or landholder, of the Gautam branch of the Bhûînhâr Brahmans, named Mansâ Râm. This man entered the service of the Nâzim Mîr Rûstam Shâh. His varied talents soon brought him into notice: and his master came to regard him as his most energetic and skilful officer. By degrees his influence extended over all the country within the jurisdiction of Rûstam Shâh, and the Nawab himself was not ignorant of his name and character. It is not astonishing, therefore, that, on occasion of the misconduct and consequent disgrace of the Deputy, Mansâ Râm should have been entrusted with the management of the Sircar. He retained charge of it until his death, about the year 1739. He was succeeded by his son, Balwant Singh, to whom, in his life-time, he had actually entrusted its administration, although continuing its nominal ruler. At his solicitation, the Emperor of Delhi granted him the title of Raja, not apparently for himself, but for his son, Balwant Singh, who was thenceforward called Raja of Benares.

Such was the origin of the Benares family. Its real founder was Mansâ Râm; but the lustre and high reputation of the family, during the last century, were due not so much to the labours of Mansâ Râm as to those of his son. Raja Balwant Singh far surpassed his father in ability. His daring and cunning, his unbounded energy, his wonderful determination, his fertility of device, his untamed rapacity, passed into a proverb. In the course of his eventful life he came into collision with all his neighbours, fought with them many a battle, which always ended in the capture of their forts and the annexation of their lands. The principle of annexation was understood in those days as well as in later times. By foul means and fair, mostly the former, Balwant Singh succeeded in obtaining ninety-six *pargannahs*, or large baronies, from which he collected the revenue, and which he governed with almost despotic power. Yet he never presumed on absolute sovereignty. He paid a large fixed sum yearly as revenue to his Suzerain, whom he acknowledged as his superior, and to whom appeals from his acts were supposed to lie. On the other hand, there is no question that he obeyed the Nawab only at pleasure. He kept a formidable body of armed retainers, with whose aid he carried on his guerillas, which the Nawab was unable either to punish or repress. On one notable occasion, the Nawab, being more than ordinarily incensed at his refractory vassal, led a large force from Oudh to Benares against him. Balwant Singh fled, and shut himself up in one of his forts. He was too wily to fight with him, and too wary to meet him peaceably. But he organized a huge system of robbery; and the Nawab's camp was beset perpetually by sharks and thieves, who pilfered day and night on a prodigious scale. The Nawab was at length wearied out, and was obliged to quit Benares, and to make terms with the Raja, who, on the departure of his master, returned to his palace in Benares.

When the battle of Buxar was fought between the British troops and the Vizier of Oudh, the latter deemed it prudent to send away Raja Balwant Singh, who had appeared in answer to a summons from his liege lord, attended by an imposing force, with the ostensible object of rendering him assistance. After the battle, the Raja made his submission to the English, which act, together with his previous neutrality, secured to him the staunch friendship and firm protection of Lord Clive. In the treaty that was subsequently made with the Nawab, a special provision was inserted in favour of Balwant Singh, in spite of the utmost efforts of the Vizier to prevent it. He cherished intense indignation towards the Raja, not so much on account of old grievances, as by reason of the part he had taken prior and subsequent to the battle of Buxar, whereby his own plans had been defeated, and the Raja had ingratiated himself with the new rulers of the country. Clive was too astute not to see through the malicious plans of the Nawab to ruin his vassal. Yet when he left for England, his weak and incapable successor, Mr. Vansittart, yielded temporarily to the wishes of the Nawab to crush the Raja, who was only saved by his own promptness and presence of mind.

Nevertheless, it is perfectly true, that the Raja of Benares would have been utterly destroyed had it not been for the aid and support of the British Government. Balwant Singh passed away, leaving a vast inheritance to Cheit Singh, a son by an irregular marriage, who, mainly through the zeal and adroitness of his faithful adviser, Babu Ausân Singh, ancestor of the late distinguished Raja Sir Deo Narain Singh Bahâdur, and not without some difficulty, became his father's successor. Cheit Singh was placed on the same footing in relation-to the British Government as that held by his father; had the same jurisdiction, and occupied the same estates; and might have been, like him, an honoured and privileged feudatory, had he chosen to be so. But falling out with his sage counsellor, and left to his own resources, he had the inconceivable folly to run counter to the wishes of Warren Hastings, who at one time was his friend, but became his bitter and relentless enemy. None can exonerate Warren Hastings from harshness and vindictiveness in his treatment of the Raja. At the same time, the demands which Warren Hastings made on him, though excessive, were within his legitimate province, if he saw fit, as Governor-General, to make; and were also not beyond the ability of the Raja to meet. The issue is well known. Cheit Singh's rebellion brought with it transient danger to Warren Hastings personally, and likewise to British domination over the Benares territory. But both kinds of danger speedily passed away; and Cheit Singh lived and died a rebel.

Yet the Rajaship, though forfeited, was, by the merciful consideration of the Government, after a season of suspension, given to a descendant of Ranee Gulab, daughter of Raja Balwant Singh; in other words, was removed from the male to the female branch of the family. Little need be said respecting the Rajas who have in succession held that title. Although all the honour and much of the influence connected with it still remain, yet the actual authority and executive power possessed by Balwant Singh, or even by Cheit Singh, have entirely disappeared; and the holder of the title is now only a great and wealthy noble occupying large estates.

The title was originally, and until lately, simply that of Raja; but the chief now in the enjoyment of it was further ennobled a few years since for the part he took in adhering to the Government, and rendering it support, in the mutiny of 1857, and received the title of Maharaja, or great Raja. From that time to the present the Government have shown him marked attention. He has had the honour of entertaining, on several occasions, the Viceroys who have visited Benares; and, in default of a son, has been permitted to adopt his nephew as his successor. When Prince Alfred came to the sacred city, the Maharaja accompanied him and Earl Mayo to his estate at Chakiya, twenty miles off, on a tiger hunt, where the prince had some excellent sport. The Maharaja is a man of prepossessing and courteous manners, and of a calm and tranquil spirit; and while endowed with the ease and perfect self-possession so peculiar to Orientals, is destitute of the haughtiness of bearing frequently displayed by them.

THE LATE RAJA SIR DEO NARAIN SINGH BAHADUR, K.C.S.I.

Of all the native residents in Benares, for many years past, the deceased Raja was the most distinguished. On several important occasions he rendered great service to the. Government, and throughout the mutiny was the chief native counsellor and helper of the local authorities. The aid he gave during the whole of that season of peril and difficulty was most efficient and praiseworthy. He had already been created Rao Bahadur, for the ability he displayed during the disturbances in Benares in the year 1852; and for his signal acts of loyalty in the mutiny of 1857, he was created a Raja. He was one of the first native members of the Legislative Council of India, and was requested by the Viceroy a second time to join the Council, but declined the honour. In 1866, he was made a Knight Commander of the Star of India at the Viceregal Durbar held at Agra. It should be mentioned also, that, in 1857, in addition to the title of Raja, Deo Narain Singh received a *khilat*, or robe of honour, of the value of ten thousand rupees, and a perpetual grant of twenty-five thousand rupees annually from the Saidpûr-Bhitrî estate.

By the death of this large-hearted, sagacious man, Benares has sustained a great and almost irreparable loss. His influence in the city was in every way beneficial. He was a kind-hearted friend and a faithful counsellor; and his door was open at all times to admit persons seeking his advice or aid. During my residence in India, I have become acquainted with a large number of natives, but I never met one who, for ability, candour, zeal in the public service, and true magnanimity, was to be compared with this noble Hindu. For these qualities he became known far and wide, and was regarded everywhere with admiration and esteem, both by Europeans and his fellow-countrymen. He was the founder of the Benares Institute, over which he presided with great tact and zeal to the day of his death. His speeches were always pithy and full of practical wisdom, exhibiting the clearness and force of his own vigorous mind. As a president he was in every way most exemplary. His numerous friends, English and native, in Benares and elsewhere, have made a subscription to defray the expense of a marble bust, to be deposited in the Town Hall about to be erected through the munificence of the Maharaja of Vizianagram, K.C.S.I.

In the second volume of Kaye's Sepoy War, in the narrative of the mutiny in Benares, sufficient prominence is not given to the very important part which was taken by Raja Deo Narain Singh, in the maintenance of order in the city and neighbourhood during that crisis. Some persons are unduly praised, but there is one to whom only a scant measure of thanks is awarded. For the honour of the Indian Government, and the satisfaction of loyal natives in Benares and elsewhere, I earnestly trust that the title of Raja will be made hereditary in the family of this illustrious man.

In a memorandum drawn up by a former Judge of Benares on the claims of the family of Raja Sir Deo Narain Singh to the consideration of the Government, the following important statement is made respecting the deceased Raja. "When the rebellion broke out in 1857, Benares was in a position of extreme danger and insecurity. The station formed the base of all our operations to the northward, and had it been abandoned, or had it fallen into the hands of the rebels, that base would have been lost, and the consequence would, in all likelihood, have been the loss of Upper India and of every European life between Calcutta and Lahore. This catastrophe was, under Providence, chiefly averted by the courage, determination, and influence of the present Commissioner (1860) Mr. Gubbins; and I believe I am asserting no more than the simple truth, when I state, that all his exertions and devotion would have been unavailing, had he not been unflinchingly and zealously supported by Raja Deo Narain Singh. With the hereditary courage and loyalty of his race, the Raja devoted his whole property, his time, and energy, and even his life itself, had it been called for, to the service of the Government. He furnished guards of faithful men for the safety of the local authorities; kept up an intelligence department, to supply information of all that occurred in the city and its neighbourhood; and raised a loyal band of three hundred retainers for the service of the Government. This body of men proceeding out with his camels and elephants was the means of rescuing the Europeans from Jaunpûr. The Raja also furnished grain and supplies for the troops, and gave up twelve horses and an elephant for their conveyance; and when the danger was most imminent, and the local authorities were most in want of the support and countenance of a native gentleman of his position and influence, he abandoned his own house in the city, and took up his quarters in that occupied by Mr. Gubbins, in order to be able at all times, and on all occasions, to give that officer all the aid and counsel in his power" (*a*).

During the latter half of the last century, an ancestor of the late Raja, Babu Ausân Singh, was a man of great power and influence. He was first the Dewan, or Chief Minister, of Raja Balwant Singh, and was his principal adviser

(*a*) Memorandum of the Saidpûr-Bhitrî Estate, compiled from original documents, p. 20.

in his long quarrel with the Vizier of Oudh, and in all those delicate political movements which eventuated in the Raja becoming the staunch friend and ally of the British Government. On the death of Balwant Singh, as there were several claimants for the Rajaship, Babu Ausân Singh, by a series of skilful manœuvres, succeeded in obtaining the public recognition of Cheit Singh as successor to his father. But Cheit Singh fell out with his faithful servant; and consequently, in the moment of his greatest difficulties, when he needed a calm and vigorous understanding to save him from ruin, he was left to himself, and rushing into rebellion, was obliged to abandon his home in Benares, to which he was destined never to return. Humanly speaking, Raja Cheit Singh would have been saved from such a disaster, had his old adviser, and the old adviser of the family, been at his side.

When Cheit Singh's rebellion occurred, and three English officers, with a large portion of their escort, were massacred, it was mainly through the energy and zeal of Babu Ausân Singh that Warren Hastings and all the British officers with him, together with their small force, were preserved from destruction. Sir Edward Colebrooke, who was with the Governor-General at the time, in the capacity of Persian translator, and was afterwards Resident of Benares, says, that Babu Ausân Singh "furnished a body of horsemen, who were stationed for the protection of the rear of the Residency during the few days which Mr. Hastings subsequently passed there; and that the Babu subsequently attended the Governor-General to Chunar; and that he knew that Mr. Hastings attributed to the interposition of Ausân Singh the withdrawal of the Ranee and her sons from under Cheit Singh's influence; and that for these services the Governor-General had selected the Babu to act as naib (deputy) of the province until the succession to the *Râj* should be disposed of" (*a*). For a time Babu Ausân Singh administered "the revenues and government of the country in the quality of naib," until the successor to Cheit Singh as Raja was determined on.

Before the disgrace of Cheit Singh, the Government had prevailed on him to make over to Babu Ausân Singh, in consideration of his distinguished services, the *pargannah*, or large barony, of "Syudpore Bhittree," with which "the Babu had been connected in the previous Raja Balwant Singh's time." On the death of the Babu, he was succeeded by his son, Babu Shiva Narain Singh, who, true to the loyal instincts of his family, rendered essential aid to the

(*a*) Memorandum on the Saidpûr-Bhitrî Estate, p. 4.

Government during "a very serious disturbance" in Benares, in the year 1811, on occasion of the introduction of a new house-tax. The Magistrate of the time, Mr. Bird, says, that "he was greatly indebted to Babu Shiva Narain Singh, jaghirdar of Syudpore Bhittree, the only native of any consequence who had supported him on that occasion. The Babu protected the bazars in the city, and, through the support he afforded to the police, the corn-markets were unmolested, and the city supplied with corn at the usual price, when no other article of consumption was procurable." The Government expressed "their high sense of Babu Shiva Narain's patriotic conduct; and bestowed a *khilat* on him as a testimony of their approval of his exertions in the maintenance of the public peace" (*a*).

It sounds exceedingly strange that the next important event in connection with this spirited and loyal family should be the successful attempt of the Government to gain possession of the *pargannah* originally granted by Raja Cheit Singh to Babu Ausân Singh. This occurred in 1828, not without great opposition on the part of Babu Shiva Narain Singh. In issuing orders on the subject for the ejection of the Babu from a tenure which for fifty years had contributed mainly to the support of the family, it was urged, whether in mockery or solemn seriousness, is hard to say, that "the necessities of the public service required the measure." "If," the Government added, "Babu Shiva Narain should resolve on contesting their orders, he would thereby forfeit every claim to the indulgence of Government" (*b*). The Babu, as was natural, would not admit this claim of the Government to seize an estate granted so long ago to his father by Raja Cheit Singh, and consequently instituted a suit against the Government for a reversal of their orders. Thereupon, the matter was re-considered, but in the meantime Babu Shiva Narain died, and was succeeded by his son, Babu Har Narain Singh, father of the late Raja Sir Deo Narain Singh Bahâdur. The result of the dispute was, that, instead of the entire revenue of the *pargannah* of Saidpûr-Bhitrî being enjoyed by the family, as formerly, the Babu was obliged to be satisfied with one-fourth of the same, amounting to 36,330 rupees, or three thousand six hundred and thirty-three pounds, the remaining three-fourths being paid to the Government.

Notwithstanding this treatment, the loyalty of the family, and its zeal for the public welfare, never flagged. Although only deriving a fourth part of

(*a*) Memorandum on the Saidpûr-Bhitrî Estate, p. 12.

(*b*) *Ibid*, p. 17.

their former income from the Saidpûr estate, yet both father and son, the latter in a very conspicuous manner, as already shown, laboured diligently to maintain the authority of the Government in the city and district generally, and in every way to promote the prosperity of the people. In 1857, however, as before stated, when the late Raja had rendered assistance to the Government, of immense importance, the sum of 25,000 rupees, or less than another fourth part, was granted in perpetuity to him and his male successors, out of the Saidpûr-Bhitrî estate.

It was my good fortune to be intimately acquainted with the late Raja Sir Deo Narain Singh for several years before his death, and I shall long remember with great pleasure the many virtues of this estimable man. For liberality of sentiment, candour, and common sense, combined with a spirit of kindness and benevolence, I have met with very few natives in India to be compared with him for an instant. He only needed Christianity to make him a perfect Hindu. He is succeeded by his son Raja Sambhu Narain Singh, who is upwards of thirty years of age, has been educated at Queen's college, Benares, and speaks English fluently. He is a man of promise, and has evidently the desire to follow in his father's footsteps. He has lately been made an honorary magistrate of Benares.

GENEALOGICAL TABLE OF THE FAMILY OF THE LATE RAJA SIR DEO NARAIN SING BAHADUR, K.C.S.I.

(From Documents in Possession of the Family.)

- **Narsingh Deo.**
  - **Bikram Shâh.**
    - **Kâshî Nâth.**
      - **Gopâl Singh.**
        - **Murâd Sâh.**
          - **Khedurâm.**
            - **Murdan Sâh.** (Sole Tâluqdâr of Auradpûr or Darekhu, A. D. 1704.)
              - **Dâya Râm.**
                - **Pahalmân Singh.**
                - **Babu Audhû Singh.** (Babu Ausân Singh made over to him the family tâluqdârî, or estate, of Darekhu, on his receiving the jaghir of Saidpûr-Bhitrî.)
                - **Babu Ausân Singh.** (Received from Cheit Singh, Raja of Benares, the jaghir of Saidpûr-Bhitrî rent-free.)
                  - **Babu Sihil Parsâd.**
                  - **Babu Durgâ Parsâd.**
                  - **Babu Shiva Narain Singh.** (Received a *khilat* from the Government in 1801, and again in 1811.)
                    - **Babu Lachminarain Singh.**
                      - **Babu Sri Narain Singh.**
                    - **Babu Har Narain Singh.**
                      - **Raja Sir Deo Narain Singh.** (Received from the Government a *khilat* of succession in 1846; in 1853, was made Rao Bahâdur; in 1857, was made Raja Bahâdur, received a *khilat* of Rs. 10,000, and a perpetual grant of Rs. 25,000 out of the Saidpûr-Bhitrî estate; in 1866, was made Knight Commander of the Star of India, of the second class. Died in the year 1870.)
                        - **Raja Sambhu Narain Singh.** (The present Raja.)
                    - **Babu Rah Narain Singh.**
                - **Badab Singh.**
                - **Khem Karûn Singh.**

BABU FUTTEH NARAIN SINGH.

This gentleman is a relative of His Highness the Maharaja of Benares. He is well known for his public spirit and for the zeal which he exhibits in all matters tending to promote the welfare of the people. For many years, the meetings of the Benares Institute, of which he was for a long time Vice-President, but of which he has been lately made President, in succession to the late Raja Sir Deo Narain Singh Bahadur, have been held in his house. He affords in himself a fine example of a Hindu gentleman.

Babu Aiswarya Narayana Sinha is a son of the preceding. Like many of the young aristocracy of Benares, he has much time on his hands, which, unlike most of them, however, he devotes to the improvement of himself and his neighbours. He has been for years one of the leading spirits of the Benares Institute, of which he is the principal secretary. He is an honorary magistrate of Benares; is active in the promotion of education of both sexes; and is secretary of a large native school in the city. The Babu is undoubtedly one of the chief promoters of progress and social reform in Benares. By reason of his liberal spirit and excellent knowledge of English, he gains ready access to the European residents, with whom, and also with his native fellow-townsmen, he is deservedly popular.

CHAPTER VI.

THE JIJHOTIYA, OR THIRD SUB-TRIBE OF KANOUJIYA BRAHMANS—GOTRAS AND CLANS.

THIRD SUB-TRIBE.

The Jijhotiya Brahmans.

THIS sub-tribe of the Kanoujiya Brahmans is found in Bundelkhand, spreading out in a southerly and westerly direction. On the north and west, it comes in contact with the Kanoujiya Brahmans Proper; and on the north and east, with the Sarwaria Brahmans. Sir H. Elliot speaks of the tribe as follows: "This is a branch of the Kanoujiya Brahmans, which ranks low in public estimation. Their more correct name is Yajurhota, derived originally, it is said, from their having made burnt-offerings according to the form of the Yajur Veda. Their sub-divisions are much of the same character as those of the Kanoujiyas; but it is needless to enumerate them. Amongst their chief families are reckoned the Chaubes of Rûpraund, the Dubes of Dauria, and the Misrs of Hamîrpûr and Karîâ." Dr. Buchanan affirms that in his day there were two thousand families of Jijhotiyas in the district of Gorakhpûr.

This tribe needs to be properly investigated. I can hardly agree with Sir H. Elliot, that the enumeration of its sub-divisions would be without profit. The Jijhotiya Brahmans are little known in Benares; there being, it is computed, not more than sixty or seventy persons of the tribe within the city. From them I have gained some information respecting themselves; but it is very imperfect. They state that the word "Jijhotiya" is derived from Jujhûta, the name of a Baghel Raja who formerly lived in Bundelkhand. This man gathered about him a number of Brahmans, whom he greatly honoured, and whose instructions he devoutly followed. In return for their spiritual services he contributed liberally towards their support. In course of time these Brahmans became a separate people, and were called after their patron. Some of the principal *gotras* and clans of the Jijhotiyas are as follows :—

Gotras and Clans of the Jijhotiya Brahmans.

Clan of the Upamanyu Gotra, bearing the title of Pâthakh :—Rora.
Clan of the Upamanyu Gotra, bearing the title of Bâjpei :—Binwâre.
Clan of the Kasyap Gotra, bearing the title of Pateriya :—Sâypûr.
Clan of the Kasyap Gotra, bearing the title of Pastora :—Bangawa.
Clan of the Gautam Gotra, bearing the title of Chaube :—Rupnouwal.
Clan of the Gautam Gotra, bearing the title of Gangele :—Maray.
Clan of the Sândil Gotra, bearing the title of Misr :—Hamîrpûr.
Clan of the Sândil Gotra, bearing the title of Ajeriyâ :—Kotke.
Clan of the Mounas Gotra, bearing the title of Misr :—Kariya.
Clan of the Bhâraddwâj Gotra, bearing the title of Tiwârî :—Aijîke.
Clan of the Bhâraddwâj Gotra, bearing the title of Dûbe :—Uthâshane.
Clan of the Vatsa Gotra, bearing the title of Tiwârî :—Pathraili.
Clan of the Ekâvashisth Gotra, bearing the title of Nayak :—Piprî.

Some of the names in this list are peculiar. The Mounas *gotra* suggests a Rajpoot origin or connection. The honorary titles of Pateriya, Pastora, Gangele, Ajeriyâ, and Nayak, so far as I am aware, are not found in other races of Brahmans.

CHAPTER VII.

THE SANADHIYA, OR FOURTH SUB-TRIBE OF KANOUJIYA BRAHMANS—GOTRAS AND TITLES.

FOURTH SUB-TRIBE.

The Sanadhiya Brahmans.

THIS race of Kanoujiya Brahmans is found immediately to the west of the Kanoujiyas Proper, and to the east of the Gaur Brahmans Proper; in other words, lying between them. Sir Henry Elliot thus carefully describes their limits: "The Sanaudhas or Sanâdhs, as they are more familiarly called, touch the Kanoujiyas on the north-west, extending over Central Rohilkhand, and part of the Upper and Central Doab, from Pilibhît to Gwalior. The boundary line runs from the north-west angle of Râmpûr, through Richa, Jahânabâd, Nawâbganj, Bareilly, Farrîdpûr, to the Râmganga; thence through Salîmpûr and the borders of Mihrabâd; thence down the Ganges to the borders of Kanouj; thence up the Kâlînaddî to the western border of Alipûr Pattî, through Bhoîgaon, Soj, Etawa, Bîbamau, and down the Jumna to the junction of the Chambal"(*a*). The districts of Agra, Mathurâ, Etawah, Mainpûri, Aligarh, Budaon, Farakhabâd, and Pilibhît, are, in whole or in part, included within these limits.

In his report on the castes of the Agra district, Mr. Sells, Officiating Deputy Collector, makes the following observations respecting the country of the Sanâdhs and of the Kanoujiyas Proper. This, he says, "may be roughly represented as a triangle, having for its western side a line drawn from Pillibheet, in Rohilcund, to the south-west of Muttra; and for its eastern, a line from Pillibheet to the junction of the Jumna and Ganges at Allahabad; and for its base, the country bordering upon the Jumna and Chumbul rivers. Of this triangle, the western half forms the country of the Sunadhs; and the eastern, of the

(*a*) Supplemental Glossary, Vol. I, p. 149.

Canojeeas" (*a*). In the district of Agra, Mr. Sells adds, the Sanâdh Brahmans "prevail in great force," outnumbering apparently "the representatives of any of the other clans" (of Brahmans). He particularly mentions the *pargannah* of Pinahat, in all the villages of which, with hardly an exception, Sanâdhs occupy the position of landholders, cultivators, or village priests.

The tradition respecting the origin of this tribe is, that, on the return of Râm from Ceylon, he wished to celebrate his victory over Râvana, the king of that island, whom he had killed, by the celebration of a jag, or great sacrifice. As Râvana was a Brahman, Râm found it difficult to induce many of the members of this caste to take part in the solemnity. The Sarwaria Brahmans declined to do so, and consequently incurred his displeasure. But the Sanâdhs were less particular, and performed the important ceremony; and thenceforward became separated from other Brahmans, and formed a distinct tribe.

Another account is, that after the ceremony of the Horse Sacrifice, Râm wished to make grants of lands to Brahmans, which were declined by the Kânkubjiya Brahmans; yet, inasmuch as religious offerings could only be made to Brahmans, and in order not to defeat the purpose of Râm, a man was chosen from each family, to whom a village was presented. Thus seven hundred and fifty villages in the province of Mathurâ were given to the same number of Brahmans, each of whom assumed the name of his village as the designation of his clan,—*e. g.*, the Dhûria clan was in possession of the village of Dhûl, and the Pachoriya clan, of the village of Pachor.

Sanâdhs in the Mainpûrî district came, it is said, in two streams: the first in the time of the Râthor princes of Kanouj, whom they served as *purohits*, or family priests; the second only about four hundred years ago. These latter came from Sambhal. The Sândil, Gautam, Vasisht, and Bhâraddwâj Gotras are among those most prevalent in this quarter (*b*).

Although it is unquestioned that the Sanâdhs are a Kanoujiya race, and therefore are properly placed among the sub-tribes of the great Kanoujiya family, nevertheless, it is a singular fact that many Sanâdhs, perhaps most, regard themselves as belonging not to that stock at all, but to the Gaur tribe. The reason of this perhaps is their geographical proximity to, and consequent intercourse with, the Gaurs of Delhi and its neighbourhood. It shows, however, that Brahmanical tribes, notwithstanding their exclusiveness and their stringent adherence

(*a*) General Report of the Census of the North-Western Provinces for 1865, Vol. I, Appendix B, p. 65.
(*b*) *Ibid*, pp. 78, 79.

to hereditary customs and prejudices, may forget their antecedent history, and even depart from the traditions of the past.

In the Etawah district, the Kanoujiya Brahmans Proper far out-number all other Brahmans. Still, in one sub-division,—namely the *pargannah* of Oreyah,—they give place to the Sanâdhs. In his report on the castes and tribes of that district, Mr. A. O. Hume, formerly Magistrate of Etawah, gives the following interesting historical account of the Oreyah Sanâdhs: "In the Oreyah *pargannah*," he says, "the Sunoreeas or Sunâdhs predominate, and are represented chiefly by Singeeas and Merhas, two well-known *gots* of that sub-family. There are a considerable number of Singeea Brahman zemindars, and these all date their origin from one Basdeo. According to them, their ancestor first settled at Suhbda, under the protection of the Senghurs, and then one of his sons went to Delhi, where he obtained service late in Shahab-ood-deen Ghoree's reign. Later, probably in Akbar's time, the family appears to have obtained a grant of land, and the title of Chowdhree (which some of the family have ever since borne), when they took possession of Oreyah and its immediate neighbourhood; and here, though greatly reduced in circumstances, they to this day continue to hold many villages. They are probably in error in dating their advent so far back as 1200 A. D., but they are unquestionably one of the first of the Brahman septs now existing that settled in the district. The Merhas profess to have been from early times the family priests of the Senghur Raj of Bhurrey; and Chowdhree Peetum Singh of Billawan, an influential zemindar, Babootee Singh of Chanderpore, and others still, with numerous younger branches, represent the family. In the Etawah pargannah, besides the gradual influx of Kunoujiyas, two distinct immigrations of other Brahmans are noticeable as having to this day left numerous representatives. Very early in the fourteenth century, when Alla-ood-deen took Runtampore, Chitorgurh, and other places, one Hurreepunt, a famous pundit, made his way to Etawah. With him came Oogursen, Muthoorea, and others of that sub-division of the Sunoreas. Oogursen's two sons, Radho and Madho, rose to more or less importance; and, at this present moment, their descendants of the twelfth, thirteenth, and fourteenth generations, as well as the descendants of their father's companions, are to be found almost throughout the Etawah pargannah. It is noticeable that, about the time Oogursen settled here, other Muthooreas settled at Jaloun, Jhansie, Gwalior, and Mynpoory, with the latter of whom chiefly our Muthooreas intermarry. Another, and far more important sept of Sunoriahs are the 'Saburn' Chowdhrees of Manikpore. Their ancestors, it is generally allowed, accompanied

Rajah Sumersa on his first settlement in the district; and from him obtained the title of Chowdhree and a grant of several villages. In later times they possessed, it is said, a *chourasee* (eighty-four) of villages. Many of these have passed away from them; but the present heads of the family still retain a few of their old villages, with the title of Chowdhree, and still affect an importance to which, numerous as they are, their present fallen state certainly gives them little claim" (*a*).

Of the original seven hundred and fifty clans of Sanâdhiya Brahmans, fifty-one are regarded as of more influence and distinction than the rest. The *gotras* and titles of some of these are as follows:—

GOTRAS AND TITLES OF SANADHIYA BRAHMANS.

Gotras.	*Titles.*
Vasisht	Vyâsa.
Ditto	Goswâmi.
Ditto	Misr.
Ditto	Parâsar.
Ditto	Katâri.
Ditto	Devaliya.
Ditto	Dûbe.
Ditto	Khemarya.
Ditto	Upâdhiya.
Bhâraddwâj	Baidya.
Ditto	Chaube.
Ditto	Dîkhshit.
Ditto	Tripâti.
Ditto	Chaturdhar.
Kâsyap	Misr.
Sâwarni	Tiwâri.
Upamanyu	Dûbe.
Gautam	Upâdhiya.
Sândil	Pânde.
	Pâthakh.
	Swâmi.
	Samâdiya.
	Monas.
	Birthari.
	Chainpuriya.
	Bhotiya.

(*a*) General Report of the Census of the North-Western Provinces for 1865, Vol. I Appendix B, pp. 86, 87.

Gotras.	*Titles.*
	Barsiya.
	Ojhâ.
	Modaiya.
	Sandaya.
	Udeniya.
	Chachondya.
Kausik.	
Viswâmitra.	
Yamadagni.	
Dhananjaya.	
Kosal.	
Singîa.	
Merha.	

The above list, together with other information, has been chiefly obtained from Pandit Raghunâth Parsâd, the late kotwal, or chief native executive officer, of Benares. From his acquaintance with the Sanskrit language and literature, he received from all classes the honorary designation of Pandit. As he is himself a Sanâdhiya Brahman, he is well qualified to speak with authority respecting his tribe.

CHAPTER VIII.

THE SECOND TRIBE OF GAUR BRAHMANS—SARASWAT. THEIR ANTIQUITY—THEIR ORIGINAL HOME—FOUR GREAT DIVISIONS, PANJATI, ASHTBANS, BARAHI, AND BAWAN OR BHUNJAHI.

SECOND TRIBE OF GAUR BRAHMANS.

SARASWAT.

THIS is unquestionably a very ancient Brahmanical tribe, which inhabits still one of the earliest seats of Hinduism, a tract in the north-west of India beyond Delhi, once watered by the famous Saraswatî river, which figures so constantly in Hindu annals and mythology. The stream is now dried up, but its site and extent can be traced. Its disappearance seems to have greatly excited the imagination of people in former times. Prayâg, or Allahabad, is still spoken of by the natives generally as *Tribeni*, or the confluence, not of two rivers, the Ganges and Jumna, which actually unite at that spot, but of three, the Ganges, Jumna, and Saraswatî, the last not being visible, but in common belief flowing underground from its ancient bed to the point of conjunction. Saraswatî is worshipped in India as the wife of Brahmâ, as goddess of speech, as the creator of the Sanskrit language and of the Devanâgarî type of letters, and as patroness of music and art. On the subject of the drying up of the Saraswatî, Mr. Campbell writes : "It is a curious problem, that lost river, the Saraswatî. The evident river-traces all the way down to the Indus, ancient Hindu history, and the universal traditions of the people of those regions, go to make it as certain as any historical fact can be, that the Saraswatî was once a fine river, and that the countries through which it flowed (now for the most part desert and barren) were once well-watered and green. No mere diminution in the amount of rainfall, caused by denudations, or the like, could have occasioned such a change. The Saraswatî is now not a stream at all, but an absolutely dry bed, which is only filled by surface flooding in the height of the rains" (*a*).

In a remote epoch Brahmans clustered in villages and towns on the banks of the Saraswatî, and cultivated the rich lands in its neighbourhood. Their posterity, heedless of the contempt cast upon agricultural pursuits by other Brahmanical tribes, have continued to the present time to follow their excellent example. "Where the low and comparatively moist tracts, in which the river once ran, still admit of cultivation, the Saraswatî Brahmans are found very industrious and good cultivators, who claim to have occupied the country before Jats and Rajpoots became dominant. Sir John Malcolm also mentions the Marwarree or Saraswatî Brahmans as forming a considerable proportion of the most industrious cultivators in Malwa. And following the Saraswatî down to the Indus, we find that (some southern immigrants excepted) they are also the Brahmans of Scinde, but said to be much looked down on by more orthodox southerners, as eaters of meat, and altogether little advanced Brahmans. The Saraswatî Brahmans were the earliest and most simple and pure Hindus of Vedic faith, that faith being now worked out and developed; those of the Ganges and the rest of India are, in various phases, the types of modern Hinduism. The settlement on the banks of the Saraswatî is a well-known stage of Hindu history. Here the Brahmans came in contact with other races; castes were recognized, and early Hinduism became literary and historical. But the extreme caste and religious system, the full-blown High-Hinduism of the Gangetic Brahmans, was not yet. The descendants of those who continued to dwell on the Saraswatî seem to have much kept to the tenets of their forefathers. They are separate from the Kashmeerees, and have a place among the recognized divisions of Indian Brahmans; but their more advanced brethren give them the lowest place in the orthodox scale, and in their native country they chiefly shine by those simple and agricultural virtues in which their remote ancestors also probably excelled" (*b*). These observations are, I have no doubt, for the most part just and true. But it is not by any means a settled question that the Saraswatî Brahmans were either the earliest tribe of Brahmans to profess the Vedic form of religion, or that the Vedas originated with them. At the same time, there is good ground for believing that the Saraswatîs are a Brahmanical tribe of very great antiquity, and that eastern tribes date from a much more recent epoch. Moreover, seeing

(*a*) Campbell's Ethnology of India, p. 62.

(*b*) *Ibid*, pp. 61, 63.

that Hindus are singularly conservative in their habits, it seems a most probable supposition that the mode of life characterizing the modern Saraswatî Brahmans was very much that followed by their ancestors.

Saraswatî Brahmans residing in Benares have furnished me with the following account of the divisions and sub-divisions of their tribe. They have four great divisions, as follows: Panjâtî, Ashtbans, Bârahî, and Bawan or Bhunjâhî. The first, as its name denotes, has five sub-divisions; but this five-fold sub-division occurs not once but twice. The word "Ashtbans" means eight races; and, consequently, the second division represents eight clans. Bârahî refers to the number twelve, and the division represents that number of clans. The fourth, or Bawan division, contains fifty-two clans.

DIVISIONS OF SARASWAT BRAHMANS.

First Division—Panjati (*five clans.*)

First Section.			*Second Section.*		
Clans.	*Gotra.*	*Title.*	*Clans.*	*Gotra.*	*Title.*
1st	Somastambh.	Morhle.	1st	....	Kâliye.
2nd	Parâsar.	Tikkhe.	2nd	....	Mâliye.
3rd	Gautam.	Jhingan.	3rd	....	Kupûriye.
4th	Vatsa.	Jetelî.	4th	....	Madhuriye.
5th	Bhârgau.	Kumariye.	5th	....	Bagge.

Second Division—Ashtbans (*eight clans.*)

Clans.	*Gotra.*	*Title.*	*Clans.*	*Gotra.*	*Title.*
1st	Bhâraddwâj.	Pâthakh.	5th	Angirâh.	Jotashi.
2nd	Kâsyap.	Sorî.	6th	Parâsar.	Shand.
3rd	Gautam.	Tiwârî.	7th	Angirâh.	Kurla.
4th	Sâvarniya.	Yasrâj.	8th	Sâvarniya.	Bhâraddwâjî.

Third Division—Barahi (*twelve clans.*)

Clans.	*Gotra.*	*Title.*	*Clans.*	*Gotra.*	*Title.*
1st	Bhâraddwâj.	Kâlîye.	7th	Garg.	Nârad.
2nd	Vashisth.	Prabhâkar.	8th	Krishanâtra.	Sârad.
3rd	Kasyap.	Lakhanpâl.	9th	Kanshik.	Jâlpotr.
4th	Angirâh.	Ai-irî.	10th	Upmanya.	Bhamvî.
5th	Sândil.	Nâbh.	11th	Vashisth.	Paranotr.
6th	Monas.	Chitrchot.	12th	Upmanyu.	Manan.

FOURTH DIVISION—BAWAN OR BHUNJAHI *(fifty-two clans).*

Of the clans of this sub-division I have succeeded in obtaining the names of only ten, without their *gotras*, as follows:—

Clans.	*Gotra.*	*Title.*	*Clans.*	*Gotra.*	*Title.*
1st	....	Basûde.	6th	....	Sûdan.
2nd	....	Bijarâ.	7th	....	Sûtrak.
3rd	....	Rande.	8th	....	Terî.
4th	....	Merha.	9th	....	Angal.
5th	....	Mustâl.	10th	....	Hastîr.

In addition to the four branches of the Saraswatî Brahmans enumerated above, I understand that the undermentioned families are also branches of the same tribe.

1. Khatbansh.
2. Dagare.
3. Surdhwaj.

The Saraswatî Brahmans of the Bijnour district number about fifty families.

CHAPTER IX.

THE THIRD TRIBE OF GAUR BRAHMANS—GAUR—THE TAGA BRAHMANS—THEIR ORIGIN—SUB-DIVISIONS—CLANS OF GAUR BRAHMANS.

THIRD TRIBE OF GAUR BRAHMANS.

GAUR.

It has been already stated that this tribe has given its name to the five Brahmanical tribes of Northern India, but that the Gaurs Proper are confined to two districts. One of these is Bengal, more particularly its central tract. The other may be described as follows: "It runs through the Râmpûr territory as far as the Râmganga; thence through Seraulî, Seondâra, Neraulî, Bahjoî, Râjpûrâ, Dubhaî, and the western borders of Koel, Chandaus, Noh Jhîl, and Kosî. The whole of the British territory to the westward of this line is in their occupation" (*a*). The Gaurs of Bengal have doubtless sprung, at some remote period of Indian history, from the Kanoujiya stock. The common belief of Hindus, that from Bengal they emigrated to the neighbourhood of Dehli, about the time of the Pândus, is utterly incredible. It is much more likely that the Gaurs occupied the two tracts at a remote epoch, and continued their intercourse with each other during succeeding ages. But even this supposition has its difficulties, and gives no clue to the origin of the tribe. Moreover, there is reason to believe that most of the Gaur Brahmans now in Bengal have emigrated from the western division at a recent period, which circumstance increases the intricacy of the entire subject.

The traditions of the Gaur Taga Brahmans would, if well sifted, very probably throw much light on the origin of the Gaur tribe. These Taga Brahmans are found in considerable numbers throughout the northern part of the

(*a*) Elliot's Supplemental Glossary, Vol. I, p. 149.

Doab and Rohilkhand, and in the district of Delhi. With few exceptions they regard themselves as an offshoot of the Gaur Brahmans. They state that, on occasion of Raja Janamajayâ ordering a sacrifice for the destruction of serpents, the Gaur Brahmans officiated; and when the sacrifice was over, some of the Brahmans returned to their homes, but that others, remaining behind in the country, became agriculturists. The name they bear, taga (properly tyâgâ, abandoned or relinquished), denotes their having thereby abandoned the position of high Brahmans, and, like the Bhûînhârs of the Kanoujiya tribe, adopted a calling not approved by the Shâstras as an occupation fit for Brahmans. The tradition is referred to in the "Mahâbhâratâ." Thus the Tagas became separated from the Gaur stock. Now, as they commonly assert that they are descendants from the Gaurs of Hariâna, and as the Gaurs occupied that territory at a remote period, and continue to do so, it is by no means improbable that this may have been their original seat, from which they spread out into other parts.

In a short paper on castes written by W. Forbes, Esquire, C.B., formerly Magistrate of Meerut, are some important observations on the Taga Gaurs, not only as to their present condition, but also as to their previous history. "The Tagas," he remarks, "next to the Jâts, are the predominating caste in the district. Their name is derived, it is said, from 'tâg denâ,' to 'give up'; but whether they gave up their religion, or were themselves given up as heretics by their co-religionists, is not clearly ascertained. Various legends are current as to the manner of their metamorphosis from priests to agriculturists. One story has it, that Rajah Chamachche called the Brahmans together for a religious ceremony, and in the customary present of *pan* each found the name of a village on a ticket hidden in the *pan* leaf. They thus became zemindars or landholders, and gave up begging for alms. They are in many respects a peculiar caste. It seems universally allowed that they are, of all the castes now existing as holders of land in this part of the country, the earliest settlers. This is the prevailing idea, although it seems strange to say so of a district which boasts the site of the old Brahmanical city of Hustinapoor. They are the people who were found in full possession of the Meerut district when the Jâts and other offshoots of the Rajpoot caste swarmed across the Jumna river as colonists, to inhabit the land. Can it be possible that they are ancient Brahmans of the country, excommunicated in the mass for evil deeds connected with the downfall and destruction of the legendary city of Hustinapoor?" (*a*). Under the supposition

(*a*) General Report of the Census of the North-Western Provinces for 1865, Vol. I, Appendix B, p. 12.

that the Tagas are a branch of the Gaurs, and that they separated from them in early Hindu times, this indirect testimony from the natives themselves, as given by Mr. Forbes, to the great antiquity of the Gaurs, and to their early occupation of this region of country, is exceedingly valuable. Mr. Forbes's conjecture, based on his knowledge of the traditions current in the neighbourhood, is strong in regard to the Tagas, but is stronger still in regard to the Gaurs, their acknowledged ancestors.

At the end of the war in which Prithi Raj was destroyed by the Mahomedans, the Tagas were taken into favour by the Mussalman emperor, who desired them to persecute the Chauhân Rajpoots, of whom Prithi Raj was the head. Many of the Taga clan came to the district of Bijnûr, where they lived for long at enmity with the Chauhâns.

The following explanation of the origin of the Gaurs is given by Mr. George Campbell, in his recent work on the "Ethnology of India:" "The principal tributary of the Saraswatî is the 'Guggur' or 'Ghargar,' which now gives its name to the main channel where it passes through the Harriana district. May not the name of 'Gour' borne by these Brahmans of Harriana be a mere abbreviation of 'Guggur' or 'Ghargar'? May not the 'Gour Brahmans be simply Brahmans of the Guggur or Lower Saraswati?" (*a*).

Respecting the location of the Gaur Brahmans in the North-West, Mr. Plowden, in his Report on the Census of 1865, states that one-half of them, or nearly so, are found in the districts of Muzaffarnagar and Sahâranpûr. There are also many, he says, in the districts of Morâdâbâd and Mathurâ (*b*). The Taga Brahmans, who, as already shown, are a branch of the Gaurs, are met with exclusively in the districts of Muzaffarnagar, Sahâranpûr, Bijnûr, Meerut, and Morâdâbâd. The Gaurs, for a non-indigenous tribe, are very numerous in the city of Benares.

The tribe has the following sub-divisions:—

Sub-divisions of the Gaur Tribe.

1. Ad-Gaur, or original Gaurs.
2. Srî Gaur.
3. The Taga Brahmans.
4. Bhârgava.

(*a*) Campbell's Ethnology of India, p. 64.
(*b*) General Report of the Census of the North-Western Provinces, 1865, Vol. I, Appendix B, p. 81.

5. Madh-Sreni (Bengali Brahmans).
6. Purbiya Gaur (Eastern Gaur Brahmans).
7. Pachhânde Gaur (Western Gaur Brahmans).
8. Hiranya or Hariyanewâlî.
9. Chaurâsiya.
10. Pushkarnî.

(Brahmans of Ajmere and Jaipûr.)

11. Thâkurâyan.
12. Bhojak.
13. Kakariya.
14. Deswâlî Chhannât. From Mâlwâ. Has six branches:—
    1. Gujar Gaur.
    2. Pârikh.
    3. Sikhwâl.
    4. Dayma or Davîch.
    5. Khandelwâl.
    6. Ojha or Gaur Sâraswat.
15. Dase Gaur.

The following is a very imperfect list of some of the clans of this tribe, together with their *gotras* and titles:—

Clans.	*Gotra.*	*Title.*	*Clans.*	*Gotra.*	*Title.*
1st	Kausik.	Dîkhshit.	17th	....	Gândharwâl.
2nd	Bhâraddwâj.	Tiwârî.	18th	....	Pândyâna.
3rd	Krishanâtra.	Chaube.	19th	....	Pântiyâ.
4th	Parâsar.	Nirmal.	20th	....	Jhundiye.
5th	Vatsa.	Nâgwân.	21st	....	Kânodiyâ.
6th	....	Chauhunwâl.	22nd	....	Gautam.
7th	Vatsa.	Marhatâ.	23rd	....	Gûgwâl.
8th	Parâsar.	Lâtâ.	24th	....	Mudhâlwân.
9th	....	Motâ.	25th	....	Nugarwâl.
10th	....	Indouriya.	26th	....	Sâthiyâ.
11th	Sândil.	Haritwâl.	27th	....	Vâjare.
12th	Kasyap.	Bhanchakkî.	28th	....	Simmanwâl.
13th	Angirâh.	Mirîchîyâ.	29th	....	Dungarwâl.
14th	Vashishth.	Ghâgsân.	30th	....	Kherwâl.
15th	Gautam.	Vidhatâ.	31st	....	Suraliyâ.
16th	....	Pharatwâl.			

Certain Brahmanical family names, such as Mukhurjee, Banerjee, Chaturjee, are extensively used, and widely known, in Bengal. The two former belong to the Kânkubjiya Tribe Proper, and the third to the Gaurs, although there are some families of this name which claim a connection with the Ḳânkubjiya tribe.

The Gaur Brahmans are found in the Sahâranpûr and Dehra Dûn districts. They are said to have come direct from the plains to the Dûn. They maintain rigidly their purity of caste, and marry only with Brahmans from the plains.

CHAPTER X.

THE FOURTH TRIBE OF GAUR BRAHMANS—MAITHILA—SUB-DIVISIONS OR BRANCHES —GOTRAS—CLANS.

FOURTH TRIBE OF GAUR BRAHMANS.

MAITHILA.

This tribe is found in Tirhût, and generally throughout the northern part of Behar. Some members of the tribe are met with in the districts of Benares, Jaunpûr, Mirzapûr, and Allahabad; but, if there be any truth in the last Census Report, not at all in the large district of Gorakhpûr, to the north-west, although lying contiguous to it. This last statistical statement, however, cannot be correct. A more careful inquiry would, I feel satisfied, reveal the existence of some families of Maithilas residing in this extensive tract. In some parts of the country, Ojha and Maithila Brahmans are considered to be one and the same. While it is quite true, on the one hand, that the Maithilas are commonly called Ojhas, it is not true, on the other, that all Ojhas are Maithilas. In Benares, for instance, the term Ojha is used to designate the person called in to exorcise evil spirits, to allay turbulent departed spirits,—who, it is supposed, work mischief in various ways,—to destroy the power and influence of ghosts and goblins, and the like. He is sometimes a Brahman; but he may proceed likewise from any of the other castes. It is possible that there may be some connection between the Ojha, as thus employed, and the Maithila Brahmans; and further investigation might perhaps show in what it consists.

This tribe has four divisions:—

I. Maithil.
II. Sârâtri.
III. Joga.
IV. Changola.

The following is a list of some of the *gotras* prevailing in the tribe:—

Gotras.	*Gotras.*	*Gotras.*
Kasyap.	Bhâraddwâj.	Parâsar.
Kâsyap.	Kâtiyâyana.	Baiyâghrapadyâ.
Sândil.	Garg.	Gautam.
Vatsa.	Gârgiyâ.	Jamdagni.
Sâvarniya.		

Like other Brahmanical tribes, the Maithilas consist of a large number of clans, many of which might easily be ascertained by any person living in Tirhût. From those residing in Benares, I have been able to gather the names of only five. These are as follows:—

Clans.	*Gotra.*	*Title.*
Barhiyâm.	Sândil.	Ojha.
Sakuri.	Kâsyap.	Pâthakh.
Dadari.	Sâvarniya.	Misr.
Nagwâr.	Vatsa.	Thâkur.
Malariyâ.	Kâtiyâyana.	Chandhrî.

The Maithilas are very numerous in the district of Bhâgalpûr, especially in the southern and western parts. In Behar also they are as influential as in their own proper country of Tirhût (*a*).

(*a*) Buchanan's Eastern India, Vol. II, p. 115.

CHAPTER XI.

THE FIFTH TRIBE OF GAUR BRAHMANS—UTKALA. FIRST DIVISION—SUPERIOR BRAHMANS. SECOND DIVISION—INFERIOR BRAHMANS. THIRD DIVISION—FIRST CLASS, DAKHIN SRENY; SECOND CLASS, JAJPUR SRENY; THIRD CLASS, PANYARY SRENY; FOURTH CLASS, UTKAL SRENY.

FIFTH TRIBE OF GAUR BRAHMANS.

Utkala.

These are Brahmans of Orissa, in which province they are found in considerable numbers. Compared with the Brahmans of the North-Western Provinces, they are very lax in their habits, and by no means adhere with such strictness to caste rules as many others of their order. The truth is, they have more common sense, and far less pride, than Brahmans of Benares, and of similar places, in which caste prejudice is very powerful, not to say, tyrannical. The Ooriya Brahmans not only engage in trade and agriculture, but also employ themselves in the lowly occupations of brickmaking and bricklaying (*a*). Yet they are not all equally sensible and free from prejudice. There are some who pretend to greater purity than the rest, meaning thereby greater strictness and rigidity. Hence, the Ooriya Brahmans might be classed under two great divisions, the strict and the lax; but it will be better to divide them into three sections. They are known by two designations, Utkala and Uddro.

Divisions of Utkala Brahmans.

First Division (Superior Brahmans).

Gotras			*Titles.*
Shambûkar	...	...	Otha.
Kâsyap	...	...	Tiwâri.
Ghratha Kausik	...	...	Misr.

(*a*) Campbell's Ethnology of India, p. 69.

Gotras.			Titles.
Bhâraddwâj	...	...	Shath-pathî.
Gautam and Mûdhgal	...	...	Pânde.
Vashisht	...	...	Raha.
Kapiladhaj	...	...	Nanda.
Dhara-Gautam	...	...	Dass.
Athrel	...	...	Shorongî.

Each of these *gotras* embraces one or more clans. None of these superior Brahmans engage in any manual labour. Some of them are addicted to study. Questions of difficulty occurring in the Courts of law, or elsewhere, respecting the law of inheritance, are referred to them for solution. Their exclusiveness renders them haughty and superstitious.

Second Division (Inferior Brahmans).

Gotras.	Titles.	Number.
Kâsyap / Gautam	Mahâpâtra	1, 2
Gautam	Pandâ	3
Gautam	Shâbûth	4
Shambûkar / Bhâraddwâj / Mûdhgal	Senâpatî	5, 6, 7
Mûdhgal	Nekâb / Mekâb	8, 9
( )	Pathî	10
Gautam	Pânnî	11
Bhâraddwâj / Gautam	Shauthrâ	12, 13
Gautam	Pash-pâloke	14
Gautam / Kâsyap	Barû	15, 16
Kâsyap	Mûdhîrath	17
Mûdhgal	Doythâ	18
Gautam	Paryhârî	19
( )	Khûntea	20
Dhara-Gautam	Garâ-baru	21
( )	Nâhâka	22

Each of these *gotras* contains one or more clans. The Nekâb and Mekâb (Nos. 8 and 9) Brahmans are cooks by profession. The Pathîs (No. 10) administer oaths in Courts of law. The Pannî, Shauthrâ, and Pash-pâloke Brahmans (Nos. 11 to 14) are pandits, doorkeepers (*darwans*), and gardeners. The Barû Brahmans perform labour in menial capacities. The same may be said of the Mûdhîrath Brahmans (No. 17). The Doythâ clans are called Bhîls, and are said to be descendants of Shabar. The Garâ-barû Brahmans (No. 21) are employed in temple service, in carrying water to be used in sacrifice. The Nâhâka clans (No. 22) are a mixed race, the offspring of a Brahman father and Chamâr (worker in leather) mother.

Third Division (Sreny).

Four classes of Brahmans found in Orissa are known by the cognomen of Sreny. These are severally Dakhin Sreny, Jâjpûr Sreny, Panyâry Sreny, and Utkal Sreny. Each of these has its *gotras*, clans, and titular designations. The clans are numerous, but the *gotras* with their titles are as follows :—

First Class (Dakhin Sreny).

Gotras.	*Titles.*
Shambhûkar	Misr.
Bhâraddwâj	Nandha.
Gautam	Kothâ.
Mûdhgal	Shath-pathî.
Dhara-Gautam	Tripatî.
Athrel	Ratha.
Vashisht	Sharangî.
Ghratha-Kausik	Achârjî.
	Mahâpâtra.
	Dâs.

Second Class (Jâjpûr Sreny).

Gotras.	*Titles.*
The same as in Dakhin Sreny, with the addition of Kapiladwâj.	The same as in Dakhin Sreny.

Third Class (Panyâry Sreny).

Gotras.	*Titles.*
The same as in Dakhin Sreny.	Misr. Pânde. Mâhinthî. Pandâ. Naik. Shâbûth. Senâpatî. Nekâb. Mekâb. Pathî. Kar. Pânnî. Pânnî-grâhî. Shauthrâ. Dâs.

Fourth Class (Utkal Sreny).

Gotras.	*Titles.*
The same as in Dakhin Sreny.	The same as in Panyâry Sreny, with the exception of Mâhinthî.

CHAPTER XII.

THE FIVE DRAVIRA TRIBES OF CENTRAL AND SOUTHERN INDIA. THE MAHARASHTRA BRAHMANS. GOTRAS. THE KAHRADE BRANCH. THE BRAHMANS OF KONKAN. THEIR GOTRAS AND CLANS. BAPU DEO SHASTRI.

THE FIVE DRAVIRA OR SOUTHERN TRIBES.

THESE are all great tribes of Brahmans belonging to one family, as already stated in the third chapter, where they are styled Drâvira, or southern tribes, in contradistinction to those in the north, which have been described under the general designation of Gaur Brahmans. It will be remembered that these five Drâvira tribes are the following, Mahârâshtra, Tailanga, Drâvira, Karnâta, and Gurjar, which are as distinct from one another as the five Gaur tribes. Moreover, they hold no social intercourse whatever with the northern tribes, and neither intermarry nor eat with them. In Benares there is a considerable number of Mahârâshtra and Gurjar Brahmans, who having resided there from generation to generation, may fairly be regarded as permanent inhabitants of the city; yet there is no intermingling between them and any of the northern tribes represented in the city, and they continue as much distinct from them as though they were a different race of beings.

FIRST TRIBE OF DRAVIRA BRAHMANS.

MAHARASHTRA.

Section I.

The Mahratta Brahmans are a very distinguished race among the Brahmanical tribes of India. For quickness of intellect, for energy, practical power, and learning, they are unsurpassed. In Benares itself, which is famous for its pandits deeply read in Sanskrit literature, they are highly respected for their intelligence and knowledge. As a people, they seem to possess, wherever they are found, those great mental gifts which formerly made the Mahrattas so formidable. Their proper country, says Mr. Campbell, extends "from Damaun to the neighbourhood of Goa, and from Bombay to Nagpore and the Wynganga." His remarks on the characteristics of this tribe are graphic and interesting. "The Maratta Brahmins," he remarks, "are the most famous and successful of their race. That their fortune is due to their talent and energy is shown by their success beyond their own bounds, in fact throughout southern and central India. But in their own country, and among their own people, they are also favoured by circumstances. The lower caste men of the pen, who have ousted the Brahmins in some countries of the north, and more than rivalled them in others, are not found in the Maratta social system. The mass of the Maratta people are of a comparatively humble class, without the pride and jealousy of Brahmins shown by Rajpoots and Jats. Hence, wherever there is a Maratta people or Maratta rule, Maratta Brahmins are the brains and directing power. At first they contented themselves with the highest administrative offices under Maratta rulers; but later, as is well known, the Peshwa and other Brahmins usurped the supreme power itself, assumed the supreme command of armies, and openly ruled the confederacy. In truth, so miscellaneous, and so loosely held together by any other tie, were Maratta confederacies and armies, that these Brahmins may be considered to be the real source of the power and fame of the Marattas as rulers in India. They were the heads of a body, of which others were but the hands guided by them. Even in the present day, in many states and places beyond their own limits, they have the chief power.

"In fact, perhaps no race, certainly no Indian race, has ever shown greater administrative talent and acuteness. The native country of the Maratta Brahmins is chiefly to the west, and especially the Concan, south of Bombay, the hilly strip near the western coast. It might be conjectured, that centuries of Mahommedan rule might have caused the retreat of the Brahmins from the more open plains to these regions; but I do not know that there is historical ground for this supposition, and think it more likely that under any rule they would hold their own, and circumvent even foreign rulers. Their personal appearance would lead one to suppose that they came from the north-west. Many of them are very fair, and I think that there is among them a much greater tendency to the common occurrence of a somewhat aquiline, or what I call sub-aquiline, type of feature than among Hindustani Brahmins. A very marked feature, not commonly met with, seems to be a light greyish kind of eye. Altogether, I cannot suppose these Brahmins to be a branch of the race which, after occupying Hindustan, extended southwards. I cannot imagine how they could, in the south, as it were, in some degree, have returned towards an earlier type, instead of step by step becoming darker and more Indian-like. It is undoubtedly the case, and is a subject of common remark, that all along the west coast of India, the people are much fairer than in the interior, even though most of the interior country above the Ghats is considerably elevated. Some have accounted for this by saying that colour does not altogether depend on the thermometer; that the inhabitants of the more umbrageous coast are less exposed to an unclouded sun and dry atmosphere than the people of the bare and treeless plains of the Deccan; and that thus the difference of colour is to be accounted for. I will not say that this cause is wholly without effect; but I think it quite insufficient to account for the whole difference. The Bengalees, in a moist atmosphere, and amid a luxuriant vegetation, are generally dark. The blackest of the aboriginal tribes live in the densest forest conutry in a moist malarious climate. Even on this very western coast I find the aboriginal helots of Malabar described as being 'of the deepest black' (*a*)."

The general conclusion at which Mr. Campbell arrives is, that the Mahrattas of the western coast are neither indigenous to the soil, nor in any degree whatever, however slight, tainted with aboriginal blood, but that they have come by sea from other countries. This subject will be again referred to presently in the section on the Konkanasth branch of the Mahratta Brahmans. The circumstance of the fair skin of the Mahratta Brahmans, as compared with other inhabitants of the same regions, is interesting, but by no means peculiar. Throughout India, Brahmans have always a much lighter complexion than other Hindus, and, in addition, a physiognomy, and bearing, not exhibited by members of other castes. In the North-Western Provinces, the Brahman is quite as fair, and exhibits quite as strongly the physical characteristics of his race, as the Mahratta Brahmans of the Konkan. He is occasionally as fair as the lightest Eurasian half-caste, and in his face the red blush is seen to come and go as in that of the Englishman. That physiological differences exist, to some extent, among Brahmans, is undoubted; but the striking Brahmanical type exists in all. There is really not so much difference between a Hindustani and a Mahratta Brahman as between a Hindustani and a Bengali Brahman. The remarks of

(*a*) Campbell's Ethnology of India, pp. 70, 71.

Mr. Campbell would go to prove, if they mean anything, an almost tribal distinction between the Mahratta and all other Brahmans, consisting in a far greater purity of Brahmanical blood and freedom from intermixture with other races. I suspect that these race distinctions among the Brahmans are in the main of a provincial character, and to be accounted for on geographical grounds rather than ethnological, for it is well known that Brahmans everywhere have been exceedingly careful in the preservation of their caste. Moreover, inasmuch as the great Brahmanical tribes have kept apart from one another, and have been little addicted to intermarriages, it is only natural that, in the lapse of ages, certain physical distinctions of a definite and noticeable kind should spring up between them.

The Mahratta Brahmans are divided into a large number of *gotras*, or generic classes, each of which has its body of separate clans with their distinctive honorary titles. The following is a list of some of the principal *gotras*, drawn up by a Mahratta pandit of Benares.

Gotras of Mahârâshtra Brahmans.

Vatsa.	Maunas.
Parâsar.	Shâlankâyana.
Kausik.	Kutsa.
Bhâraddwâj.	Srîvatsa.
Vashisht.	Raibhya.
Kasyap.	Angiras.
Atri.	Shâktâyanâ.
Upmanyu.	Mudgal.
Krishanâtri.	Mândavya.
Garg.	Gâlava.
Sândil.	Gritsamad.
Gautam.	Vaitahavya.
Vâtsyâyana.	Sunak.
Vâtsya.	Kanva.
Gargya.	Aghmarkhana.
Bhargava.	Trinvindeo.
Jamadagni.	Paithînas.
Agasti.	Aupgava.
Kaundinya.	Dhriti.
Viswâmitra.	Chawar.
	Anrau.

There are fourteen great divisions or sub-tribes of Mahratta Brahmans.

Principal Divisions of Mahratta Brahmans.

1. Karhâde.
2. Konkanasth or Chitpâwan.
3. Deshasth.
4. Yajurvedî.
5. Abhîr.
6. Maitrayana.
7. Charak.
8. Nârmadî.
9. Mâlwî.
10. Deoruke.
11. Kânnau.
12. Kirvant.
13. Savashe.
14. Trigul.

I am unable to furnish a separate account of each of these divisions, although it is likely they are all represented in Benares. An elaborate printed account of the Karhâde Division is in my possession. In addition, I have received from Sivâ Râma Govinda, a teacher in the Anglo-Sanskrit department of Queen's College, Benares, and a Brahman from Konkan, an extensive list of clans of the Konkanasth branch of Mahratta Brahmans. It is one of the most complete lists of Brahmanical families that I have been able to obtain; and yet, it will be seen, that only a small number of *gotras* is described. The truth is, that every sub-division of the Brahmanical tribes has ordinarily quite as many, and, in some cases, more clans than those here given. I shall not shorten the list, but shall furnish it in full, as a specimen of the wonderful ramification of the Brahmanical race.

Section II.—The Karhâde Branch of Mahratta Brahmans.

As I am giving the names of many clans of *gotras* of the Konkanasth Brahmans, it were wearisome to the reader to peruse a somewhat similar list of the Karhâde branch of the same tribe. I shall content myself therefore with stating the names of all the *gotras* of this branch, and with the simple mention of the number of clans which each contains.

Kâsyap Gotra	eighty-two clans.
Atri Gotra	seventy-five clans.
Bhâraddwâj Gotra	seventy-seven clans.
Jamadagni Gotra	seventy-five clans.
Vasisht Gotra	eighty clans.
Kausik Gotra	forty-seven clans.
Naidhruva Gotra	twenty-four clans.
Gautam Gotra	fifteen clans.
Gârgya Gotra	sixteen clans.
Mudgal Gotra	eight clans.
Vainya Gotra	six clans.
Sândilya Gotra	six clans.
Kulsa Gotra	three clans.
Vatsa Gotra	two clans.
Bhârgau Gotra	two clans.
Pârthiva Gotra	two clans.
Viswâmitra Gotra	one clan (Kâle).
Vâdrâyana Gotra	one clan (Bharbhare).
Kaundinya Gotra	one clan (Ringe).
Upmanyu Gotra	one clan (Tike).
Angiras Gotra	one clan (Dhamankar).
Lohitâksh Gotra	one clan (Ojhe).

Section III.—The Konkanasth Brahmans, or Brahmans of Konkan.

These Brahmans inhabit the thin band of country on the western coast of India, known as Konkan. They have been already somewhat described in the introductory account of the Mahârâshtra Brahmans. The chief question that remained was as to their origin. Properly, this is not the place to investigate a subject of such a nature, as it is not the intention of this work to enquire at all into the origin of the Brahmanical race. That is a distinct subject, requiring for its due consideration an amount of philological and ethnological knowledge which few possess, and perhaps which no man has yet adequately acquired. Much light, however, has been of late years thrown upon it by the labours of men like Professor Max Müller, Dr. Haug, Dr. John Muir, and others. Although by their assiduity the intricate thread of the primitive condition of India is being gradually unravelled, yet it still remains very tangled and knotty, though not so hopelessly as formerly. The object of this dissertation on Indian tribes and races, more especially on those represented in the city and province of Benares, is practical, not speculative, and is chiefly confined to a statement of things as they are.

Conjectures unsubstantiated are always open to suspicion, yet sometimes a happy hit is made. I hardly think that the conjectures of Mr. Campbell respecting the origin of the Konkanasth Brahmans can be so regarded; nevertheless they are interesting, suggestive, and worthy of record, and may probably contain a modicum of truth. His argumentative statement is this: "All along the southern portion of the west coast, a large part of the population is notoriously to a great degree of foreign blood. The Moplahs are, to a great extent, Arabs; the 'Teers' or 'Teermen,' are also said to be immigrants (as their very name indicates); and there are many Jews and Christians, though the latter I believe have not much trace of Western blood. All along the Bombay coast also from Goa to Kurrachee, are the descendants of Persian, Arab, Portuguese, and other Western immigrants. Hence I did not think it by any means absurd when an educated Bramin of Poonah suggested to me as a theory, that the Bramins owed the light eyes and light complexion noticed among them to an intermixture of Western blood. The Bramins would be less liable, however, to casual and recent intermixture than other races; and I incline rather to the theory, that these Bramins of this part of the coast may have more directly come from the original seats of the race by the route of the Saraswatee and the Indus, and thence perhaps by sea, without passing through Hindustan and Central India, and there suffering any infiltration of aboriginal blood. Is it not probable enough that in very early days, when they were pressed by Rajpoots and Jats, they may have colonized the Konkan, reduced to subjection the rude aborigines, and transmitted to descendants features preserved from great deterioration by caste rules, and forms only somewhat deteriorated in size and robustness by a Southern climate and the absence of manual labour? If such an immigration took place so early as I suppose, it might well happen that, in long contact with Southern elements and Southern creeds, the colonists in the Maratta country would separate themselves from the old Saraswatee Bramins, and become a separate division" (*a*).

Where all is speculation and theory, it is sufficient to reply to this argument, that it is certainly quite as likely a supposition that the Saraswatee Brahmans, if they migrated to the Konkan at all, went by land as by sea, especially as caste difficulties alone have, throughout their entire history, proved an invincible

(*a*) Campbell's Ethnology of India, pp. 71, 72.

barrier to Brahmans taking a voyage, even for a few days, on the sea. Yet supposing they went by this route, I fail to see why on arriving in Konkan they should be imagined to have suffered less from 'any infiltration of aboriginal blood' than Hindustanee Brahmans, proceeding from the same spot to the countries in the north-east, to which they came, and in which they settled.

The remarks of Mr. Campbell, on the present condition and habits of the Konkanasth Brahmins, are valuable. "In the Maratta Concan the Bramins are at the head of the agricultural community. Most of the '*Kotes*' or village zemindars, who rule over and claim the proprietary right in each village, are of this caste. I have not been able to ascertain what proportion of the actual cultivators are of the same class. For the rest, office of every kind, including the village and *Pergunnah* accountantships all over the country, and every service of the head and the pen, seem to be their great resources. They are not military, nor generally in any way men of the sword; though they have, in their prosperity, taken the command of Maratta armies. Nor do they seem to have any great commercial proclivities. Among the various races who push to so great a point mercantile enterprise in Bombay, I cannot find that the Bramins have any great share. Under our Government, they have almost a monopoly of office in Western India. In the towns of the North Canarese coast, the Hindu traders are said to be chiefly 'Konkanee Bramins who trade and keep shops'" (*a*).

Gotras and Clans of the Konkanasth Brahmans.

Gotras of Kasyap Rishi and his Descendants.

Kasyap.
|
Avatsâra.
|
Naidhruva.

Clans connected with these Gotras.

Josî.
Joga.
Lele.
Lavâte.
Umale.
Phalake.
Sintare.

Gotras of Sândil Rishi and his Descendants.

Sândil.
|
Asita.
|
Daivala.

Clans connected with these Gotras.

Josî.
Dâtâra.
Kelhakara.
Mâile.
Thathe.
Tulaputhe.
Kâlhe.

(*a*) Campbell's Ethnology of India, p. 73.

Clans connected with these Gotras.

Bhânu.
Kânere.
Gokhale.
Khâdilakara.
Bivalakara.
Velanakara.
Sunkale.
Badaye.
Karamarakara.
Chhatre.
Bhatu.
Dâtîra.
Petakara.
Kâtarane.
Thosara.
Khetare.
Taitra.
Gânu.
Sithore.
Kâmde.
Godase.
Pâtanakara.
Vidwânsa.
Vidasure.
Nidasure.
Ghânavatakara.
Tâvânakara.
Ugula.
Naravane.
Kutumbâthe.
Palhanîkara.
Râne.
Bedare.
Bandare.
Govalakara.

Clans connected with these Gotras.

Ganupule.
Kâne.
Sahasrabudhe.
Risabuda.
Takale.
Somana.
Sintare.
Bâhire.
Tilhaka.
Bhoyale.
Thânkara.
Dâmale.
Parchure.
Vyâsa.
Pâvagî.
Donare.
Kosarekara.
Amadekara.
Mânte.
Lâvanakara.
Sidhye.

The clans descended from Kasyap Rishi do not intermarry with those descended from Sândil Rishi, in spite of the circumstance of their having different ancestors.

Gotras of Rishi, and his Descendants.

( )

Pourukutsa.	Pourukutsa.
Trasadasya.	Trasadasya.
Vishnuvrudha.	Nityundana.

Clans connected with these Gotras.	*Clans connected with these Gotras.*
Mahedalhe.	Sahasrabudhe.
Kidamide.	Bhide.
Deva.	Pimpalhakâre.
Parânjape.	Vaisampâyana.
Okilhakara.	Bhâdabhonke.

The clans mentioned in the one column do not intermarry with those given in the other, because they have a common ancestor.

Gotras of Atreya Rishi, and his Descendants.

Atreya.
|
Archanâuasha.
|
Shyâvâascha.

Clans descended from these Gotras.

Jogalekara.	Chitathe.
Bhâdabhoge.	Athavale.
Châpekara.	Bâdakara.
Phadeke.	Mone.
Chipolakara.	Cholakara.

These clans can intermarry with any of the clans of the *gotras* previously given.

Gotras of Bhârgava Rishi, and his Descendants.

Bhârgava.

- Chyâvana.
  - Apnava.
    - Aurva.
      - Jâmadagnya.
- Chyâvana.
  - Aurva.
    - Jâmadagnya.
      - Vatsa.

Clans descended from these Gotras.	*Clans descended from these Gotras.*
Bhâgawata.	Josî.
Pendase.	Gâgare.
Kunte.	Kâlhe.
	Ukâdave.
	Mâlhase.

These two sets of clans do not intermarry, because they are descended from a common ancestor.

Gotras of Angiras Rishi, and his Descendants.

Angiras.

Bârhaspatya.	Saiyanya.	Amahîyava.
Bhâraddwâj.	Gargya.	Auruksha.

Clans sprung from these Gotras.	*Clans sprung from these Gotras.*	*Clans sprung from these Gotras.*
Golhe.	Josî.	Sâne.
Vidya.	Thorâta.	Limye.
Manohara.	Ghâuekara.	Dalâla.
Ghâgalakara.	Bhâgavata.	Jâila.
Ghaisâsa.	Karve.	Khâbhate.
Deva.	Khângalekara.	Sarâte.
Sovanî.	Ketakara.	Vidvânsa.
Rânade.	Gore.	Karandîkara.
Tenekara.	Londhe.	Golhe.
Josî.	Vatse.	Ratâte.
Ghângurde.	Bhusakute.	Mâideva.
Achavala.	Mâte.	Bhâgavata.

Clans sprung from these Gotras.	*Clans sprung from these Gotras.*	*Clans sprung from these Gotras.*
Akhache.	Sutâra.	Limaye.
Râhâlakara.	Vaidya.	
Kâralekara.	Vedekara.	
	Bhata.	
	Dâbaka.	
	Gâdgila.	
	Mhasakara.	
	Khânbete.	
	Paulbudhe.	

The clans of these three columns cannot intermarry, because they are descended from a common ancestor.

Gotras of Vasisht Rishi, and his Descendants.

Vasisht.

Indrapramada.	Maitrâvaruna.
Abhiradvasu.	Kaundinya.

Clans descended from these Gotras.	*Clans descended from these Gotras.*
Modaka.	Patvardhana.
Dândekara.	Achâri.
Dâtâra.	Phanase.
Vinoda.	Bâgula.
Bhâtakhande.	Vinjhye.
Kârlekara.	Mahabala.
Bâpata.	Bhabhe.
Penthye.	Sâvarakara.
Sâthye.	Divekara.
Dhâru.	
Oka.	
Gokate.	
Bodasa.	
Donakara.	
Ghârapure.	
Koparakara.	
Sâthe.	
Abhyankara.	
Nâtû.	
Kârulhakara.	
Ponkase.	
Dântye.	
Govate.	
Vaidya.	
Paravatye.	

The families enumerated in these two columns do not intermarry, as they are descended from Vasisht, a common ancestor.

Gotras of Viswâmitra Rishi, and his Descendants.

Viswâmitra.

Aghamarshana.	Amarshana.
Babhravya.	Kausika.
Clans descended from these Gotras.	*Clans descended from these Gotras.*
Bâlha.	Khare.
Behare.	Gadre.
	Devadhara.
	Vartaka.
	Bâda.
	Bhâvaye.
	Barave.
	Palhande.
	Apate.
	Phâtaka.
	Satakara.
	Bâma.
	Bapaye.
	Kânitakara.
	Devala.
	Kâvanakara.
	Godabale.
	Sende.
	Kolatakara.
	Pedakara.
	Agâse.

The clans mentioned in these two columns do not intermarry, as they are descended from Viswâmitra, a common ancestor.

BAPU DEO SÁSTRI.

One of the most learned and accomplished natives of Benares, is the Pandit whose name is given above. He is a Brahman of the Konkanasth Branch of the Mahârâshtra tribe. Bapu Deo Sâstrî has greatly distinguished himself as a scholar, and has, by his works, shed a lustre both on the Sanskrit college, in which for many years he has been a professor of Mathematics and Astronomy, and on the city in which he lives. The titles of some of his numerous books are as follows: on Trigonometry, in Sanskrit; Translation of the Surya Siddhânta into English; on Algebra, in Hindî, for which he received from the Government of the North-Western Provinces a present of one thousand rupees, and a valuable shawl; on Geography, in Hindî; on Arithmetic, in Sanskrit; Symbolical Euclid, in Sanskrit. This list is sufficient to show the versatility of the Sâstrî's mind, as well as the importance of his labours in the cause of education.

In consideration of his great services rendered to science and education in India, the Sâstrî has been made an Honorary Member of the Royal Asiatic Society of Great Britain, and also of the Asiatic Society of Bengal. He is a Fellow of the Calcutta University. In addition, the Government has taken public notice of his labours on several occasions. A modest and retiring man, free from the pride so frequently found in his order, of great energy and perseverance, of patience in research, and of liberal and advanced sentiments in regard to the religious and social problems in process of solution in India, Bapu Deo Sâstrî is not merely an intellectual leader of the educated classes of Benares, but also presents in himself an excellent illustration of the good results of European learning.

CHAPTER XIII.

SECOND TRIBE OF DRAVIRA BRAHMANS—THE TAILANGA. ITS EIGHT DIVISIONS.

SECOND TRIBE OF DRAVIRA BRAHMANS.

Tailanga.

This great tribe of Brahmans inhabits those tracts of country in which the Telugu language is spoken, extending from the Northern Circars through Vizagapatam, Râjmandry, Gantûr, Masulipitam, Cuddapah, Nellore, to Bellary, and spreading over the eastern division of Hyderabad. The number of persons speaking Telugu is computed to be about fourteen millions.

The Tailanga Brahmans have a great many *gotras*, or orders, among them; but their chief divisions are limited to eight, as follows:—

Divisions of Tailanga Brahmans.

1. Tilaghâniyam.
2. Vellanâtî.
3. Veginâtî.
4. Murkinâtî.
5. Kâsalnâtî.
6. Karankamma.
7. Niogî.
8. Prathama-Shâkhi.

These eight divisions of the Tailanga Brahmans neither intermarry nor eat together. They all observe the ceremonies either of the Rig Veda or Yajur

Veda. The Karankamma Brahmans follow the ritual of the Rig Veda exclusively. These various divisions are not distributed geographically, as they may all be found in one and the same city or district. They are scattered over the Northern Circars in considerable numbers.

It is roughly calculated that there are about two hundred and fifty Tailang Brahmans in Benares, who are representatives of the first four divisions in the above list, and of the seventh, or Niogî. Yet it is possible that one or two members even of the remaining divisions may be there also.

I am indebted to Bâpu Sâstrî, a Tailang Brahman of Benares, for the above information.

CHAPTER XIV.

THIRD TRIBE OF DRAVIRA BRAHMANS—THE DRAVIRA. ITS TEN DIVISIONS.

THIRD TRIBE OF DRAVIRA BRAHMANS.

Dravira.

The third great tribe of the Drâvira family of Brahmans receives the designation applied to the entire race. Its proper geographical position is at the southern extremity of India, embracing Chingleput, Madras, Pondicherry, Trichinopoly, Arcot, Tanjore, Tinnevelly, Travancore, Kumbakonam, Madura, and the country inclusive.

Some of its principal divisions are as follows:—

Divisions of Drâvira Brahmans.

1. Warma.
    1. Chola-Des.
    2. Wara-Des.
2. Bruhat-Charana.
3. Asht-sahasra.
4. Sanket.
5. Arama.
6. Tannaiyar.
7. Tannamuâyar.
8. Nambûrî.
    (In Cochin, Travancore, as far as Calicut.)
9. Konshûn.
10. Munitrya.

The first six speak the Tamil language; the last, or Nambûrî Brahmans, the Maliyâlim. None of these divisions intermarry, or hold social intercourse with one another. The Drâviras observe the ceremonies enjoined in the Rig Veda, Yajur Veda, and Sâm Veda.

There are very few, perhaps not more than one hundred, Drâvira Brahmans resident in Benares; yet Drâvira pilgrims from Southern India are constantly coming to the sacred city for religious purposes. At the moment of my writing, a Ranee is there who has journeyed all the way from Calicut. The Drâvira Brahmans of Benares, although few, seem to be representatives of all the seven divisions given above. It is computed that in Southern India there are twelve millions of Hindus that speak Tamil, and six millions that speak Maliyâlim.

The above information was given me by Bâpu Sâstrî, a Tailang Brahman of Benares.

CHAPTER XV.

FOURTH TRIBE OF DRAVIRA BRAHMANS—THE KARNATA. LIST OF SEVENTEEN PRINCIPAL CLANS. EIGHT DIVISIONS—HAIGA, KIVATA, SHIVELRI, BARGINARA, KANDAWAR, KARNATA PROPER, AND MAISUR-KARNATAK, SIRNAD.

FOURTH TRIBE OF DRAVIRA BRAHMANS.

KARNATA.

THESE are Brahmans of the Carnatic in Southern India. The other four great Drâvira tribes hold little intercourse with them. They never intermarry with them, and will eat only rice in their company. In their own country the Karnâta Brahmans do not seem to be regarded with that intense religious veneration and awe in which Brahmans are held in Northern India. Mr. Campbell says, that 'a very large proportion of the Canarese people are of the ultra-Sivite Linayet sect, who altogether ignore Brahmans in their sacerdotal character' (*a*). Many Karnâta Brahmans are employed in the public offices, and in writing public accounts; and in the hilly parts of the country a large number are cultivators of the soil. This latter circumstance alone shows the social inferiority of this tribe to Northern Brahmans, who despise and rigidly avoid agricultural pursuits. It is, however, greatly to their credit that they are less scrupulous on this question.

In Benares there are about one hundred and fifty Karnâta Brahmans. These are, for the most part, engaged in literary pursuits, and reside chiefly in a *math* or monastic institution at Hanumân Ghât, in the city. Some of them, together with many other Brahmans, are supported by the Maharaja Scindia of Gwalior. Wilson, in his Glossary, remarks that the tribe is divided into two great branches,—1, Badgalnâd, 2, Sîlnâd. Bapu Sâstrî, the Tailang Brahman of Benares, who has given me valuable information respecting the Tailang and

(*a*) Ethnology of India, p. 74.

Drâvira tribes, has furnished me with the following classification of the Karnâta Brahmans.

Divisions of Karnâta Brahmans.

1. Haiga.
2. Kwâta.
3. Shîvelrî.
4. Bargînâra.
5. Kandâwa.

To which should be added,

6. Karnâta Proper.
7. Maisûr-Karnâtak (Brahmans of Mysore).
8. Sîrnâd.

The Karnâta Brahmans follow the instructions of the Rig Veda and Yajur Veda. About six millions of persons speak the Canarese language. Some of the principal clans of the Karnâta Brahmans are as follows:

List of Seventeen Principal Families or Clans.

	Clans.	*Rank.*	*Gotras.*
1.	Mahisur	Ad-karnâtak	Kasyap.
2.	Biangalur	Karnakang	Gautam.
3.	Sringerî	Murkinâru	Bhâraddwâj.
4.	Sri-rangapatan	Byalanâru	Vasisht.
5.	Dewandahâlî	Karnkambulû	Viswamitrâ.
6.	Hosurubâgaloru	Murkinâru	Sândil.
7.	Mâgadî	Navîn-Karnatak	Garg.
8.	Mulûbâgalu	Perî-Charan	Angirâ.
9.	Mâlorû	Deshastha	Vatsa.
10.	Sarjâpûran	Halekaranrû	Bhâraddwâj.
11.	Syamrâj-nagaram	Prâchîn-Karnâtak	Upamanyu.
12.	Nanjan-gurû.		
13.	Kuchî.		
14.	Kurak	Perî-Charan	Kâsyap.
15.	Shiomagî	Murkinâru	Bharaddwâj.
16.	Chitra-durg	Murkinaru	Gautam.
17.	Hâgalbârî	Prâchîn-Karnâtak	Sândil.

This list has been supplied to me by Baijnâth Sâstrî, a member of the tribe residing in Benares.

That there should be a marked difference in the names of these clans as compared with Brahman clans in Northern India, is matter for no surprise, inasmuch as, most clans, whether in the north or the south, derive their names from villages, towns, and other localities. But the names of Brahmanical titles are, for the most part, the same over the greater portion of India. Yet the titles designating the various ranks of the Karnâta Brahmans are, in almost every instance, of a peculiar and apparently of a special character and significance. The only one that I can trace elsewhere is that of Deshastha, a title also found among Mahratta Brahmans. There is, however, no difference whatever in the names of the *gotras*.

Mr. Campbell has gathered the following information respecting the Brahmans of the Canarese country. "In the north-western part of the Canarese country," he remarks, "in the district of North Canara, in the high and hilly country above and about the *ghats*, and the adjoining parts of Mysore, there is a large population of Brahman cultivators, who are, on all hands, represented as exceedingly industrious, thriving, and in every way good. Most of these people are called Haiga Brahmans; and they seem to be of pure race, and of no bastard or doubtful caste. They especially affect the cultivation of the betel-nut, and both own and cultivate the land over a large extent of country. In the Canara district they constitute one of the most numerous castes. In the Nagar district of Mysore they are also very numerous, and they are there described as 'very fair, with large eyes and aquiline noses,' a description which would seem to imply for them a derivation from an uncorrupted and little intermixed northern source. They are stated not to be very literary, or highly educated, being more devoted to agriculture" (*a*).

Moreover, he says, "in South Canara, and what is called the Talava country, there are again many Brahmans who do much cultivation; and on the whole West Coast, down to the extreme South of India, the country is said to have been extensively colonized by the Brahman colony led from Kalpi by Parasrâm, who caused the sea to retire for their convenience. In the centre of this tract, in Malabar, the Brahmans, owing to political circumstances and hostile rule, have been, to a great extent, driven away; but they are very numerous in Travancore and Cochin; and in the Palghaut valley the Brahmans seem to be very numerous as cultivators, and are industrious and good in that capacity. The principal class of Brahmans on the South Coast are called Namberees; and they have some very peculiar customs. They affect, however, much of the sacerdotal character, and seem to be very influential in Travancore and Cochin" (*b*).

(*a*) Mr. Campbell's Ethnology of India, p. 74.

(*b*) *Ibid*, pp. 74, 75.

CHAPTER XVI.

FIFTH TRIBE OF DRAVIRA BRAHMANS—THE GURJAR. EIGHTY-FOUR TRIBES. CLANS OF THE GUJERATI BRAHMANS OF BENARES FROM SITPUR-PATAN. THE NAGAR BRAHMANS. TWO TRIBES—BHIKHSHU AND MEHTA.

FIFTH TRIBE OF DRAVIRA BRAHMANS.

GURJAR.

Section I.

THIS race of Brahmans comes originally from Gujerât. Mr. George Campbell says that they trace their descent from Kâsyap (*a*). Doubtless, this is true of some, perhaps of many, but not of the whole. In Benares the Gujerâtî Brahmans profess to be descended from eight Rishis, of whom Kâsyap is one.

These Brahmans are divided into eighty-four branches, all which, or nearly so, are represented in Benares. They have the reputation, in the North-Western Provinces, of being largely devoted to the study of Sanskrit literature; yet, in their own country, many are employed in trade, and in the public service. By reason of certain social peculiarities, they hold but little intercourse with the other great Drâvira tribes, which, although they do not intermarry, yet can eat together; but all, for the most part, keep aloof from the Gujerâtîs.

The accounts given by the Gujerâtî Brahmans on this point differ considerably. Some state that no intercourse of a social character subsists between themselves and other tribes, while others will not admit this position, but say that, to some extent, there is intercourse between them and other tribes, that is that certain Gurjar clans can eat with some members of the other Drâvira tribes. It is manifest, however, that, if this be really the case, it is occasional and exceptional.

The eighty-four sub-tribes or divisions of Gurjar Brahmans keep separate

(*a*) Campbell's Ethnology of India, p. 70.

from one another, on the subject of marriage, yet some of them will eat together. These sub-tribes or branches are as follows.

Section II.—Eighty-four Branches of Gurjar Brahmans.

1. Sahasr Udîchya.
2. Shihora Udîchya.
3. Tolikiya Udîchya.
4. Badnagara.
5. Bisannagarâ.
6. Sathodarâ.
7. Vishanodarâ.
8. Varakârâ.
9. Shahchorâ.
10. Udumbarâ.
11. Narsâmparâ.
12. Balodarâ.
13. Pagorâ.
14. Nâdodarâ.
15. Giranârâ.
16. Somaparâ.
17. Harsorâ.
18. Sajoḍurâ.
19. Gangâputrâ.
20. Motmaitrâ.
21. Gomitrâ.
22. Chitrorâ.
23. Srîgorâ.
24. Gurjargorâ.
25. Karorâ.
26. Vayadâ.
27. Bhadmevâvâ.
28. Travâdîmevârâ.
29. Drâvirâ.
30. Dîmâwâl.
31. Rayakowâl.
32. Rorwâl.
33. Kherâwâl.
34. Sinduwâl.
35. Pallîwâl.
36. Gomtîwâl.
37. Itâwâl.
38. Meratwâl.
39. Gyâwâl.
40. Agastwâl.
41. Pretwâl.
42. Yâgrikwâl.
43. Gorwâl.
44. Pudwâl.
45. Unewâl.
46. Rajwal.
47. Kanoujiyâ.
48. Tilok Kanoujiyâ.
49. Kandoliyâ.
50. Karkheliyâ.
51. Parwâliyâ.
52. Sorathiyâ.
53. Tangnoriyâ.
54. Sanoriyâ.
55. Sanoviyâ.
56. Motâlâ.
57. Jhârolâ.
58. Raypula.
59. Kapilâ.
60. Akshymamylâ.
61. Guglâ.
62. Nâpalâ.
63. Anavalâ.
64. Srîmâlâ.
65. Trivedâmorh.
66. Chaturvedîmorh.
67. Bâlmîk.
68. Nârmadik.
69. Gargawî.
70. Mâlwî.
71. Kalingâ.
72. Talingâ.
73. Niduwânâ.
74. Bharathânâ.
75. Pushkaranâ.
76. Sâraswat.
77. Kharaytâ.
78. Mâru.
79. Dâhimâ.
80. Chambêsa.
81. Jâmbu.
82. Marowâ.
83. Dadhîch.
84. Lalâth.

Respecting the Gujerâtî Brahmans of Central India, Malcolm says that they "are very numerous." Some of them, he adds, "are employed in the offices of religion, while others trade, and gain a respectable livelihood as writers and accountants. Many of the Marwar or Joudhpûr Brahmans are also traders; but the great mass from that country, as well as from Udaipûr, are labourers and cultivators, forming indeed a very considerable proportion of the most industrious husbandmen of Central India" (*a*).

(*a*) Sir John Malcolm's Memoir of Central India, Vol. II., p. 122.

Section III.

The Gujerâtî Brahmans of Benares number, I am told, several thousand individuals, belonging to five hundred families. Many of them are of the Udîchya branches and came from Sîtpûr-pâtan, in the Bombay presidency. Their clans are as follows:—

Gujerâtî Brahmans of Benares from Sîtpûr-Patan, of the Udîchya branches.

Clans.	Gotras.	Titles.	Clans.	Gotras.	Titles.
1st.	Gautam ...	... Pandyâ.	9th.	Mudgal ...	... Râwal.
2nd.	Vatsya ...	... Thâkar.	10th.	Gautam ...	... Jyotikhî.
3rd.	Ditto ...	... Pâthakh.	11th.	Ditto ...	... Mahate.
4th.	Ditto ...	... Sukal.	12th.	Bhârgawa	... Sukal.
5th.	Bhârgawa	... Dave.	13th.	Dâlabhiya	... Tarwâdî.
6th.	Bhâraddwâj	... Jânî.	14th.	Vashista .	... Biyâs.
7th.	Bhârgawa	... Upâdhiya.	15th.	Gautam ...	... Bauhure.
8th.	Kasyap ...	... Pancholî.			

A large proportion of the Gujerâtî Brahmans of Benares are well off. They reside mostly in the neighbourhood of Râm Ghât and Durgâ Ghât of the city. Not a few are teachers of the Vedas, Vyakaran, Nyâya, Purânâ, and other Hindu systems and books, as well as expounders of the ceremonies of Hinduism.

Section IV.—The Nâgar Brahmans.

The Nâgars are an important, though not numerous, sub-tribe of Gujerâtî Brahmans in Benares. The head of them is an influential and respectable man, named Beni Lâl, who is possessed of considerable wealth. His family, he states, came first to Benares on pilgrimage upwards of one hundred years ago, and then settled there. He affirms that the Nâgars are divided into two distinct classes, which seldom intermarry, as follows:—

1. Bhikhshu.
2. Mehta.

The Bhikhshu Nâgars have maintained the strictness of their Brahmanical training and associations, which the Mehtas have not done. They have consequently retained amongst them most of the Brahmanical titles in vogue in Northern India, such as, Tiwâri, Dûbe, Upâdhiya, and so on, which the Mehtas have entirely discarded. The cause of this distinction between the two branches of the clan is curious. Babu Beni Lâl states, that, originally, before the Mahomedan conquest of India, the Nâgars inhabited the city of Barnagar (Varâhanagar), near Mount Abu. After several attacks on the city by Mahomed of Ghaznî, a portion of the Nâgars determined to aid in opposing him. Since that time they have continued separate from the non-combatant Nâgars, the latter engaging in the strict observance of Brahmanical rites, the former devoting themselves to fighting, trade, and other occupations, and so becoming very lax in their Brahmanical usages. The Bhikhshus, as the name indicates, mostly subsist on charity, while the Mehtas work for their own livelihood. The Mehtas, moreover, are spoken of as writers, and apparently hold the position of the Kayasth, or Writer caste, in Northern India.

The Nâgar Brahmans are landholders in the district of Bulandshahr, where they are famous for their knowledge of medicines and charms. They are also found in Farakhabâd and other places of the North-Western Provinces. The Gujerâtî Brahmans generally have small branches in many parts of these provinces. In the Bijnûr district they number some fifty families.

CHAPTER XVII.

SUPPLEMENTARY TRIBES OF BRAHMANS—THE SAKADWIPI, OR MAGADHA BRAHMANS—THE MATHURA CHAUBI BRAHMANS—THE MALWA BRAHMANS—THE KURMACHALI TRIBE—THE NAIPALI TRIBE—THE KASHMIRI BRAHMANS—THE SAPT-SHATI TRIBE—THE SHENEVI BRAHMANS—THE PALASHE TRIBE.

SUPPLEMENTARY TRIBES OF BRAHMANS.

In addition to the ten great tribes of Brahmans, five Gaur, or northern, and five Drâvira, or southern, of each of which a brief account has now been given, there are several tribes, which, although regarded as Brahmanical, yet have never been included within the ten-fold division of the race. Some of these are found in Northern India, and others in Southern India.

Section I.—The Sâkadwîpî or Magadha Brahmans.

The original country of this tribe of Brahmans is the ancient kingdom of Magadha. As this tract is always regarded by Hindus as particularly impure, so that in their view whoever dies there becomes in the next birth an ass, it is very probable that the indigenous Brahmans of that territory are, on this account, considered unworthy to be ranked with other Brahmanical tribes. The Sâkadwîpîs are found in considerable numbers in their primitive seat, yet many families have migrated to other parts of the country. They do not, however, form alliances with other Brahmans, though they freely intermarry amongst themselves. Their test applied to a stranger pretending to be a Sâkadwîpî, is to offer him what is called *jhûthâ pani*, or water from a vessel from which another person has drunk; a custom prohibited by all strict sects of Hindus. Should the stranger not be a Sâkadwîpî, he will refuse the water, probably with some indignation, as, by drinking it, his caste, whatever it was, would be broken. If a Sâkadwîpî, however, he will take it readily.

Although this tribe, like all others, is loth to depreciate itself, yet it is unquestionably of lower rank than the ten tribes. In the district of Behar, many belong to the sect of Râmanand. Some of the Rajas of Oudh are of this race.

There are said to be several hundred families of Sâkadwîpî Brahmans in Benares. Many are engaged in the study of the sacred books, though not all. Some are devoted to trade. Jethu Misr, a banker of considerable wealth in that city, is a Brahman of this tribe. The following is a list of some of the *gotras*, clans, and titles, of these Brahmans:—

Clan.	*Gotra.*	*Title.*
Urwâr	... Bhâraddwâj	... Misr.
Khantwâr	... Kaundiniya	... Pâthak.
Makhapawâr	... ( )	... Misr.
Bhaluniyâr	... Sândil	... Pandit.
Chheriyâr	... Garg	... Pânde.
Panchhaiya	... Sândil	... Misr.
Paraniyâr	... Ditto	... Pânde.
Dedhâ	... Kaundiniya	... Misr.
Bilsaya	... Kâsyap	... Ditto
Adrawâr	... Bhâraddwâj	... Misr.
Onariyâr	... ( )	... Ditto
Jamwârt	... ( )	... Pâthak.
Thâkurmirao	... Sândil	... Ditto.
Sri Mauriyor	... Parâsar	... Pânde.
Anwadhiyâr	... Vatsa	... Misr.
Kukurandhâ	... Parâsar	... Ditto
Deokuliyâr	... Bhâraddwâj	... Pânde.
Pawaeyâr	... Ditto	... Misr.

All these various classes and ranks hold intercourse with one another, and intermarry.

Section II.—Mathurâ ke Chaubî, or Brahmans of Mathurâ.

Chaubî is a title assumed by certain classes of Brahmans, of various tribes and sub-divisions of tribes, in many parts of India. Its proper meaning is one who can read the four Vedas, an honour doubtless highly coveted in ancient times. Like many other titles, however, it has entirely lost its original purport, and is borne by a multitude of persons, who not only are unable to read these ancient writings, but are totally ignorant of all knowledge of the Sanskrit language. The Chaubîs of Mathurâ are distinct from all other Chaubîs, and constitute a separate class, or order of Brahmans, having no relation to other Brahmans, and holding no social intercourse with them. In their customs, they are very similar to other tribes.

There is a tradition among the Chaubîs that their ancestors, at a remote period of Indian history, were compelled by persecution to retire from Mathurâ for a time, and to place themselves under the protection of king Sarsen, grandfather of Krishna, and that they resided near Jateshwar, on the Jumna.

There is one custom peculiar to this people, arising, it is supposed, from the smallness of the tribe. On occasion of a girl being given in marriage by one family to another, an agreement is made that the second family shall, if required, give a girl in return to a youth of the first. This custom is altogether repudiated by high-caste Brahmans, who will give their daughters in marriage to young men of lower Brahmanical rank, but will by no means take their sisters for their sons.

The Chaubîs are a fine manly race, and are famed throughout the North-Western Provinces for their skill and muscular strength, exhibited in wrestling, boxing, and other athletic sports. Yet not merely are the Mathurâ Chaubîs celebrated for such exercises, but also other Chaubîs.

There are a few members of this tribe in Benares, from whom I have learnt the following account of their chief divisions.

The Chaubîs are primarily divided into seven *gotras*, or branches, with their seven clans, which are further sub-divided into sixty-four minor clans.

Primary *gotras* and clans of the Mathurâ Chaubî Brahmans:

	Clan.	*Gotra.*	*Title.*		*Clan.*	*Gotra.*	*Title.*
1.	Kakora	... Daksha	... Chaubî.	5.	Battiya	... Bhargau	... Chaubî.
2.	Mihârî	... Kautsa	... Ditto.	6.	Uthauhiya	... Bhâraddwâj	... Ditto.
3.	Purohit	... Sausravas	... Ditto.	7.	Gagoliya	... Dhûm	... Ditto.
4.	Kâhî	... Vashisht	... Ditto.				

A few of these Mathurâ Chaubî Brahmans are found in the Agra district, where, it is said, they accept offerings at times and places when they would be refused by Brahmans of higher rank and greater strictness. They are, for the most part, landholders and traders. Some also are known to reside in the Mainpûrî district, where, as indeed in many other places, they are termed "Mathuriyas," in contradistinction to the Chaubî Brahmans which have no connexion with the Mathurâ tribe. Those in Mainpûrî came originally from Chittore.

Chaubî Brahmans—a distinct race from the Mathurâ tribe, and belonging to many separate clans and *gotras*, and even to different Brahmanical tribes,—are scattered over the districts of Azimgarh, Jaunpûr, Gorakhpûr, Mirzapûr, and Benares, in considerable numbers. They are a martial, high-blooded people, distinguished for energy and courage, and other manly virtues.

Section III.—The Mâlwâ Brahmans.

It is a matter of doubt whether the Mâlwâ Brahmans belong to any of the principal tribes of Brahmans. If they do so at all, they probably are akin to their neighbours, the Gujerâtî Brahmans. And yet I am not aware that they claim or acknowledge any such connexion. It is remarkable that the Deswâlî Chhanâtî Brahmans, consisting of six separate divisions, though regarding Mâlwâ as their home, do not associate with the Mâlwâ Brahmans. That the same tract of country should have produced two distinct and independent classes of Brahmans, is very remarkable. The history of both might probably be gained upon the spot, but nowhere else.

Some of the Mâlwâ Brahmans in the province of Benares are said to have been in those parts for many generations. The tradition current amongst them is, that, about four hundred years ago, their ancestors left their native country, and established themselves in that province. Gradually, intercourse between them and their kindred in Mâlwâ fell off, until at length all caste relations ceased; so that now they are virtually two separate tribes, and do not intermarry or eat food together.

The Mâlwâ Brahmans are divided into thirteen and-a-half *gotras*, which are practically fourteen, as follows:—

Gotras of the Mâlwâ Brahmans.

1. Bhâraddwâj.
2. Parâsar.
3. Angiras.
4. Gautam.
5. Sândil.
6. Tilkâksh.
7. Vatsa.
8. Kautsa.
9. Kasyap.
10. Katyayan.
11. Kaundinya.
12. Maitraya.
13. Ardha-Vasisht.
14. Vasisht.

The members of all these *gotras* can intermarry, and eat cooked food together at the same festival.

Section IV.—The Kurmâchali Brahmans.

The hilly regions of the province of Kumaon are inhabited partly by a race of Brahmans of undoubted antiquity. It is unknown whence they came; indeed, they are regarded as aboriginal. Yet by some persons the Kurmâchalî Brahmans are reckoned among the divisions of the Gaur tribe proper. As the matter is doubtful, I have preferred to place them in the list of supplementary Brahmanical tribes.

The Kurmâchalî Brahmans have two branches, as follows:—

I. Deshasht.
II. Karpûrî.

Each of these branches is divided into a number of clans, the names of some of which I have been able to ascertain. Those given below are all found in the city of Benares.

Sub-divisions of the Deshasht Branch.

	Clan.	Gotra.	Title.
1.	Gangâwalî	... Bhâraddwâj	... Pant.
2.	Khûta	... Ditto	... Ditto.
3.	Tilârî	... Bhâraddwâj...	Pant
4.	Gangâwâlî	... Viswâmitra ...	Bhatt.

Sub-divisions of the Karpûrî Branch.

	Clan.	Gotra.	Title.
1.	Pâtiawâl	... Bhâraddwâj	Pânde.
2.	Paliyâû	... Gautam ...	Ditto.
3.	Almorha	... Ditto ...	Tripâtî.
4.	Gangâwalî	... Bhâraddwâj	Pâthak.
5.	Shimaltia	... Kâsyap ...	Pânde.
6.	Palludâ	... Angiras ...	Joshi.
7.	Jhîjâra	... Garg ...	Ditto.
8.	Pâtiawâl	... Bhâraddwâj	Kândapal.
9.	Lohinî	... Bhâraddwâj	Misr.
10.	Tilârî ...	... Ditto ...	Joshi.
11.	Karnâtak	... Ditto ...	Pâthak.
12.	Hât ...	... Ditto ...	Pânde.
13.	Chansâra	... Gautam ...	Tripâtî.
14.	Mâlâ ...	... Bhâraddwâj	Pânde.
15.	Kholâ ...	... Gautam ...	Ditto.

The Kurmâchalî Brahmans keep aloof from other Brahmanical tribes, and although, as before remarked, they are sometimes ranked with the Gaurs, yet the latter do not intermarry with them, or eat cooked food in their company; indeed, the Kurmâchalî clans do not all hold marriage relations with one another. In addition to the two-fold division of the tribe already noticed, they are, on ceremonial and religious grounds, further divided into the Vaishnavas, who worship Vishnu, and refrain from animal food, and the Shaivas, who worship Shiva, and eat meat.

It is worthy of remark, that one of the divisions of the Kurmâchalî Brahmans,—namely, the Deshasht,—is also found as the designation of one of the principal divisions of the Mahârâshtra Brahmans.

Besides the Kurmâchalîs Proper, there are several other Kurmâchalî tribes having no connexion with one another. It will be sufficient to give their designations merely, leaving their descriptions to those better acquainted with them than the author :—

Kanoujiya Kurmâchalî.
Mahârâshtra Kurmâchalî.
Gurjar Kurmâchalî.
Purâne Kurmâchalî.

Section V.—The Naipâlî Brahmans.

The Naipâlî Brahmans are now separate from all others, but a tradition exists that, in the time of Nanda Raja, they sustained intimate relations with other tribes, and intermarried with them. Their lax ceremonial habits, however, in eating the flesh of buffaloes and other animals, and in drinking ardent spirits, would alone lead them to be despised, and to be regarded as a degenerate race by the stricter Brahmans of the plains. The tradition prevalent amongst them, and which probably is true, is that they sprang from the Kanoujiya stock. The disavowal of the relationship by the Kanoujiyas is in itself no valid reason for rejecting the tradition.

The divisions and sub-divisions of this tribe are very numerous. The following list of some of the principal has been furnished by the Nepalese Brahmans of Benares. While the names of their *gotras* are, for the most part, similar to those found among other Brahmanical tribes, nevertheless, the titles which they assume are, with few exceptions, peculiar :—

Clans, Gotras, and Titular Rank of the Nepalese Brahmans.

Clans.	*Gotras.*	*Titles.*	*Clans.*	*Gotras.*	*Titles.*
Lagantol	... Kausik	... Regumî.	Tâlî	... Bhâraddwâj	... Bhadârî.
Ditto	... Ghrita-kausik	... Khadâl.	Asantol	... Ditto	... Bhatt.
Makhantol	... Vasisht	... Bhattrâî.	Lunjung	... Kausik	... Tiwârî.
Pokaldyân	... Ghrita-kausik	... Naipâl	Bhachchpâk	... Kâsyap	... Adhikârî.
Jhosetol	... Kausik	... Regamî.	Sahar	... Viswamitra	... Aijanputr.
Jhiltumbh	... Vasisht	... Bhattrâî.	Pîrâ	... Garg	... Lamichhânya.
Buddh-Singh	. Kâsyap	... Ghimire.	Naipâl	... Bhâraddwâj	... Dyaukota.
Jîûnpûr	... Kausik	... Regamî.	Phirkyâp	... Ghrita-kausik	... Khadâl.
Borlâng	... Upmanyu	... Dhakâl.	Khinchpât	... Atreya	... Paudyâl.
Dahachok	... Atreya	... Sikghal.	Naipâl	... Kaudinya	... Pâkumpâl.
Pîrâ	... Vatsa	... Rûpâkhetî.	Sidhulî	... Ditto	... Sâpkotâ.
Gorkhâ	... Upmanyu	... Dhakâl.	Gaukaru	... Kausik	... Dungânâ.
Agarkhû	... Atreya	... Pandyâl.	Ditto	... Vasisht	... Châlispâ.
Dolkhâ	... Kaudinya	... Achârya.	Dyaurâlî	... Kaudinya	... Bâskotâ.
Gokaru	... Garg	... Rishâl.	Bûrhâ-nîlkanth	Kâsyap	... Adhikârî.
Gaikur	... Gautam	... Tiwârî.	Kalherî	... Atri	... Khatiwâra.
Gokaru	... Vasisht	... Chalise.	Pharping	... Atreya	... Pandyâl.
Sindhu	... Kausik	... Dhumgânâ.	Pokharâ	... Bhâraddwâj	... Pokharnyâl.
Borlâng	... Bhâraddwâj	... Pokhyâl.	Bhedangâ	... Atri	... Gotâmya.
Dângsalyâng	... Atri	... Gotâmyá.	Goganpânî	... Kasyap	... Gartaulâ.
Maidhi	... Bhâraddwâj	... Silwâl.	Mandan	... Ghrita-kausik	... Naipâl.
Pokhaliâng	... Atreya	... Arjâl.	Koteswar	... Vatsa	... Dâlân.
Dhâding	... Upmanyu	... Dhakâl.	Nalâng	... Mohuliya	... Timisirâ.
Nârânnîti	... Vasisht	... Bharrârî.	Adhikholâ	... Atreya	... Kâphle.
Mânkhu	... Dhananjaya	... Rijâl.	Vâsdol	... Bhâraddwâj	... Bâgle.
Shipâ	... Kâsyap	... Ghimire.	Pâlpâ	... Angiras	... Josî.
Gorkhâ	... Maudgal	... Timisirâ.	Dhâpâkhel	... Dhananjaya	... Rijâl.
Indra-chok	... Atreya	... Arjyâl.	Pokhlyâng	... Atreya	... Arjpâl.
Châugu	... Kaudinya	... Newâpâr.	Pharping	... Kausik	... Rimâl.
Pashupatitâr	... Ghrita-kausik	... Naipâl.	Adhikholâ	... Kaudinya	... Neopâne.
Ghyâl-chok	... Atreya	... Regamî.	Dah-chok	... Bhâraddwâj	... Suvetî.
Tukuchâ	... Atri	... Pokhyâl.	Indra-chok	... Ditto	... Bâgle.
Kavilâs	... Ditto	... Misr.	Parbat	... Gautam	... Pânde.
Nigâlpânî	... Dhananjaya	... Rijâl.	Pâlpâ	... Maudgalya	... Koirâlâ.
Palân-chok	... Vasisht	... Kharryâl.	Nuvâkot	... Kaudinya	... Pârjulî.
Pâlpâ	... Gautam	... Pant.	Târuka	... Upmanyu	... Dhakâl.

Section VI.—The Kâshmîrî Brahmans.

That Kâshmîr, or as it is usually spelt, Cashmere, is one of the primitive seats of the Brahmans in India, is beyond dispute. Situated on the highway from Central Asia to India, it was only natural that the Aryan race should select this beautiful country, with its hills and valleys, for one of its first settlements. It is singular, however, that the only Hindu caste known to the province is the Brahmanical. While innumerable castes have sprung up on the plains, the Brahmans have appropriated Cashmere exclusively to themselves. This circumstance furnishes an argument for the original unity of the Hindu tribes. If this unity did not exist in very ancient times, it is difficult to account for the fact that only Brahmans have occupied Cashmere. The Honorable George Campbell, in his "Ethnology of India," gives, in a few lines, a condensed view of the relation of the Brahmans to Cashmere, and also of their personal characteristics.

"Kashmir," he says, "is a Bramin country. The lower classes have long been converted to Mahomedanism; but they seem to be ethnologically identical with the Bramins; and tradition also asserts that they are of the same race. At the present day no other Hindu caste, save the Bramin, is known; nor is there any trace (so far as I could find) that there ever was any other in the country. The Bramin population is numerous; but it would seem as if, while the illiterate multitude adopted the religion of the ruling power, the better educated and superior class maintained their own tenets: and at this day, the Bramins (or Pandits, as they are usually called) form quite a sort of aristocracy. They are almost all educated, and exceedingly clever; and so, being to a great degree above manual labour, they are an excessive and somewhat oppressive bureaucracy, which not only has ruled Kashmir under every successive Government, but sends out colonies to seek a livelihood throughout Northern India.

"The Kashmir Brahmans are quite High-Arian in the type of their features, very fair and handsome, with high chiselled features, and no trace of intermixture of the blood of any lower race. It may be partly race, and partly occupation, but they have certainly a greater refinement and regularity of feature than the Affghans and others of a rougher type, with, however, a less manly-looking physique, and a colour less ruddy, and more inclining to a somewhat sallow fairness. The high nose, slightly aquiline, but by no means what we call Jewish or nut-cracker, is a common type. Raise a little the brow of a Greek statue, and give the nose a small turn at the bony point in front of the bridge, so as to break the straightness of line, you have then the model type of this part of

India, to be found both in the living men and in the statues dug up in the Peshawar valley. There are also a good many straight noses, and some varieties, as in all places, but much less departure from an ordinary handsome standard than in most countries. The figure of the ordinary working Kâshmîrî is strong and athletic. But none of them are martial; and the Bramins are, in this respect, no exception. They rule by the brain and the pen, and not by the sword. It is this character that has gained them the favour of so many rulers of a different faith. Kashmir long belonged to the Cabul kingdom; but it was never in any degree colonised by Affghans, and is singularly free from any modern intermixture of foreign races. The fact seems to be, that the valley never belonged to the Affghan nation, but was always retained as a Crown appanage of the kings, who were very jealous of admitting into it subjects whom they might find it difficult to turn out again, and much preferred to govern through the Pandits. Others have, to a great extent, followed the same policy. The Kâshmîrî Pandits are known all over Northern India as a very clever and energetic race of office-seekers. As a body they excel in acuteness the same number of any other race with whom they come in contact" (*a*). By the last observation Mr. Campbell does not mean to imply that the Kâshmîrî Brahmans are more intelligent and clever than some other Brahmanical tribes, but that they are unsurpassed in this respect by other races. He compares them with Mahratta Brahmans, to whom, probably, they are in no respect inferior; but he says they have not had the same advantage in the plains of India as the Mahratta Brahmans have had among the inferior races of their own country. He acknowledges, too, that as foreigners among energetic races they have had a much harder struggle than Mahratta Brahmans, and have not made themselves conspicuous.

The Kâshmîrî Brahmans, although of such acknowledged antiquity, have in reality no status among Brahmanical tribes. Some of the Benares Pandits rank them among Kanoujiya Brahmans, but most erroneously, I conceive, inasmuch as the Kâshmîrîs are of older date than the Kanoujiyas. Why the Kâshmîrîs have not been admitted among the ten principal Brahmanical tribes is owing, I imagine, to two reasons. In the first place, as inhabitants of a mountainous region they have been separated from them geographically; and secondly, the cold climate of the hills has induced among them, as among the Brahmans of Naipâl, certain lax habits which Brahmans on the plains regard with abhorrence. Foremost of these is the habit of eating the flesh of animals,

(*a*) Ethnology of India, pp. 57-59.

which, during the severe winter, they feel to be necessary, not only for the preservation of health, but even for the support of life. Mr. Campbell thinks it not improbable that the ten tribes have actually sprung from the Kâshmîrî Brahmans. He states a very interesting circumstance, and one of considerable importance in relation to primitive Brahmanical genealogy, regarding the connection of the Rishi Kâsyap,—who is the founder of so many *gotras* or great families among the Brahmans throughout India,—with the Brahmans of Cashmere. The founder of the Kâshmîrî Brahmans is the same Kâsyap, he remarks, 'who drained the lake, colonised the valley, gave his name to Kâshgâr and Kâshmîr, and to the people originally called Kâshas or Kâssias' (*a*).

The Kâshmîrî Pandits are said to be descended from three brothers, Kabit, Mimit, and Omit, who in former times distinguished themselves for their knowledge of Sanskrit poetry and logic, and for their acquaintance with the Vedant philosophy.

This tribe of Brahmans has three great divisions, as follows:

Divisions of Kâshmîrî Brahmans.

I. Bhatt.
II. Pandit.
III. Râjdân.

Each of these has its clans and *gotras*. How many they number, I am unable to say: the undermentioned sub-divisions are found among the Kâshmîrî Brahmans residing in Benares.

Branches of the Bhatt Division.

Clan.	*Gotra.*	*Title.*
Hawâkadal	Viswâmitra	Bangu.
Ahalmar	Kâsyap	Kanoujî.

Branches of the Pandit Division.

Clan.	*Gotra.*	*Title.*
Pampol	Kâpisthal	Jâdu.
Ranawalî	Kausik	Kachro.
Hawâkadal	Ditto	Majju.
Janâkadal	Ditto	Munju.
Jogîlankar	Ditto	Photdâr.
Chhachabala	Bhâraddwâj	Batphulo.
Ahalmarî	Ditto	Ditto.
Chhachabala	Dad-Bhâraddwâj	Dar.
Alîkdal	Ditto	Ditto.
Ranâwâlî	Upmanyu	Sum.
Jogîlankar	Dattâtraiya	Bân.
Pampol	Pâlvâs-gârgya	Photdâr.
Ranâwalî	Bhârgau	Jâdu.

(*a*) Ethnology of India, p. 58.

Branches of the Râjdân Division.

Clan.	*Gotra.*	*Title.*
Baldîmar	Swâmin Gautam Laugâkshi	Laburkar.
Hawâkadal	Datt	Kaul.

Section VII.—The Sapt-Shati Brahmans.

A tribe of Brahmans found in Bengal, and so far as I am aware, unconnected with any of the ten Brahmanical tribes. It occupies a low position among Brahmans. There is a tradition that originally it was associated with one of the superior races, and that it lost its position through the ceremonial delinquencies of its members. At one time it held no intercourse with the Kanoujiya Brahmans of Bengal; but of late years a bond of union has been cemented between it and the orthodox Rârhiyâ branch of the Kanoujiya Brahmans of Bengal, so that now the latter will partake of food together with the Sapt-Shatîs.

This tribe eats animal food, and drinks spirits at pleasure, both which practices are abhorred by most Brahmans. There are but few Sapt-Shatî families in Benares, and these, as far as possible, endeavour to hide their caste, and to disavow their connexion with the tribe. The term is derived from *sapt*, seven, and *shat*, a hundred.

The Sapt-Shatîs have sixteen branches, as follows:

	Branch.	*Gotra.*
1.	Sagai	Gautam.
2.	Sogai	Parâsar.
3.	Nânashi	Kausik.
4.	Jagai	Vatsa.
5.	Alanî	Sândil.
6.	Malani	Gautam.
7.	Karlâ	Kâsyap.
8.	Pitadî	Parâsar.
9.	Bâlthopî	Gautam.

The *gotra* of this branch was originally Bhâraddwâj.

	Branch.	*Gotra.*
10.	Bâgadî	Parâsar.
11.	Ulukî	Ghrita-kausik.
12.	Chhuturî	Sândil.
13.	Malluk-jorî ...	Vatsa.
14.	Nâchadî	Gautam.
15.	Katânî	Ditto.
16.	Kâsyap-Kânadî	Vatsa.

The *gotra* of this branch was originally Kâsyap, but lost its position from disobedience to caste rules.

Section VIII.—The Shenevi Brahmans.

The Shenevi Brahmans are a supplementary tribe found in Southern India, holding no relations with the five great Drâvira races. Wilson says of them, that they are "a class of Hindus in the Mahratta country, who maintain that they are Brahmans, and wear the characteristic cord; but who are not recognized to be so by the other Brahmans, from whom they differ chiefly in eating fish" (*a*).

Section IX.—The Palashe Brahmans.

This is an independent tribe of Brahmans in Southern India, neither included among the five Drâviras, nor apparently connected with any of them.

The remaining supplementary tribes of Brahmans are of little weight or importance, except perhaps locally. As already observed in a previous chapter, I am not aware that any one of them has representatives in Benares, a circumstance sufficient to show their insignificance.

(*a*) Wilson's Glossary, p. 474.

PART II.

THE KSHATRIYA OR RAJPOOT TRIBES.

CHAPTER I.

SOCIAL POSITION OF RAJPOOTS—LIST OF THE THIRTY-SIX ROYAL TRIBES—RAJPOOT TRIBES OF BENARES--RAJPOOT TRIBES OF OUDH.

THIS is the second of the great Hindu castes, and is called Kshatriya and Rajpoot almost indiscriminately. A distinction is sometimes drawn between these terms, however; but it has always appeared to me to be more nominal than real. It is certain that, throughout the Benares province, the two mean precisely the same thing. Whether they do so elsewhere, I am unable to affirm.

The Rajpoots, like the Brahmans, were once very powerful and influential. Although in the deadly contentions between these two primitive tribes, in the early Hindu epoch in India, the Rajpoots, whether by force of arms, or by intrigue and artifice, succumbed to the sacerdotal class, yet it is incontestible that, for many long ages, they were the principal rulers of India. The great Hindu families, descendants of mighty potentates, are still, in the main, of Rajpoot blood. The Chauhâns and Râthors trace back their lineage to the period when they had not yet united to resist Mahomedan incursions, and were content to expend their strength in their conflicts with one another. Among the noble houses of the nations of the earth, there are none that can boast of a longer pedigree, or of a more splendid history, than the Rajpoots of India.

Much might be written on this subject. The discussion of Rajpoot annals and heroic deeds is not the object of this work, although in itself confessedly an object of great interest and moment. Not a little has been written at various times by European authors on this topic. It would be mere presumption for me to follow in their wake, by saying anything respecting the political and national history of this people. I shall limit myself chiefly to an account of their actual condition at the present moment, and to an enumeration of some of the divisions of the caste, especially with reference to Benares and its vicinity.

In ancient times the two functions of this race were ruling and fighting. Only one of these, the latter, still remains. A large proportion of the sepoys of the Indian army have ever been, and still are, Rajpoots. The number, I imagine, has somewhat diminished since the mutiny. Yet this occupation is regarded by all classes as a legitimate and natural one for the members of this caste. The *physique* of the Rajpoot, in the opinion of military men, peculiarly adapts him for the life of a soldier. He is generally tall and well made, with a good development of muscle, but with a smaller proportion of bone. He is of somewhat larger build than the Brahman, yet does not display in his countenance the Brahman's high intelligence and commanding dignity, nor has the Brahman's thinness of skin and delicacy of complexion.

The other special function of these tribes, that of ruling, has, with the spread of British power in India, nearly passed away. Some of the great chiefs, such as the Maharajas of Udaipûr, Joudhpûr, Jaipûr, Kapurthala, Pattiâla, Rewah, and others, still possess some form of monarchical authority; but the greater proportion of Rajpoot princes and nobles are of mere titular rank. In many cases they are owners of large estates; and in virtue thereof, and of the ancient name they bear, with its accompanying degree of honour, exert a considerable amount of local influence—an influence, however, with not much authority attending it. Regarding the Rajpoot nobles as the chief components of the aristocracy of India, and therefore as representatives of the entire order, it may be well to enquire for a moment into the aims and purposes which they pursue. Formerly, they could command armies, or divisions and sub-divisions of armies, and were employed as rulers over provinces and districts, or else governed in their own right. Such occupations gave scope to their ambition, and an object on which their intelligence and energy might expend themselves. But all this has been changed. Not being employed now in such offices, or in any other of great national or social interest, life is to many of them without a purpose. The majority of the higher classes of course are satisfied with an existence of luxurious indolence; yet not all. They feel, however, that it is useless to be ambitious, for that there is nothing for them to do, and very little for them to gain. A few make themselves conspicuous by their liberality and public spirit, in laying out vast sums of money on colleges, schools, hospitals, asylums, and the like. Yet their secret personal ambition is mostly directed to very inferior objects. To secure a higher place in the Governor-General's Durbar, or more frequent salutes, or a greater number of guns at each salute, some will devote years of time, and lacs of rupees, and will engage in a course of intrigues of the most intricate character.

This is pitiful, but by no means surprising. The truth is, that want of employment is the great bane of the aristocracy of India in the present day. It is not a healthy condition, nor a safe and satisfactory one.

A large number of the Rajpoot caste are addicted to agriculture. As traders, or manufacturers, Rajpoots are little known. The general conclusion, therefore, is, that, although, socially, this tribe occupies a high position, and although, under more genial circumstances and conditions, it was authoritative and influential, yet it is now in a state of great depression. Educated men, and men of commanding prominence as writers, thinkers, or actors, do not spring from it as they do from some others of a much lower grade in Hindu opinion. It is notorious that both Brahmans and Rajpoots, or the members of the two highest and most distinguished races in India, are, speaking generally, fast losing ground, and giving place to the lower castes.

In confirmation of some of these views, Mr. Campbell, in his account of the Rajpoots, makes the following pregnant remarks:—" They are chiefly known to Europeans in their military character and as feudal conquerors. But, in reality, in their own villages in the plains of the Ganges, they are simple agriculturists, of a constitution very much like that of the Jats, only less pure and complete. The fact is that the Rajpoots have had their day, and are now a down-going race. Partly the furnishing of armies and feudal hosts has exhausted the material, and corrupted the simplicity of their original villages; partly infanticide and other causes tend to diminish their numbers. The result of all which is, that over great tracts of country, we find them rather a minority, trying to maintain a failing rule over a scarcely subject majority, than forming full democratic bodies of free Rajpoots. Still, in some parts of the country, the agricultural Rajpoot villages are strong and numerous ; the land is divided among them; every Rajpoot is free and equal; and the commune is administered on democratic principles. Wherever this is so, their institutions are like those of the Jats. Although they have never cared much for Bramins, they have, unlike the Jats, the ceremonies and superstitions of Hindu caste. They cook once a day with great fuss and form, almost every man for himself, after the most approved Hindustani fashion ; and are very particular about caste-marks. Their widows may not re-marry; and it is their excessive point of honour to marry their daughters to none but men of the best tribes (a feeling allied to our chivalry, no doubt), that renders the daughters such a burden to them, and makes female infanticide unfortunately so common among them. Their wives, again, are shut up after the Mahomedan fashion, and are lost for agricultural labor.

Altogether, Rajpoot females are a very unsatisfactory institution; and this goes far to weigh down and give a comparatively bad name to men who are often industrious enough" (*a*).

Infanticide as practised by the Rajpoots arises, in the first instance, from the custom of the race to prohibit intermarriages among members of the same tribe. No matter how extensive the tribe may be, or how many soever the ramifications it may have, it properly forms one family, of which the men are all brothers, and the women are all sisters. Just as a brother cannot marry a sister, so a man cannot marry a woman of the same tribe, though there may be no blood relationship whatever between them. This produces another custom equally pernicious, namely, that of endeavouring to marry a girl into a tribe of a higher rank than that to which she belongs. The lower tribes of Rajpoots have consequently a motive of great strength to induce them to spare the lives of their girls, inasmuch as their ambition is gratified by the superior alliances which are thus formed. But this motive becomes less powerful the higher the rank of the girl, until in tribes of the highest rank it has no force at all. The marriage of a girl in such case is attended with prodigious expense, with no counterbalancing circumstances gratifying the pride or ambition of her family. The result has been infanticide. It will thus be found that this fearful crime has been practised almost exclusively by higher caste Rajpoots, and to a small extent only by Rajpoot tribes of inferior degree. It is not the purpose of this work to suggest remedial measures for an evil of this character; yet it is manifest to the writer, that one of the most effectual would be to encourage and facilitate marriages between the sexes in the highest tribes, and, if practicable, to induce the sexes, not related by consanguinity to one another in the same tribe, to intermarry.

The Kshatriyas were originally divided into two principal and co-ordinate branches, styled Sûrajbansî, or the Solar Race, and Chandrabansî, or the Lunar race; to which were added the four Agniculas, or Fire Tribes. Afterwards they were further divided into thirty-six Royal Tribes, each of which has had, or still has, its own princes and nobles; and many of them were still further separated into clans and families. The Kshatriyas, therefore, are almost as extensive in their ramifications as the Brahmans. Various lists of the royal tribes have been given by writers. The following is that drawn up by Colonel Tod (*b*).

(*a*). Campbell's Ethnology of India, pp. 86, 87.

(*b*). Tod's Rajasthan, Vol. I., p. 80. He also gives several other lists.

Thirty-six Royal Tribes of Rajpoots.

1. Surya (Solar Race.)
2. Som, or Chandra (Lunar Race.)
3. Grahilot, or Gahilot ... 24 Branches.
4. Yadu ... ... 8 ditto.
5. Tuâr ... ... 17 ditto.
6. Râthor ... ... 13 ditto.
7. Kashwaha, or Kachwâha.
8. Pramara ... ... 35 Branches.
9. Chahuman, or Chauhân 26 ditto.
10. Chalûk, or Solanki ... 16 ditto.
11. Parihâra ... ... 12 ditto.
12. Chawara.
13. Tâk, or Takshak.
14. Jit, Get, or Jât.
15. Han or Hûn.
16. Katti.
17. Balla.
18. Jhala ... ... 2 Branches.
19. Jaitwa, or Kamari.
20. Gohil.
21. Sarwaiya.
22. Silar.
23. Dabi.
24. Gaur ... ... 5 Branches.
25. Doda, or Dor.
26. Gaharwâl.
27. Bir-Gûjar ... ... 3 Branches.
28. Sengarh.
29. Sakarwâl.
30. Bais.
31. Dahia.
32. Johya.
33. Mohil.
34. Nikûmpa.
35. Rajpali.
36. Dahima.

Many of these royal tribes are represented in Benares; while many others, not of the royal families, are found there likewise. Scattered over the North-Western Provinces are numerous clans of Rajpoots, more or less connected with the royal races, which, from intermarriages with them and with one another, and, in some cases, probably with non-Rajpoot families, and also by reason of local associations, have established for themselves the position of separate tribes bearing their own distinctive names. Such as can trace their Rajpoot lineage, and are of undoubted purity of blood, are recognized as belonging to the great Rajpoot brotherhood, and frequently intermarry with the ancient houses.

In giving a sketch of the tribes represented in Benares, it will be necessary, for the sake of completeness, to show in what respects they are connected with other parts of these provinces, as well as to furnish, as far as practicable, some account of their origin and history. Little, hitherto, has been accomplished in a consecutive manner on this subject. I hope, therefore, that the following connected description of most of the leading tribes of Rajpoots now existing in these Provinces, and of some of the inferior and less known tribes, although in no case so full and complete as the subject deserves, will be of some use, if only in presenting a picture of each in succession.

At the head of the Kshatriyas of Benares is His Highness the Maharaja of Vizianagram, who, although properly belonging to the Northern Sircars, in the Madras Presidency, where he possesses large estates, yet resides for the most part in Benares. His father lived there many years, and the present Maharaja's early days were spent in that city. So that it has come to pass that he is recognized as the head of the Rajpoots of the city and neighbourhood.

During the year 1870 great efforts were made by the members of the Benares Institute to induce the leading castes of Benares to agree to lessen greatly the expenses incurred at marriage festivals. The Maharaja of Vizianagram undertook to preside over the meetings of the Rajpoot tribes, which assembled at his palace in considerable numbers. I may here add, that the results of these meetings were very successful, so far as the attainment of their special object was concerned. The representatives of the tribes agreed to adopt three different rates of expenditure, according to the rank and condition of the persons to be married. It is yet to be seen whether the promises which have been made on this subject, not only by the Kshatriyas, but also by many other castes in Benares, will be fully observed. Should they be so, it is unquestionable that a great social reform will have been accomplished. Marriages will no longer be a heavy burden, and infanticide, as practised on female children with the view of saving the expense of the marriage ceremony, with its attendant festivities, will cease. Thirty tribes were represented on these occasions at the house of the Maharaja. During the last great marriage season, in the spring of the year 1871, some of the castes observed the promises which had been made by their representatives, and performed the marriage ceremony for a sum considerably less than what had been customary for many years. The Kayasths were especially conspicuous for their observance of the new rules of marriage expenditure.

The following is a list of Rajpoot tribes in Benares, including the district and province of that name, which are more or less described in the following pages:—

Rajpoot Tribes of Benares.

1. Grahlot.
2. Sisodiya.
3. Karchuliya.
4. Tomara.
5. Barwar.
6. Râthor.
7. Kachhwâhâ.
8. Pramara, Ponwar, Pomar or Puar.
9. Dore.
10. Parihârâ.
11. Narauliya.
12. Châlukiya or Solankhi.

13. Baghel.
14. Chauhân.
15. Bhadauriya.
16. Bachgotî.
17. Bilkhariya.
18. Dhrigubansî.
19. Râjkumâr.
20. Rajwâr.
21. Hârâ.
22. Khichî.
23. Naikumbh.
24. Bargyân.
25. Gaharwâr.
26. Kinwâr.
27. Chandela.
28. Sengarh.
29. Sakarwâr.
30. Kausik.
31. Bais.
32. Gautam.
33. Dikshit.
34. Sirnet.
35. Raghubansî.
36. Hayobans.
37. Bachalgotî.
38. Monas.
39. Bisen.
40. Jât.
41. Bhattîgûjar.
42. Raikwâr.
43. Donwâr.
44. Lautamia.
45. Kâkan.
46. Kulhan.
47. Sûrajbansî.
48. Chandrabansî.
49. Sombansî.
50. Nâgbansî.
51. Bhrigubansî.
52. Mahrawar.
53. Jâdubansî.
54. Sonak.
55. Sarwar.
56. Ujain.
57. Dhanawast.
58. Chaupata Khambh.
59. Banâfar.
60. Niniarwâr.
61. Hardwâs.
62. Baharwaliya.
63. Pachtoriya.
64. Nanwag.
65. Rikhibansî.
66. Bhanwag.
67. Karamwâr.
68. Bîûrihâ.
69. Garg or Gargbansî.
70. Horiya or Horaiya.
71. Patsariya.
72. Bhathariya or Batauriya.
73. Chanamiya or Chanamiyan.
74. Sangjal.
75. Dhanis.
76. Lathor.
77. Rora.
78. Teha.
79. Sarpakhariya.
80. Amethiya.
81. Sonwan.
82. Palwâr or Palîwâr.
83. Patîlî.
84. Singhel or Singalî.
85. Surhaniya.
86. Srî Mat.
87. Agastwâr.
88. Bijheriya.
89. Bhâlâ-sultân.
90. Bîjheniya.
91. Baheriya.
92. Barhaiya.
93. Chakwâîn.
94. Durgbansî.
95. Janûtûrwâ.
96. Kachhaura.
97. Dangast.
98. Gâîn.
99. Bundela.

Respecting the Rajpoot tribes of the Province of Oudh, Mr. P. Carnegy, Deputy Commissioner and Settlement Officer of Fyzabad, who, during his many years' residence in that Province has been a keen observer of its different races, respecting which he has at various times written interesting accounts, makes the following observations: "I believe I am well within the mark when I say, that, at the present moment, there are about thirty Kshatriya clans in the Province, which are presided over by more than one hundred and fifty chiefs, who have a seat at the Viceregal Darbar. But there are, besides these, numerous other important colonies also, which are, however, without a chief at their head; as for instance, the Sakarwârs, the Chandels, the Râthors, the Kachwâhâs, the Raghubansîs, and many others" (*a*). The list is as follows:—

Rajpoot Tribes of the Province of Oudh.

No.	*Tribe.*	*Number of Chiefs.*
1.	Amethia	2
2.	Bais	24
3.	Bisen	13
4.	Bundelgote	3
5.	Bachgote	15
6.	Bilkarria	2
7.	Baharia	1
8.	Barelliân	1
9.	Chandel	2
10.	Drigbansî	1
11.	Chouhân	1
12.	Gaur	6
13.	Gargbansî	2
14.	Gautam	1
15.	Gamohâ	1
16.	Janwar	11
17.	Katyar	2
18.	Kânpuria	15
19.	Kalhans	8
20.	Kachar	1
21.	Nikumbh	1
22.	Palwâr	5
23.	Ponwar	5
24.	Râjkumâr	8
25.	Raikwâr	5
26.	Rajpoot Pahâri	2
27.	Rajwâr	1
28.	Sombansî	2
29.	Surajbansî	3

(*a*) Mr. P. Carnegy's Races of Oudh, p. 37.

CHAPTER II.

GAHLOT OR GRAHILOT TRIBE—SISODIYA BRANCH—THE MAHARAJA OF VIZIANAGRAM—THE KARCHULIYA CLAN.

GAHLOT OR GRAHILOT.

MEMBERS of this tribe are, it is said, scattered over a considerable portion of the North-Western Provinces; yet, if this be so, the last Census Report, with the exception of two districts, barely acknowledges their existence elsewhere. They are only noticed altogether in five districts (*a*). Elliot says they are in great numbers in Bulandshahr; but the Census Report is silent about them (*b*). They are landholders in the districts of Mirzapûr, Ghazipûr, Azimgarh, Cawnpûr, Mathurâ, Farakhabâd, Aligarh, and Bulandshahr.

The tribe has twenty-four branches, as follows: Aharya, Mangaliya, Sîsodiya, Pîpara, Kâlam, Gâhor, Dhorniya, Gaura, Magarsâ, Bhimalâ, Kamkotak, Kutechâ, Sorâ, Uhar, Useba, Nirrûp, Nadoriya, Nâdhotâ, Ujârkâ, Kutacharâ, Dusaudh, Bateorâ, Pâhâ, Purot (*c*).

The Rana of Udaipûr is of the Sîsodiya branch of this tribe, and lays claim to a long and distinguished lineage. His ancestors were formerly rulers in Gujerat, from which country they were expelled. In the time of Prithi Raja (with whom many Rajpoots of the present day like to link themselves), it is said, one of the members of this family intermarried with that famous house. Rai Durgâ, of the Sîsodiya clan of Gahlots, was a general in Akbar's army, and accompanied Prince Murâd on his expedition against Mirza Mahammad Hakîm of Cabul. He also went on several other expeditions (*d*). The Sîsodiya and

(*a*) Report of the Census of the North-Western Provinces for 1865, Vol. II.; General Statement No. II., p. 11.

(*b*) Elliot's Supplemental Glossary, Vol. I., p. 90. See also the Report of the Census of 1865, Vol. I. Appendix B., p. 69.

(*c*) Tod's Rajasthan, Vol. I., p. 84.

(*d*) Ain i Akbari, Mr. Blochmann's Translation, ol. I., p. 417.

Aharya branches are amongst the most important of the tribe. The former term is sometimes applied to the entire race. Indeed, Colonel Tod asserts, that Sîsodiya was the last change of name which the Rana of Udaipûr's family underwent. It was first, he says, Surajbans, then Grahilot or Gahilot, Aharya and Sîsodiya. These changes arose from revolutions and local circumstances.

This race, according to the testimony of tradition, is descended in a direct line from Râma. The name "Grahilot" is said to have been given to it by Grahaditiya, of the family of the Balabhi kings, who became the head of the small principality of Edar. The appellation "Grahilot" continued to designate the tribe for a time ; but, on its taking possession of Ahar, was changed to Aharya, by which name it was known till the twelfth century, when, says Tod, "the elder brother, Râhap, abandoned his claim to the throne of Chittore, obtained by force of arms from the Mori, and settled at Dongarpûr, which he yet holds, as well as the title 'Aharya,' while the younger, Mâhap, established the seat of power at Sîsoda, whence Sîsodiya set aside both Aharya and Gahlot" (*a*). Although the tribe, as already stated, is sometimes styled Sîsodiya, yet this term is properly only applicable to one branch of the twenty-four into which the Gahlots are divided. Sir John Malcolm remarks, "that of the Rajpoot families who have exercised power, and who stand first in reputation, are the Sîsodyas, Râthors, Kachwâhas, and Chauhâns. The Sîsodiyas, which include the Udaipûr family, are considered the highest in rank, from their rule being the most ancient" (*b*).

In the Agra district the Grahilots are found chiefly in the sub-divisions of Ferozabâd and Khandauli, where they have been settled for a long period extending over several hundred years. Those in Farakhabâd state that they received a tract of country there from Prithi Raja, for the good services their ancestors performed in the wars against Jai Chand, the Râthor Raja of Kanouj. There are several families of Chirar Rajpoots, calling themselves Gahlots, in the employ of the Raja of Mainpûri ; but their claim to this relationship is not recognized by Rajpoots generally, and their habits are very low, indeed not superior to the lowest Hindu castes. The Gahlots are said to be landholders in Karauli, Manikpûr, and Jhanti. There are also a few of them in other places (*c*).

In his Memorandum on the Castes of Etawah, Mr. A. O. Hume has an

(*a*) Tod's Rajasthan, Vol. I., pp. 83, 84; and 211, &c. See in this Volume a very interesting account of the Udaipûr family.

(*b*) Sir John Malcolm's Memoir of Central India, Vol. II., p. 128.

(*c*) Report of the Census of the North-Western Provinces for 1865, Vol. I., Appendix B., pp. 69, 74, 76.

interesting notice of this tribe. "In the East a good many of the Gahlor, or, as it is sometimes written, Gahlot Thakurs, are to be found. The head-quarters of this clan, hereabouts at least, is in Pargannahs Rasulabâd and Tirûa Thatea, Zillah (district of) Farakhabâd. They profess to have made their way, about 400 A. D., from Mathurâ and Delhi, to assist Sultan Mahmud Tuglak in maintaining order in and about Kanouj; and to have received the six hundred villages, they still profess to hold, in reward for their service. That they obtained their present holdings about the time that that most blood-thirsty ruffian, Tamerlane, had reduced the whole of Upper India to a state of anarchy, is, I deem, probable enough; but, although Mahmud Tuglak was residing for a short time at Kanouj, it was as a mere refugee, and I doubt whether he ever attempted to keep order anywhere, or possessed any power to reward allies. I suspect by their own good swords they won those lands, as certainly later 'by those same swords they kept them'" (*a*).

The Gahlots have twelve villages in the district of Oonao situated in the Harha Pargannah, in Tuppah (or sub-division of a Pargannah) Konrârî, which is also the name of the principal village. They have occupied the country from the time of the emperor Aurungzebe, when they appear to have ejected the former Korî inhabitants (*b*).

The chief city of the Gahlots in ancient times is reputed to have been Balabhipûr near Surat. "They became sovereigns, if not founders," says Colonel Tod, "of Balabhi, which had a separate era of its own, called the Balabhi Sambat, according with Sambat Vicrama 375." Raja Partâb Chand Sîsodiya established a kingdom at Chitrgarh, in Maiwar, and married the daughter of Naushirawan, from whom therefore the Rana of Udaipûr is said to be descended. In the time of Rai Pithora, one of the Chittore family occupied a portion of the territory now included in the Bulandshar district. His descendants gained possession of as many as sixty villages. Twenty-five of these, situated in the Dadrî Pargannah, are inhabited solely by Gahlots (*c*).

In the Pargannah of Rasûlabâd, in the Cawnpûr district, the Grahilots and Gaurs are the most numerous tribes of Rajpoots. The former are reported to have come originally from Kanouj.

The Gahilots are of the Kâsyap *gotra* or order.

(*a*) General Report of the Census of the North-Western Provinces for 1865, Vol. I., Memorandum by Mr. A. O. Hume, Appendix B., p. 84.

(*b*) Mr. Elliot's Chronicles of Oonao, p. 53.

c) Census of the North-Western Provinces, Vol. I., Appendix B., p. 18.

HIS HIGHNESS THE MAHARAJA MIRZA VIJIARAMA GAJAPATTY RAJ MANEA, SULTAN BAHADUR, K.C.S.I., OF VIZIANAGRAM,

OF THE SISODIYA BRANCH OF GAHLOTS, AND HEAD OF THE RAJPOOTS IN BENARES.

The Maharaja of Vizianagram is descended from the Ranas of Udaipûr, one of the most ancient, and, in popular estimation, most illustrious families in India. He is consequently of the Grahilot tribe; and speaks of himself as belonging to the Sîsodiya branch, and of the Vasisht gotra. According to the traditions of this famous house, Bijaibhûp, one of its members, at a very early period, settled in Ajudhiya, the modern Oudh, whence, in the year 514 of the Sâka era, corresponding to 592 A.D., his descendant, Mâdhavavarma, emigrated to the Telingâna country, accompanied by representatives of the Vasisht, Dhanunjaya, Kaundinya, Kasyap, and Bhâraddwâj *gotras* of his own tribe.

The colonists established themselves at Bejamârah, on the river Kristna, which country they occupied for 921 years. In course of time they became a numerous people. Gradually disputes broke out among them, which ended in the loss of their independent sovereignty, and in their submission to Sultan Kali, A.D. 1512, the founder of the Kutbshâhi dynasty of Golcondah. Under Abdallah, the fifth king of that line, Pusapati Tummerâj, otherwise called Raghunadharaj, was appointed as Subadar of the Sircars, A.D. 1652, and received a *Jaghir*, or landed estate, consisting of the Kamila and Bhogaporam *Pargannahs*. This was the first distinction conferred on the ancestors of the Vizianagram family by the Golcondah princes. When the Golcondah territory fell into the hands of the Emperor Aurungzebe, Tummerâj was confirmed in his office of Subadar, and received a present of a two-edged sword from the emperor, which furnished the device of the coat of arms still used by the family.

The office, however, was not to be a sinecure. Tummerâj received orders from his master, first to expel the English from his territory by every means in his power, and to take possession of or destroy their property, wherever found; and, secondly, on their renewal of friendly intercourse with the emperor, his orders were to let them trade freely as heretofore.

In 1690 Tummerâj was succeeded by his son Sîta Râm Chandrulu, who added ten *Pargannahs*, or baronies, to the family estates, and assumed the title of Kalinga Maharaj, in virtue of his acquiring Potturu, in the Kalinga territory. He had a retinue of 125 cavaliers and 450 foot soldiers, for his guard of honour, and maintained several detachments of armed men in various parts of the country over which he exercised jurisdiction.

Sîta Râm was succeeded by his son Veda Ananda Râj, who had two sons, Sîta Râm Râj, and Veda Vijiarâm Râj. The latter entered upon the duties of the administration of the Circars in the room of his father. He expelled Jaffir Ali Khan, the Nawab of Chicacole, and, as a reward for his faithful services, was honoured by the emperor with the title of Manea Sultan, or Chief of the Hill Districts. Thereupon, he took up his residence in the town of Vizianagram, where he erected the present fort, in the year 1730, a quadrangular stone edifice with an enormous bastion at each corner.

The Circars were only in nominal subjection to Aurungzebe, and were in reality in the hands of the Hindu chiefs who ruled over them. This state of things continued until 1724, when Yusufjah, the great Viceroy of the Deccan, took them under his control, and at once inaugurated a thorough system of civil and military government. At his death, the French endeavoured to obtain a footing in these provinces, in consequence of the disputed succession. Eventually, Salâbat Jang, of the family of Yusufjah, granted to the French, at the close of 1753, the four Circars of Mustafanagar or Kondapilly, Ellore, Rajamandry, and Chicacole, which were taken possession of by Bussy, the French General, through his subordinate M. Morasin, then at Masulipatam.

At that time the most powerful Hindu noble in the Chicacole Circar was Veda Vijiarâm Râj, head of the Vijianagar family, who became a valuable ally of Bussy. In the winter of 1756 the French general began his march into the Circars, accompanied by 500 European soldiers and 4000 Sepoys, and on the 19th December arrived at Rajamandry. Here he was met by Raja Vijiarâm Râj, and other Indian chiefs, at the head of a force numbering 10,000 men.

Raja Ranga Row, chief of the Poligars in the neighbourhood, whose large estates, extending over twenty square miles, were contiguous to those of Raja Vijiarâm Râj, having made himself obnoxious to the latter, it was proposed to Bussy that Raja Ranga Row should be compelled to quit his hereditary lands of Bobily for others of greater extent, situated at a distance from Vijiarâm Râj's territories. As Ranga Row declined the proposal, when made to him, it was resolved to force him into submission. With the aid of his native friends, Bussy made an attack upon him at day-break on the 24th January 1757, and sustained it till the afternoon. Perceiving the hopelessness of further defence, Ranga Row formed the resolution of putting to death all the women and children in the fort, to prevent their falling into the hands of the enemy. Assembling his principal men, he explained to them his determination, which was at once put in execution. Ranga Row was presently killed by a musket ball, and the fort captured.

Raja Vijiarâm, however, paid dearly for his avarice, for, on the third day after the capture, at midnight, while asleep, four men from Bobily entered his tent, and assassinated him.

On the news of his death spreading abroad, a crowd of people collected together, and while they were in full debate on the catastrophe, an old man was observed advancing leading a boy. 'This is the son of Ranga Row, whom I have preserved against his father's consent,' said the old man. On hearing this, Bussy presented to the boy the estate which he had offered to Ranga Row in exchange for Bobily, and retained him for a while in his camp.

Leaving Bobily, Bussy marched through the northern part of the Chicacole province, and on his return to Hydrabad, defeated the British troops at Vizagapatam, and established his power there, as well as in the other parts of the Northern Circars.

Raja Vijiarâm Râj was succeeded by his nephew Gajapati Anand Raj Maharaj. The new Raja, soon after the departure of Bussy, made an attack on Vizagapatam, expelled the French garrison, and sent intelligence of his exploit to Madras, offering to surrender to the English the places he had captured. He also asked for the aid of a force wherewith to proceed against the French in the Deccan. Being unsuccessful in his application to Madras, he turned to Bengal for assistance. Lord Clive, with his accustomed promptness and far-sightedness, sent an expedition by sea to his support, under the command of Colonel Forde, which disembarked at Vizagapatam on the 12th September 1758.

Some difficulty arose at the outset respecting the amount of pecuniary aid which the Raja was to give to the English force, the remuneration which he was ultimately to receive for the same, and the help he would give in the war, which having been removed by a treaty concluded between the two parties, the united army attacked the French at Peddapûr, and defeated them. The enemy abandoned their camp, which together with large stores of ammunition fell into the hands of the allies. The French retreated to Rajamandry, whence they were driven by Colonel Forde, who shortly after laid siege to Masulipatam, and took it by assault.

The Raja now refused all further supplies to Colonel Forde, who hearing that Salâbat Jang had advanced to within forty miles of Masulipatam, in the emergency paid a visit to him in his camp. Salâbat Jang gladly made peace with the invader, and a treaty was made, whereby the Circar of Masulipatam with eight districts, the Circar of Nijampatam, and the districts of Condavir and Wakalmanuer, were given to the English.

On the expulsion of the French the Sircar came again under the charge of the Subadar of the Deccan. His authority over them, however, was more nominal than real until the year 1765, when a Firman was issued by the Emperor Shah Alam, conferring the Circars on the British as a free gift unfettered by the intervention of third parties. Yet strange to say, on the 12th November, 1766, as though these treaties were both unsound, another treaty was ratified with the Nizam at Hyderabad, by which the East India Company agreed to pay the Nizam an annual tribute of nine lakhs of rupees for the Circars.

Meanwhile, Raja Anand Râj had fallen a victim to small-pox in the year 1759, soon after the termination of the war with the French. He died without issue, and his wives performed the horrid rite of suttee by immolating themselves on his funeral pile. The selection of an heir was entrusted by the family to the Ranee of the late Raja Vijiarâm Râj. This lady chose Pusapati Râm Bhadra Râj, a boy of twelve years of age, second son of her husband's cousin, as the successor to Anand Râj; who assumed the name of Vijiarâm Râj, by which he was afterwards known. The elder brother, Sîta Râm Râj, was excluded by Hindu law, yet owing to Vijiarâm's minority, all real authority fell into his hands. The influence he thus gained, he never lost, and during the greater portion of his life-time Vijiarâm Râj, although Raja, was in truth under the subjection of his brother.

The young Raja was confirmed in his titles by the Nizam at Rajamandry in April 1760, since which year the title of Mirza, granted at the same time by the Nizam in virtue of a Firman from the emperor of Dehli, has been attached to the Rajaship.

Sîta Râm's first efforts were directed to supplant the ancient Diwan, in which he was successful. He next proceeded to bring to terms Vengal Row, one of the old Bobily family, a determined opponent of the authority of the Pusapatis. He next made an attack on the large estates of Narain Deo of Parla Kemedi, while that Chief was absent on pilgrimage to Jagannath. Narain returned, however, with a body of five thousand Mahratta horse, and defended his territory with great spirit. Nevertheless, Sîta Râm defeated him, and the issue of the struggle was the annexation of a considerable portion of the Ganjam District.

After this, the two brothers, like freebooters, bent on seizing their neighbour's property, marched southwards into the Rajamandry Circar, which, after some fighting with the Nawab, they added, it is said, to their already enormous possessions.

A negotiation was now commenced between the East India Company, on the one side, and Vijiarâm Râj and Sîtâ Râm on the other, which ended in the latter agreeing to pay to the former the annual sum of three lacs of rupees, as tribute for their country, and to resign all claims of conquest in the estates of Narain Deo of Kemedi.

In the year 1775, a strong faction of leading Rachwârs caused Sîtâ Râm to resign his office of Diwan, on Vijiarâm Râj's covenanting to acknowledge Sîtâ Râm's son, Narsingha Gajapati Râj, as his successor, in the event of no male issue being afterwards born to him. It is manifest from the whole course of Sîta Râm's proceedings, that, although he administered his brother's estates with great tact and energy, he had, nevertheless, by his overbearing arrogance made himself very obnoxious to him. Vijiarâm Râj was, therefore, glad to be at last delivered from a yoke that had become intolerable.

But Sîta Râm was not to be shelved so summarily. On the appoinment of Sir Thomas Rumbold to the Governorship of Madras, Raja Vijiarâm Râj, and many other landholders, were summoned to Madras, in order that arrangements for the collection and payment of tribute and revenue might be made with them personally. Sîta Râm found this to be the opportunity he had desired. There is good ground for the belief, moreover, that, when he went to Madras, he took with him a large sum of money, which he distributed with great adroitness, and, further, that while there he entered into engagements for additional payments to those persons who signally aided him in his projects. Whatever may have been the means he employed, it is certain that he succeeded in attaining his own ends, and in utterly defeating those of his brother. Sir Thomas Rumbold re-instated him in the post he formerly held.

The Court of Directors, to their honour, repudiated the arbitrary and harsh course taken by the Governor. "Our surprise and concern were great," they write on the 10th January, 1781, "on observing the very injurious treatment which the ancient Raja of Vizianagram received at the Presidency, when, deaf to his representation and entreaties, you, in the most arbitrary and unwarrantable manner, appointed his ambitious and intriguing brother, Sîtâ Râm Râj, Diwan of the Circars, and thereby put him in possession of the services of his elder brother, who had just informed you that he sought his ruin.

A Resolution moved by Mr. Dundas, afterwards Lord Melville, in the House of Commons, on the 25th April 1782, was to the same effect—"that the

Governor and a majority of the Council of Fort Saint George did by menaces and harsh treatment compel Vijiarâm Râj, the Raja of Vijianagar, to employ Sîta Râm Râj as the Diwan, or manager, of his zemindary, in the room of Jaggannath, a man of probity and good character; that the compulsive menaces made use of towards the Raja, and the gross ill-treatment which he received at the Presidency, were humiliating, unjust, and cruel, in themselves, and highly derogatory to the interests of the East India Company, and to the honour of the British nation."

Sîta Râm was ejected from his office, and, eventually, under the orders of the Government, took up his residence in Madras. His brother, the Raja, left to his own weak judgment, was deficient in all the qualities necessary to his high and important position. Sîta Râm had proved himself an obstinate, self-willed, tyrannical steward, yet he had administered the Raja's estates with singular sagacity, and had kept him from difficulties in his relations with the Indian Government. The estates were now mismanaged, and were soon incapable of paying the enhanced tribute imposed upon them. The consequence was, that, first of all, remonstrances, and, then, threats, were employed to obtain it from the Raja. On his part, Vijiarâm Raj, unable to appreciate the danger he was courting, neglected the demands of the Government, and at length defied its authority. Thereupon, the Governor of Madras determined to bring him to reason by force. Troops were led out against him, and on the 10th July 1792, a severe conflict took place between them and the Raja's men, which ended in the death of the Raja and of many of his followers.

The Raja had placed the ladies of his family with his young son, Narain Babu, a boy of eight years of age, at a village four miles distant from the scene of the engagement; and on the eve of the battle, he sent instructions to the boy, to surrender himself to the British force and the Madras Council, in case of his own death. After the battle, however, the child was carried away by his attendants, and notwithstanding that Sir Charles Oakley, Governor of Madras, gave repeated assurances in writing that if he surrendered he would be protected, and would receive all the respect due to his rank, yet the relatives of the lad listened to none of the overtures thus made. The Governor, being wearied with their foolish and pertinacious opposition, issued a final order, that he was to return to his own country within the space of thirty days. This order also, like the rest, was disobeyed.

Had it not been for a change in the Government of Madras at this time, there is ground for supposing, that the family of the late Raja Vijiarâm Râj would have come to ruin. Sir C. Oakley was succeeded by Lord Hobart; the Provisional Council was abolished; and Collectorates were established. The Government issued a proclamation, calling upon the Hill Poligars to return peaceably to their respective villages, guaranteeing to them a consideration of their just claims. Before the close of 1796, agreements had been made with most of the Hill landholders. Narain Râj was ordered to pay four lacs of rupees, or forty thousand pounds, by way of compensation for the claims of the Company against his late father, and his estates were at the same time greatly curtailed.

At the Permanent Settlement the sum of five lacs was fixed as the annual tribute to be paid by Narain Râj, exclusive of the revenue from salt, sugar, port dues, and other imposts. Moreover, the Government granted to Narain Râj the following title, Mirza Raja Sri Pusapati Narayana Gajapati Râj Bahâdur Manea Sultan, Zemindar of Vizianagram, together with a salute of nineteen guns whenever he visited the chief authorities in the district.

By the year 1817 the Raja had incurred a debt of twelve lacs of rupees. He therefore requested the Government to take charge of his estates until the debt was paid off, under the stipulation that he should meanwhile receive eighty thousand rupees a year for his personal expenses. The debt was cleared off in the year 1822, and the estates were restored to their owner.

In 1827 the Raja again made over his estates to the Government, and proceeded to Benares on an allowance of one lac of rupees a year. There he resided until 1845, when he died. His debts, however, instead of diminishing, had increased from seven lacs to eleven, a considerable portion of which was contracted during his residence in Benares.

The present Maharaja Vijiarâm Gajapati Râj visited his estates in Vizianagram for the first time in 1848, when, on his entering the Fort, he was received with a salute of nineteen guns, fired from the cantonments by order of Government. In 1852 the estates were handed over to the Maharaja free of debt, and with a surplus of upwards of two lacs of rupees. In 1863 the Maharaja was requested by Sir John Lawrence, the Viceroy and Governor General, to become a Member of the Legislative Council of India; and in the following year was created a Maharaja, as a personal distinction, in consideration of his liberality in endowing a hospital in Vizagapatam, to the extent of twenty thousand rupees, and of the example which he had set to neighbouring *Zemindars*, or landholders, in the general good management of his estates. The further honour has been recently conferred upon him, of Knight Commander of the Star of India.

For the princely sums which the Maharaja devotes to public institutions in Madras, Bengal, and the North-Western Provinces, and for the great public spirit he displays in promoting the prosperity of the country generally, it is unquestionable that he occupies the very highest position among the nobles of India. Only lately he has erected a new Dispensary in Benares, and has engaged to build a Town Hall, at a cost of not less than five thousand pounds. Yet this generosity is insignificant compared with one act of large-handed and splendid liberality which he performed in the early part of the past year, in offering to present twenty thousand pounds to the Medical College of Allahabad, which it was proposed to establish. Although this object has not been sanctioned by the Governor General in Council, yet the sum is not withdrawn, but is offered for some other object in connection with the proposed Allahabad University. The Maharaja is, moreover, not merely an ornament of native society in Benares and elsewhere, but by his excellent knowledge of English, his great politeness, his fondness for field sports, and his general manliness of character, is cordially welcomed everywhere among the Europeans settled in the country.

GENEALOGY OF THE FAMILY OF THE MAHARAJA OF VIZIANAGRAM.

Descended from the brothers, Sri Pusapati Râmavarma and Mâdhavarma, who formerly ruled over the Kalinga Country.

I. Raja Raghunadharâj, A. D. 1652.
II. Raja Sîtâ Râm Chandrulu, A. D. 1685.
III. Raja Ananda Râj 1696. IV. Raja Tamonirâj, 1696.
V. Raja Vaneatapatirâj, 1699. VI. Raja Anandarâj, 1699.
VII. Sîta Râm Râj, 1717. VIII. Raja Peda Vijearâm, 1731.
IX. Raja Ananda Râj, 1756.
X. Raja Vijiaram Gajapati Râj, 1762.
XI. Raja Narsinga Gajapati Râj. XII. Raja Naraina Gajapati Râj, 1796.
XIII. The present Maharaja Vijiarâm Gajapati Râj, recognized in the room of his father, 1845.

Kumar Maharaja Narain Gajapati Râj, born February 10th, 1850, died September 29th, 1863.

Kumar Maharaja Anand Gajapati Raj, born December 31st, 1850.

Also Maharaj Kumarika Appala Kundayya Devi, born February 17th, 1849; married, July 11th, 1866, to Kumâr Maharaja Râma Râj Singh, heir apparent and cousin of the Maharaja of Rewah.

KARCHULIYA.

This is reputed to be a branch of the Sîsodiya Rajpoots. They are very numerous in the Kopâchit *pargannah* of the Ghazipur district, where they hold possession of about two hundred villages. They affirm that the name Karchûliya, which is derived from the Sanskrit 'kar,' a hand, and 'chalânâ,' to make use of, was given them by the emperor Allauddîn, in token of their bravery. Eighteen generations have passed away since Hem Shâh, the progenitor of the clan, founded the colony at Kopâchit; and they are able to state the names of each in succession (*a*). A small number of Karchûliya Rajpoots are also settled in the Banda district.

(*a*) Dr. W. Oldham's Statistical Memoir of the Ghazipûr District, Part 1, page 62.

CHAPTER III.

THE TOMARA OR TUAR, BARWAR, RATHOR, AND KACHHWAHA TRIBES.

Tomara or Tuar.

THIS tribe of Rajpoots is of great antiquity, and although now of little importance, was once held in much honour. In the North-Western Provinces, where it formerly possessed extensive power, it numbers little more than four thousand souls, of whom upwards of three thousand inhabit the Agra district. But these statistics rest on the very doubtful authority of the Census Returns of 1865. These Returns, however, are singularly inconsistent with each other. For instance, in one volume, the Tomars of Bulandshahr and Meerut, are said to be descended from Anek Pâl, and to be in possession of ten villages, besides portions of other villages situated in the former district. The narrative states that these Tomars are of two kinds, Hindu and Mahomedan, the latter having been converted to Islamism as far back as the reign of Kutb-uddîn (*a*). The next volume, containing the tabular list of all the tribes and castes of these provinces, does not represent a single Tomar as residing in those districts (*b*).

The Tomars of Budaon are traditionally descended from Raja Sank Pâl, who, many ages ago, conquered that part of the country, and settled in it with a large number of his followers. The Ujhânî division of the district has still a considerable population of Tomars. They state, moreover, that their ancestors were subdued by Raja Hirand Pâl of Kampil, since which time they have been styled 'Jangarah' (*c*). On the termination of the Tomar rule over the ancient kingdom of Delhi, many of the family seem to have migrated southwards and settled in various parts of Gwalior, whence they pushed out to the northward again, and some entered what is now the Agra district (*d*). In the

(*a*) Census of the North-Western Provinces, for 1865, Vol. I., Appendix B., pp. 19, 20.

(*b*) *Ibid*, Vol. II. General Statement of Castes, No. 4, p. 11, list Towmur.

(*c*) Census of the North-Western Provinces, for 1865, Vol I., Appendix B., p. 46.

(*d*) *Ibid*, p. 68.

district of Etah the Tomars are partly descended from the Gwalior Tomars, and partly from Tomars who came direct from Delhi and Hastinapûr. They are found in numerous villages in this district, although their existence is ignored by the Census Tables (*a*). There are some also in the district of Mainpûrî.

The Tomar dynasty was reigning in Delhi when the Mahomedans first entered India. It commenced with Anang Pâl I, in the year 736 A. D., according to the traditional statement, but, in the judgment of General Cunningham, who has paid great attention to the matter, the more correct date is 733 A. D. It lasted for a period of four hundred and nineteen years, when Delhi was captured by the Chauhân Raja of Ajmere, Visala Devâ. There were nineteen Kings of the Tomar dynasty, of whom General Cunningham has given a list, with the dates of their accession, and the duration of their several reigns, in his Archæological Survey of Delhi, page 16. The two royal families were united by the marriage of Visala Devâ's son or grandson with the daughter of the last king, Anang Pâl III. The issue of this union was the very famous Prithi Raj, or Prithvi Raja, or Rai Pithora, as he is variously styled (*b*). This prince was conquered by Muazuddîn Sâm in 1193.

After this, says Mr. Beames, in his account of this tribe of Rajpoots, in Elliot's Supplemental Glossary, "the Tomars make no mark in history till the reign of Alâuddîn Khilji, or shortly after the death of that sovereign, when Bîr Shing Deo, an obscure Tomar, became possessed of Gwalior, which had been previously held successively by the Kachhwâhas, the Parihârs, and the Mahomedans. After him a long line of illustrious princes ruled, subject more or less to Musalman influence, among whom Dungar Singh is noteworthy, inasmuch as in his reign the celebrated rock-sculptures of Gwalior were executed. They appear to have been sometimes at feud with, and sometimes faithful allies of, the Musalman rulers of Delhi. The princes of the house of Lodi, Bahlol, Sikandur, and Ibrahîm, attacked and defeated them, or were defeated by them, several times in those troublous and unsettled ages. The strong fortress of Gwalior, however, more often defied the Mogul forces. Raja Mân Singh was a prince of great power and ability, and in his reign the power of the Tomars was at its height. He was a wise ruler, a patron of the arts, and himself a skilful musician, and a beneficent administrator" (*c*). His successor, Vikramaditya, was subdued by the Mahomedans, and was killed at the battle of Panipat, fighting in

(*a*) Census of the North-Western Provinces, for 1865, Vol. I., Appendix B., p. 94.

(*b*) General Cunningham's Archæological Survey, pp. 16—23.

(*c*) Elliot's Supplemental Glossary, Vol. I., p. 163.

their behalf. He is supposed to have possessed the celebrated Kohinoor diamond, which he gave to the emperor Bâbar. The family gradually sank into insignificance, and at length removed from Gwalior and settled in Udaipûr. It retains, however, the memory of its ancient prestige (*a*).

The Tomars, although once so powerful and illustrious, possess now no independent territory. Vikramaditiya, who established the Sambat era, dating from the year 56 B. C., is believed, on good grounds, to have sprung from this tribe. "The chief possessions left to the Tuârs," remarks Colonel Tod, "are the district of Tuârgar, on the right bank of the Chumbal towards its junction with the Jumna, and the small chieftainship of Patan Tuârvati, in the Jaipûr State, and whose head claims affinity with the ancient kings of Indraprastha" (*b*).

In the Gorakhpûr district are a few families of this tribe, there styled Tongâr. They are not of high rank in popular estimation. Small communities also are found in the Fathpûr district. A few likewise are met with in the districts of Benares and Shâhjahânpûr.

The tribe is divided into seventeen branches.

Barwar.

The Barwar clan of Majhosi and Manîâr, in the Ghazipûr district, profess to be a branch of the Tomar tribe. They came thither in association with the Naraulia branch of the Parihâr Rajpoots, and assisted them in the expulsion of the Cherus. Their traditions state that they first of all settled in the Azimgarh district, and afterwards entered Kharîd. The name 'Barwar,' they say, is derived from Barnagar, formerly the principal village of the tribe. Other Barwars are found at Deochandpûr, a village in the Saidpûr *pargannah* of the Ghazipûr district; and others still at Bârîpûr in the Chapra district (*c*).

"It is worthy of notice," says Dr. W. Oldham, "that the Barwars of Majhosi and of Manîâr *tuppehs*, though they claim a common origin, are entirely distinct from each other. They will only eat together on the occasion of some great gathering, when the people of the other clans of the *pargannah* are present. The population of Manîâr, the chief town of the Barwars, is 6,124. It is the seat of an extensive grain trade" (*d*).

(*a*) Elliot's Supplemental Glossary, Vol. I., pp. 163-64.
(*b*) Tod's Rajasthan, Vol. I., pp. 88, 89.
(*c*) Dr. W. Oldham's Statistical Memoir of the Ghazipur District, Part I., p. 61.
(*d*) *Ibid*, p. 62.

Râthor.

Although the Râthors have lost much of their ancient renown, nevertheless, they are still reckoned among the most distinguished of the Rajpoot tribes. At the period of the first Mahomedan incursions into Hindustan, they ruled over Kanouj, which was then a flourishing kingdom, surpassing in power and influence all other states in the country. It is impossible to define the exact limits of the Kanoujiya kingdom at that time; but there is reason to believe that it embraced a considerable portion of the tract now called the North Western Provinces. The present house of Joudhpûr boasts its descent from the Râthor monarchs. Many of the subordinate chiefs of the Raja of Joudhpûr's territory are of the same race.

The Râthor dynasty of Marwâr was established by Sevajî, son of Jai Chand, whose descendants for many years maintained a high character for their bravery and heroism. 'The Mogul emperors were indebted for half their conquests to the Lâkh Talwâr Râhtoria, the hundred thousand swords of the Râthors.' Rai Sing of this tribe was a famous captain in the armies of Akbar. His father, Khalyân Mall, received Akbar with great respect at Ajmere, in the fifteenth year of his reign, and then entered his service (*a*).

The Râthors are divided into twenty-four principal clans, descendants, tradition affirms, of Kusha, a twin son of Râma. Some of these are as follows: Dhandal, Bhadail, Chakkit, Duhariya, Khokrâ, Baddrâ, Chaîjrâ, Râmdeo, Kabriya, Hattûndiya, Mâlâwat, Sundu, Kataicha, Maholi, Gogâdeo, Mahaicha, Jaisingh, Mursiya, and Jorâ (*b*). These branches are found, for the most part, in Rajpootana; and, if any reliance is to be placed in the statistics obtained by the Government, exist only in small numbers in the North-Western Provinces. Here they are said to be fewer than five thousand persons, three-fourths of whom are in the districts of Cawnpûr and Gorakhpûr. But this is, doubtless, an error. Tod says that a doubt hangs over the origin of this race, and that the Surajbansi bards deny them the honour which they claim, of being connected with the genuine Solar Race (*c*)

In the district of Farakhabad, the ancestor of the Râthors was one Karan Singh, who received from Shamsuddin Ghori a grant of land in Mohamadabâd, together with the title of Rao. Some three hundred years ago they occupied, in addition, the *pargannah* or barony of Imratpûr, and founded the villages of Râjapûr, Râthorî, and others (*d*).

(*a*) Aîn i Akbarî, Mr. Blochmann's Translation, Vol. I., p. 357.

(*b*) Tod's Rajasthan, p. 88.

(*c*) *Ibid.*

(*d*) Report of the Census of the North-Western Provinces, for 1865, Appendix B., p. 74.

In the southern part of the district of Shâhjahânpûr the Râthors occupy the village of Kajarî, which they acquired four hundred years ago by the marriage of one of the tribe with the daughter of Sahdal, a Rajpoot of Barah Kalan (*a*).

There are a few of the tribe in the Khandaulî division of the Agra district, whose family has resided there for the last hundred years. In the Karouli division of Mainpûrî they possess eighty-eight villages, some of them recently obtained. The head of the clan in Karoûlî is Chandhri Lakshman Singh (*b*). In the last Census Report of the Mainpûri district the Râthor Rajpoots are not even noticed; yet one would suppose, from their possessing so many villages, that, at least in the tract which they occupy, they must be somewhat numerous.

On the defeat of Raja Jai Chand of Kanouj by Mohamad Ghori his family seems to have sought refuge in the Barna territory, in the present district of Etah, which it subsequently left, and settled in Sonhar, in the same district, where it came in conflict with the Bhayar tribe, and defeated it. These Râthors divided the Sonhar country among themselves. The Raja of Râmpûr, of the barony of Azimnagar, and the Rao of Khemsaipûr, of the barony of Shamsabâd, are Râthors in the direct line from Jai Chand (*c*). There is no mention of the Râthors in the last Census Report of the Etah district. A small colony of them is located on the right bank of the Sot, in the Kot *pargannah* of the Budaon district.

A small community of this tribe is said to reside in the Benares district, but the insignificance of its numbers is sufficient reason for its influence not being felt. Only one family is to be found in the city of Benares.

The Râthors are of the Sândil *gotra* or order.

Members of this tribe inhabit the Gorakhpûr district; but, strange to say, they are regarded as much inferior to some other Rajpoot tribes, and are not permitted to intermarry with them (*d*).

Kachhwâhâ or Kashwâhâ.

Like the Râthors, but on better grounds, this tribe of Rajpoots is also said to be descended from Râma, King of Ajudhiya, through his twin son Kusha, from whose lineage the present Maharaja of Jaipûr professes to have sprung.

(*a*) Report of the Census of the North-Western Provinces, for 1865, Appendix B., p. 56.

(*b*) *Ibid*, p. 78.

(*c*) *Ibid*, p. 93.

(*d*) Buchanan's Eastern India, Vol. II., p. 458.

The tribe prevails in the country of Jaipûr, sometimes called Amber, and is very numerous in the capital city of that name. It is traditionally affirmed, that the ancient seat of the Kachhwâhâs, down to the period of Raja Nala, was Narwargarah, when the fort of Amber became their chief abode, and remained so for many centuries until the time of Raja Sawai Jai Singh, who built the city of Jaipûr (*a*). In taking possession of the Amber territory, they expelled therefrom the Mîna and Badgûjar tribes (*b*).

Respecting the primitive history of the Kachhwâhâs, Mr. Beames, on the authority of General Cunningham, states, "that their original seat was Kuntipûra or Kutwâ. One of their kings, Suraj Sen, is alleged to have founded the city of Gwalior, forty miles south-east of Kutwâr; and they became independent under Vajra Dâma, one of whose inscriptions is dated A. D. 977. They retained the sovereignty of Gwalior, together with that of Narwar, till 1129, when Tej-karan, 'the bridegroom prince,' as he is called, eighty-fourth in descent from Suraj Sen, left his capital of Gwalior, and went to Deora, to marry the king's daughter of that place, and was so charmed with her society that he never returned. His nephew, Parimâl, a Parihâra, supplanted him in Gwalior and Narwar. The Kachhwâhâs then migrated to Dundâr (or Jaipûr, as it was subsequently called,) where they established themselves a new principality" (*c*).

We learn from the Aîn i Akbarî, that Kachhwâhâ nobles were in high position in the Court of Akbar. Raja Bihârî Mall of this tribe, was the first Rajpoot, says Mr. Blochmann, that joined Akbar's Court. The emperor gave him the command of five thousand troops. Three sons of the Raja were in Akbar's service, namely, Bhagwân Dâs, Jagannâth, and Salhadî (*d*). Raja Bhagwân Dâs was also, like his father, commander of five thousand men, and Governor of Zabulistân. His daughter was married to prince Salîm, eldest son of the emperor; the offspring of which marriage was Prince Khusrau (*e*). Raja Mân Singh, a son of Raja Bhagwân Dâs, was one of the most illustrious men of the time. He was born at Amber, the ancient home of the family, and was one of Akbar's great generals and governors. At his death sixty of his fifteen hundred wives immolated themselves on the funeral pile (*f*). Rai Sâl Darbârî was another Kachhwâhâ in Akbar's service. He was in charge of the royal harem. During

(*a*) Census of the North-Western Provinces for 1865, Vol. I., Appendix B., p. 17.

(*b*) Elliot's Supplemental Glossary, Vol. I., p. 158.

(*c*) *Ibid*, p. 158, 59.

(*d*) Aîn i Akbarî, Mr. Blochmann's Translation, Vol. I., pp. 328, 329.

(*e*) *Ibid*, p. 333.

(*f*) *Ibid*, p. 339—341.

the reign of Jahângîr, Akbar's son, he was sent on an expedition to the Dakhin. Rai Singh entered early Akbar's service; for he was present in the battle of Khairabâd, in the fight at Sarnâl, and accompanied the emperor on his forced march to Patan and Ahmadabâd (*a*).

The tribe is divided into twelve clans, which are found scattered about in many parts of the country. In the district of Bulandshahr, Kachhwâhâ landholders exist in the Khurja division; and Kachhwâhâ cultivators inhabit the villages of Manikpûr and Khalilpûr Rath, in the Baran division. A few of the race have of late years entered the Agra district, and settled in Kheragarh. There are some also at Devapûra close to the city of Mainpûrî. These state that they came originally from beyond the Chambal, and that the reason of their quitting their native country was, the marriage of a Kachhwâhâ Rajpoot into the family of the Raja of Mainpûrî (*b*). Rhotâs on the Sone was also founded by them.

The tribe is represented, says Mr. A. O. Hume, in the district of Etawah. "The Kaurs of Baylah were once rather important landholders, and, with their numerous kinsmen, still hold Baylah itself, and a few other villages. They are Kachhwâhâs, of the same family, if we are to believe them, as the Raja of Râmpûra, in Jalaun; and they claim, of course, like the rest of their clan, to be descended from Kusha, one of the sons of Râma. The Kachhwâhâs appear to have emigrated at an early period from Gwalior, or its neighbourhood, to that tract of country now known as Kachhwaihî Ghar. Thence, in 1656 A. D., came one Ajab Singh, who took service with the then Raja of Rûrû, and later, through his master's influence, obtained possession of Baylah and other villages. Besides this family, there are a good number of this caste (all emigrants from Kachhwaihî Ghar) sprinkled here and there about the eastern *pargannahs* of this district; but none are landholders of any importance, and none seem to have resided here for more than two hundred years" (*c*). In this district there were, in 1865, according to the Census Returns, nearly six thousand members of this tribe of Rajpoots. The territory called by Mr. Hume Kachhwaihî Ghar (more properly Kachhwaihî Garh, from *garh*, a fort), lies between the Sindh and Pahauj rivers, and was ceded to the Indian Government in 1844 by Scindiah, in consideration of his receiving a British contingent (*d*).

(*a*) Aîn i Akbarî, Mr. Blochmann's Translation, Vol. I., pp. 419, 420.

(*b*) Census of the North-Western Provinces, for 1865, Vol. I., Appendix B., pp. 17, 68, 77.

(*c*) *Ibid*, Memorandum of Mr. A. O. Hume, p. 35.

(*d*) Elliot's Supplemental Glossary, Vol. I., p. 158.

The Kachhwâhâs claim to have once had possession of three hundred and sixty villages in the district of Muzaffarnagar. "This," says Sir H. Elliot, "may have been the case, for amongst those who went to aid the Chauhân Prince Bisal Deo, in his invasion of Gujerat, we find the Kachhwâhâs of Antarbed enumerated ; and as they are not found in any numbers elsewhere in the Doab, except in Etawah, those of Muzaffarnagar are perhaps indicated. But they must have been in much greater strength than they are now, whether we consider them as occupants of Muzaffarnagar or Etawah, to have been honoured with any notice in such a gathering of Rajpoots. The mention of the Kachhwâhâs of Antarbed, in the middle of the eleventh century, is interesting, as showing that those of Amber had not yet risen into notice ; and that those of Narwar, who are recorded by Chand as proceeding to the defence of Chittore in the beginning of the ninth century, must have been on the decline" (*a*). In the Census Report for 1865, the Kachhwâhâs of Muzaffarnagar are unnoticed.

This tribe is also found at Akbarpûr, Tamraura, and Sekandarpûr, in the district of Etah. In Jalaun it is represented by Raja Mân Singh, of Râmpûr, who is the proprietor of an estate free of revenue, valued at three thousand pounds a year. The Raja of Gopâlpûr, and the Raja of Sikrî, now in needy circumstances, are of the same tribe. Some of the finest soldiers in the old Sepoy army were Kachhwâhâ Rajpoots (*b*).

Colonies of Kachhwâhâs are met with more or less in Cawnpûr, Etawah, Azimgarh, Jaunpûr, and other places in these provinces.

(*a*) Elliot's Supplemental Glossary, Vol. I., p. 158.

(*b*) Census of the North-Western Provinces, for 1865, Vol. I., Appendix B., pp. 95, 96.

CHAPTER IV.

THE AGNIKULAS OR FIRE RACES.

1—THE PRAMARA TRIBE; THE DORE CLAN; 2—THE PARIHARA TRIBE; 3—THE CHALUKIYA OR SOLANKHI TRIBE—THE BAGHEL TRIBE—THE BHAL OR BHALA-SULTAN TRIBE.

THE AGNIKULAS OR FIRE RACES.

There are four tribes of Agnikulas, as follows:

I. Pramara, called also Ponwar and Pomar.
II. Parihârâ.
III. Châlukiya or Solankhi.
IV. Chauhân.

These will be described in order.

First Division of the Agnikulas or Fire Races.

Pramara, Ponwar, Puar or Pomar.

In ancient times the Pramaras were amongst the most powerful of the Rajpoot tribes. 'The world is the Pramar's,' remarks Colonel Tod, is an ancient saying, denoting their extensive sway. He also gives the names of some of the most important capitals of the kingdoms they either conquered or founded, such as, Maheshwar, Dhâr, Ujain, Chittore, Abu, and Chandravati. 'Though the Pramara family never equalled in wealth the famous Solanki princes of Anhalwâra, or shone with such lustre as the Chauhân, it attained a wider range and an earlier consolidation of dominion than either, and far excelled, in all, the Parihâra, the last and least of the Agnikulas, which it long held tributary.' The Pramaras took possession of Maheswar, the capital of the Haiya kings, in which apparently they first exercised regal authority. 'The era of Bhoj, the son of Munj,' says Colonel Tod, 'has been satisfactorily settled; and an inscription in the nail-headed character carries it back a step farther, and elicits an historical fact of infinite value, giving the date of the last prince of the Pramaras of Chittore, and the consequent accession of the Gahlots' (*a*).

'The nine gems' will always be associated in Hindu literature with the name of Bhoj Pramara. The first Chandragupta mentioned in Hindu annals, who was contemporary with Alexander the Great, was of the Mori branch of this tribe. The Moris were held to be of the Takshak or Serpent Race. The power and influence of the Pramara tribe are represented in the following analysis of its branches prepared by Colonel Tod:

Branches of the Pramara Tribe.

1. Mori—of which was Chandragupta, and the princes of Chittore prior to the Gahlots.
2. Soda—Sogdi of Alexander, the princes of Dhat in the Indian desert.
3. Sankla—Chiefs of Pugal; and in Marwâr.
4. Khair—Capital Khairâlu.
5. Umra and Sumra—Anciently in the desert, now Mahomedans.
6. Vihil or Bihil—Princes of Chandravati.
7. Maipawat—Present chief of Bijolli in Mewâr.
8. Bulhâr—Northern desert.
9. Kâbâ—Celebrated in Saurâshtra in ancient times: a few yet in Sirani.
10. Ummata—The princes of Ummatwârâ in Mâlwâ there established for twelve generations. Ummatwârâ is the largest tract left to the Pramaras. Since the war in 1817, being under the British interference, they cannot be called independent.
11. Rehâr,
12. Dhunda,
13. Soratiah,
14. Harair,

(11–14) Grasia petty chiefs in Mâlwâ.

Besides others unknown, as Chaonda, Khejar, Sagra, Barkota, Puni, Sâmpâl, Bhîba, Kâlpusar, Kalmoh, Kohila, Papâ, Kahoriya, Dhand, Deba, Barhar, Jîpra, Posra, Dhûnta, Rikamva, and Taika. Most of these are proselytes to Islamism, and several are beyond the Indus (*b*).

Sir John Malcolm affirms, that, in ancient times, this race was the most celebrated of all the Rajpoot tribes of Central India. But he adds, the Pramaras having intermarried into Mahratta Sudra families, have become degraded in rank, so 'that the poorest of the proud Rajpoot chiefs, whom they count among their dependants, would disdain to eat with them, or to give them a daughter in marriage' (*c*).

(*a*) Tod's Rajasthan, Vol. I., pp. 91—93.
(*b*) *Ibid*, pp. 91—93.
(*c*) Malcolm's Central India, Vol. II., p. 130.

This tribe of Rajpoots is found in considerable numbers in the districts of Agra and Cawnpûr; and many families inhabit other districts, such as Banda, Allahabad, Gorakhpûr, Jaunpûr, Azimgarh, Jhânsî, and some portions of Oudh. It is said that the original seat of the tribe was Ujain. Its appearance in the neighbourhood of Agra is thus accounted for. "Raja Bijîpâl of Baiâna wished to bring about an alliance between his daughter and the son of Tindpâl, of Ujain, and with this view sent an embassy with presents. Tindpâl, however, objecting to the proposed marriage, ordered the ambassador to return, but his son Lakansî meeting them on his own account, accepted the proposal, and in spite of Tindpâl's objections, brought back the party to Baiâna, and there the marriage took place. Villages were then assigned to the prince and princess for maintenance. These, however, proving insufficient, the daughter was sent back to her father, some little time after, to solicit a further grant. But all that Tindpâl gave his daughter, was a sword, which she was instructed to deliver to her husband. Lakansî, then, interpreting the gift, whether rightly or wrongly, to mean that he should extend his possessions with its aid, seized and added to his territory 1400 villages, giving them over to his followers. At various times they have migrated northwards, their first halting-place in this district being the *pargannah* of Kheragarh, where they are zemindars and cultivators. They have in course of time become dispossessed of a great many of their states, bartering them for less substantial wealth to Goojurs and Brahmins" (*a*).

The Ponwars are spread over the Jaunpûr district. They are said to have settled in the Jhânsî district, in Bundelkhand, some time after the conquest of the country by the Bundelas. In the Farakhabâd district they have been attached to the *pargannah* of Amritpûr for the last six hundred years, where their ancestor, Bhûprao, obtained lands from Raja Jai Singh Deo, ruler of Khor or Shamsabâd (*b*). There are a few in the Etah district, in the subdivision of Azimnagar.

There are two colonies of this tribe in the district of Unao in Oudh. One is in the Morawan *pargannah*, occupying thirty villages. It is said, "that their ancestor, Narhar Singh Ponwar, distinguished himself in the siege of Chittore, under Akbar Shah, and received a grant of this tract of land as a reward for his services. He founded the village of Narri-chak, which is called after his name. These Ponwars must have been a powerful clan once; but the

(*a*) Report of the Census of the North-Western Provinces, for 1865, Appendix B., pp. 67, 68.

(*b*) *Ibid*, p. 74.

great encroachment of the Baises, one hundred and fifty years ago, reduced them to complete insignificance, and deprived them of a large portion of their land."

Respecting the other colony of Ponwars, "there is," says the same writer, "still less to be said. They are an offshoot of the Ponwar Raj of Etonja (in the Lucknow district), and obtained a tract, about twelve villages, through the favour of Raja Newal Rai, Diwan of Newab Safdar Jang, Governor of Oudh, in 1740 A. D." (*a*). The Ponwars of Oudh have five great landholders who possess the privilege of a seat at the Governor General's Durbar.

Dr. Wilton Oldham has collected some important historical facts concerning a branch of this tribe in the Ghazipûr district. "The large *taluqa* of Shivapur Dîr, Pargannah Bulliah, belongs to a brotherhood of Ujain or Ponwar Rajpoots, of the Agnikula race; and there are some fraternities of the tribe in the Doâbî and Mahaich *pargannahs*. The Ujains of two villages, Dayaparsatha and Dharaon, in the latter *pargannah*, became Mussalmans during the empire of the Moguls. The head of the clan is the Raja of Dumraon. He traces back his pedigree eighty-six generations, from Raja Bikramadat, or Vikramajît, from whom the Sambat era of the Hindus is reckoned. Of these ancestors, sixty-nine were the rulers of Ujain in Mâlwâ; and the first settler in the Bhojpûr *pargannah* of Shahabâd was Raja Sameo Sah, from whom the present Raja, Maheshwar Bakhsh, is the seventeenth in descent.

"The Raja of Dumraon owns nearly the entire of Doâbî Pargannah, which, at the Permanent Settlement, belonged to Shahabâd; and as he and his ancestors have purchased many estates in other *pargannahs*, he is now the largest proprietor in the district. A Bhûînhar family of Pândê Brahmans, settled at Bairîah in Doâbî *pargannah*, have for generations past been the Tahseldars, or land-agents, of the Dumraon family. They are now themselves a very wealthy and powerful family; and became, by auction-purchase, owners of extensive estates in *pargannahs* Kharîd, Kopâchit, and Mahaich. The Dumraon estates are badly managed; the tenantry are always discontented; and the Raja never has a rupee to spare. The present Raja, Maheshwar Bakhsh, with a view of adopting the life of a religious recluse, made an attempt to resign in favour of his son, which the Government would not confirm. From want of energy of mind, and possibly of physical courage, he is sometimes called the Banya Raja, and has not much influence in the country. His kinsman Babu Kûnr Singh, a man of embarrassed means, but of great courage and energy, was always looked upon as

(*a*) Mr. Elliott's Chronicles of Oonao, pp. 55, 56.

the real chief of the Ujain tribe. As is well known, he became a conspicuous rebel, was shot while crossing the Ganges, and died in his house at Jagdispûr.

"The great Raja Siladitya, who, in the beginning of the seventh century, overthrew the Gupta dynasty, was Raja of Mâlwâ, and no doubt belonged to this clan. His name is not to be found in the Dumraon pedigree. This, however, is easily accounted for, owing to the common practice of styling the same person by more than one name. Thus King Asoka, in his columns, is called Priyadarsi, and most of the Gupta sovereigns had two names. *Pargannah* Bhojpûr, in Shahabâd, is said to take its name from Bhoj Raja, tenth in descent from Raja Bikramadat. It is inhabited by a numerous clan of Ujain Ponwars" (*a*).

The Ponwars are found in the Fathpûr district, in considerable numbers, but the Census Returns make no allusion to them. Those in the *pargannahs* of Ghazipûr Khâs, Mahammadpûr, and some other places, are said to be descended from Purba Rai Singh, who received a present of lands from Ghazî Khân, the Nazim of that day, after whom the *pargannah* of Ghazipûr has been named (*b*).

The Ponwar race was expelled from Ujain, it is supposed, by the emperor Shahab-ud-dîn Ghorî, together with their leader Raja Mitrsen, and became scattered in different directions. Some of them settled in what is now the Bulandshahr district, and their descendants are found in the *pargannahs* of Dibbaî and Jîwar. The Khidmatiyas, a low class of Rajpoots, are an offshoot of them. This tribe inhabits three villages in the Baran *pargannah* of the same district (*c*).

It is numerous in the district of Shâhjahânpûr, where it is designated Pomar, and holds from seventy to eighty villages in two *pargannahs*. The Ponwars of Gorakhpûr came originally from the west, and settled at Balwa, where they received a grant of several villages from the Raja of Majhaulî. Ponwars from Gwalior have resided for many years in association with the Bais Rajpoots, at Ghâtampûr, in the district of Cawnpûr. They are said to have come there originally in company with Hasua Deo, Raja of Hamîrpûr, in Bundelkhand. They were lately in possession of fifteen villages in the *pargannah*.

Members of this tribe are found in Benares, but they are few in number. They profess to have come from Dhûranagar. The Pramaras are of the Kasyap *gotra*.

(*a*) Dr. W. Oldham's Statistical Memoir of the Ghazipûr District, pp. 56, 57.

(*b*) Census of the North-Western Provinces, for 1865, Appendix B., p. 105.

(*c*) *Ibid*, p. 17.

Dore.

The Dore Rajpoots are said to be descendants of the Ponwars. One of the Rajas of Mainpûrî having offered his head to the Gadîs Dehi, was called Dhund after his death; and his successors were called Dores. At present, the Hindu representatives (for some have become Mahomedans) of the Dore clan are found at Deoganw, Bhainsakhar, and Bahampûr, in the Bulandshahr districts (*a*). In the Morâdabâd district also are more than two hundred families of this tribe.

SECOND DIVISION OF THE AGNIKULAS OR FIRE RACES.

Parihâra.

This is the least famous of the Agnikulas. Although not occupying the first position in ancient times, they were, nevertheless, a tribe of considerable power. Their capital was Mandawar, formerly the chief city of Marwâr, which was once subject to them, before its occupation by the Râthors. They are still a numerous tribe, and abound in many parts of these provinces. They are found in the south-eastern tract of the Agra district in association with the Bhadaurias; but their settlement there appears to be of recent date. In the Etawah district they inhabit the country to the south of the Kuârî and Chambal rivers, called the Taluqa Sandaus. This region is full of ravines, and therefore difficult of access. Consequently, the Parihârs, taking advantage of their position, "have ever been a peculiarly lawless and desperate community. Nay, they even ventured some fifty years ago to murder Lieutenant Maunsell, who was then on duty with Mr. Halhed in pursuit of thugs, of whom Sandos had long been one of the chief strongholds."

"The great ancestors of these Parihârs, says Mr. Hume, was Belan Deo. From him, in the seventh generation, descended Nahir Deo, one of whose fourteen sons, Puop Sing, founded this particular clan, who were then located in Biana, Zillah (district of) Amritpûr. Very early in the eleventh century, and consequent on (though why consequent, none can explain) the defeat of Anang Pâl by Mahmud of Ghaznî, Samit Rai, the then surviving head of the house, fled to Sandos, and colonized the country thereabouts, which his clan still continue to occupy. Besides their thirteen or fourteen villages in Sandos, a few villages in Bhartenan, Dalelnagar, &c., have from time to time been occupied, and are now inhabited by offshoots of the Sandos clan. In quite recent times two families of Parihârs, represented at the present moment by Lala Laik Singh, of

(*a*) Report of the Census of the North-Western Provinces, for 1865, Vol. I., Appendix B.; account of Castes of Etawah by Mr. A. O. Hume, p. 85.

Harchandpûr, and Raja Bijai Singh, of Malhajanî, have risen into importance in the Pheepûnd and Etawah pargannahs, by marriages into the Sengarh and Chauhân families respectively, to whom they owe alike their lands and titles" (*a*).

In the Jhânsî and Hamîrpûr districts, and contiguous Native States, this tribe occupies twenty-seven villages, the head man of the tribe living at Jignî, a pseudo-independent State on the right bank of the Dassan river. The Parihârs of the Jhânsî district are said to have sprung from Gobindeo and Sarangdeo, grandsons of Raja Jûjhar Singh, the traditional head of the family. They have been inhabitants of that tract of country for ages, even from before the Bundela conquest. They came, in all likelihood, from Marwâr, of which country they held possession to the beginning of the twelfth century (*b*). The Parihârs of Hamîrpûr were in that portion of the district anciently called Garhkattar, several generations subsequent to Sarang Deo. This chief had two wives. The descendants of the first inhabited the country west of the Dassan; and of the second, the places known as Jignî and Malehta. By degrees they spread over the district (*c*).

Dr. Buchanan regards the Parihârs of Gorakhpûr and Shahâbad as originally Bhars, yet he says the Bhars do not pretend to any relationship with the Parihârs, and the latter are held to be not only a pure, but a high Rajpoot tribe (*d*).

Mr. C. A. Elliott, formerly Assistant Commissioner in Oudh, and latterly Secretary to the Government of the North-West Provinces, in his admirable little work entitled 'Chronicles of Oonao,' has given a very interesting and exceedingly important account of the Rajpoot tribes settled in the district of Unao in the Province of Oudh. Respecting the Parihârs, he says, that they form one of the four Agnikulas, or Rajpoot tribes born out of fire. He prefaces his further remarks on this clan by a quotation from the works of Colonel Tod respecting the creation of these four tribes, observing that 'it is too grand and impressive to be omitted.' "When the Daityas (or evil demons) made a determined attack on the sacred mount Abu, the Munis (or devotees), who reside there, created four tribes for their defence. They kindled a sacred fire, and assembling round it, prayed for aid to Mahadeo. From the fire-fountain a figure issued forth; but he had not a warrior's mien. The Brahmans placed him as a guardian of the gate, and called him Prithi-dwâra (Earth's door), or Parihâra."

(*a*) Report of the Census of the North-Western Provinces, for 1865, Vol. I., Appendix B.; account of Castes of Etawah by Mr. A. O. Hume, p. 85.

(*b*) *Ibid*, p. 100.

(*c*) *Ibid*, p. 108.

(*d*) Buchanan's Eastern India, Vol. II., p. 463.

" A second issued forth, and being formed in the palm of the hand (challû), was called Chalûk. A third appeared, and was named Pramara. He had the blessing of the Rishis, and with the others went against the demons; but they did not prevail.

" Again, Vasishta, seated on the lotus, prepared incantations—again he called the gods to aid—and as he poured forth the libation, a figure arose, lofty in stature, of elevated front, hair like jet, eyes rolling, breast expanded, clad in armour, with his quiver filled, a bow in one hand, and a brand in another, four-handed, whence his name, Chauhân.

" Vasishta prayed that his hopes might be fulfilled. As the Chauhân was despatched against the demons, Susti-devi, on her lion, armed with the trident, descended and bestowed her blessings on the Chauhân, and promised to hear his prayer. He went against the demons ; their leaders, he slew. The rest fled, nor halted till they reached the depths of hell. The Brahmans were made happy; of his race was Prithi Raja (Prithora)."

Mr. Elliott proceeds to narrate various incidents concerning the Parihârs of Unao. " The Parihârs at the time of Shahâb-ud-dîn Ghorî (1194 A. D.) were in possession of Mandawar, the capital of Marwâr; and received with hospitality the fugitive Râthors, whom the Mahomedan invader had driven from Kanouj. Their hospitality was repaid with treachery; and the Parihârs, in their turn, were expelled from Marwâr by their guests, and never rose to any distinction again. The present Parihârs in the Oonao district inhabit the Pargannah of Sârosî, or, as it has recently become habitual to call it, Sekandarpur, and possess the mystic number of eighty-four villages, a tract of land which is called a Chaurâsi. Strictly speaking, they possess eighty-three; but it is possible that one village may have been washed away by the Ganges without any record of it remaining. According to their local traditions, they came from a place called Jignî, which is not to be found on the map, or Srinagar, that is Cashmere.

" This is a curious instance of the immense vitality of traditions. In a book called the Khoman Râsa, which was written in the ninth century, to commemorate the defence of Chittore by Khoman against the Mahomedans, a list is given of the tribes who came to assist in the defence, and among them we find the Parihâra from Cashmere (*a*). From that high hill country they were driven, we know not by what cause, to inhabit the sandy plains of Marwâr; expelled thence, they were broken into innumerable little principalities, which found no abiding place, and have undergone continual changes, till we meet

(*a*) Tod's Rajasthan, Vol. I., p. 248.

with a small portion of the clan, who settled comparatively a short time ago in a little corner of Oudh, and even here the name of the beautiful valley, from which they came ten centuries ago, is still common in the mouths of men.

"The story of the settling of the ancestors of the clan in Sarosî is thus told. About three hundred years ago, in the time of Humayun, king of Delhi, a Dikshit girl from Parenda was married to the son of the Parihâr Raja, who lived in Jignî, across the Jumna. The bridegroom came with a large escort of his friends and brotherhood to celebrate the marriage; and the party on their journey passed through Sarosî. As they sat down around a well (the locality of which is still shown, though the well has fallen in), they asked who were the lords of the fort which stood not far off. They were told, that the fort was held by Dhobis (washermen), and other Sudras, who owned the neighbouring country. The procession then went on to Parenda, and returning conducted the bride to her home. Just before the Holi festival, a party headed by Bhagay Singh returned, waited for the evening of that riotous feast, and then, when the guards of the fort were heavy with wine, and no danger was looked for, suddenly attacked and slaughtered them, and made themselves masters of the fort and the surrounding country.

"Bhagay Singh had four sons; and they divided the eighty-four villages he had conquered, at his death. Asîs and Salhu, the two eldest sons, took the largest portion of the estate, twenty villages falling to the former, and to the latter forty-two. The third son, Manik, was a devotee, and refused to be troubled with worldly affairs. All he asked for was, one village on the banks of the Ganges, where he might spend his life in worship, and wash away his sins, three times a day, in the holy stream. The youngest son, Balîdân, was quite a boy at the time of his father's death, and took what share his brothers chose to give him, and they do not seem to have treated him badly.

Genealogy of the Parihâr Taluqdâr.

Bhagay Singh.

Asîs. | Salhu. | Manik. | Balidân.

Asîs.
Sakat.
Mangal.
Dîpchand.
Zorâwar.
Jindh Sâh.
Hîra.

Risal. | Laik. | Kalandar. (Subadar Major). | Atbal. | Pancham.

Pancham.
Golâb Singh.

The four eldest sons died childless.

"The law of primogeniture did not exist among the family; and every son, as he grew up, and married, claimed his right to a separate share of his father's inheritance; and thus the ancestral estate constantly dwindled as fresh slices were cut off it, till at last the whole family were a set of impoverished gentlemen, who kept up none of the dignity which had belonged to the first conquerors, Bhagay Singh and his sons. For six generations they stagnated thus, no important event marking their history, till the time of Hîra Singh. The family property in his time had grown very small, and he had five sons to divide it amongst; and, to add to his misfortunes, he was accused of some crime, thrown into prison at Faizabad, and loaded with chains. With the chains on his leg he escaped, arrived safely at Jarosî, and lay in hiding there. His pride being thus broken, he resolved to send his third son, Kalandar Singh, to take service in the Company's army. He rose to be Subadar Major in the 49th Regiment of Native Infantry; and in this position, through his supposed influence with the Resident, became a very considerable man. He knew that, as long as he was at hand, no chakladar would venture to treat the Parihâr Zemindars with injustice, but on his death they would be again at the mercy of the local authorities. He therefore collected all the members of the brotherhood who were descended from Asîs and persuaded them to mass their divided holdings nominally into one large estate, of which his nephew Golâb Singh should be the representative Taluqdâr, so that while in reality each small shareholder retained sole possession of his own share, they should present the appearance of a powerful and united Taluqa, making Golâb Singh their nominal head. Thus the chakladars would be afraid to touch a man who seemed to hold so large an estate, though in reality he only enjoyed a small portion of it. The brotherhood consented to this, and from 1840 till annexation, the estate was held in the name of Golâb Singh alone, and they had no farther trouble from the oppressions of the chakladars.

"It must have been before this fusion of the divided holdings that an attack was made on the Jarosî fort by some Government troops, of which only a vague tradition still exists. The leader of the troops was Mustafa Beg, or, in the village dialect, Musakka Beg. He was killed in the assault, and his ghost is said still to haunt the tree under which he was standing at the time of his death. To this day no villager, Hindu or Mussulman, passes that tree without making a low salaam to Musakka Bir Baba" (*a*).

The Parihârs are divided into twelve separate families or clans. One of them is called Narauliya from Narwal, possibly that in the Gwalior territory. These are found in the Ghazipûr district, and their ancestors were Khegol and Mingal Deo, who were in the service of Raja Malûpa, a Cheru, whom they killed on his insulting them in a fit of intoxication. The Narauliyas are "inordinately proud, passionate, and extravagant. They have lost a considerable amount of their property; but still retain probably more than half of their original possessions." Their chief village is Bansdîh with a population of upwards of six thousand persons. They hold the considerable estates of Sukhpûra and Kharaunî (*b*).

In the Allahabad district the only colony of the Parihârs is found to the south of the Jumna. This branch, it is said, came originally from Mainpûrî. Until recently they were addicted to female infanticide. There is good reason to believe, however, that they have now abandoned the horrid custom, as the Census Returns show a proper proportion of births of the two sexes. It is necessary to add, that the clan has been carefully though unobtrusively watched for the last thirty years (*c*).

This tribe is also represented by a few families in the district of Benares. It is of the Kasyap *gotra* or order.

(*a*) The Chronicles of Oonao, by C. A. Elliott, Esq., B.C.S., pp. 56—60.

(*b*) Dr. Wilton Oldham's Statistical Memoirs of Ghazipur, p. 61.

(*c*) Report of the Census of the North-Western Provinces, for 1865, Vol. I., Appendix B., p. 129.

Third Division of the Agnikulas or Fire Races.

Chalukiya or Solankhi.

The historical celebrity of this tribe cannot be discussed in this place. Its numbers in these provinces are but few. Yet it is well represented by the Baghels, who have sprung from it. There is ground for believing that, before the Râthor monarchs commenced their rule in Kanouj, princes of this tribe were established at Sûra on the Ganges. Their celebrated chief, Siddh Rai Jai Singh, was, according to Tod, at the head of twenty-two principalities, 'from the Karnatic to the base of the Himalaya Mountains' (*a*). This tribe has sixteen branches, respecting which the same writer gives the following account (*b*).

Branches of the Solankhi Tribe.

1.	Bhagela.	...	Raja of Bhagelkhand (capital Bandugarh), Raos of Pitapûr, Theraud, and Adalaj, &c.
2.	Bîrpûra.	...	Rao of Lunawarra.
3.	Behila	...	Kaliyânpûr in Mewar, styled Rao, but serving the chief of Salumbra.
4.	Bhurta.	...	In Baru, Tekra, and Chahir, in Jessalmer. Famous robbers in the deserts, known as Malduts.
5.	Kalacha	...	(as above)
6.	Langaha	...	Moslims about Multan.
7.	Togru	...	Moslims in the Panjnad.
8.	Briku	...	Ditto Ditto.
9.	Surki	...	In Dekhan.
10.	Sirwarcah	...	Girnar in Saurashtra.
11.	Raoka	...	Thoda in Jaipûr.
12.	Ranikiya	...	Daisûri in Mewar.
13.	Kharura	...	Allote and Jâwara, in Mâlwâ.
14.	Tantia	...	Chandbhar Sâkanbari.
15.	Almecha	...	No land.
16.	Kalamor	...	Gujerât.

Solankhi Rajpoots are found in the district of Etah. Some say that they came thither from Gujerât; others affirm that they came from Tonk. A small community of the race reside in the district of Benares, in the direction of Sultânpûr; but none in the city itself.

Baghel.

This clan, in the opinion of Tod and Elliot, is a branch of the Solankhi tribe of Rajpoots, though Wilson affirms that it is a branch of the Sîsodiya

(*a*) Tod's Rajasthan, Vol. I., p. 98.
(*b*) *Ibid*, p. 100.

tribe. It is agreed that these Rajpoots came originally from Gujerât, where their ancestors ruled over the country, and where some of their descendants are still found. But their peculiar territory now is that to which they have applied their own name, Baghelkhand, or Rewah, lying on the line of railway to the south of the district of Allahabad. The Maharaja of Rewah is at the head of the Baghel clan, and is descended from Siddh Rai Jai Singh, ruler of Anhalwara Pattan from A. D. 1094 to 1195. "His Court," says Elliot, "was visited by the Nubian Geographer, Edrisi, who distinctly states that at the time of his visit the chief adhered to the tenets of Buddha."

The Raja of Barrah and the Chief of Kotah also claim their descent from the Baghels of Gujerât. Together with the Maharaja of Rewah they consider their common ancestor was Bagherdeo, a Gujerât chieftain, who, in Sambat 606, or upwards of thirteen hundred years ago, undertook a pilgrimage from Gujerât to the famous Hindu shrines in Northern India.

This pilgrimage, says Mr. G. Ricketts, in his Report on the castes of Allahabad, was, according to tradition, "abandoned by this famous chief, who seized on Kirwee, Banda, and the southern portions of this district, which formed the original possessions of one of his sons, from whom the Barhar Raja claims his descent. The name of Baghardeo, and the name of the clan 'Baghel,' have a common derivation in the legend, that this famous warrior chief was fed when a child on a tigress's milk. It is the notion of a savage to prefer this to the more natural food of an infant; but the whole clan take great pride in this quaint tradition. A Baghel may not marry but with a Baghel under penalty of excommunication. The most notorious gang of dacoits who for three generations has infested the south of this district are of this clan; and this claim of consanguinity with the Rewah Maharaja has ensured their constant protection in his territories: and certainly the savage nature of the prototype of their race has pervaded the acts of these noted robbers. Each of their feats has shown the extremes of craft, treachery, and the meanest cowardice. When armed, and in numbers, they have murdered the single and unarmed; they have beaten women, and killed children" (*a*).

Among the Baghels of Rewah is a community of Mahomedans who have apostatized from the Hindu religion. They are the posterity of a chief who was warmly attached to Akbar Shah. The emperor, it is said, in return for his fidelity, permitted the Baghel chief to take possession of as much land as he

(*a*) Elliot's Supplemental Glossary, Vol. I., p. 50.
Census of the North-Western Provinces, for 1865, Vol. I., Appendix B., p. 129.

could conquer from the aboriginal Bhars inhabiting the country across the Ganges. The Baghel, in token of his gratitude for the favour, embraced Islamism (*a*).

The Rewah Baghels were possessed of considerable power and influence in the time of Akbar, who "in his youth was for a long time a companion of Raja Râm Baghel; and whose mother was indebted to him for protection during the troubles of Humayun" (*b*).

Baghel Rajpoots are numerous in the districts of Mirzapûr, Allahabad, and Banda. They are also met with in Cawnpûr, Etawah, Hamîrpûr and Jaunpûr; in Chabrâmau, Tirûâ, and Thattia, of Farakhabâd,—the Raja of Thattia being a Baghel—in Bhaddi, an extensive *pargannah* belonging to the Maharaja of Benares; in Gorakhpûr; and also in Sohâgpûr.

The word 'Baghel' means tiger's cubs; but Colonel Tod derives the word from 'Bhâg Rao,' the assumed founder of the clan. 'There are many chieftainships,' he remarks, 'still in Gujerât of the Bhagel tribe. Of these Pitapûr and Tharaud are the most conspicuous' (*c*).

The few families of Bhagels in the Benares district are doubtless colonists from the Rewah territory. They are employed in trade, and in the service of native chiefs.

The Baghel tribe is said to be of the Kasyap and Bhâraddwâj *gotras*.

Bhâl or Bhâlâ-Sultân.

This tribe is said to have sprung from the Solankhi Rajpoots. The family, according to tradition, obtained the title of Bhâlâ-Sultân from Shahâb-ud-dîn Ghorî, who conferred it on Siwai Singh, its common ancestor, for distinguished services performed by him in the war with Prithi Raj. 'Bhâlâ' means a spear, and 'Sultân,' a sovereign or lord, so that the title bears the signification of 'spear-king.'

The Bhâl Rajpoots of Bulandshahr claim descent from Sidhrao Jai Singh of Parpatan, in Gujerât. They have been in possession of eighty-four villages in the Khurja *pargannah* of that district from time immemorial. The estate, however, is divided into two great branches, each consisting of forty-two villages. Some members of the tribe embraced the Mahomedan faith in the reign of

(*a*) Census of the North-Western Provinces, for 1865, Vol. I., Appendix B., p. 130.
(*b*) Elliot's Supplemental Glossary, Vol. I., p. 50.
(*c*) Tod's Rajasthan, Vol. I., p. 99.

Akbar; and their descendants, although recognized as Bhâlâs, have continued their adherence to that religion down to the present time (*a*).

The Bhâlâ-Sultâns are also found in Gorakhpûr. Sir H. Elliot conjectures that the Bhâlâs are connected with the Ballas, who are included in the Rajkula, and were lords of Bhâl in Saurâshtra. He says, moreover, that there is a distinction between the Bhâls and Bhâlâ-Sultâns, the former being of inferior rank to the latter (*b*). A small colony of the tribe has settled in the district of Allahabad.

(*a*) Report of the Census of the North-Western Provinces, Vol. I., Appendix B., pp. 18, 19.

(*b*) Supplemental Glossary, Vol. I., pp. 16, 17.

CHAPTER V.

THE CHAUHAN TRIBE. THE BHADAURIYA, BACHGOTI, BILKHARIYA, RAJWAR, RAJKUMAR, HARA, KHICHI, BARGYAN, AND NAIKUMBH TRIBES.

Fourth Division of the Agnikulas or Fire Races.

Chauhan.

This tribe has twenty-four branches, as follows: Chauhân, Hârâ, Khîchî, Sonigarra, Deora, Pabia, Sanchora, Golwâl, Bhadauriya, Narbhân, Mâlâni, Purbiya, Sura, Madraicha, Sankraicha, Bhuraicha, Balaicha, Passaira, Chachairah, Rosiah, Chanda, Nacumpa (Naikumbh), Bhawar, and Bankat (*a*). Sir H. Elliot adds to these the Thûn, Bachgotî, Râjkumâr, Bilkhariya, and Bandhalgotî clans (*b*). Wilson mentions other branches, such as, the Deoras of Sirohi, the Sonagaras of Jhalore, and the Pawaichas of Powagarh (*c*).

The Hârâs, says Colonel Tod, have well maintained the Chauhân reputation for valour. Six princely brothers shed their blood in one field in the support of the aged Shah Jahan against his rebellious son Aurungzebe; and of the six, but one survived his wounds. 'The Khîchîs of Gagraun and Ragugarh,' he observes, 'the Deoras of Sirdhi, the Sonagaras of Jhalore, the Chauhâns of Sûî Bah and Sanchore, and the Pawaichas of Pawagarh, have all immortalized themselves by the most heroic and devoted deeds. Most of the families yet exist, brave as in the days of Prithi Raj. Many of the chiefs of the Chauhân race abandoned their faith to preserve their lands: the Kaim-khani, the

(*a*) Tod's Rajasthan, Vol. I., p. 97.
(*b*) Elliot's Supplemental Glossary, Vol. I., p. 63.
(*c*) Wilson's Glossary, p. 434.

Sarwânis, the Lowânis, the Kararwânis, and the Baidwânas, chiefly residing in Shekavati, are the most conspicuous. No less than twelve petty princes thus deserted their faith. Ishwar Das, nephew of Prithi Raj, was the first who set this example' (*a*).

The Chauhân Raja, Visala Deva, of Ajmere, attacked Anang Pâl III., King of Delhi, of the Tomara dynasty, and conquered him, about the year 1152. The two families were united in marriage, the offspring of which was the celebrated Prithi Raj. The Chauhân rule in Ajmere was brought to an end by Mahomed Ghorî and Kutb-ud-dîn, in the years 1193—1195. Colonel Tod remarks, that 'the genealogical tree of the Chauhâns exhibits thirty-nine princes, from Anhal, the first created Chauhân, to Prithi Raj, the last of the Hindu emperors of India.' But the chain of succession is, he conceives, imperfect. The founder of Ajmere was Ajipal, a name greatly celebrated in Chauhân annals. Yet Sambhar, on the banks of the Salt Lake, of the same name, was probably, according to the same authority, anterior to Ajmere, and 'yielded an epithet to the princes of this race, who were styled Sambri Rao. These continued to be the most important places of Chauhân power, until the translation of Prithi Raj to the imperial throne of Delhi threw a parting halo of splendour over the last of its independent Kings' (*b*).

The Chauhâns are found in many districts of the North-Western Provinces; but they are most numerous in Bijnour and Etawah, especially in the former, where they are divided into three classes, Choudhrî Chauhân, Padhan Chauhân, and Khagî Chauhân. The last is least in degree, and among them the re-marriage of widows is permitted. The only distinction between the first and second of these classes is, that the Choudhri Chauhâns will marry the daughters of the Padhan Chauhâns, but will not give their own to them. It is said that all these Chauhâns of Bijnour are merely so in name, but not in reality, and that they are promiscuous assemblages of several clans of Rajpoots (*c*).

The Chauhâns of Etawah appear to have entered that district about the year 1266 A. D., under Sumarsa, their Raja, and his two brothers, the founders of the Rajaships of Rajor and Mainpûrî. These were the sons of Raja Uram

(*a*) Tod's Rajasthan, Vol. I., pp. 96, 97.

(*b*) *Ibid*, pp. 95, 96.

(*c*) Census Report of the North-Western Provinces, for 1865; Memorandum of Kunr Luchman Singh, Appendix B., p. 34.

Rao, grandsons of Hamîr Shah, who was killed at the taking of Ratanpûr by Altamsh, in the year 1230, and descendants of the celebrated Prithi Raj. They came from Nîmrânâ, and took possession of the whole of the western division of the district. Mr. A. O. Hume, formerly Magistrate of Etawah, from whose report the above information has been obtained, remarks, that "Pertabnere, the present head-quarters of the Chauhâns of Etawah, was founded by Pertab Shâh, in the eighth generation from Somer Sah; and in the twelfth, Rajah Modh Singh abandoned the Etawah Fort as a residence. It continued for long to be the head-quarters of the representatives of the Government, till finally destroyed under the orders of the Nawab Soojah-ood-dowla, in consequence of the protest of the Etawah towns-people that so long as the Aumils occupied such an impregnable residence, they would never do anything but oppress the people. This is an undoubted fact, and is curiously typical of the spirit of the times. From this stem (of Rajah Sumarsa) the Rajahs of Pertabnere and Chuckkernugger, the Rana of Sikroree, the Rows of Jasohan and Kishnî, and other princely houses, sprang; and though they probably no longer hold more than a fifth at most of the eleven hundred and twenty-two villages over which Sumarsa once exercised regal authority, the Chauhâns are still the dominant race of the west, as the Senghurs are of the east of the Etawah district" (*a*). The Chauhân Rajpoots have been a ruling class in that part of Etawah for fully six hundred years. It is singular that in the Chail division of the Allahabad district is a clan of Chauhân Mahomedans, a race of Chauhân Rajpoots converted to Islamism.

The most influential branches of the Chauhân tribe in the North-Western Provinces are "those of the Central Doab, in Khandauli of Agra; in Lakhnau, Jânib Râst, Deolî Jakhan, and the Hazûr Tahsîl of Etawah; in Akbarpûr of Cawnpûr; and in Mûstafabâd, Gihror, Sonj, Etah, Kishnî Nabîganj, and Bhûngânw, in the district of Mainpûrî. Of these the most conspicuous are the families of Rajor, Pratâbnîr, Chakarnagar, and Manchana, the head of which latter is usually known as the Raja of Mainpûrî. These four families, as well as their relatives, do not allow other Chauhâns to associate with them on terms of equality, being descended from the illustrious Prithi Raj, and therefore connected with the regal stem of Nîmrânâ" (*b*). The title of Raja is attached to the heads of these four great houses. The title of Rana is given to the Sakraulî family of Etawah; and of Rao, to each of the families of Jasohan and Kishnî.

(*a*) Census Report of the North-Western Provinces, for 1865, Mr. A. O. Hume's Memorandum on the prevailing Castes of Etawah, Appendix B., p. 83.

(*b*) Elliot's Supplemental Glossary, Vol. I., p. 64.

The Bhadauria Chauhâns also have a Raja, a Dewan (possessed by the family of Parna in Bah Panahat), a Rai (held by the family of Chitauli in Atair), and six Raos, held by six different families (*a*).

A descendant of Prithi Raj was Lâh Rao of Mandâwar, whose territory is called Râth. The Chauhâns of this family are styled Alanot. A brother of Lâh was Laure, Raja of Nîmrânâ, whose descendant always receives his investiture of the Rajaship from the Rao of Mandâwar, who shows his superiority over the Raja by applying the *tilak*, or mark, on the forehead between the eyes, not with the finger, as is customary, but with the great toe (*b*). The Chauhâns of Benares are few in number, and without note. Although the tribe can boast of so many chiefs of distinction elsewhere, yet in Benares it is not represented by one. They are of the Vatsa *gotra*.

Chauhân Khand is a district between Sirgûja and Sohâgpûr in Central India, inhabited by a clan of Chauhân Rajpoots sprung from those in Mainpûrî. Their chief formerly was Chandarsen, who has given the name to Chandwâr. The Chauhâns of Upper Rohilkhand are generally regarded as of low rank, and are sometimes not reckoned among Rajpoots at all. The names of their clans are: Nihtor, Haldaur, Sherkot, Afzalgurh, Nâgînâ, Chandpûr, and Mandâwar (*c*).

At Sambhal, Bilârî, and Hassanpûr, in the Morâdabâd district, Chauhân Rajpoots have resided for ages. They settled in Thâkurdwâra and Kâshîpûr, in the same tract, five hundred years ago, having come from Chittore, Meerut, and Rohilkhand. The Chauhân population in these parts greatly increased in the reign of the emperor Bahlol Lodi (*d*) The present Chauhân Raja of Mainpûrî traces his pedigree through no fewer than ninety-three ancestors, beginning with one Raja Jag Dutt; of these Prithi Raj was the seventieth (*e*) In the district of Etah, the Chauhâns are said to be descended from Raja Sangat, otherwise called Sakat Deo, a name of some repute, who sprang from Chabur Deo, brother of Prithi Raj. The towns of Etah, Marehra, and Bilrâm, and the villages of Tilokpûr, Prithipûr Kapâta, Bhadwâs, and Dhoulaiswar, were founded by these Rajpoots. The Raja of Etah is of this tribe; the town bearing his name dates from the fourteenth century (*f*). In the Census Statistics of 1865, no notice is taken of the Chauhâns of Etah.

(*a*) Elliot's Supplemental Glossary, Vol. I., p. 64.
(*b*) *Ibid*, p. 65.
(*c*) *Ibid*, p. 67.
(*d*) General Report of the Census of the North-Western Provinces, for 1865, App. B., pp. 39, 40.
(*e*) *Ibid*, Memorandum by Mr. Growse, B.C.S., pp. 75, 76.
(*f*) *Ibid*, Memorandum by Mr. Crosthwaite, p. 93.

From the inveterate tendency of nearly all the Chauhâns to trace their descent from the celebrated Prithi Raj, it is manifest that the traditions respecting most of their pedigrees are of little worth. The same may be said of the pedigrees of the Râthors, who profess to be descended from Jai Chand, the last monarch of the ancient kingdom of Kanouj. Some scores of Rajas and Rais in these provinces indulge the pleasant conceit that they are lineally descended from the one or the other. All such family traditions should be received with great caution.

In the district of Bulandshahr are several Chauhân families or clans, all professedly of the lineage of Prithi Râj. Some settled under their chief Rao Kalaka in the Agautha division, where they laid the foundations of a number of villages. Others were led by Tej Pâl, and inhabited first the village of Badlî, from which they removed to Khataolî, and at various times occupied as many as fourteen villages. Others, again, settled in Raipûr Katauri, whence they expelled the former Brahman proprietors. Their chief was Rao Kalû, who married into the Tomar family of Rajpoots. Rao Kalû, however, came to a bad end, for both himself and his son were hanged by the Chaklidâr of Karaurî Secundrabâd for their conduct to the unfortunate Brahmans. But the grandson of Kalû, Patrâj, avenged their death by the slaughter of the Chaklidâr, for which act he received a free pardon from the Emperor of Delhi, on condition of his embracing the Mahomedan faith. All the Brahman villages also were assigned to him. Several villages are still held by this clan, though many have passed away from them (*a*).

It is conjectured that the Chauhâns entered Oudh shortly after the Dikshit Rajpoots. "They colonized," says Mr. C. A. Elliott, "a tract of land, which lies south of Dikhthîânâ, with the Ponwars, Bachils, and Parihârs between it and the river Ganges. Chauhânâ is the name given to this tract, which is popularly said to consist of ninety villages" (*b*). Mr. C. A. Elliott states, that the great Rajpoot clans bearing the names of Bachgotî, Râjkumâr, Rajwâr, and Khânzâda, which exercise authority over a large portion of the Fyzabad and Sultânpûr districts, are really Chauhâns, whose ancestors quitted Mainpûrî about the same time. The chief ground for this statement is, that they all belong to the same *gotra*, or great family stock (*c*). This, however, is not true in Benares, for there the Chauhâns are of the Vatsa *gotra*, and the Râjkumârs of

(*a*) Census of the North-Western Provinces, for 1865, Vol. I., Appendix B., p. 18.

(*b*) Mr. C. A. Elliott's Chronicles of Oonao, p. 42.

(*c*) *Ibid*, p. 43.

the Kasyap. In the Bangarmau sub-division of the Unao district is another colony of Chauhâns, possessing twenty-seven villages. They have no family traditions; and, consequently, are not generally regarded as genuine Chauhâns, nor are permitted to sit on an equality with other members of the tribe (*a*).

Two Chauhân families of high lineage occupy lands to the North-West of the Mangalsi Pargannah of the Fyzabad district of Oudh, having come originally, they assert, from Bhûînganj or Bhûînagar, in the Mainpûrî district. "They marry their sons in the east," says Mr. P. Carnegy, "among the Bais of Kotsarâwan, the Bais of the Chaurâsî of Salehpûr Sarauja near Shahganj, and also the Gautams of Trans-Gogra. Their daughters they marry in the west to Ponwars, the Chamâr-Gaurs of Amethia, Surajbans, and Raikwârs. They consider themselves of much purer and higher family than the Chauhâns of the great Southern family of this district, of five hundred and sixty-five villages" (*b*).

The Chauhâns are powerful in the district of Cawnpûr. The pargannah of Akbarpûr Shâhpûr, in the year 1848, belonged almost exclusively to this tribe. They are said to have come thither upwards of three hundred years ago. They are a branch of the Mainpûrî family. The Chauhâns are also found in the Sarh Salîmpûr pargannah. In 1848 Raja Sanwal Sing was their representative (*c*).

They are also met with in the Fathpûr district, where they hold a few estates. The Chauhâns of Gorakhpûr are descended from Nâg Sen, son of a Rajah of Chittore.

Bhadauriya.

The Bhadauriya Chauhâns have six clans, namely, Athbhaiya, Kulhaiya, Mainu, Tasselî, Chandarsenia, and Râût, and are found in the districts of Shâhjahânpûr, Etawah, Cawnpûr, and Saugor in Central India. "They are in chief force," says Sir H. Elliot, "in Bâh Panâhat of Agra, and to the country to the South, which after them is called Bhadâwar. Some say their name is derived from Badara, between the Chambal and the Jumna; others, more correctly, from Bhadaura, in the neighbourhood of Atair" (*d*). He also states that "the

(*a*) Mr. C. A. Elliott's Chronicles of Oonao, p. 43.

(*b*) Mr. P. Carnegy's Historical Sketch of the Fyzabad District, Appendix by Mr. J. Woodburn Settlement Officer, pp. 4, 5.

(*c*) Report of the Cawnpûr District.

(*d*) Elliot's Supplementary Glossary, Vol. I., p. 25.

family of the Raja of Bhadâwar aspires to a high antiquity;" and that "we are led to infer from a passage in Tod's Rajasthan, that the Bhadauriyas were established on the Chambal by Monika Rai, Prince of Ajmere, or at least shortly after his reign. Now, as he flourished towards the close of the seventh century, the Bhadauriyas must have preceded the Chauhâns of the Doab, if reliance is to be placed on his statement" (*a*). The Raja of Panâhat, of the Bhadauriya branch of the Chauhân tribe, claims for his family great antiquity. He owns an estate of thirty villages.

The family was held in consideration under the later Mogul emperors. Mr. Hume says, that the Bhadauriyas "are allowed precedence by the Chauhâns of Manchhâna or Mainpûrî and Pertabnere; but in reality these Bhadauriyas were of no importance when the great Chauhân houses were founded hereabouts (Etawah), and only rose into notice when the Chauhâns of Etawah had been for nearly four hundred years the rulers of the whole country round about. It was during the time of Shâh Jahân and his successors, that the Bhadauriyas (always a troublesome and disreputable set) obtained a permanent hold, which they still retain, on much of the Chauhân territory. The Rao of Barpûra is a Bhadauriya, and the head of the clan in this district" (*b*). In the district of Benares many of the Rajpoots, on the right bank of the Ganges, are of this branch of Chauhâns. There are several thousands in Agra; and they form an important community in Cawnpûr.

Bachgoti.

The Bachgotî Chauhâns are said to have sprung from four brothers,—named Gûge, Gâge, Gautam, and Rânî. Some of the tribe are located in the country on the confines of Oudh and Jaunpûr, and on the borders of Gorakhpûr. The Raja of Kurwar, and the Diwan of Hasanpûr Bandhiva, in the south-east tract of Oudh, although a Mahomedan, are of this clan. The Diwan, strange to say, applies the *tilak* to the foreheads of the Hindu Rajas of Binaudha, on their investiture of the title of Raja. These Mahomedan Bachgotî Chauhâns are of considerable antiquity, and are referred to before the Mogul Period of Indian History. The Bilkhariyas, Rajwârs, and Râjkumârs are said to have sprung from the Bachgotî Chauhâns.

(*a*) Elliot's Supplementary Glossary, Vol. I., p. 25.

(*b*) Report of the Census of the North-Western Provinces, for 1865, Vol. I., Appendix B., Memorandum by Mr. A. O. Hume, p. 84.

This tribe is exceedingly numerous in Jaunpûr, where they number between twenty and thirty thousand persons. There are many also in the country about Benares. A few are to be found in Allahabad and Azimgarh.

The Bachgotîs of Oudh are second in rank of all the Rajpoot tribes, and have the privilege of sending no fewer than fifteen chiefs to the vice-regal Durbar. The tribe is of the Vatsa *gotra* or order.

Bilkhariya.

This tribe is said, both by Wilson and Sir H. Elliot, to be a branch of the Bachgotî Chauhâns, and to derive their name from Bilkhar in Oudh (*a*). Mr. P. Carnegy, however, states that they are an offshoot of the Dikshit tribe settled in the Partâbgarh district of Oudh; and that they took their name from Belkar-kot, a fort which they captured (*b*). The Dhuriapûr *pargannah* of the Gorakhpûr district, contains a considerable colony of Bilkhariya Rajpoots. In Oudh the tribe boasts of two chiefs of high position.

Rajwâr.

An insignificant tribe of Rajpoots. A few families are found in Benares, and about one hundred in Jaunpûr. There is also a colony in Oudh, which possesses some influence, and sends one *taluqdâr*, or large landholder, to the Governor-General's Durbar, whenever he holds his court in that Province.

Râjkumâr.

The term Râjkumâr is properly a compound word, meaning the son of a Raja; and is commonly so applied. It also designates a distinct Rajpoot tribe, of considerable wealth and influence, inhabiting various tracts in the North-Western Provinces, and engaged, for the most part, in the pursuit of agriculture. Families of the tribe are to be found in Benares and several neighbouring districts. It is numerous in Jaunpûr, where there are upwards of a thousand families. The members of this tribe in the district of Benares, Wilson remarks, were once "notorious for the murder of their infant daughters" (*c*). Whether they have improved of late years in this respect, is worthy of careful inquiry. The somewhat rigid surveillance, under which some of the Rajpoot tribes are now placed, must, I fain hope, have had the effect of diminishing this inhuman crime, formerly so prevalent in the Benares province.

(*a*) Elliot's Supplemental Glossary, Vol. I., p. 38.

(*b*) Mr. P. Carnegy's Races of Oudh, p. 39.

(*c*) Wilson's Glossary, p. 434.

The Râjkumârs of Benares are of the Kâsyap *gotra*. They are a very influential community in the Province of Oudh, where as many as eight *taluqdars* have a seat in the Governor-General's Durbar as representatives of the tribe.

Hârâ.

The Hârâ Rajpoots, although a branch of the great Chauhân family, have, nevertheless, a distinct tribal existence. The province of Hârâwatî is called after this clan; and two of its most important chiefs, the Rajas of Kota and Bundi, have principalities of the same name within its compass. This tribe has few representatives in the North-Western Provinces. A small community, however, is in Benares, some of whom are attached to the Bundi Raja, who has property in the city. There are also some families in Ratanpûr Bansî, in the district of Gorakhpûr.

Rai Surjan, of this clan, entered the service of the Emperor Akbar. He was first attached to the Rana, and was governor of Ratanbhûr, at which time he steadily opposed the emperor's troops. Eventually, he saw the uselessness of resistance, and made his submission to Akbar, by whom he was made governor of Gadha-Katangah, and afterwards of the fort of Chunar (*a*). A son of Rai Surjan, Rai Bhoj, served under Raja Mân Singh, in Akbar's army, against the Afghans of Orissa, and under Shaikh Abulfazl in the Dakhin (*b*).

A few families of the Hârâ Rajpoots possess small estates in the Gorakhpûr district, and are accounted as of the highest rank.

Khîchî.

A branch of the Chauhân Rajpoots. A few families only are scattered among the North-Western Provinces; some of which are found in Benares, and others in Allahabad and Cawnpûr. The Khîchîs of Raghugarh are important members of this tribe (*c*).

Bargyân.

The members of this tribe state that they are Chauhâns, and originally came from the Mainpûrî district. They affirm that they received the title of Bargyân on account of some great enterprise which their ancestors performed. Some are found in the Ghazipûr district. Upwards of fifty years ago, they

(*a*) Aîn-i-Akbarî, Mr. Blochmann's translation, Vol. I., p. 409.

(*b*) *Ibid*, p. 458.

(*c*) Wilson's Glossary, p. 434.

foolishly allowed themselves to fall into arrears in the payment of land revenue, on account of which most of their estates were sold off. Consequently, their present condition is one of poverty not unmingled with discontent. They formerly possessed fifty-two villages (*a*).

This tribe has also branches in the Azimgarh district, representing a small community of about a hundred families.

Naikumbh.

This tribe is sometimes reckoned among the thirty-six royal races as distinct from the Chauhâns; but there is reason to suppose that it really belongs to that great tribe. It is found in considerable numbers in the tract of country embracing the districts of Gorakhpûr, Azimgarh, Jaunpûr, and Ghazipûr. It belongs to the Vashisht *gotra* or order. There is a powerful clan in Hardui, at the head of which is Thâkur Bharat Singh.

Those in Gorakhpûr, remarks Dr. Oldham, have the title of Sirnet, which was given to them by one of the emperors of Delhi, from the following singular circumstance. "The Naikumbhs then, as now, only raised the hand to the head; and never bowed the head when making obeisance. The emperorannoy, ed by this apparent want of respect of some Naikumbh chiefs in attendance at his court, ordered that, before their entrance, a sword should be placed across the doorway, in such a manner that they, on entering his presence, should be compelled to stoop. Some of the Naikumbh chiefs maintaining their position were decapitated. The emperor, satisfied with this exhibition of their firmness and determination, permitted them in future to make their *salams* in their own fashion, and gave to them the title of Sirnet" (*b*). Mr. C. A. Elliott believes the Sirnets to have sprung from the Dikshit Rajpoots. See the section on the Sirnet tribe further on.

The Naikumbhs of the Bastî *pargannah* of Gorakhpûr are stated to have come originally from Srinagar, together with the Raja of Satâsî, and for a time to have served him and also the Raja of Bansî. Subsequently receiving grants of lands in the Bastî *pargannah*, they settled there. The Rajas of Bastî, Unwal, and Rudrapûr, in the Gorakhpûr district, all belong to this tribe.

In the Jaunpûr district, the *pargannah* of Mariâhû has the largest number of this clan. The entire district, at the last Census, contained upwards of twelve

(*a*) Dr. W. Oldham's Statistical Memoir of the Ghazipûr District, p. 65.

(*b*) See Dr. W. Oldham's Statistical Memoir of the Ghazipûr District. He gives two possible derivations of Sirnet, one from the Sanskrit *sar*, a head, and *net*, a leader; the other from the Persian *sir-nest*, headless.

thousand individuals. There is a small community of the tribe in Benares, consisting of traders and servants.

The Naikumbhs of Ghazipûr are in the Reotî Tuppeh or sub-division. They consider themselves to have sprung from Bekram Deo, brother of Raja Akhraj Deo, of Unwal of Gorakhpûr, who founded a colony of his own race there several hundred years ago, on occasion of his visiting the confluence of the sacred rivers, Ganges and Sarju, on pilgrimage. They strive earnestly to keep up their intercourse and associations with the original family. In order to cement the family bond a head-man of the Ghazipûr branch, Babu Raghunâth Singh, visited Unwal some sixty or seventy years ago, and there dug wells and planted groves. The Naikumbhs of this district hold a high position among Rajpoots. In the mutiny they rebelled, and gave some trouble; but were afterwards pardoned. They are a fine, handsome race. The late Raja of Haldî married a Naikumbh lady. A small number of the clan became Mussalmans during the Mahomedan rule (*a*).

This tribe has settlements in Oudh, and sends one *talukdar*, or native chief, to the Governor-General's Durbar.

(*a*) See the Report of the Census of the North-Western Provinces, Vol. I., Appendix B., pp. 110, 115; and Dr. W. Oldham's Statistical Memoir of the Ghazipûr District, pp. 59, 60.

CHAPTER VI.

THE GAUR, AMETHIYA, KATHARIYA, GAHARWAR, BUNDELA, KINWAR, BIJHONIYA, BIJHERIYA, AGASTWAR, AND GAIN TRIBES.

Gaur.

LIKE the Gaur Brahmans, the Gaur Rajpoots are found in large numbers in some parts of the North-Western Provinces. Yet there does not appear to have been any original blood-relation between the two races. Nevertheless, it is not improbable that they inhabited the same country simultaneously; and hence received the same appellation. What this country was, is a problem hard to solve; but most likely it was the tract around Delhi. Other tribes have sub-divisions or clans bearing the name of Gaur. It is given to the twelfth clan of the Kayasths; it is one of the seven clans of the Dirzîs; and it is borne also by the Taga Brahmans.

The Gaur Rajpoots are, in these Provinces, divided into three classes, known as Bhat-Gaur, Bâhman-Gaur, and Chamâr-Gaur, names originating, it is supposed, from the intercourse of this tribe of Rajpoots with the Bhats, the Brahmans, and the Chamârs. Colonel Tod enumerates five branches, which are very different from these,—namely, Untâhir, Silhâlâ, Tûr, Dûsena, and Budânu; and says, that repeated mention is made of the Gaurs in the wars of Prithi Râj, as leaders of renown. He states also that they were most probably possessors of Ajmere prior to its occupation by the Chauhâns (*a*). "The Chamâr-Gaur," says Sir H. Elliot, "who are sub-divided into Rajas and Rais, rank the highest, which is accounted for in this way. When troubles fell upon the Gaur family, one of their ladies, far advanced in pregnancy, took refuge in a Chamâr's house, and was so grateful to him for his protection, that she promised to call her child by his name. The Bhats and Brahmans, to whom the others fled, do not appear to have had similar forbearance; and hence, strange as it may appear, the sub-divisions called after their name rank below the Chamâr-Gaur.

(*a*) Tod's Rajasthan, Vol., I., p. 116.

The Chamâr-Gaur themselves say, their name is properly Chaunhar-Gaur, from a Raja who was called Chaunhar. Sometimes they say their real name is Chiman Gaur; and that they are called after a Muni, whose name was Chiman. The fact is, they are ashamed of their name, as it presumes a connexion with Chamârs, which they are anxious to disclaim" (*a*).

The tribe is very numerous in the districts of Agra and Cawnpûr. They seem to have occupied the Etawah territory from a remote epoch. Their own traditions state, says Mr. A. O. Hume, "that they migrated from Sopar, in the West, as early as 650 A. D., and took up their head-quarters at Parsû, reclaiming much of the surrounding country from the everlasting Meos whom everybody was always conquering, without, it must be confessed, their appearing much the worse for it. In about 1000 A. D., the Gaur Thakurs were, they assert, in great force in that tract of country now known as the Phapûnd, Akbarpûr, Oraiyah, Bidhûna, Rasûlabâd, and Dera Mangalpûr Pargannahs, having their head-quarters at Mahhousî, and founding fifty-two or *bâwan garhis*, or forts, amongst which Phapûnd, Umrî, Burhadânâ, and many others lately granted to the Kayasth Chaudhris, are enumerated." These Gaur Rajpoots affirm, that, at the beginning of the twelfth century, they were utterly ruined by Ala and Udal, Rajahs of Mahoba, especially by the agency of Udal, who was an archer of consummate skill. They never regained their importance in Etawah, although their influence in other places greatly augmented. The tribe still holds Sahail, Karchalla, Jaura, and other villages, situated in the districts of Etawah and Cawnpûr (*b*).

There are a few Gaur Rajpoots in the district of Etah. Bâhman-Gaurs are landholders of the village of Barhola; and Chamâr-Gaurs, of the village of Barona. Sanorî is another village occupied by the tribe (*c*). The Gaurs in the Jhânsî district affirm that their ancestors came from Indûrkhî, in Scindiah's country, some three hundred years ago.

A colony of Gaurs has been established at Zîrakpûr and Mela, in Oudh, from about the time of the emperor Baber. They possess still nearly all the thirty-six villages originally founded by the family. They are Bâhman-Gaurs of the Modal *gotra*.

A second colony of Bâhman-Gaurs occupies twenty-eight villages in the Harha *pargannah* of Unao. Their tradition is, that the country they now

(*a*) Elliot's Supplemental Glossary, Vol. I., p. 105.

(*b*) Report of the Census of the North-Western Provinces of India, for 1865, Appendix B., Vol. I., pp. 83, 84.

(*c*) *Ibid*, p. 94.

possess was formerly inhabited by a race of cowherds, who lived by pasturage. Having in some way offended the Government, a force was sent against them by the emperor Akbar under the command of Garapdes Gaur. This commander extirpated the cowherds, and obtained a grant of their lands, on which he forthwith settled ; and they have been in the hands of his family ever since (*a*).

Sir H. Elliot states, "that the strongest clan of Gaur is in the Central Doab. They say that they came from Narnâl, from which place Nar in Rasûlabâd, the residence of a Gaur Raja, derives its name. The Rajas of Saket, Kishtawar, Mandî and Keonthal, in the Himalayas, between Simla and Kashmîr, are all Gaur Rajpoots. He of Saket is a Chamâr-Gaur. They all state that their families came originally from Bengal" (*b*).

The Gaur Rajpoots hold a number of villages in the district of Shâhjahânpûr. In addition to some in the north of the district, they also possess about fifty near Powayan, Seraman, and Khotar. Their tradition is, that they entered the district about nine hundred years ago under the leadership of Khag Kai and Bagh Rai, two chiefs who originally came from Oudh, and took possession of sixty-two villages, of which their descendants still hold fifty. The Raja of Powayan is the head of the Gaurs in that part of the country.

The Amethia Rajpoots of Oudh are said to be a branch of the Chamâr-Gaurs. In this province the Gaur occupies a position of considerable influence, and sends as many as six representative chiefs to the vice-regal Durbar.

The Gaurs are numerous in the Rasulabâd *pargannah* of the Cawnpûr district. They have been in that neighbourhood for several hundred years, and came originally under the leadership of Abas Deo. The Raja of Nar is the representative of the family by lineal descent. The landholders of Makraudpûr Kahnjarî are more wealthy and influential than the Raja (*c*). The Gaur Rajpoots in the Dera Mangalpûr *pargannah* are a branch of the Rasûlabâd family. In 1848 their principal men were Rana Umrao Chand of Mangalpûr, Rawat Tej Singh of Bhandemau, and Rawat Sundar Singh. The first is highest in rank, and receives offerings during the Dasahra festival from the men of his tribe in acknowledgment of his superiority. Not long before this, Rawat Sunder Singh's family possessed fifty-two villages; but it has been ruined by extravagance (*d*). The Gaurs were also at that time the principal landed proprietors of the *pargannah* Sikandrah Bilâspûr.

(*a*) Mr. C. A. Elliott's Chronicles of Oonao, p. 52.
(*b*) Sir H. Elliot's Supplemental Glossary, Vol. I., pp. 185, 186.
(*c*) Report of the District of Cawnpûr, p. 60.
(*d*) Report of the Cawnpûr District, p. 68.

This tribe is located in Sîtâpûr, Hardui, Unao, and Bahraich, of Oudh, and boasts of six chieftains. It is found also in considerable numbers on the borders of Rohilkhand. The head of them in the province of Oudh is taluqdâr of Kateswar in Sîtâpûr. He is a Bâhman-Gaur: his clansmen possess the large number of thirty-seven villages. Dâl Singh, a taluqdâr of Kagrâla, is the second in rank. He is a Chamâr-Gaur. His clansmen occupy ninety-six villages (*a*).

Amethiya.

The small clan of this name sprang from Amethi, in Oudh. They are a branch of the Chamâr-Gaurs. Wilson says that they spring from the Chauhân family (*b*). They have colonies in Binaudha, and in Salîmpûr Majhaulî, in the Gorakhpûr district ; and also in the district of Azimgarh.

Kathariya.

This clan is allied to the Gaur tribe, and the two tribes, it is said, are found generally dwelling together. This seems to be true of those inhabiting the provinces of Rohilkhand and its neighbourhood. Whether it is true of the tribes elsewhere, I am unable to say. Formerly, Rohilkhand was called Kather from its being inhabited by the Kathariya tribe, who, it appears, were not subdued until the time of the emperor Shâh Jahân. The province, however, had been previously frequently invaded by the Mahomedan armies, and many villages once belonging to the Kathariyas had been brought within the Sircar of Budaon as belonging to the district of Gola. Still, this tribe claims 'to have been independent of the emperor of Delhi for three generations after Akbar's fiscal divisions of Sircars and Pargannahs were framed.'

The head of this tribe is the Raja of Khotar. His family has possessed the estate of Khotar from a comparatively recent date, having received the grant of it originally from a Vizier of Oudh. The country inhabited by the Gaur and Kathariya Rajpoots in Rohilkhand is nearly contiguous to the *Pargannah* of Gola, as described in the district records of Akbar's reign ; 'but they spread themselves into parts of the modern divisions of Pilibhît and Lakîmpûr (in Bareilly and Oudh), which were not altogether included in Gola.' The Kathariyas state that formerly the eastern division of Rohilkhand was in the hands of the Bachal Rajpoots, who were defeated by an army from Delhi, and their lands given to the Kathariyas (*c*).

(*a*) Mr. P. Carnegy's Races of Oudh, p. 53.
(*b*) Wilson's Glossary, p. 22.
(*c*) Census of the North-Western Provinces for 1865, Vol. I., Appendix B., p. 57.

Gaharwâr or Gaharwâl.

This is included by Colonel Tod among the thirty-six royal tribes of Rajpoots. Its chief seat is in Mirzapûr, in which district there were in 1865 nearly twenty-seven thousand Gaharwârs, at the head of whom was the Raja of Bijaipûr, a large village some ten miles from the city of Mirzapûr. Formerly, the Gaharwâr Raja was styled Raja of Kantit, an extensive *pargannah* or barony including the city of Mirzapûr and the country beyond it, as far as the fort of Chunar twenty miles distant. In the middle of the last century, Balwant Singh, the powerful Raja of Benares, made war against the Kantit Raja, and expelled him from his territory, which his family had occupied for more than five centuries. Some time after the rebellion of Raja Cheit Singh of Benares, the son of the fugitive Raja was re-called by the Governor General of India, and re-placed in the home of his fathers. His estates, however, were not returned; but he was granted certain lands, yielding a comparatively small income, together with the old palace at Bijaipûr. This the family still enjoys. Had it not been for the British Government the family would have been utterly ruined.

The predecessors of the Gaharwârs in Kantit, and in vast tracts of country lying contiguous to it, were the Bhars, an indigenous race of great enterprise, who although not highly civilized were far removed from barbarism. They have left numerous evidences of their energy and skill, in earthworks, forts, dams, and the like. For some time, tradition states, they were able to cope with the Gaharwâr immigrants, but eventually they were entirely subdued by them. At the present time, large numbers of the Bhars are still found scattered all over this region; yet, for the most part, they are degraded and despised.

The Gaharwâr Rajpoots are said to be connected with the Râthors. They claim to have been once rulers over the ancient kingdom of Kanouj, and there is good reason to believe that the claim is a just one. Sir H. Elliot considers it probable that the Gaharwâr kings preceded the five Râthor monarchs of Kanouj, and "fled to their present seats on the occupancy of the country by the Râthors; or, it may be, that after living in subordination to, or becoming incorporated with, the Râthors, they were dispersed at the final conquest of Kanouj by Mahomed Ghorî." Those who inhabited Kantit were under the leadership of Gadan Deo, whom some have supposed to be Manik Chand, brother of Jai Chand, the Râthor king *(a)*. The Raja of Dyah is of this tribe, to whom, and also to the Raja of Bijaipûr, the Raja of Mânda is related. This

(a) Elliot's Supplemental Glossary, Vol. I., pp. 121, 123.

chief has extensive possessions in the Allahabad district. Formerly, his property lay likewise in the neighbouring districts of Mirzapûr, Jaunpûr, and Benares. He is a man of considerable influence, and is said to be descended in a direct line from Jai Chand, of Kanouj (*a*). The Gaharwârs of the *pargannah* of Khera Magror, in the Benares district, belonging to the Maharaja of Benares, have been converted to Mahomedanism. Gaharwârs are found at Singrâmpûr in the Farakhabad district, in some other parts of the Doâb, and in Bandelkhand, Ghazipûr, and Gorakhpûr ; and are rather numerous in the district of Cawnpûr.

This tribe occupies an important position in the Ghazipûr district. "The greater part of Pargannah Mahaich, south of the Ganges, belongs to a tribe of Gaharwâr Surajbans Rajpoots, who claim," says Dr. W. Oldham, "descent from Babu Kûnr Manik Chand Singh, a cadet of the family of the Raja of Kantit in the Mirzapûr district. He is stated to have been in the military employment of the emperors of Delhi, and to have taken the *pargannah* at a higher revenue than the Brahmans who had held it before him, and who, it appears probable, were the descendants of some of the Brahmans of the Gupta period. The villages held by the Gaharwârs are divided into *tarafs*, called by the names of Kûnr Singh's three sons, Sîdhan, Jamdarg, and Râdhâ Rai. Two or three centuries ago, ten of the descendants of Sîdhan Rai entered into a warlike confederation, and built eight forts, the ruins of which still remain at Dhanapûr, the chief village of the *pargannah*. They, by force of arms, extended on every side the limits of the *pargannah*, and their own property.

"During the government of the first Raja of Benares, Balwant Singh, Babu Mardan Singh, a Gaharwâr, was his deputy in the government of the *pargannah*. He is described as a man of great liberality, who, in a famine which occurred in A. D. 1763, when five seers (or ten pounds) of peas or *gram* (a kind of pea) sold for a rupee, daily fed hundreds of every caste with food cooked by Brahmans. The Gaharwârs of the *pargannah* have retained about half of the one hundred and eighty-four villages formerly owned by them; but the chief village of the clan, Dhanapûr, though still nominally their property, is irretrievably mortgaged. One small branch of the clan became Mahomedans during the empire of the Moguls.

"For several generations past all connection between the branch of the Gaharwârs in Mahaich and the parent clan of Kantit has ceased; and the

(*a*) Census of the North-Western Provinces for 1865, Vol. I., Appendix B., p 129.

members of the two branches will not eat together. There is also a small colony of Gaharwârs in the Pachotar Pargannah" (*a*).

This tribe is scarcely known in Rajpootana; and the Rajpoot clans there will not permit any marriage connexions with it. Col. Tod, in his Rajasthan, states that the Bundelas have sprung from the Gaharwârs in the following manner. The great ancestor of the latter, he says, "was Khortâj Deva, from whom Jessonda, the seventh in descent, in consequence of some grand sacrificial rites performed at Bindabasi, gave the title of Bundela to his issue. Bundela has now usurped the name of Gaharwâr, and become the appellation of the immense tract which its various branches inhabit in Bundelkhand, on the ruins of the Chandelas, whose chief cities, Kalinjar, Mohini, and Mohoba, they took possession of "(*b*).

It is sometimes asserted by natives of the country that the Gaharwârs are descended from ancient kings of Benares; yet no satisfactory authority is given for the assertion (*c*). At the present day very few of the race are to be found either in the city or district of Benares, although the tribe is confessedly numerous in the neighbouring district of Mirzapûr. The small number, however, residing in Benares, occupy a respectable position as landholders.

Raja Bhawânî Singh of Akbarpûr, in the district of Cawnpûr, was, in 1848, the chief of the Gaharwârs of the *pargannah* of Bilhaur Deohah, and the owner of eighty villages. Being of imbecile mind his wife managed his estates (*d*).

The Gaharwârs are of the Kâsyap *gotra* or order.

Bundela.

A race of Rajpoots inhabiting Bundelkhand, to which territory they have given their own name. They have sprung, it is said, from the union of a Gaharwâr of Kantit in Mirzapûr with a slave girl, or, as others affirm, with the daughter of a Khangar Raja. In any case, it is acknowledged that they are not genuine Rajpoots (*e*).

The wars between the great Rajpoot families of Delhi and Kanouj, and between the Mahomedans and the Hindû tribes of the north-western portion of India, six or seven hundred years ago, bore an abundant harvest of confusion and disorder, which ended in the destruction of a multitude of ancient tenures

(*a*) Dr. Wilton Oldham's Statistical Memoir of the Ghazipûr District, pp. 58, 9.

(*b*) Tod's Rajasthan, p. 116.

(*c*) See Buchanan's Eastern India, Vol. II., p. 459.

(*d*) Report of the District of Cawnpûr, p. 64.

(*e*) Elliot's Supplemental Glossary, Vol. I., p. 46.

over a large tract of country, and the establishment of new ones, many of which last to the present day. The Bundela tribe had its origin at this period and under these circumstances.

This tribe has a few colonies in several districts of the North-Western Provinces. They are found in Benares, Cawnpûr, and Agra, and probably in other places. There are several thousands in Banda, Jhânsi, and Lallatpûr. The latter district alone contained, at the last Census, nearly ten thousand Bundelas (*a*). Wilson remarks that there are few members of the tribe inhabiting the British portion of Bundelkhand, except in the *pargannah* of Panwârî (*b*).

The Bundelas are said to differ in many important respects from other Rajpoot tribes. For instance, they marry amongst themselves, while other Rajpoot tribes marry with one another. They have a peculiar way of shaving their heads. They work with their own hands in the field, in ploughing, sowing, and so forth, which Brahmans and Rajpoots generally are too proud to do. The Bundela is a sturdy, manly fellow, with abundance of native energy and force (*c*).

Kinwâr.

This is a small tribe sprung from a union of Gaharwâr and Bhûînhâr families with Dikshit Rajpoots. Hence it has two branches:

1. Kinwâr Rajpoots.
2. Kinwâr Bhûînhârs.

The Kinwâr Rajpoots are settled in the Sahatwâr or Mohatpâl sub-division of the Kharîd *pargannah*, in the Ghazipûr district. There is a considerable number also in the Baliah *pargannah* of the same district, where they possess two extensive estates called Châtâ and Sârî. These are descended from the Sahatwârs, who affirm respecting themselves, that they received their lands from the Ujain Raja of Bhojpûr, by the marriage of Kulkul Sah, their ancestor, and the founder of their clan, with his daughter. There are upwards of eight thousand inhabitants in the town of Sahatwâr, a place of great trade. The tribe once held three other important positions in the neighbourhood; but they were subdued by the Sahatwârs, who seized their lands, and reduced them to the condition of labourers.

(*a*) Report of the Census of the North-Western Provinces for 1865, Vol. II., p. 9.
(*b*) Wilson's Glossary of Indian Terms, p. 94.
(*c*) Report of the Census of the North-Western Provinces for 1865, Vol. I., Appendix B., p. 106.

The Kinwâr Bhûînhârs are ignorant of their early family association with the Kinwâr Rajpoots. They, however, assign the same place as their primitive home as that given by the latter, namely Karnât Padampûr, that is, Padampûr in the Carnatic, which they imagine to be near Delhi, instead of in Southern India (*a*).

The Kinwârs, like many other Rajpoot tribes, while of high rank in one district, are of comparatively inferior rank in others. For instance, in the district of Bhâgalpûr, the Kinwârs are numerous, and are held in high estimation; but in Gorakhpûr, where there are between six and seven thousand members of the tribe, they are held in little consideration.

Bijhoniya.

A tribe found in the district of Jaunpûr, where it numbers a few hundred families. It does not seem to have branches in other districts.

Bijheriya.

A small community of Rajpoots inhabiting the Gorakhpûr district, and claiming to be a distinct tribe.

Agastwâr.

An inconsiderable colony of Rajpoots found at Mauhgahnî and Havelî, in the Benares district.

Gain.

These Rajpoots are found in small numbers both in Benares and in Kopâchit of Ghazipûr (*b*). The tribe is of the Kasyap *gotra*.

(*a*) See Dr. W. Oldham's Statistical Memoir of the Ghazipûr District, Part I., pp. 60, 61.

(*b*) Elliot's Supplemental Glossary, Vol. I., p. 89.

CHAPTER VII.

THE CHANDELA, SENGARH, SAKARWAR, KAUSIK, DANGAST, KACHHAURA, BARHAIYA, AND HORIYA OR HORAIYA TRIBES.

Chandela.

THIS tribe of Rajpoots is found in many parts of the North Western Provinces. Its original seat is Bundelkhand, where the city of Mahoba was the capital of its territory, which seems to have extended to the Narbuddha, and was called Chandelî. It does not occupy a high position among Rajpoots, as is manifest from its not intermarrying with the superior races. "In the lower Doab," says Wilson, "they are divided into four tribes, bearing the several Hindu designations of a ruler or king, as, Raja, Rao, Râna, and Râwat." "The chiefs of the Sheorâjpur Chandels are known as the Rajah of Sheorâjpûr, the Rao of Sânpai, the Râna of Sakrej, and the Râwat of Râwathpûr. The chiefs of Nâlagarh, Kahlûr, and Bilâspûr, are Chandels, and the first-named acknowledge a connection with the Raja of Kumaon" (*a*).

The Chandelas of Azimgarh number seven thousand, and came, it is asserted, from Khaparha in Jaunpûr. They settled in the *pargannah* of Nathupûr, where they acquired much land. A *char*, or embankment, formed on the bed of streams by a stoppage or diversion of their course, was thrown up between the Kutabî lake and the river Ghogra. "Of this *char*," says Mr. Thomason, "the Chandels took possession. Their prosperity kept pace with the increase of the *char;* and the Chandels of the Deobârî are now one of the most flourishing clans" (*b*). The Chandelas of Gorakhpûr are not permitted to marry the daughters of the principal tribes of the district.

There are many of this race in the Mirzapûr district. Those living in the south are said to have been excommunicated from their tribe on account of their intermarriage with the aborigines of that neighbourhood, and consequently are

(*a*) Elliot's Supplemental Glossary, Vol. I., p. 72.

(*b*) Mr. Thomason's Report of the Ceded Portion of the Azimgarh District, p. 18.

in effect a separate caste. This people appear to have held possession of Bundelkhand for several hundred years; but their power and influence have, to a great extent, died away. In the Jhânsî district they do not retain a single village.

Mahoba, their ancient capital, was evidently the great centre whence they emigrated in various directions. Those that entered Mirzapûr fled from Prithi Raj when he defeated Brimaditya, the son of their leader Parimal. They expelled the Bâland race; and were themselves subdued and driven away by Raja Balwant Singh of Benares about the middle of the last century. The Chandel Rajas of Agorî, Barhar, and Bijaigarh, would have been completely exterminated had it not been for the generosity of the Indian Government, who, on gaining possession of the country, restored them to their former homes (*a*). In the *pargannahs* of Agorî, Barhar, Bijaigarh, and Singrauli, the Chandel Rajpoots still possess a great portion of the villages. A list of the former Rajas of Agorî will be found at the end of this section.

The Rajpoot races have ever delighted in warfare, which circumstance has mainly contributed to their diffusion throughout the country. When their own principalities fell into the hands of their enemies, or a sharp reverse occurred even perhaps of less magnitude than this, instead of remaining in their old towns and villages, numbers started in various directions under leaders or chiefs for regions more or less distant, where they might be their own masters again, and live in comparative security. Here they either formed new clans, or new branches of the old tribe. The absorption of their lands by their enemies would be ill-brooked by a proud and courageous people. And, moreover, in those earlier days, extensive tracts of country seem to have been entirely in the hands of aboriginal tribes, like the Bhars, Kols, Gonds, and the like, whose lands must have appeared very tempting to a warlike people dispossessed of their own estates.

The Chandels entered the province of Oudh as emigrants from the south, at a distant period of Indian history. They first settled at Surajpûr in the Cawnpûr district; and subsequently some of the clan crossed over the Ganges and dwelt in the *pargánnah* of Bangarmau, where their descendants still occupy twelve villages. Even up to the time of the Mutiny, the Raja of Surajpûr was a man of great importance, both for the antiquity of his family and the extent of his possessions. It is not improbable that the cause of the original emigration

(*a*) Elliot's Supplemental Glossary, Vol. I., pp. 72, 3.

of the tribe from the south was the terrible conflict waged between the Chandel and the Chauhân Rajpoots, in which the former were defeated (*a*). The tribe in Oudh sends two chiefs to the Governor General's Durbar.

This tribe is numerous in the district of Shâhjahânpûr, where it has possession of no fewer than one hundred and ninety-seven villages. It is most powerful to the south of the district, and years ago the Chandelas of that tract gave much trouble to the Government, by whom they were called Kandhar Thâkurs, from the name of their chief village. The large estates of the clan are in the hands of nearly three hundred proprietors, the head of whom is Raja Dalel Singh (*b*).

The large village of Sakhrej, in the Cawnpûr district, is divided into four portions, two being occupied by Brahmans, and two, called severally Dhakan and Hîraman, from two chiefs, by Chandel Rajpoots. These two tribes have been located there for many generations (*c*). The Chandels prevail throughout the entire *pargannah*. Râna Siva Râj Singh and Râna Kadam Singh were formerly the recognized leaders of the clan. In the Sivarâjpûr *pargannah* the Raja of that name was the head of the Chandels. His family was a branch of the Kanouj Chandels. In the Bithûr *pargannah*, not long since, they held as many as sixty-five villages. Their principal men were Raja Durga Parshâd, of Bahâdurnagar, Raja Kûber Singh, of Pankî Gangâ Gangî, Raja Pahalwân Singh, of Sapaî, and Râût Ghansiam Singh, of Rawalpûr, who were all related to the Sivarâjpûr family.

The Chandels of Fathpûr came originally from Mâlwâ. They afterwards emigrated to Kalingar in Bundelkhand, and thence moved on to Mahoba. The Raja of Seorâjpûr is the head of the clan in the district of Fathpûr.

The descendants of the family of the Chandels which settled in Agorî, in the southern part of the Mirzapûr district, and, in the commencement of the thirteenth century, subdued the Baland Raja, of the aboriginal Kharwâr tribe, taking possession of his fort and territory, have preserved a brief record of their race from those early times nearly to the present day. It is prefaced by a list of Rajas of Mahoba prior to the migration of the Chandels to Agorî.

(*a*) Mr. C. A. Elliott's Chronicles of Oonao, p. 23.

(*b*) Census of the North-Western Provinces for 1865, Vol. I., Appendix B., p. 56.

(*c*) Report of the Cawnpûr District, p. 69.

Lords of Mahoba Nagar before the Defeat of the Chandels by Prithi Raj.

Raja Suraj Brahm.
„ Nal Ghokh.
„ Kol Brahm.
„ Par Mal Brahm.
„ Kâl Brahm.
Raja Ranjît Brahm.
„ Puran Brahm.
„ Chitur Brahm.
„ Barang Deo.
„ Harang Deo.

Chandel Rajas of Agori.

1. Raja Bharî Mal.
Came from Mahânagar, and settled in Agorî, killing the ancient Baland Raja ruling over the aboriginal Kharwârs, and dispersing his family.
2. „ Nârâyan Deo.
3. „ Hari Singh Deo.
Was attacked by the descendants of the old Baland Raja, and put to death, together with all the members of his family except one of his Ranees, who, escaping, gave birth to a son, Oran Deo (*a*).
4. „ Oran Deo.
Was married to the daughter of the Gaharwâr Raja of Kantit, by whose assistance he recovered the fort of Agorî and the possessions attached to it.
5. „ Dûlah Deo.
6. „ Darak Deo.
7. „ Râj Mal Deo.
8. „ Râj Dhar Deo.
9. „ Daryau Deo.
10. „ Dându Kai.

Had three sons :—
1. Prithi Râj.
2. Darp Nârâyan.
3. Chatur Bhoj Rai.

Prithi Râj became Raja of Bijaigarh ; Darp Nârâyan remained in Agorî ; Chatur Bhoj Rai received the Talluqa or estate of Iman Darâwal consisting of forty-two villages.

11. Raja Darp Nârâyan. Had two sons, Madan Singh, and Babu Mâdhu Singh.
12. „ Madan Singh. Had four sons.
13. „ Sûjan Sâhî. Had two sons.
14. „ Lâl Sâhî. Had two sons.
15. „ Ikshal Sâhî. Had two sons.
16. „ Fath Bahâdur. Had two sons.
17. „ Sankar Sâhu. Had two sons.
18. „ Sambhû Sâh. Was expelled from Agorî Barhar, by Balwant Singh, Raja of Benares. Had one son.

(*a*) See a full account of these events in the description of the aboriginal tribe of Kharwârs.

19. Raja Lâl Sheodit Nârâyan. Had three sons.

20. Adil Sâh. Was restored to the Rajaship of Agorî Barhar in 1781, from which Sambhû Sâh had been expelled. He died childless in 1794, and was succeeded by his nephew.

21. „ Ran Bahâdur Sâh. Was invested with the *tilak* of Raja during the life-time of Adil Sâh. Had two sons.

22. „ Makaradhwaj Sâh. Died a few months after his father.

23. „ Raghunâth Sâh. Waived his claim in favour of his son.

The Chandelas of Benares are few in number, yet possess wealth and influence. They are mostly landholders. They profess to belong to the Chandrayan or Chandrasen *gotra* or order.

Sengarh.

This tribe of Rajpoots is much less known, and is much less famous, than some of those already described. Nevertheless, it has points of interest attached to it of a special character. The origin of these Rajpoots is said to be as follows. "Claiming, like the Gautam Rajpoots," remarks Mr. A. O. Hume, "to be descended from Singhî or Siringhî Rish, and a daughter of the then monarch of Kanouj, they pretend that their own immediate ancestor, Purandeo (or Surandeo, as some have it), son of Padam Rish, and grandson of the horned sage Singhî Rish, having received the *tilak* from Raja Dalîp of Antar, migrated southwards, and established an important kingdom in the Deccan, or, as most will have it, Ceylon This constant allusion to a monarchy of Rajpoots in Ceylon, which haunts us at every turn of the irold traditions, may embalm some long-forgotten reality ; but nothing as yet discovered warrants our treating it as any thing but a pure myth. For seventy-two generations the Sengarhs ruled in the far south, whence, moving to Dhara (Dhar ?), for fifty-one more generations their sovereignty remained intact. Thence they appear to have been forced to migrate to Bandhu; whence, again, six generations later, they moved to Kanar, a place near Jaggamanpûr. Here it was that, in the one hundred and thirty-seventh generation from Singhî Rish—or Sukdeo, as he is indifferently called—the founder of the modern fortunes of the Sengarh Raj first saw the light. I entertain no doubt that he is a real historical personage. He married Deokulah, the daughter of Jai Chand, apparently the Râthor Raja of Kanouj, who, in 1194 A. D., was defeated somewhere in the Etawah district by Shahâb ud-dîn Ghorî, who, it is said, plundered Etawah itself about the same time."

Mr. Hume goes on to show in what way the fall of the great and ancient kingdom of Kanouj paved the way for the establishment of the principalities, of the Sengarh and Chauhân tribes of Rajpoots. "Bisakdeo took possession of the whole of the western parts of the present district. His descendants allege that he received it in dower, on his marriage with the daughter of the Kanouj Raja, on condition of exterminating the Meos, who were then ravaging the whole country. But this seems scarcely likely, since at the time of his marriage, the Kings of Delhi claimed sovereignty over this tract, and had made, about the time of the famous battle of Tirourî, a grant of a portion of it to one of their own employés" (*a*). It seems that after the downfal of the Delhi and Kanouj kingdoms, in 1193 and 1194 severally, the Mahomedan conqueror showed favour to the Sengarhs, and permitted them to retain possession of some portions of the present district of Etawah, which they had forcibly occupied. From that time to the present, the clan has held the lands acquired in those early times. One other family, descendants of the famous Chandan Singh, entered the district during the last century, when the country was governed by the Nawab of Oudh, and by force and fraud gained immense estates. "To this day," says Mr. Hume, the Sengarh river, along whose rugged banks they fought in old times so many bloody battles, remains a lasting monument of their former greatness and importance. Not many petty tribes have had the name of a considerable river changed in their honour ; yet such has been the case with the Sengarh, since the Sengarh, if tradition speaks truly, once bore the name of Besind" (*b*).

It is interesting and instructive to note the course taken by officers of Government in the settlement of the revenue of this part of the country. If six hundred years of uninterrupted possession of lands does not constitute a substantial legal claim to them, it is hard to see by what title any lands can be held at all. Hear what Mr. Hume, the magistrate and collector of the district, says. "Amongst the Sengarhs," he remarks, the "only important family that has not held its present estates for many generations, is that which the sons and grandsons of the famous Chandan Singh now represent. Chandan Singh's father, Saddan Singh, a Biswahdâr of a single village, but prime favourite of the great Aumil Bhagmal (the representative here, shortly before the introduction of our rule, of the Oudh Government)—partly by force, partly by fraud, but mainly by the favour of his patron—acquired immense landed possessions, to

(*a*) Census of the North-Western Provinces for 1865, Vol. I., App. B., Memorandum by Mr. A. O. Hume, pp. 81, 2.

(*b*) *Ibid*, p. 82.

which he had no equitable claim. While numbers of those villages which the Sengarh princes had ruled for full six hundred years were *settled away from them*, with servants, retainers, farmers, family priests, and the like, several of Chandan Singh's ill-gotten *mehals*, which he had forfeited by failure to pay the Government demand and to which he seems not to have had the remotest right, were settled with his sons, in total disregard of the real owners." Well may Mr. Hume remark on a system characterized by such shortsightedness and injustice that "in Oudh it cost us many of our best and bravest, and all but lost us India" (*a*).

This tribe is also numerous in the districts of Cawnpûr and Azimgarh. In Jalaun likewise it holds many villages, which are to the north-east of the district near the Jumna, and is represented by the Raja of Jagmohanpûr. There are a few hundreds of this clan in the Jhânsî district. Those residing in the Ghazipûr district are distinguished for their determined resistance to Balwant Singh, Raja of Benares, in the last century (*b*). This chief had acquired immense authority and enormous estates stretching over some thousands of square miles of territory, from which he had ruthlessly expelled their former owners. He was, however, stoutly opposed by the Sengarhs of Ghazipûr. These belonged to the Laknesar barony, where they had been for a long period. The Raja, incensed at the spirit they displayed, conducted a large force into the heart of their fastness. But here he was greatly hampered by the ravines and the jungle. For two days they resisted his successive attacks. From their loop-holed forts and houses they dealt deadly destruction upon the Raja's retainers. The issue of this famous fight was gratifying to the brave clan, and has been a subject of exultation among their descendants down to the present time. The Raja was obliged to agree to a compromise, and permitted the Sengarhs to retain their estates on the payment of a small revenue. The fruit of their bravery is conspicuously seen now that the country is under British rule, for the amount of land revenue annually paid by the Sengarhs, settled in accordance with the original arrangement made by them with Raja Balwant Singh, is now only nine *annas*, or thirteen pence half-penny, per acre, the lowest sum paid in the whole of the Benares Province, excepting the sums paid by the hill-people in the Mirzapûr district.

(*a*) Census of the North-Western Provinces for 1865, Vol. I., App. B., Memorandum by Mr. A. O. Hume, p. 83.

(*b*) See Balwant-nâma or an Historical Account of Raja Balwant Singh.

Further information respecting these Sengarhs of Ghazipûr, is given by Dr. Wilton Oldham in his very valuable work on the Ghazipûr district, to which I have had occasion repeatedly to refer. "An important and interesting branch of the Sengarh tribe of Rajpoots occupy part of Zuhurâbâd, and the whole of the adjacent *pargannah* of Laknesar. The Sengarhs state that their ancestors, Harî and Bîr Thâkurs, came from Phuphûnd, of Zillah (district of) Etawah, and took service with the Bhar Raja of the northern part of the district. On one occasion, having been struck by the Raja, they and their adherents attacked and killed him, and took possession of the country. The descendants of Harî Thâkur occupied Laknesar *pargannah*. Those of Bîr Thâkur are settled partly in *pargannah* Zuhurâbâd, and partly in a portion of Sekandarpûr, in the Azimgarh district, which, prior to 1840 A. D., was included in the Kopâchit *pargannah* of this district. Fifteen generations are counted from the time of the first founders of the clan to the present day.

"The Sengarhs are all devoted to the worship of a deified member of the tribe named Amar Singh, who lived, I believe, about two hundred years ago. He is worshipped under the designation of Nâth Bâbâ; and several temples to his honour have been erected in Rasserah, the chief village of *pargannah* Laknesar.

"Before the establishment of the British authority, the Sengarhs, of Laknesar, had managed to establish for themselves an unrivalled reputation for courage, independence, and insubordination. This reputation they preserved unimpaired during the first years of our administration. When Mr. Duncan, resident of Benares, visited the *pargannah*, arrows were fired at his body-guard from the forts of the Sengarhs. This offence was pardoned by Mr. Duncan, whose forbearance and moderation were only surpassed by his abilities. Murders committed in a blood-feud were condoned. The entire *pargannah* was settled, as the undivided estate of the whole clan with their Chaudhris or headmen, on the same easy terms on which they had previously held it under the Raja of Benares and the Nawab Vizier of Oudh. The Sengarhs, nevertheless, failed to pay the Government revenue; and the Collector of Benares, in 1798, was obliged to proceed against them with military force. With some trouble he arrested the Chaudhris, reduced them to submission, induced them to agree to pay an enhanced revenue, and levelled their forts. On their failing to pay this enhanced revenue, the *pargannah* was sold by auction for balances to the Raja of Benares. The Raja in vain attempted to get possession; and, subsequently, the sale was cancelled by the order of Government, and the Sengarhs re-admitted to settlement on their former revenue. No detailed record of ownership has hitherto been prepared for this *pargannah;* but it is now in course of preparation. The properties of the different shareholders are intermixed in a most intricate manner. No decree of the Civil Court giving possession to any purchaser by auction or by private sale, has ever been executed, owing to the impossibility of identifying the property of any one of the proprietors. The Sengarhs have abandoned their old habits of contumacy and insubordination. They behaved well during the Mutiny ; and are now peaceful and loyal citizens. Their chief town, Basserah, contains a population of 5,689, and is a place of great trade (*a*)."

The Sengarhs of Oudh first entered the country in the time of the emperor Baber, when two Rajpoots of the clan, Jagat Sâh and Gopâl Singh, proceeded thither from Jagmohanpûr across the Jumna, in the service of Shaikh Bayazîd, who had been placed in charge of the province. These settled in Kantha, and were followed by another family which settled in Parsandan. The families remained peaceably for eleven generations, during which time they kept the Lodhs, who had been the original landholders, and whom they had apparently dispossessed, in subjection. But in the eleventh generation the Lodhs suddenly fell upon the Sengarhs of Kantha with such fury that they killed most of the men, but suffered the women and children to escape. This outrage, however, was soon avenged by the surviving Sengarhs with the aid of their clansmen, whom they brought with them from Jagmohanpûr, whither they had fled. They not only recovered the lands which had been lost, but also drove out a considerable body of Pathans, who, for some time, had been encroaching on their territory.

These Sengarhs now occupied two places, Kantha and Manora ; and the other family of Parsandan also broke up into two branches, one remaining in the original home, the other establishing itself at Kosarî. At the present day, the Sengarhs of Parsandan possess eight villages; those at Kosarî, eight; those at Manora, nine; and those at Kantha, eight. See a very interesting descriptive account of the Sengarhs of Oudh in Mr. Elliott's Chronicles of Oonao, from which this information has been derived.

This clan has also possessions in the Fathpûr district. They are said to have come from Bundelkhand. They are found in several *pargannahs.* A few also are met with in the Agra district. They have representatives likewise in Benares.

(*a*) Dr. W. Oldham's Statistical Memoir of the Ghazipûr District, pp. 57, 58.

The Sengarhs hold many villages in the north-eastern part of the Etah district, near the banks of the Jumna. The principal man amongst them is the Raja of Jagmohanpûr. They are a turbulent race, and gave trouble in the Mutiny. There are a few hundreds of them in Jhânsî, to which place they are said to have come from Jagmohanpûr, some three hundred years ago.

Sakarwâr.

There is some doubt whether this tribe is of Brahmanical or Rajpoot origin. Its numerous members in the Agra district profess to belong to the Solar Race of Rajpoots, and to have come, several hundred years ago, at different times, from Sakarwârî, a small district of Gwalior, on the right bank of the Chambal. They first settled in the Kheragarh *pargannah*, where they held possession of twelve villages (*a*). The name, says Colonel Tod, was derived from Fathpûr Sikri, which was once an independent principality. They are of the Sândil *gotra*, or order.

The Sakarwârs are powerful and very wealthy in the Zamânîah *pargannah* of the Ghazipûr district. They affirm that their ancestors emigrated from Fathpûr Sikri, in the Agra district. They are evidently therefore related to the Agra Sakarwârs, and yet, strange to say, claim to be descended not from Rajpoots, but from Misr Brahmans. This claim, however, cannot be allowed. They look up to the mythical Raja Gadh, as their common ancestor, who had, they say, four sons, Achal, Abchal, Sâran, and Rohî. Considerable confusion has sprung up among the descendants of these sons, for while some regard themselves as Sakarwâr Rajpoots, others speak of themselves as Sakarwâr Bhûînhârs. This will be manifest by examining the following genealogical chart.

Sakarwârs of Zamânîah Pargannah, Ghazipûr.

Raja Gadh.

Achal.	Abchal.		Sâran.	Rohî.
	Sainu.	Pûran Mal.		
His descendants are Sakarwâr Bhûînhârs, and inhabit Sohwal, Patkania, and other villages in the North-East of the Zamânîah Pargannah.	His descendants are Sakarwâr Rajpoots. They are powerful and numerous. They inhabit the large village of Gahmar and other villages.	His descendants are Sakarwâr Bhûînhârs, and are very numerous. Two of their villages are Sherpûr and Reotipûr, each having a population of about 10,000 persons.	His descendants are Sakarwâr Bhûînhârs—and are settled in Saringa and Rohanîû, in the Shahâbâd district.	His descendants are Sakarwâr Bhûînhârs—and are settled in Saringa and Rohanîû, in the Shahâbâd district.

The distinction here drawn between Rajpoots and Bhûînhârs, who are really of the same race, is strange and inexplicable. The truth is that the word Bhûînhâr

(*a*) Report of the Census of the North-Western Provinces for 1865, Part I., Appendix B., p. 67.

applies to Rajpoots as well as to Brahmans; yet why the same clan should make use of both terms, is by no means apparent.

Some ten generations ago, Marhar Rai, a descendant of Pûran Mal, became a Mahomedan. His family now occupies fourteen villages on the banks of the Karamnâsa, called Kamsar. The Sakarwâr Rajpoots are, for the most part, poor, while the Sakarwâr Bhûînhârs are generally in good circumstances (*a*.)

In the district of Unao, in Oudh, the Sakarwârs occupy nine or ten villages in the Asoha *pargannah*. They have lost their family traditions, and are weak and inconsiderable. Mr. C. A. Elliott thinks, however, there is reason to believe "that they are a portion of the same Sakarwârs who, immigrating into Oudh from the west, settled in the Fyzabad district, near Dostpur. These latter," he adds, "certainly are earlier colonists than the Bachgotî Râjkumâr Rajas, who have now nearly succeeded in reducing them to servitude, and whose immigration was contemporaneous with that of the Chauhâns of Chauhânâ. The latter probably colonized their present position in 1350 A. D., and belong to the first class of colonists; and, consequently, if the above line of reasoning be correct, the Sakarwârs, who are earlier than they, belong to the first class also" (*b*).

The Tuppeh of Harbanspûr, in the Azimgarh district, seems to have been long in the hands of the Sakarwârs, a remnant of whom still survive in Unchagâon. The Rajas laid waste their lands in order to strengthen their forts by encouraging the growth of jungle upon them, and the Sakarwârs were expelled (*c*). There is a small though flourishing colony of the tribe inhabiting certain parts of the Benares district. They are chiefly *zamindars* or landholders.

Kausik.

These are Rajpoots of the Lunar race, and are found in the Kopâchit *pargannah* of the Ghazipûr district. Like the Sakarwâr Rajpoots they claim to be descended from Raja Gadh, the mythical founder of the Gadhipûr district, which is supposed by some natives, though probably erroneously, to have been the original name of the Ghazipûr district. The Kausik traditions affirm that the two branches of the clan were founded as follows: that in Ghazipûr by two brothers, Del Chand and Sel Chand; and that in the Gorakhpûr district by the Raja of Gopâlpûr, whose descendant is still at the head of the Kausiks there.

(*a*) Dr. W. Oldham's Statistical Memoir of the Ghazipûr District, Part I., p. 64.

(*b*) Mr. C. A. Elliott's Chronicles of Oonao, p. 44.

(*c*) Mr. Thomason's Report of the Ceded Portions of the Azimgarh District, p. 17.

Although the Kausiks are worshippers of idols, yet their *gurus*, or spiritual guides, are not so, but belong to a monotheistic sect peculiar to Ghazipûr (*a*).

The Kausiks of Gorakhpûr inhabit the territory which their ancestors are said to have taken from the Bhars, the original occupiers and lords of that part of the country. This aboriginal race is elsewhere noticed in detail.

There are several thousands of this tribe in Hamîrpûr. There is likewise a small community in Benares, who are mostly engaged in trade of various kinds, or as higher class servants. The tribe is strong in various parts of Azimgarh; for example, in Deoganw, Mahul, and Gopâlpûr. According to the Aîn i Akbarî, they were formerly landed proprietors in the district of Jaunpûr (*b*).

Dangast.

A tribe of Rajpoots in the Ghazipûr district. They are found both in the Shâdîabad and Pachhotar *pargannahs* (*c*).

Kachhaura.

One of the numerous small tribes of Rajpoots found in the province of Benares. A few families are met with in the Gorakhpûr district.

Barhaiya.

A considerable community in the Azimgarh district, where it numbers about a thousand families, or nearly five thousand persons. It is found also in Sikandarpûr and Bhadaon, and also in Saidpûr-Bhitri, in the Ghazipûr district (*d*).

Horiya or Horaiya.

A few families of this small tribe of Rajpoots are found in the village of Sarsawân, of the district of Benares, and also in Mirzapûr. A much larger community is settled in the neigbouring district of Jaunpûr, especially about Mariâhû, amounting to between three and four thousand persons (*e*). They are said to be of the Sombansî or Lunar race of Rajpoots.

(*a*) See further information respecting this tribe in Dr. W. Oldham's Statistical Memoir of the Ghazipûr District, Part I., pp. 62, 63.

(*b*) Supplemental Glossary, Vol. I., p. 157.

(*c*) *Ibid*, p. 89.

(*d*) *Ibid*, p. 56.

(*e*) Report of the Census of the North-Western Provinces for 1865, Vol. II., p. 9.

CHAPTER VIII.

THE BAIS, CHANANIYA OR CHANAMIYAN, AND GARG OR GARGBANSI TRIBES.

Bais.

This is said to be the most numerous tribe of Rajpoots in the North-Western Provinces. Their common home is the district of Baiswâra in Oudh, a tract of country bounded on the west by Cawnpûr, on the east by the river Sai, on the south by the Chûâb stream, and on the north by Dikhtan. The tribe is considered by Tod and others, but erroneously, to belong to the thirty-six royal tribes of Rajpoots. It was the opinion of Tod, that the clan is a subdivision of the Surajbansi tribe. Dundia Khera in Baiswâra seems to have been, according to tradition, the spot where the tribe sprang from; yet they assert that their remote ancestors came from Mungi Paitun in the Dekhan. They regard themselves as of the same lineage as Sâlivâhana, the king of that place in A. D. 78, and the author of the Sâka era (*a*); but there is no proper foundation for this notion. The tribe can intermarry with the Chauhâns, Kachhwâhâs, and other distinguished Rajpoot races. The branch styled Tilak-Chandra, professes superiority to all the rest, and only gives its daughters in marriage to Rajpoots of high blood (*b*). There are four divisions or clans of these Tilak-Chandra Bais Rajpoots, namely, Rao, Raja, Naithâ, and Sainbasi, who look upon the Gautam Raja of Argal as the founder of their fortunes. The Bais Rajpoots have, if their own statements can be believed, three hundred and sixty separate clans (*c*).

In Bulandshahr, the ancestor of the Bais landholders of Karan obtained from the emperor of Delhi a grant of twelve villages, which they hold to the present day. In the district of Badaon this tribe has occupied the barony of Kot Salbhan for the last three hundred years. There are two principal families

(*a*) Elliot's Supplemental Glossary, Vol. I., pp. 13, 14.
(*b*) Wilson's Glossary, p. 48.
(*c*) Elliot's Glossary, Vol. I., p. 15.

which are descendants of the two sons of Dulîp Singh, their original chief, who is reputed to have come from Baiswâra, in Oudh. The head of one has the title of Rai, and of the other, of Chaudhri. In the district of Agra the tribe is found, for the most part, in the Khandauli division, where they have been for a hundred years or so. About four or five hundred years ago, some of the tribe, having left Singrâmpûr, took service under the Behar Taluqdars, or great landholders, of Saurik and Sakatpûr, in the district of Farakhabâd; but they were too strong for the Taluqdars, and wresting their lands from them, gave the name of Baispûr to their own village. In Etah they possess the villages of Nardauli and Sekandarpûr-Bais, in the division of Nidhpûr. They are people of considerable influence and importance in Fathpûr; and are described as having come from Harha, in Oudh. One of their number, Ghîsa Sâh, has the honour of having planted the villages of Dûndrâ, Banarsî, Hariâpûr and Bamrauli; and his brother, Daya Sâh, the village of Baijânî. But the tribe in those parts has become weakened of late years.

A detachment of these Rajpoots seems to have settled at Jhânsî, in Bundelkhand, at the close of the fifteenth century, or thereabouts. A class of Ban-Bais Rajpoots is found in the Allahabad district, who, having come in contact with the Bhar and Kol aborigines, dispossessed them of their lands, which they have retained for several hundred years. The prefix *ban* means jungle, and refers to the condition of the country when they acquired it (*a*).

The Bais Rajpoots are found in the *pargannah* of Bahariabâd in the Ghazipûr districts, and are descended from one Baghel Rai, who is supposed to have colonized a portion of jungle-land there some fifteen generations ago. They are proprietors of ten or twelve villages at the present day (*b*).

In regard to intermarriages with other clans, Sir. H. Elliot observes, that "the ordinary Bais of our Provinces give their daughters in marriage, amongst others, to Sengarhs, Bhadaurias, Chauhâns, Kachhwâhas, Gautams, Parihârs, Dikshits, and Gaharwârs; and receive daughters in marriage from Banâphars, Jinwars, Khîchars, Ragbansîs, Raikwârs, and the Karcholi Gahlots" (*c*).

This tribe is very powerful in the province of Oudh, where it takes the leadership of Rajpoots of every clan. Mr. C. A. Elliott, in his 'Chronicles of Oonao,'

(*a*) Report of the Census of the North-Western Provinces for 1865, Appendix B., pp. 16, 46, 69, 74, 94, 100, 103, 124.

(*b*) Dr. W. Oldham's Statistical Memoir of the Ghazipûr District, p. 65.

(*c*) Elliot's Supplemental Glossary, Vol. I., p. 14.

has paid special attention to the Bais annals, and from the minuteness and care displayed in his account, may be regarded as the chief authority respecting the tribe. His information has been gained by personal and extensive intercourse with leading men of the clan. I shall proceed to give an outline of his narrative.

While acknowledging that the Bais Rajpoots assert themselves to be descended from Sâlivâhana, conqueror of Vikramajît, of Ujain, Mr. Elliott gives his own opinion, that the tribe sprang from the union of a Chauhân and a Kumhâr. "About 1250 A. D., the Gautam Raja of Argal refused to pay tribute to the Lodi king of Delhi, and defeated the Governor of Oudh, who sent a force against him. Soon after this defeat the Ranee, without his knowledge, and with no fitting escort, went secretly to bathe in the Ganges at Buxar (*a*), on the festival of the new moon. The Governor of Oudh heard of it, and sent men to the *ghât* to capture her. Her escort was dispersed, and she was on the point of being made prisoner, when she lifted the covering of her litter, and cried, 'Is there here no Kshatriya who will rescue me from the barbarian, and save my honour?' Abhai Chand and Nirbhai Chand, two Bais Rajpoots from Mungî Pâtan, heard her and came to her rescue, beat off her assailants, and guarded her litter till she arrived safely in Argal. Nirbhai Chand died of his wounds; but Abhai Chand recovered; and the Raja, in gratitude for his gallant rescue, though he was of inferior caste, gave him his daughter in marriage, and with her as dowry all the lands on the north of the Ganges over which the Gautam bore rule. He also conferred on his son-in-law the title of Rao, which is still the highest dignity among the Baises" (*b*). Sir Henry Elliot adds, that "the Gautam Raja offered the bride all the villages of which she could pronounce the names without drawing breath. She accordingly commenced; and after reciting five lines of names, had proceeded as far as Panch-gânw, when the Raja's son, fearing that his possessions would be lost to him, seized hold of the bride's throat, and prevented further utterance" (*c*).

(*a*) "Buxar is close to Dundia Khera. Sir H. M. Elliot, in his article on the word Bais in the Supplemental Glossary, places the locale of this story at Allahabad. I have given here the tradition current in Baiswâra, which I think more probable (1), because Buxar is closer to Argal, and is the nearest *ghât* she could have gone to; (2) because Allahabad, being a much-frequented *ghât*, the Ranee would hardly have gone there without escort in any case; (3) because the town being the residence of the Governor of a Subah (or Province), she would have been running into the lion's mouth by going there." p. 66.

(*b*) "I state this after careful enquiry from the best Pandits and Bhats. The common belief is, that the Raja is the higher title; but this probably arises only from the fact that it is so with the neighbouring clans. The Bais Raja never had as large a territory as the Rao, a fact which in itself is conclusive." p. 66.

(*c*) Elliot's Supplemental Glossary, Vol. I., p. 117.

"Abhai Chand fixed his home in Dundia Khera; and the title and estate descended in an unbroken line through seven generations to Tilakchand, the great eponymous hero of the clans, who are called after him Tilakchandi Baises, in contradistinction to other branches of the same tribe. He lived about 1400 A. D., and extended the Bais domination over all the neighbouring country; and it is from his victories that the limits of Baiswâra became definitively fixed. The tract is universally said to include twenty-two *pargannahs* (or sub-divisions); and though there is considerable discrepancy in the various lists of those *pargannahs* which are furnished from different quarters, the following list is probably correct.

The Baiswâra Territory.

Districts (according to present distribution).	Pargannahs (or sub-divisions) of the district.
Rai Bareilly	Dundia Khera.
ditto	Unchgaon.
ditto	Kûmhî.
ditto	Bar.
ditto	Kehenjar.
ditto	Ghatampûr.
ditto	Serhupûr.
ditto	Makraid.
ditto	Dalmau.
ditto	Bareilly.
ditto	Behar.
ditto	Pâlhan.
ditto	Panhan.
ditto	Salhanpûr.
Oonao	Harha.
ditto	Purwa.
ditto	Morawan.
ditto	Sarwan.
ditto	Asoha.
ditto	Gorinda.
ditto	Parsandan.
Lucknow	Bijnour.

Tilakchand, in his capacity of premier Raja of Oudh, took upon him to ennoble persons of low caste at pleasure. His own palankeen-bearers (Kahârs) he raised to the position of Rajpoots. It is said also that he elevated a number of torch-bearers to the same rank. His creation of a Brahman from a Lodh is very curious. "Hunting one day, he was overpowered with thirst, and seeing a man drinking by a pond under a mango tree, went up to him, and without a word took his *lota* (brass drinking vessel) from his hands, and drank. His thirst appeased, the consequences of his act occurred to him (he was liable to be degraded from his own caste), and he asked, 'what caste are you?' 'Maharaj,' said the other, standing on one leg, 'I am a Lodh.' 'No,' said he, 'you mistake, you are an Am-târa Pâthakh, a Brahman of the mango and the pool' (*a*). The creation held good; and to this day the descendants of this Lodh rank as Brahmans, and perform the religious duties of the caste without giving offence to any of their purer brethren" (*b*).

Before he had sons of his own he adopted a Kayasth; but after the birth of Prithi Chand and Harhiar Deo, he separated him from his family, giving him estates of the value of ten thousand pounds near Rai Bareilly, which are still in the possession of the Kayasth's family (*c*). In the time of Deorai, grandson of Tilakchand, the head of the Bachgotî Rajpoot tribe in Oudh, who had possessed the right of confirming the title of Raja in every Rajpoot family in the province by applying the *tilak* or mark to the brow, abandoned Hinduism, and became a Mahomedan. On this the Rajpoots permitted Bhojrai, the second son of Deorai, to assume the title of Raja, and also the office of affixing the *tilak*. The Raos of Dûndia Khera have sprung from the eldest son, Bhairo Dâs; the Rajas of Morar Mou from the second son, Bhojrai; and the Chot-bhais, from the third, Kaliyân Mal. Harhiar Deo, brother of Prithi Chand, had two sons, who belonged to the villages of Sumbassî and Nuhesta in the *pargannah* of Behar. These two form separate branches of the Tilakchand stock, making with the other two, the descendants of Prithi Chand, four distinct branches.

Mr. Elliott has drawn out a very useful Genealogical Table of the Bais tribe, which will be found at the end of this section. Of the families descended from these four branches, only three, it seems, besides the Rao of Dûndia Khera, "possess estates in the Oonao district. They are the Sumbassî family of Pâhu, the Nuhesta house of Pachimgâon, and the Chot-bhaiya of Sandânâ. The Sandânâ family are much impoverished; and now possess only two villages

(*a*) From *âm*, mango, and *tâl*, a pool.

(*b*) Mr. Elliott's Chronicles of Oonao, p. 68.

(*c*) "The prefix 'Rai' in Rai Bareilly, is said to arise from this, as it is a very common suffix to a Kayasth's name."

where they once had sixty. The Pâhu Taluqa is also much fallen away from what it was when Mitrajît first founded it; but Bhûp Singh has still some twenty villages in his estate" (*a*).

"Mitrajît is a favorite hero with the bards, who tell many stories of his prowess, and of the amusement which his rustic plainness occasioned at the Delhi Court." Rao Mardan Sing, ninth in descent from Tilakchand, about 1700 A. D., regained the extensive estates, consisting of seven *pargannahs* or large baronies, which had been taken from Baiswâra in the life-time of Tilakchand. In addition, he seized from the Sumbassî branch the greater part of Pâthan and Behar. Mr. Elliott gives some account of the wild life and bravery of Chaitrai, an illegitimate son of Sadauli, whose memory still lives in the numerous ballads of the country. For further information respecting the Bais tribe in Oudh, see Mr. Elliott's Chronicles of Oonao, pp. 66—82.

Mr. P. Carnegy mentions that, in the Pachhimrath Pargannah, there are five distinct families of Bais Rajpoots, which entered the *pargannah* at different times. These are :—

1. The Bais of Malethû.
2. The Bais of Sohwal and Rûrû.
3. The Bais of Uchhâpali.
4. The Bais of Râmpûr Bhagun, Tikrî, &c.
5. The Bais of Gondor.

All these families settled in the *pargannah* at periods varying from two to four hundred years ago, and all encountered the Bhars, whom they subdued, and occupied their lands.

There are four other families, divided into eastern and western, of the Bais tribe, in the neighbouring *pargannah* of Mangalsi; and one in Haveli Oudh. It is a singular circumstance, that all these Bais families are despised as well as disowned by the Tilakchandî Bais Rajpoots. This is attributed by Mr. Carnegy to their low origin, for he conjectures that they have only been admitted within the last few centuries to a place among Rajpoot tribes (*b*).

The Bais Rajpoots have great influence in the Ghâtampûr *pargannah* of the Cawnpûr district. Their ancestor, Ghâtam Deo, it is said, drove out the

(*a*) Mr. Elliott's Chronicles of Oonao, p. 70.
(*b*) Mr. P. Carnegy's Historical Sketch of Fyzabad.

Ahîrs, and gave his name to the *pargannah* (*a*). They recently occupied sixteen villages. Those in the Sarh Salîmpûr *pargannah* of the same district, are of a different family; and came from Dundia Khera in Oudh. They hold no intercourse whatever with the Ghâtampûr branch.

This tribe possesses many villages in the district of Fathpûr. In the year 1848, it had, in one *pargannah* alone, as many as thirty-seven separate estates.

There are many tribes of Rajpoots inhabiting the city and district of Benares; but the most numerous of all, are of the race which forms the subject of this chapter. As a class they are not wealthy, and therefore do not occupy the commanding social position which some other tribes enjoy. They are of the Bhâraddwâj *gotra*.

(*a*) Report of the Cawnpûr District, p. 108.

GENEALOGICAL TABLE OF THE BAIS TRIBE.

- Abhai Chand (rescuer of the Gautam Ranee at Buxar).
  - Karaurai.
    - Jarûrai.
      - Purûrai.
        - Ghâtam Deo.
          - Jajhan Deo.
            - Rambhîr Deo.
              - Raitâs.
                - Asârâm.
                  - Jathuna.
                    - Tilakchand.
                      - Prithichand.
                        - Deorai.
                          - Rao Bhairo Dâs.
                            - Rao Târâchand.
                              - Rao Sangrâm.
                                - Rao Kanak.
                                  - Rao Prithi Râj.
                                    - Rao Pûrandar.
                                      - Rao Mardan Singh (Nazim of Baiswâra.)
                                        - Rao Raghunâth Singh. (Of Dûndia Khera.)
                                          - Rao Bhairî Tâl Singh.
                                            - Rao Hari Singh. (He died childless, but adopted Basant's son.)
                                              - Rao Râm-bakhsh Singh.
                                        - Udat Singh. (of Behar.)
                                          - Hindu Singh. (Who was driven out of Behar by the Sumbassîs.)
                                            - Basant Singh.
                                              - Rao Râm-bakhsh Singh.
                                        - Raja Achal Singh (Of Pûrwa; Nazim of Baiswâra.)
                                          - Ajît Singh.
                                            - Umar Singh.
                                              - Babu Debî-Bakhsh Singh. (Of Pûrwa.)
                          - Bhojrai. He received the title of Raja, and is ancestor of the present Maharaja Dirgbijai Singh, of Morarmou.
                          - Kalyânmal. His descendants are called Chotbhâis. Among these is the house of Sandána.
                      - Harhiar Deo.
                        - Khemkaran (Ancestor of the Sumbassî sub-division.)
                          - Sakat.
                            - Donmu Deo.
                              - Ajît Mal.
                                - Nihâl (Ancestor of Rana Beni Mâdhu Bakhsh (Rebel Leader.)
                                - Umrao (Ancestor of Rana Raghunath Singh, of Kajargâon) [Hon. Assistant Commissioner.]
                              - Mitrajît.
                                - Kaliyân Sâh.
                                  - Indrajît
                                    - Fath.
                                      - Jai Singh Rai.
                                        - Mardan.
                                          - Hindupat.
                                            - Achal.
                                              - Bhûp Singh (of Pâhu.)
                              - Pahâr (Ancestor of the Taluqdar of Kûria Satâwan.)
                            - Rûdsâh (Ancestor of the Taluqdar, of Simar-pahâr.)
                            - Kaliyân Mal. (Ancestor of the Taluqdar of Chandania.)
                        - Karan Rai. (Ancestor of the Nuhesta sub-division.)
                          - Gobind Rai. (Whose descendants are small Nuhesta landholders.)
                          - Râm Singh.
                            - Rûp Narain.
                              - Ban (Ancestor of Hind Pâl Singh, Taluqdar or landed proprietor of Pachimgâon.)
                              - Bal (Ancestor of Jaggarnâth, Taluqdar of Simri.)
                              - Bîrbhau.
                                - Bhairo Dâs.
                                  - Chatarpat (Ancestor of Sîtâ Bakhsh, Taluqdar of Gaura.)
                                  - Bakt (Ancestor of Mahâbal Singh of Behar.)
                                  - Shamsher (Ancestor of Jagmohan Singh, of Chandâpûr.)

Chananiya or Chanamiyan.

A tribe calling themselves Rajpoots in the Jaunpûr district, where they number upwards of a thousand families, or more than five thousand persons (*a*). They are also found in Azimgarh and Gorakhpûr. Wilson says, they are Chandrabansî Rajpoots. Sir H. Elliot states that they are commonly regarded as an inferior branch of the Bais tribe.

Garg or Gargbansî.

A tribe found scattered about in small numbers among several districts to the east of the Jumna. There are five hundred families in Azimgarh, and upwards of a hundred in Mirzapûr. There are also communities of Gargbansîs in the province of Oudh, and two *taluqdars*, or chiefs, represent the tribe at the Darbar of the Governor-General on occasion of his visiting the province. They are likewise met with in Gorakhpûr. These came from Ajudhiya in Oudh as *chaklidars* of Amorha, in which *pargannah* they eventually settled (*b*). They are also found in Ratanpûr, Bansî, and Rasûlpûr Gaur, in the same district.

The Gargbansîs are of the Kasyap *gotra*.

(*a*) Report of the Census of the North-Western Provinces for 1865, Vol. II., p. 12.
(*b*) *Ibid*, Vol. I., p. 109.

CHAPTER IX.

THE GAUTAM, DIKSHIT, PACHTORIYA, SIRNET, DURGBANSI, DHRIGUBANSI, RAGHUBANSI, SRI MAT SONWAN, BIURIHA, AND BHATHARIYA OR BATAURIYA TRIBES.

Gautam.

THIS tribe is met with in great numbers in the North-Western Provinces, especially in the districts of Mirzapûr, Fathpûr, Azimgarh, Cawnpûr, Gorakhpûr, Benares, and Jaunpûr, which are inhabited by many thousands. They are also found in several other districts, but not apparently so numerously. The Census of 1865 gives no account of any existing in Ghazipûr, yet Sir Henry Elliot says that they are there in large numbers; and his statement is corroborated by Dr. W. Oldham, in his Statistical Memoir of the Ghazipûr district.

It is traditionally stated that the tribe sprang from Siringî Rikh, who married the daughter of Raja Ajaipâl, of Kanouj; and that their principal seat, during a long period, was Argal, a village on the Rhind river, in the Kora *pargannah*, in the district of Fathpûr. They seem to have been a people of influence and power throughout that tract of country. Their descendants, however, have not been able to maintain the ancient prestige and distinction of the race. There is still a Gautam Raja, who preserves the memory of the noble deeds and glory of his ancestors. The fort of Kora was originally built by one of them, named Bijai Singh, who, in the time of the emperor Humáyun, abandoned Hinduism and became a Mahomedan. The Gautam Rajpoots now living in Kora, it is generally known, were converted to Islamism about that period. They now bear the title of 'Khân,' which is borne likewise by other families of this tribe attached to the Mahomedan faith in the *pargannahs* of Tuppehjar and Kûtiagûnar (*a*)

(*a*) Report of the Census of 1865, Vol. I., Appendix B., p. 103.

There are other Gautam Rajpoots in the sub-division of Kaliyânpûr, in the same district, who, it is believed, came from the same stock, and, like those in Kora, have mostly become Mahomedans. They still practise, however, various rites like the Hindus. "Baryâr, or Baray, Gautam having become a Mussalman, was known afterwards as Bahâdur Khân; and receiving a *jaghir* from the emperor Akbar, built the village of Khunta, on the Rhind, and the fort known as Garhî Jar, which, although ruined, still exists, and is held by his descendants, Abdul Rahmân Khân, and others. Garhî Jar is in *Pargannah* Tuppeh-Jar, one of the three composing the Kaliyânpûr (formerly Bindkî) *Tahsîldârî* (revenue district)" (*a*).

The tribe is very numerous in the district of Mirzapûr. The branches found in Azimgarh are said to be of the family of Raja Chandar Sen, of Argal, who, arriving in that country with an armed force, settled down in the village of Mahnagar, where he erected a fort and established a bazar, which are still existing. His son, Abhman Rai, having quarrelled with his father, paid a visit to Delhi, where he became a Mahomedan. He received certain titles of rank from the emperor, and was succeeded at his death by his nephew, who likewise abandoned Hinduism for the Moslem faith. The present Raja of Azimgarh, a Mahomedan, is descended from this stock (*b*). A somewhat different account is given by Mr. Thomason, formerly Collector of Azimgarh, and afterwards Lieutenant-Governor of the North-Western Provinces. "The Gautam Rajpoots," he states, came from the Doâb under two leaders, Gen Rai, and Men Rai. They established themselves in Tuppeh Daulatabâd, and there founded two villages. Mahannagar was the residence of Men Rai, and Goura of Gen Rai. To one of these two stocks all the Gautams of that part of the country trace their origin" (*c*).

The Gautams are very numerous in the *pargannah* of Aurangabâd Nagar in the Gorakhpûr district, and came originally from Chanda, where their Chief married the daughter of the Raja of Gonda, who gave her the Nagar estate as her dowry (*d*).

Respecting the Gautams of Ghazipûr, Dr. Oldham, in his Statistical Memoirs of that district, makes the following observations. "Proceeding north of the Ganges from Mahaitch, we find, in *Pargannah* Karrandah, a very numerous clan

(*a*) Report of the Census of 1865, Vol. I., Appendix B., p. 103.

(*b*) *Ibid*, 112.

(*c*) Mr. Thomason's Report of the Ceded Portion of the District of Azimgarh, p. 13.

(*d*) Report of the Census of 1865, Vol. I, App. B., p. 110.

of Gautam Sombans, or Lunar Rajpoots, who own the greater part of the *pargannah.* These Gautams trace their descent from the main branch of the clan, which has its head-quarters at Argal, in *Pargannah* Kora of the Fathpûr district. They appear to have settled in this district about four or five hundred years ago; and are stated to have conquered and expelled the Seorees, under the leadership of Birnî and Ijrî Kûnr, Gautam Chiefs. The Gautams in four villages became Mussalmans during the empire of the Moguls. The settlement of the head village of *Pargannah* Mainpûr was concluded with the head man; not, as in other estates throughout the district, in the name of the entire proprietary body, but as sole owner. The result of this procedure has been a long-continued feud, and frequent litigation between him and the descendants of shareholders, now reduced to the position of cultivators (*a*). Other portions of this tribe are found in Saidpûr and Zamânîah, in the same district.

It is undoubted that the general testimony, as already shown, is in favour of the Gautam tribe having had its origin at Argal in the Fathpûr district. "They are divided, says Sir H. Elliot, into the tribes (meaning titled clans of) Raja, Rao, Râna, and Râwat. The representative of the Rajas lives at Argal; of the Raos at Birâhanpûr, in Bindkî; of the Ranas at Chillî, in *pargannah* Majhâwan, now included in Sarh Salîmpûr; and of the Râwats at Bhâûpûr, in Bindkî. Besides the possessions which they themselves retained, they are said—and here probability is in favour of the tradition—to have bestowed upon their allies several large tracts, which are to this day tenanted by the grantees. Thus the Chandels of Sivarâjpûr in Cawnpûr are represented to have received from them sixty-two villages in that *pargannah*, having been induced to leave their original seat of Mahoba, after the defeat of their chief Brimaditiya by Prithî Râj. The Jaganbansî Kanaujiya Brahmans of Kora are said to have received the Chandrahat of that *pargannah* from Birsingh Deo, a Gautam Chieftain. The Thatbarar Kanaujiya Brahmans are said to have been Bakhshîs of the Argal family. The Athya Gautams, who are reckoned inferior to the general stock, and considered to have been originally Jinwar Rajpoots, are said to have received twenty-eight villages in Bindkî from the Argal Raja, with whom they had contrived to ingratiate themselves by teaching him the game of chess. But the largest assignment of land which was attributed to their bounty, is that of Baiswâra in Oudh" (*b*).

(*a*) Dr. W. Oldham's Statistical Memoirs of the Ghazipûr District, Part I., p. 59.

(*b*) Elliot's Supplemental Glossary, Vol. I., pp. 116, 117.

The conclusion which Sir H. Elliot draws is, that "the Gautam country must really have been an important tract, extending from Kalpî to the neighbourhood of Gorakhpûr, since we find a Gautam Raja still residing, as head of his tribe, in Nagar in that district; and that the Azimgarh family, now Mussalmans, were, before their conversion, Rajpoots of the Gautam stock. We find it also stated in Buchanan (Eastern India, Vol. II., p. 458), that the Gautams of Gorakhpûr considered that their ancestors were once in possession of Bundelkhand" (*a*). From all these statements it is plain that the Gautam Rajpoots held an extensive tract of land in the Lower Doâb in former times.

There is indeed some probability that these Gautams are of the same family as that of the Sâkyas, from whom sprang the renowned Sâkya Muni or Buddha. "As the Bais (Rajpoots) are descendants of Sâlivâhana, and a Sâlivâhana was sovereign of Pratisthâna, the modern Jhûsî, it gives at once an established antiquity to the Gautams, which makes it possible that we may have in them the descendants of the illustrious Sâkyas" (*b*).

Respecting the later history of this tribe, we have this further information. "For some generations the Gautams of Argal seem by their own accounts to have continued in great prosperity, dating their decline from the period of Humayun's return to India, who avenged himself upon them for their zealous adherence to the cause of his victorious rival, Shîr Shâh. Mussulman history, however, is silent on this subject, both of this warfare of extermination, and of the presumed importance of Argal and the Gautams; and it is therefore difficult to say what portions of truth are mixed up with the fictions of these relations.

"The Gautams of Jaunpûr and the eastward give their daughters in marriage to Sombansî, Bachgotî, Bachalgotî or Bandhalgotî, Bajwâr, and Râjkûmâr Rajpoots. Those of the Doâb give their daughters to other tribes, the Bhadauria, Kachhwâha, Râthor, Gahlot, Chauhân, and Tomar; and they vary as much with respect to the tribes whose daughters they receive" (*c*).

This tribe seems to have entered Oudh at a very early period, so early indeed that Mr. C. A. Elliott speaks of it as pre-historic. He says with justice that the history of the Bais Rajpoots shows that when they settled in that country the Gautams had large possessions. "They themselves claim," he states, "to have dowered the daughter of their house with one thousand four hundred and forty villages, when she wedded her Bais bridegroom and her

(*a*) Elliot's Supplemental Glossary, Vol. I., pp. 117, 118.

(*b*) *Ibid*, p. 118.

(*c*) *Ibid*, pp. 118, 119.

mother's preserver; but this claim is probably exaggerated, and is not supported by the traditions of the Baises themselves" (*a*). The influence of the Gautams is not great in Oudh in the present day, as is sufficiently manifest from the circumstance that only one *taluqdar* or Chief represents them at the Durbar of the viceroy.

The Gautam Rajpoots occupy thirty-seven villages to the south of the district of Shâhjahânpûr. They have considerable possessions also in the Cawnpûr district. In the *pargannah* of Sarh Salîmpûr alone, they had, a few years since, as many as thirty-nine villages. The Raja of Argal in *pargannah* Kora was the head of the clan.

In many of the districts of these Provinces, the Gautams are among the most powerful and wealthy of the Rajpoot tribes. In Mirzapûr they number nearly twenty thousand persons. There are likewise many in the Benares district, where their influence is extensive. None of them, however, are large landholders. A considerable proportion of them are traders and servants. In the latter district, the Gautams are sometimes confounded with the Bhûînhâr Brahmans of the Gautam *gotra*, who are generally designated by the natives by the simple term Gautam.

The Gautam Rajpoots are of the Bhâraddwâj and Garg *gotras* or orders.

Dikshit.

This tribe is spread over a considerable tract of country extending from Oudh southwards to Bundelkhand, and eastwards to Ghazipûr. The account of the origin of the clan is thus given by Mr. Elliott.

"The traditions of the clan relate that the Dikshits are descended from the Surajbans Rajas, who for fifty-one generations ruled over Ajudhiya. In the fifty-first generation from Ikswaku, Raja Durgban left Ajudhiya, and migrated to Gujerât, where his descendants took the title of Durgbansis, or children o Durg. In the twenty-fourth generation from him Kaliyân Sâh Durgbans went to pay homage to Raja Vikramajît, the great Raja of Ujain. From him (about 50 B. C.) he received the title of Dikshit, which his descendants bore, instead of Durgbans. For many centuries they remained stationary in Gujerât; till, at the time when the Raj of Kanouj was at its zenith, Balbhadra Dikshit, the younger son of Samarpradhân, entered the service of the Râthor Raja. From him he received as a gift the Samonî *pargannah*, which lies across the Jumna in

(*a*) Mr. C. A. Elliott's Chronicles of Oonao, p. 21.

the Banda district ; and he settled down in this estate with his family and his followers. But the Hindoo monarchies were already drawing to their close, and the grandson of Balbhadra, Jaswant, saw the death of the Raja of Kanouj, and the destruction of the power and the family of his benefactor. Samonî was too near Kanouj not to be affected by this great dynastic revolution ; and the Dikshit colony was disturbed and broken up by these disastrous events. Jaswant Singh had four sons. The eldest remained in Samonî, and his descendants possess the estate to this day. "The second, Udîbhan, migrated into Oudh, and colonized the district of Dikhthîânâ. "The third, Banwârî, went still further north, crossing the Gogra and the Raptî, and choosing a safe retreat in the Sub-Himalayan forests, founded there the great Sirnet Raj of Bansî. "The fourth, Khairâj, migrated to the east, and settled down in the district of Partâbgarh, and took the town of Bilkhar, whence his descendants are called Bilkhariyas" (*a*).

Udîbhan held possession of fourteen *pargannahs*, forming the country termed Dikhthîânâ, which extended from the borders of Baiswâra, on the east, to Sândî Pâlî, on the west, and from the Gûmtî to the Ganges. This tract was previously inhabited by the Lodhs, whose subjugation, in the absence of all tradition on the subject, seems to have been effected with ease. Udîbhan became Raja, and the title was handed down through six generations. As a proof of the high position of this Rajpoot clan, it is sufficient to state, that other Rajpoot tribes of Oudh were in those days eager to form alliances with it. Unfortunately, the desire for separate ownership destroyed the unity of the clan and the integrity of the Dikhthîânâ territory, which were parcelled out into six divisions by the six sons of Râna Singh, and appropriated by them severally. The names of these sons, and of their possessions, are as follows:—

Sons of Râna Singh.	Their possessions.
1. Bîr Nâth	Chamraulî.
2. Pathimal	Pathiora.
3. Bîrsâh	Bholî.
4. Sadan	Sanânâ.
5. Gandarâj	Mushkâbâd.
6. Gûrdat	Gaura.

The descendants of Pathimal, the second son, are the Parenda family, who are now the acknowledged head of the entire clan.

(*a*) Mr. Elliott's Chronicles of Oonao, pp. 34, 35.

On the return of the emperor Humayun, the Dikshit tribe received a blow, from which it has never recovered. Pathimal declined to acknowledge the emperor, and, supported by a large number of Rajpoots, opposed him with great pertinacity. In the end, a severe battle was fought, which resulted in the destruction of Pathimal and other chiefs, and of many Rajpoots of various clans. Dikhthîânâ being thereby left without a leader, the Chandel Raja of Surajpûr attempted to annex it to his estates. This was stoutly opposed, however, by the remaining Dikshits, who elected a young son of one of the wives of Pathimal as their Raja. This child was called Nirbahan. He lived at Unao. His grandson, Bîr Singh Deo, founded the village of Bîrsinghpûr; and his son Khîrat Singh removed thence, and built the fort of Parenda, which his descendant inhabits. Yet the tribe never recovered its prestige; and, to make matters worse, the lands were divided into small portions, and given to one and another of the family. Weak, impoverished, and without honour and position, the fortunes of the house became at length wretched in the extreme, so that the Raja was unable to afford the expenses of receiving the *tilak*, or mark of Rajaship, applied to the forehead in the presence of Rajas and other men of rank—a ceremony always accompanied by the feasting of all present, together with liberal donations to Brahmans. The representative of the clan of late years has been Raja Daya Shankar, a man of great spirit and determination, who, in the maintenance of his imagined rights, on four separate occasions, has fought severe fights with Chakladârs, persons superintending a large district of country (*a*).

In the Ghazipûr district, nearly the whole of Pachotar is occupied by a branch of the Dikshit clan, called there Pachtoriya. They state that their ancestor was Manik Rao, who, about twenty generations back, migrated from Bulandshahr to this tract (*b*).

The tribe is also found in the Fathpûr district, inhabiting the *pargannahs* of Katia, Fathpûr, Ekdalla, Mutaur, and Ghazipûr; and also in Bundelkhand and the Benares district. Those in Fathpûr are in part descended from Simaunî, who came from Banda, and settled at Kurra Kanak, on the Jumna, in the *pargannah* Mutaur. Some of the family have embraced the Mahomedan faith. One named Râm Singh went to Delhi, after his marriage with the daughter of Nandan Raī Gautam, where he also became a Mahomedan, and was then called

(*a*) Mr. Elliott's Chronicles of Oonao, pp. 34—41.
(*b*) Dr. W. Oldham's Statistical Memoirs of the Ghazipûr District, p. 58.

Malikdâd Khân. His posterity occupy the village of Lalaulî, on the Jumna, which he founded, and, although professedly Mussalmans, practise a number of Hindu ceremonies (*a*)

The Dikshits of Hamîrpûr came originally from Koel or Aligarh. Their existence in the district, however, is not recognized by the last Census Report.

There is a considerable colony of Dikshits in Azimgarh; and a few in Jaunpûr. There is also an insignificant community of Dikshit *Zamindars* in Benares. The tribe is of the Kâsyap *gotra* or order.

Pachtoriya.

A tribe of very small extent is called by this name, and is found in Benares, Azimgarh, and Ghazipûr. In Benares, it occupies no very honourable position, and is engaged in trade, and in other employments.

The Pachtoriyas of Ghazipûr came thither from Bijaipûr Bhalkhand, under their leader Talkasî Rai, and took possession of the tract now known as the Pachotar *pargannah*. They claim to be Dikshits, although bearing the name Pachtoriya. The other Rajpoots of the district recognize them, and intermarry with them. Some of the tribe apostatized to Mahomedanism in the time of Abdulla Khan, and their descendants are found scattered about the *pargannah*. They mingle with other Mahomedans, and live according to their habits and manners (*b*).

The tribe is of the Kasyap *gotra.*

Sirnet.

This tribe is mostly found in the Gorakhpûr district, where it is very numerous and influential. It is said to have come from Srinagar with the Raja of Satâsî, and to have received grants of lands in the Bastî *pargannah*, on which it settled. There is considerable doubt as to what Srinagar is intended, as there are several places of this name in India. Some hold that it is the Srinagar of Garhwâl, on the lower slope of the Himalayas, though without sufficient reason. Others that it is the Srinagar of Bundelkhand. The family of the Raja of Unaula, the most important chief of the clan, states, that they came originally from Assam (*c*). Raja Bhagwant Singh of Satâsî had

(*a*) Report of the Census of the North-Western Provinces, for 1865, Appendix B., pp. 104, 105.
(*b*) *Ibid*, p. 122.
(*c*) Buchanan's Eastern India, Vol. II., p. 457.

three sons, among whom he divided his property. Unaula and Bhowaparia fell to Jagdhir Singh, from whom the present Raja is descended. Several branches of the tribe trace their relationship to the Raja of Bansî. The Babus of Dadupûr are descended from Rudra Singh, Raja of Satâsî. Other respectable families of this clan are found also in the Havelî Gorakhpûr and Silhet *pargannahs.*

A few families of Sirnets have established themselves in the Azimgarh and Allahabad districts. It is the opinion of Mr. Elliott, that this clan is a branch of the Dikshit Rajpoots of Dikhitiânâ in Oudh. Dr. W. Oldham, however, considers that they belong to the Naikumbh tribe, which, in the Gorakhpûr district, receives the title of Sirnet.

The Sirnets are found in small numbers in the Benares district, and are employed as cultivators.

Durgbansîs.

The Durgbansîs, although of the same family originally as the Dikshits, yet in several parts of the country have a separate name, and are regarded as a distinct tribe. They occupy lands in Garwâra, Ghisera, and Râri, in the Jaunpûr district, and also in Mâhul of Azimgarh. They intermarry with some of the highest tribes of Rajpoots. The Raja of Garwâra belongs to the Durgbansî tribe (*a*).

Dhrigubansî.

This tribe sprang from the province of Oudh. It is numerous in the district of Jaunpûr, where it possesses several thousand families. Colonies also are in the neighbouring district of Azimgarh. In Mirzapûr are a few hundred individuals; and in Benares likewise is a small community. In Oudh the Dhrigubansîs have one chief, whom they are permitted to send as their representative to the Governor General's Durbar.

Raghubansî.

This tribe is scattered over a considerable portion of the North-Western Provinces, from Farakhabâd, in the west, to Azimgarh and Ghazipûr, in the east. In the district of Azimgarh alone there are thirty thousand, while in the

(*a*) Supplemental Glossary, Vol. I., p. 87.

Mirzapûr district there are upwards of forty thousand. Their common *gotra* is Kasyap.

The Raghubansîs hold three villages in the neighbourhood of Ghiror, in the Mainpûrî district. They came, they say, from Ajudhiya, in the time of Raja Jai Chand of Kanouj. Those in the Nidhpûr *pargannah*, of the Etah district, state, that their ancestors proceeded from the same place. It is believed that Raja Raghu, of the Solar Race, made Ajudhiya his seat of Government. Hence, all his descendants are called Raghubansîs. They are numerous in some parts of Ghazipûr, particularly Saidpûr and Cawnpûr; in the Dûbî *pargannah*, of Jaunpûr; and in the *pargannahs* of Katehâr, Bârah, and Mahûârî, of Benares. In the days of Domon Deo, a powerful Raja of Chandraulî, in the reign of the emperor Shîr Shâh, 'the Raghubansîs of Katehâr, (in the Benares district), crossing the Gumtî, took possession of ten villages, which they still hold' (*a*).

A tradition exists at Râmbhîrpûr, in Oudh, that the Raghubansîs of that neighbourhood were all slain together with their Raja by the troops of Shahâb-ud-din Ghorî. Mr. C. A. Elliott, who mentions the tradition, considers that it is without foundation, as he cannot conceive it possible that a race could be almost completely exterminated, seeing that only one family of the entire clan now exists there. It is hardly necessary to suppose that an utter destruction of the tribe was effected. It may have been so thoroughly subdued that the survivors emigrated in a body to other regions (*b*).

The Raghubansîs occupy a considerable number of villages in the district of Fathpûr. They are said to have come from the other side of the Jumna; but they have been in the district for several hundred years. A few also are met with in the Agra district.

This tribe is numerous in Benares, yet less so than the Bais Rajpoots. They have come hither from Ajudhiya. Many of them are employed in the cultivation of the ground. Some are landholders, occupying a position of high respectability. At their head is Lâl Bahâdur Singh, who is in the possession of large estates. They form an important colony at Chandraulî, a few miles from Benares, in the direction of Ghazipûr, whence they extend to the Dûbî *pargannah* of Jaunpûr.

(*a*) Dr. W. Oldham's Statistical Memoir of the Ghazipûr District, Part I., p. 65.

(*b*) Chronicles of Oonao, p. 22.

Sri Mat.

A small tribe from Satâsî, in the Gorakhpûr district, which, in former times, migrated to the tract now comprised in the Azimgarh district, where it assisted other Rajpoot tribes in the subjugation and expulsion of the aboriginal races, and participated with them in the estates which they seized.

Sonwan.

In the Jaunpûr district this tribe is exceedingly numerous. According to the last Census its numbers fell little short of ten thousand. The tribe seems to be confined to this tract.

Bûtrihâ.

A small tribe of Rajpoots in the Benares district engaged in the cultivation of the ground. It belongs to the Bhâraddwâj *gotra* or order.

Bhathariya or Batauriya.

An inconsiderable community of Rajpoots in the Jaunpûr district, numbering, at the last Census of 1865, about two or three hundred families. It seems to be of local origin.

CHAPTER X.

THE HAYOBANS, BACHALGOTI, MONAS, BISEN, RAJPUSI, RAIKWAR, SARPAKHARIYA, DHANIS, LATHOR, AND PATSARIYA TRIBES.

Hayobans, Haiya, Haihaya, or Harihobans.

This was once an important tribe of Rajpoots, and occupied a very extensive territory on the banks of the Nirbuddha in Central India, where under their leader, the famous Sahasra Arjuna, they founded the city of Maheswarî, the original capital of the Sombansîs, or Rajpoots of the Lunar Race. A dynasty of Hayobans kings, says Mr. R. Egerton, in a recent paper, occupied Ratanpûr, in Central India, where they continued for fifty-two generations. The last representative of the family was Raja Raghunâth Singh, who died only one hundred and ten years ago (*a*). A few of the tribe are found at Sohâgpûr; but it seems to have lost entirely its ancient rank and splendour, and, like many other Indian races, to have been well nigh obliterated. This people were powerful and warlike in former times, and were sufficiently strong to cope with aboriginal races. To them is attributed the expulsion of the Cherûs, a numerous and energetic tribe of aborigines, from the country on the southern bank of the Ganges.

In the district of Ghazipûr, however, the Hayobansîs hold the highest rank among Rajpoots of the neighbourhood. They claim to be descended from the kings of Ratanpûr. Dr. W. Oldham gives the following account of the tribe, taken from what he terms an 'historical pedigree,' in the possession of the family, and from other sources.

"Chandra Got, a cadet of the Ratanpûr house, in the year 906 Sambat, or 850 A. D., migrated northwards, settled at Manjha on the Ghogra, now included in the Sâran district, and waged successful war with the aboriginal Cherûs.

(*a*) Dr. W. Oldham's Statistical Memoirs of Ghazipûr, p. 55; Elliot's Supplemental Glossary, Vol. I., p. 128.

After a couple of hundred years, his descendants left Manjha, and settled south of the Ganges, at Bahîa, where they remained five centuries, and subdued the Cherûs. In or about the year 1584 Sambat, or 1528 A. D., the Raja Bhopat Deo (or perhaps one of his sons) violated Mahem, a Brahman woman of the house of the *parohit*, or family priest, of the Hayobans clan. She burned herself to death; and in dying imprecated the most fearful curses on the Hayobans race. After this tragedy, the clan left Bahîa, and passed beyond the Ganges to the Balliah *pargannah*, where they for a while were located at Gae Ghât, and finally settled at Haldî, from which place the Hayobans Raja now takes his title. The tomb of Mahenî, under a peepul tree, close to the railway at Bahîa, is still visited by women of every caste, who come in numbers either to invoke her as a deified being, or to offer oblations in commemoration of her. There are still a few Hayobans residing in the neighbourhood; but nothing will induce them to enter the village of Bahîa, once the chief seat of the clan, and in which the remains of their ancestors' fort are still to be seen" (*a*).

The Rajas of Haldî, it appears, were, for a time, lords of the Balliah *pargunnah*, and most probably paid revenue for the whole of it to the Mogul emperors. Balwant Singh, Raja of Benares, dispossessed them of their rights in the *pargannah*. Some years afterwards, when the country had come into the hands of the British Government, Mr. Fowke, the Agent for the Governor-General in Benares, conferred upon Bhûabal Deo, Raja of Haldî, a perpetual grant of sixteen thousand rupees per annum, in recognition of his ancestral right over the Balliah *pargannah*. Afterwards, as a further confirmation of this right, when the permanent settlement of the lands in this part of the country was made by Mr. Duncan, Resident of Benares, five estates of sixteen thousand acres in extent, were settled with the Raja at a revenue of upwards of twenty-four thousand rupees. The annual allowance or pension was continued during the life-time of the Raja, and also of his son Isharî Bakhsh; but it was diminished to the third Raja, Dalganjan Singh, in 1806; and was altogether discontinued on the accession of Raja Harak Nâth Deo, in 1825, and has never been renewed, notwithstanding urgent and repeated applications to the Government for its restoration.

The present Raja, a boy of eleven years of age, says Dr. W. Oldham, is "miserably poor, as all the estates of the family were sold by his ancestors to the Raja of Domraon. A couple of small villages conferred on him by Government, for good conduct during the disturbances of 1857 and 1858, and five hundred

(*a*) Dr. W. Oldham's Statistical Memoirs of Ghazipûr, p. 55.

beegahs of land allowed to him by the Domraon Raja, at a moderate rent, is all that remains to support the dignity of a family once illustrious and powerful, and still, in their fallen state, ranking higher in popular estimation than even the house of the Raja of Domraon, who is the possessor of immense estates, and can boast a pedigree of eighty-six generations from the greatest of Indian kings" (*a*).

Several Hayobans families inhabit villages in various parts of the Balliah *pargannah*, of complexion so dark, and features so non-Aryan, that Dr. Oldham is somewhat inclined to agree with Mr. P. Carnegy, that the Hayobans tribe is really an aboriginal Tamil race. This too is the opinion of Mr. Hodgson, a high authority on the aboriginal tribes of India. Mr. P. Carnegy gives the statement of General Sleeman, that the ancient Hayobans sovereigns of Ratanpûr and Lahanjî were subdued by Gond Rajas.

Bachal or Bachalgoti.

This tribe has been established in the district of Shâhjahânpûr from ancient times. They formerly were in possession of the eastern portion of Rohilkhand, but were driven out by the Mahomedans, and their lands given to the Kathariya Rajpoots. They are said to have come originally from the neighbourhood of Farakhabâd, about the year 1000 A. D., under the leadership of a chief named Dâran Pâd. They proceeded in a northerly direction. One of their celebrated men was Raja Ben, who founded Mâtî. The famous Raja Deo belongs to this clan, who had twelve sons, the descendants of whom are found scattered over a considerable extent of country. In the middle of the sixteenth century, 'Chabi Singh, one of the tribe, obtained, partly by a grant of the emperor, and partly by violence, a territory extending over parts of the Kânt, Powayan, Tilhar, and Shâhjahânpûr *pargannahs*; and, at a later date, one of his descendants obtained possession of Samarîya, which, along with seventy other villages in these parts, is still in the possession of this tribe. One Raja Tilak Chand Bachal is said to have occupied Tilhar, and to have settled his tribe in Patah Chircola, now called Jalâlpûr, driving out the Gûjars and Banjâras' (*b*).

This tribe, according to Sir H. Elliot, is of the Lunar Race of Rajpoots. 'We find them,' he says, 'in Jalâlî of Aligarh; Kot Sâlbâhan, Ujhânî, and

(*a*) Dr. W. Oldham's Statistical Memoirs of Ghazipûr, pp. 55, 6.

(*b*) Census of the North-Western Provinces for 1865, Vol. I., Appendix B., p. 58.

Nidhpûr, of Budaon ; Sahâr and Arîng of Mathura; and in Tilhar and Shâhjehânpûr.' Moreover, he states, that the landholders of Farîda and of Kânt Gola, the old name of Shâhjehânpûr, as recorded in the Aîn-i Akbarî, were of the Bachal tribe (*a*). The Bachals appear to be the earliest recorded occupants of the entire tract lying to the north of this district.

The Bachals are met with also in the Khandaulî and Ferozabâd *pargannahs*, to the north of the Agra district. They are, however, few in number, and of recent date. A small community also is found in the Benares district.

Monas.

This clan is divided into two branches, of which the elder is found at Amber or old Jaipûr. The younger branch is traditionally stated to have migrated from this country and to have entered the *pargannah* of Bhadohî, in the Mirzapûr district, at a time when an aboriginal race of Bhars held possession of that territory. Accounts differ as to the origin of their dispute with the Bhars; but they agree in this, that Rajpoots of the Mon race, while pursuing their pilgrimage to the sacred city of Benares, were attracted by the Bhar fields, through which they passed, and decided on settling upon them. The number of the immigrants was at first small; but it was increased by accessions from the original stock in Jaipûr. When they became strong enough, a desperate effort was made by the clan to expel the Bhars, which ended in the complete destruction of the latter. The *pargannah* fell into the hands of the conquerors, and remained in their possession for many generations.

In an elaborate account of the Bhadohî *pargannah*, Mr. Duthoit, Deputy Superintendent of the Family Domains of the Maharaja of Benares, has given some interesting particulars respecting the history of the younger branch of this clan. "The Monas have a pedigree," he says, "which goes back for thirty-two generations; but much dependance cannot be placed on it. In this country about five generations go to a century; so that the pedigree would place the family in the *pargannah* almost from the date of the Mahomedan conquest. For twenty-six generations the names of father and son succeed one another without any further detail. Sâgar Rai is the first head of the family of whom anything authentic would seem to be known. He had three sons, Harbans Rai, Râm Chandra, and Jagdîs Rai. The share of Jagdîs Rai long remained distinct : the

(*a*) Elliot's Supplemental Glossary, Vol. I., pp. 8, 9.

rest of the *pargannah* seems to have fallen to Râm Chandra. Râm Chandra was succeeded by his son, Bîrbhadra Singh. Bîrbhadra had five sons ; but two only, Jodh Rai and Madan Singh, need be mentioned. Jodh Rai obtained a Zemindari *sanad* (or land-grant), for the whole of the *pargannah*, from the emperor Shâh Jahân ; but was killed by the Subahdar of Allahabad not long afterwards. Upon this, the emperor is said to have given a fresh *sanad* to Jodh Rai's widow ; and she, it is asserted, delegated the management of the Zemindâri (or estate) to Madan Singh" (*a*).

This Madan Singh is regarded as the second founder of the family. He was evidently a crafty man, and not so honest as he might have been. He managed to gain possession of nearly the whole of the *pargannah*, and was very powerful and prosperous. In the early part of the last century feuds broke out among his descendants; and the Raja of Partâbgarh in Oudh, Pirthîpat Singh, was invited to render assistance. The Raja embraced the opportunity of gaining the control of the *pargannah*, and after a time made it over, certain portions excepted, to Balwant Singh, Raja of Benares. By the year 1776 only one estate remained with the Monas Rajpoots ; all the rest of the *pargannah* having by that time been absorbed by the Benares family.

The Monas Rajpoots still reside, for the most part, in the Bhadohî *pargannah* of Mirzapûr. Some families, however, have settled in the Allahabad and Jaunpûr districts, and a very small number in the Gorakhpûr and Benares districts. In the last mentioned district they are chiefly husbandmen. The tribe is of the Maunî *gotra*, or order, a name peculiar to themselves.

Bisen.

This tribe is scattered over most of the districts among the eastern tracts of the North Western Provinces, but is not found west of Cawnpûr. In some places it is met with in considerable numbers, as in the districts of Allahabad, Gorakhpûr, Azimgarh, and Jaunpûr. In Oudh, they are said to occupy three hundred and sixty villages.

Mr. C. A. Elliott affirms that they came originally from Salîmpûr Majhoulî, in Gorakhpûr. The Raja of this place is, says Sir Henry Elliot, the acknowledged chief of the Bisen stock. " The founder of the political influence of the family was Mewar Bhat, whose ancestors had for many generations resided as devotees in the neighbourhood of Nawâpûr, now known as Salîmpûr Majhaulî.

(*a*) Report of the Bhadohi Pargannah by Mr. W. Duthoit, B.C.S., pp. 8, 9.

Mewat Bhat, though himself a religious man, was not able to withstand the solicitations of ambition; and, taking up arms, after returning from a pilgrimage to Benares, acquired possession of the greater part of the country between the Ganges and the great Gandak. Mewat had four wives. By one, a Râjputnî, he had issue, Bisu Sen, the founder of the name of Bisen, and the ancestor of the Raja's family. By a Bhûînhâr, he had Bagmar Sahî, the ancestor of the Kawarî and Tamakhoî Rajas. By a Brahminî, he had Nages, whose descendants hold a few villages in Salîmpûr Majhaulî. By a Kurmî, he had the ancestor of those now resident in Ghosî of Azimgarh. The present incumbent of the Raj is said to be in the hundred and fifteenth generation from Mewar Bhat" (*a*).

From Gorakhpûr the Bisens stretched out westward to Manikpûr, and from the colony located there sprang the Unao branch, which retains, in that district, a number of villages, in spite of all the efforts of the Mahomedans to dispossess them. An ancient Bisen Raja, by name Unwant, gave his name to Unao, but at what era, is not known (*b*). From the testimony of a grant inscribed on a copper-plate found in the Fyzabad district, in which a Kanouj Raja bestows the present of a village in Oudh, it would seem that Oudh was once a part of the Kanouj dominions. Moreover, there is a tradition that the Bisen Raja of Unao rendered military service to Jai Chand in resisting Mahomed Ghori (*c*). In the Kopâchit *pargannah* of Ghazipûr, there are a few families of this clan, having possession of some ten or twelve villages to the north of the *pargannah.*

The Bisen Rajpoots of Gorakhpûr, where they are a very influential people, claim descent, says Buchanan, from Bhrigu, a Brahman Rishi of the Vedic or pre-Vedic period ; but this is mere wild imagination (*d*). The Raja of Majhaulî, who, as already stated, is at the head of the Bisen Rajpoots, is descended, according to local tradition, from Cheit Mal. This surname is still retained by the head of the clan.

The clan has estates in the district of Fathpûr. It is numerous in the Haswa *pargannah.*

The Bisens of Oudh number thirteen chiefs, and are found chiefly in Partâbgarh, Bahraich, Gondâ, Dariabâd, and Sultânpûr. "The local heads of the family," remarks Mr. P. Carnegy, "are Raja Hanwant Singh of Kâlâkankar—as fine a specimen of the oriental yeoman as is to be found anywhere,

(*a*) Elliot's Supplemental Glossary, Vol. I., p. 42.
(*b*) Mr. C. A. Elliott's Chronicles of Oonao, p. 22.
(*c*) *Ibid.*
(*d*) Buchanan's Eastern India, Vol. II., p. 459.

and one who will ever be respected by our countrymen for the asylum he offered to the officers of this district, in the rebellion—and also the Rajas of Mankâpûr and Bhingâ" (*a*).

A few Bisen families are found in Benares, both in the city and district. They are mostly engaged in trade, or in the cultivation of the ground; and have no Rajas or Chiefs to give them social distinction. They belong to the Sândil and Parâsar *gotras* or orders.

Râjpusi.

This clan exists in considerable numbers in the Hardui and Sîtapûr districts of Oudh. Formerly, its chief seat was at Râmkot (the Fort of Râm). "Little is known of the early history of this town; but its ruins, which lie in the west corner of the district overlooking the river Sai, still testify to its grandeur and extent. Some of the mounds which mark the site of the ancient buildings are still one hundred feet in height; and the ruins extend over a circumference of several miles. This was the seat of the Râjpusî power, which extended far to the west and north of Râmkot. The last of the lords of Râmkot, Raja Santhar by name, threw off his allegiance to Kanouj, and refused to pay the annual tribute. On this, Raja Jai Chand gave to Alâ and Udal the grant of all the Ganjar country; and they attacked and destroyed Râmkot, leaving it the shapeless mass of ruins we now find it. 'The streams, which run between the various mounds, cut away the *debris*, and lay bare at times the massive walls made of enormous bricks, uncemented; or sometimes turn up relics of the past, caskets full of dust, which once was embroidered apparel, but which crumbles to the touch,—or gold coins and jewels with quaint and uncouth legends. But to those that find them, such treasures ever are as fairy gifts, bringing misfortune and misery into the family, and dragging the possessors down to irretrievable poverty" (*b*).

It would be interesting to excavate some of these mounds 'one hundred feet in height,' in which ancient buildings lie entombed; and doubtless, the result would be of value to the archæology, as well as to the history, of India.

Raikwâr.

This clan is scattered about various districts of these provinces, especially on their eastern borders. It has branches in Farakhâbâd, Cawnpûr, Allahabad,

(*a*) Mr. P. Carnegy's Races of Oudh, p. 49.
(*b*) Mr. C. A. Elliott's Chronicles of Oonao, p. 24.

Benares, Gorakhpûr, Azimgarh, Jaunpûr, and also in Oudh. Yet the tribe seems to be of small dimensions in comparison with many others.

The Raikwârs have a dozen villages in the *pargannah* of Rangarmau, of the district of Unao in Oudh; and are called by the name of Shâdîpûr Gauria. "They claim kindred," says Mr. C. A. Elliott, "with the Raikwâr Rajas of Bondî and Râmnagar, in the Baraich and Dariabâd districts; and assert that, at the same time that those larger colonies were founded, their ancestors settled down in the twelve villages they now hold. The Bondî Raja's ancestor immigrated to Oudh from the hill-country about Cashmere eighteen generations, or four hundered and fifty years, ago, that is, about 1400 A. D. The connection of these Raikwârs with the great Rajas on the banks of the Gogra had been entirely broken off; but when they began to rise in political importance they sought to renew it. About sixty years ago, Mittû Singh and Bakht Singh, two of the leading *zemindars*, went to Râmnagar, and claimed brotherhood with the Raja. He heard their story, entertained them with hospitality, and sent them out food, and, among other things, tooth-brushes made of wood of the *nîm* tree. All other Rajpoots place a special value on this wood; but the Raikwârs alone are forbidden to use it, and the rejection of these tooth-brushes proved to the Raja that his visitors were truly of his own kin" (*a*). Mr. Elliott adds to this interesting narrative a brief account of the Raikwârs of Shâdîpûr Gauria, in regard to the turbulent and disloyal spirit they have manifested.

The Raikwârs of Dariabâd in Oudh are in possession of thirty-one villages. Their chief is the Raja of Râmnagar. They possess great influence in the Amsin *pargannah* of the Fyzabad district. They are said to have come from Râmnagar-Dhimari, in the Barabanki district, some three hundred years ago. The tribe in Oudh has five representative chiefs at the Governor General's Durbar. There are only a few members of the tribe in the Benares district; but they number several hundred families in the districts of Azimgarh and Gorakhpûr. The Raikwârs are of the Kasyap *gotra*.

Sarpakhariya.

An inconsiderable tribe of Rajpoots inhabiting the district of Azimgarh, where they are supposed to number upwards of a thousand persons (*b*). They are said to have come originally from Tuar Kasar.

(*a*) Mr. C. A. Elliott's Chronicles of Oonao, pp. 44, 45.
(*b*) Report of the Census of the North-Western Provinces for 1865, Vol. II., p. 15.

Dhanis.

A race of Rajpoots in the Gorakhpûr district, numbering a few hundred individuals. About one hundred families have also settled in Azimgarh.

Lathor.

A Rajpoot tribe rather numerous in the Azimgarh district. I am not aware that it is found in other places.

Patsariya.

An insignificant community of Rajpoots found in the Jaunpûr district, and apparently of local origin, numbering a few hundred families.

CHAPTER XI.

THE YADU OR JADUBANSI, BANAPHAR, BHRIGUBANSI, RIKHIBANSI, BAHARWALIYA OR BARHAULIYA, SURAJBANSI, CHANDRABANSI, SOMBANSI, NAGBANSI, KANPURIYA, JANUTURWA, SONAK, TASHAIYA, SARWAR OR SURWAR, UJAIN, DHANAWAST, CHAUPATA KHAMBH, BHANWAG, NINIARWAR, NANWAG, KARAMWAR, SANGJAL, SURHANIYA, PALWAR OR PALIWAR, SINGHEL OR SINGALI, PALILI, AND HARDWAS TRIBES.

Yadu or Jadubansî.

THIS tribe is especially illustrious as the representative of Buddha, the founder of the Buddhist religion, whose direct descendants are always regarded as Yadus. The original name has become strangely corrupted, and the race is now seldom designated as Yadu or Yaduvansa, but commonly by the term Jâdu, or Jâdun, or Jâdubansî.

The Yadus inhabited, says Colonel Tod, a tract of country beyond the North-Western frontier even as far as Samarkhand, at a remote period of Hindu history. It is not known when they re-crossed the Indus and returned to India. Having obtained possession of the Panjab, they were unable to retain their hold upon it; and, after a time, passing over the Satlaj and Gara, entered the Indian desert, where expelling various tribes, such as the Langahas, the Johyas, and the Mohilas, they founded Tannot, Darrawal, and Jessalmer, in the year 1157, A. D. The last city is the present capital of the Bhattis, one of the branches of the Jadubansî race.

This tribe has eight divisions, or branches, as follows:

1. Yadu—The head of this branch is the prince of the small state of Karauli.
2. Bhatti—Represented by the head of the Jessalmer state.
3. Jhareja—Represented by the Raja of Cutch.
4. Samaicha—Represented by Mahomedan nobles in Scinde.
5. Madaicha.
6. Bidman.
7. Buddha.
8. Soha.

Next to the Bhattis the Jharejas are now the most important clan of this tribe. They are supposed to have settled in the valley of the Indus on the frontier of Seistân. The modern Jharejas have largely intermingled with the Mahomedans of Scinde. Colonel Tod, to whom I am indebted for this information respecting the Yadus, has given a further account concerning this tribe (*a*).

The Jâdus are very numerous in the two districts of Mathurâ and Agra, where it embraces a population of upwards of thirty thousand persons. In Agra, the chief settlement is in the Ferozabâd *pargannah*, especially round Kotlah, where the tribe is very influential. They are said to have been established in that region for several hundred years. The Jâduns of the western part of the district are an inferior branch of the stock. Those inhabiting the Mathurâ district allow second marriages, and are consequently despised and shunned by the Jâduns of Karauli and other places (*b*).

The Jâduns of Jewar have the title of Chaukarzada; but the term Bâgrî is applied to the inferior members of the tribe by way of reproach. The family of Awa Mîsa, in the Mathurâ district, has gained for itself a high position, and the Taluqdar, or head man, says Elliot, now lays claim to a direct descent from Anand Pal, the son of the Kirauli Raja, Kumâr Pâl; and asserts that the Bareshwarî, Jaiswâr, and other self-styled Jâduns, are altogether of an inferior stock. Jâduns are also found, he adds, in Hoshangabâd, whither they emigrated after Akbar's conquests on the Nirbuddha (*c*). A few families of this tribe are likewise met with in Morâdabâd, Etawah, Cawnpûr, Azimgarh, and Benares.

Banâphar.

A tribe of Rajpoots inhabiting the country districts, a few miles from Benares. They are found in the direction of Marîâhû, a thriving town on the borders of Oudh.

This tribe is not confined to Benares, but is scattered over a considerable extent of country, and has its colonies in various places between Benares and Cawnpûr, to the west, and as far south as Banda. Its numbers appear to be greatest in the district of Mirzapûr, where it has a community of several thousand persons.

Wilson regards this tribe as connected with the Yadubansî Rajpoots; and states that it is chiefly settled in Oudh, but is likewise found as far as

(*a*) Tod's Rajasthan, Vol. I., pp. 85—87.

(*b*) Census Report of the North-Western Provinces, for 1865, Vol. I., pp. 64, 65.

(*c*) Supplemental Glossary, Vol. I., p. 129.

Bundelkhand (*a*). Mr. P. Carnegy, in his list of the Rajpoot Races of Oudh, makes no mention of the Banâphar tribe.

The famous warriors, Alâ and Udal, whose names are household words throughout a large portion of the North Western Provinces, and whose achievements are sung by Nats and bards in all directions, were of this tribe.

The clan is scattered about the southern parts of Oudh in considerable numbers. "There are some also," says Sir H. Elliot, "in Karra of Allahabad; in Narwan, Havelî, and Katehar of Benares; in Garra Mandla; and in Bundelkhand. Their original seat is Mahoba" (*b*).

The Banâphars are of the Kasyap *gotra* or order.

Bhrigubansî.

The Bhrigubansîs, says Wilson, derive their origin from Parasrâma. A few members of the tribe are found in the Benares district, and a few others in the neighbouring district of Azimgarh.

The tribe belongs to the Sâvaran *gotra* or order.

Rikhibansî.

A numerous community of Rajpoots in Semrîpuârî and other parts of the district of Benares, where as landholders they occupy an influential position. Colonies also are found in the Azimgarh and Mirzapûr districts. The tribe is of the Kasyap *gotra*.

Baharwaliya or Barhauliya.

This small Rajpoot tribe is found in Benares. They are of inferior position socially, and are engaged in the pursuit of trade, or in the service of merchants and others. They are of the Sâvaran *gotra* or order.

This tribe is, I suppose, the same as that called Barhauliya of the Bhrigubansî stock, and chief proprietors of Barhaul in Benares. They are said to have come originally, says Sir H. Elliot, from Raingarh in Marwâr, and instead of pursuing their journey to Jagannâth, as they had intended, to have staid with the aboriginal chief either of the Seori or Cherû tribe, who presented Narctam Rai, their leader, with several villages, as a reward for certain medical services which he had rendered.

(*a*) Wilson's Glossary, p. 57.

(*b*) Supplemental Glossary, Vol. I., p. 51.

The usual consequence of Rajpoot intimacy with the aborigines ensued, for, on the death of the Raja, Narotam Rai took possession of his estates, and governed them in behalf of his own people (*a.*)

Sûrajbansî.

This tribe must not be confounded with the great Sûrajbansî family, or Solar Race. It is simply a distinct tribe separate from the rest. Its origin, like that of the subordinate Chandrabansî and Sombansî tribes, is mysterious. Manifestly, it is connected with the Sûrajbansî stock, and probably contains many of the degraded members of its numerous branches who, suppressing their individuality and professing only their relationship to the Sûrajbansî family, have gradually formed themselves into a new and separate Rajpoot tribe.

Members of the tribe are found in Benares, and in many other places in these Provinces. Several thousands are located in Gorakhpûr and Fathpûr. In some districts, such as Jaunpûr, Azimgarh, and Allahabad, it numbers only a few families. Altogether, it is not a numerous tribe. The Sûrajbansîs are of the Sâvaran *gotra* or order. An influential community of this tribe is settled in Oudh, and has the privilege of sending three representative *taluqdars,* or large landholders, to the Viceroy's Durbar.

Chandrabansî.

Properly the Lunar Race, from "Chandra," the Moon, and 'bans," race, yet in reality, as here used, meaning a separate and subordinate tribe of Rajpoots sprung originally from the great Chandrabansî family.

The tribe is somewhat largely represented in Dehra Dûn, where it numbers about thirty thousand individuals. It is in considerable force also in the district of Fathpûr. Benares, Allahabad, and other districts, likewise, have small communities of this tribe. They are of the Sânkrat *gotra* or order.

Sombansî.

The Sombansî Rajpoots properly comprise the whole of the Lunar Race. From some unexplained cause, however, instead of being a generic term denoting a number of tribes, it has come to represent only one tribe. Moreover, it is a singular phenomenon that there is a special Sonbansî tribe and also a special

(*a*) Supplemental Glossary, Vol. I., p. 57.

Chandrabansî tribe, although Som and Chandra have precisely the same meaning, that is, the 'Moon.' There must be some great anomaly in such tribes.

The Sombansîs are not numerous, nor are they found in many places. There are about two thousand Sombansîs in the Cawnpûr district, and the same in Jaunpûr. In the Azimgarh district also there are upwards of a hundred families. A small number reside in Benares. Some are traders; others are servants.

The Sombansîs of Saidpûr, in the Ghazipûr district, occupy four villages, named Kutgurra, Jîwar, Tûrna, and Jânî Chak. They came originally from Partâbgurh in Oudh, under Raja Jotik Deo and Motik Deo. The tribe once held possession of the Masaun Fort, which, judging from the extensive artificial mound on which it stood, must have been of considerable dimensions.

This tribe has colonies at Sândipâli, in Gorakhpûr, and also in Banauda, in the province of Oudh. The Sombansîs of Oudh are of sufficient importance to send two representative chiefs to the Governor General's Durbar. The Sombansîs, according to one authority which I have consulted, are of the Sânkrat *gotra*, and according to another, of the Byâg *gotra*. As both are good native authorities in Benares, I am unable to decide which is the correct statement.

Nâgbansî.

These Rajpoots are traditionally descended from the Serpent Race of early Hindu history. At the head of the race stands the famous Raja Takshak, who probably was a real personage. In the period preceding that when Buddhism became the dominant faith in India, and coeval with the period when Greece extended her dominions to the banks of the Indus, the Serpent Kings were possessed of great power in the country, and continued to hold their authority during several generations. Nâga and Takshak have the same meaning in Sanskrit; and in the early heroic period of Indian history both refer to the Serpent Race. It is not yet settled, and perhaps will never be, what relation subsisted between the Serpent Race and the aboriginal races of the country. It has been conjectured, that the Takshaks, or Nâgbansis, are of Scythian origin, and invaded India under their leader Shesnâg about six or seven centuries before the Christian era. If this be so, then the Nâgbansîs of the present day, if they are true descendants of the Serpent Tribe, and there is no reason, so far as I know, to doubt it, are not properly a Hindu tribe at all; and exhibit the anomaly of a strange and alien race being incorporated in the great Hindu family, and, while retaining their distinctiveness and historical associations, being permitted to rank among the highest castes. The Nâgbansîs are regarded as genuine Rajpoots.

Another interesting question connected with the Serpent Race in ancient Hindu annals is, to what extent the snake worship which they practised affected Hinduism. There is not the smallest ground for supposing that in the very earliest Hindu epochs the Aryan immigrants worshipped the snake; yet it is quite certain that long before the Christian era some of the great Hindu sects had introduced the worship into their religious ceremonies, and that, at the present day, all Hindu sects, without exception, pay divine homage to the snake. In a work of a purely practical character it would be out of place to enter upon a lengthened disquisition on a subject of this nature. I shall content myself by merely stating the belief, that the Aryans received their snake worship from the aboriginal races, probably at a time when they were in political subordination to them.

Various communities in India are designated after the Nâga or snake. Several Nâga or Serpent Tribes are found among the hills to the south of Assam. There is also a class of Hindu mendicants scattered about the country who call themselves Nâgas, that is, belonging to the Serpent Race. In our judgment, there is every likelihood that all these Nâga or Serpent Tribes, including the Nâgbansî Rajpoots, were primarily connected with each other. This conjecture cannot be established by historical records, yet a careful comparison of the peculiar social customs which they practise would go far to settle the question of its validity.

A few families of the Nâgbansî tribe reside in Benares, chiefly in the Râmâpûra quarter of the city, where they have been for as many as five or six generations past, having come originally from Chotâ Nâgpûr, in which province the tribe is found in considerable strength. The head of the Nâgbansîs of Benares is Sankar Khan Datt Singh, a landowner of wealth and influence. Colonies of the tribe are found at Sultânpûr, a few miles from that city in the direction of Chunâr. The Nâgbansîs of Benares and its neighbourhood belong to the Vatsa *gotra*.

In the Census Returns of the North Western Provinces for 1865, no account whatever is taken of this class of Rajpoots.

The Nâgbansîs are numerous in the district of Gorakhpûr, some of whom, says Buchanan, call themselves by this name, while others assume the name of Vayâsa, a town between Lucknow and the Ganges, although acknowledging themselves to be Nâgbansîs. He also states that the Nâgbansî Rajpoots are remnants of the aboriginal Cherûs, 'once the kings of at least the Gangetic provinces' (*a*).

Kânpûriya.

A small tribe of Rajpoots in the district of Benares, sprung from Cawnpûr, whence it derives its appellation of Kânpûriya. Families also of the same tribe are found in other districts, such as those of Jaunpûr and Allahabâd, and of Cawnpûr itself. The Kânpûriyas are powerful and wealthy Rajpoots in the Province of Oudh. No fewer than fifteen chiefs have the right and privilege of sitting in the Viceroy's Durbar as representatives of the tribe.

Janûtûrwâ.

A small community of Rajpoots of this name inhabit the town of Gangâpûr, in the Benares district. The town is famous for its connexion with the family of the Maharaja of Benares.

Sonak.

A Rajpoot tribe long established in the Bhadohî *pargannah* of the district of Mirzapûr. A few families also are met with in the neighbouring district of Jaunpûr. The tribe is small.

Tashaiya.

A tribe of Rajpoots inhabiting the district of Allahabad, respecting whom Mr. G. Ricketts remarks as follows. In *pargannah* Meh there is a caste called 'Tussaiyah,' whose cognomen is susceptible of explanation. They were Kshatriyas of Etawah; and tradition has it that the founder of this clan was sent by Timûr Shâh to take possession of a tract of country from the Bhars. This was done; and the name Tussaiyah is a corruption of 'Teg Shahiyah,' the sword of the king, explanatory alike of the nature of the mission and its originator' (*b*).

Sarwar or Surwâr.

A tribe of Rajpoots inhabiting the districts of Jaunpûr and Mirzapûr, where they are met with in considerable numbers. A few likewise are found

(*a*) Buchanan's Eastern India, Vol. II., p. 460.

(*b*) Report of the Census of the North-Western Provinces for 1865, App. p. 129.

in the village of Surwân, Benares, and also in Azimgarh, and even as far as Cawnpûr. I am unable to give any information respecting the origin of the tribe. It is worthy of remark, that there is a great similarity between the name of this race of Rajpoots and that of the Sarwaria branch of the Kanoujiya Brahmans, sprung from the Sarwar lands beyond the Sarju. A similarity of this nature, however, amounting even to an exact correspondence, is frequently found subsisting between Brahmans and Rajpoots. Both races have their Gautams, their Bhûînhârs, their Kinwârs, and likewise have the same *gotras*, thereby professing to be descended from the same *rishis*, or sages of primitive Hinduism. The Sarwars belong to the Garg *gotra*.

Ujain.

This tribe has the tradition of being descended from Raja Bhoj. A few families are in Benares, where they hold the position of *zamindars*. Some however, are engaged in trade, and in other ways. There is a considerable community of the Ujain Rajpoots in the district of Cawnpûr. Several clans are found also in Farakhabâd and Azimgarh; and a small number of families in Gorakhpûr.

The Ujainîs have been for many generations settled at Sasserâm and Hussainpûr. They are of the Sâvaran *gotra* or order.

Dhanawast.

A tribe not found in the district of Benares, yet inhabiting certain tracts in the neighbouring district of Jaunpûr, where it is found in considerable strength. According to the Census Returns of 1865, there were in that year upwards of six thousand members of the tribe in that district alone. There were also a few families in the adjoining district of Azimgarh. The tribe is called Dhusat as well as Dhanawast. It is of the Kasyap *gotra* or order.

Chaupata Khambh.

A tribe claiming to be Rajpoots found in the city of Benares. Its numbers are few; these are, for the most part, engaged in the manufacture of fine wire used in the frames in which cloth of various descriptions is woven. Some families are devoted to trade.

The tribe is very strong in the district of Jaunpûr, where it numbers upwards of fifteen thousand individuals. A few families are also found in the neighbouring district of Azimgarh.

The tradition of the Chaupata Khambhis is, that two Brahmans, named Baldeo and Kuldeo, came from Sarwar, beyond the Ghogra, and settled down in the Patkholi village of the Kirakat *pargannah*, in the district of Jaunpûr. It appears that Raja Jai Chand, of the Lunar Race of Rajpoots, gave his daughter in marriage to Baldeo, which circumstance was a source of great vexation to Kuldeo, who determined to show his indignation by setting up a pillar, or *khambh*, as a sign that Baldeo's family had become degenerate. The descendants of Baldeo consequently received their designation from the pillar, and were called Chaupat Khambhs (*a*).

Bhanwag.

A class of Rajpoots numbering from fifty to a hundred families, holding the position of *zamindars*, or landholders, in the district of Benares. The tribe is very numerous in the neighbouring district of Jaunpûr, where nearly a thousand families, or between four and five thousand members of the tribe, are located. It bears the appellation of Bhanwa as well as Bhanwag. There is a colony of the tribe at Saidpûr Bhitri in the Ghazipûr district.

Niniarwâr.

This tribe is of the Sombansî or Lunar Race of Rajpoots. Its tradition is, that, in former times, it came from Delhi and settled in Partâbgarh, in Oudh, whence it extended itself to Ghazipûr, in which district, at the present day, the tribe is found located in four villages.

Nanwag.

A large and important tribe in the district of Jaunpûr, where it numbered at the last Census between twenty and thirty thousand persons. There are colonies of the tribe amounting to a hundred families, or more, in each of the districts of Allahabad, Mirzapûr, and Benares. A small number also is found in Azimgarh (*b*). In Benares the Nanwags are landholders. At their head is Sangrâm Singh, a *zamindar* of influence and position. The Nanwags appear to have entered the Bhadohî *Pargannah* of the Mirzapûr district, and to have

(*a*) Report of the Census of the North-Western Provinces for 1865, Vol. I., p. 115.
(*b*) *Ibid*, Vol. II., p. 10.

settled there with the sanction of Raja Balwant Singh, head of the Benares family, in the middle of the last century.

The tribe is of the Kasyap *gotra.*

Karamwâr.

A few members of this tribe, consisting of some four or five families, inhabit the Benares district, where they are *zamindars,* or landholders. Several hundred families are located in the Azimgarh district. The tribe belongs to the Bhârgau *gotra* or order.

Sangjal.

An insignificant race in the Gorakhpûr district claiming to be of the Rajpoot stock. Its numbers are small. A small community of the tribe has established itself in the district of Azimgarh.

Surhaniya.

A numerous tribe in the Sagrî *Pargannah* of the Azimgarh district. Sâgar Rai, the common ancestor of the race, is traditionally regarded as having come from Purpachura, in the district of Fyzabad in Oudh, about three hundred years ago, and as having entered the service of the Raja of Azimgarh. Here a grandson of Sâgar Rai, by name Dhandi Rai, had an opportunity of distinguishing himself. A notorious bandit was at that time committing great depredations in the district, and no effort of the Raja was sufficient to check him. Dhandi Rai obtaining the permission of the Raja, made a gallant attack upon the bandit, captured, and killed him. In testimony of his gratitude, the Raja presented Dhandi Rai with an extensive estate of fourteen miles in circumference, now known as the Taluqa Nainijaur (*a*).

Palwâr or Paliwâr.

A tribe found in considerable numbers in several districts to the east of Allahabad. The name is apparently the same as that of the Paliwâl Banyas, the *l* and *r* being interchangeable. But I suppose the similarity is accidental. The Paliwâr Rajpoots have colonies in the five districts of Benares, Mirzapûr, Jaunpûr, Azimgarh, and Gorakhpûr. In Azimgarh, they numbered at the

(*a*) Report of the Census of the North-Western Provinces for 1865, Vol. II., Appendix B., p. 112.

last Census upwards of thirteen thousand persons. In Benares the community is very small.

The origin of the tribe is said to be as follows. Tradition states that a man named Patrâj, of the Sombansî tribe of Rajpoots, migrated from the neighbourhood of Delhi to the village of Bandîpûr, in the Fyzabad district, where he made himself famous by his conflicts with the Râj Bhars, with whom he successfully fought, and whom he defrauded of their estates. He had four wives of four different castes, namely Rajpoot, Ahîr, Bhar, and another unmentioned. Their descendants were called Palwâlâ,—the name of the father, afterwards contracted to Palwâl,—Ahiriniya, Bhariniya, and Dyniya (*a*).

Singhel or Singali.

A tribe of Rajpoots found exclusively in the Azimgarh district, where it numbers about a thousand families. The Singhels are of the Kasyap *gotra.*

Patîli.

A tribe peculiar to Benares, where it numbers a few hundred families. I am not aware that it is found in any other district.

Hardwâs.

A small community of Rajpoots residing in the city of Benares, engaged in trade or as servants. They are of the Bhâraddwâj *gotra.* Some families also of this tribe are found at Deoganw, in the Azimgarh district, and at Salîmpûr Majhauli, in the Gorakhpûr district.

(*a*) Report of the Census of the North-Western Provinces for 1865, Vol. II., pp. 112, 113.

CHAPTER XII.

THE JAT AND GUJAR TRIBES.

Jât.

It would be out of place to venture on a discussion respecting the origin of this numerous and exceedingly interesting tribe. This will be found elsewhere, especially in Colonel Tod's Rajasthan. Although the Jâts are included among the thirty-six royal tribes of Rajpoots, yet they are not commonly spoken of as Rajpoots, nor do they intermarry with other tribes. There is very good reason, however, for the belief that alliances have been at times formed between them and other Rajpoots. Much curious speculation has been expended on the origin of the Jâts, which it is not the object of this work to discuss, much less to augment.

The race is variously designated. It is called Yati, Get, Jaut, Jhat, Jit, Jat, and Jât. It is very numerous in the Panjab and Râjputâna, and in both places is known as Jit. On the Jumna and Ganges, and in the North Western Provinces generally, the tribe bears the name of Jât. Its traditions state that its-ancient home was to the west of the Indus.

Sir Henry Elliot affirms, that in these Provinces the tribe has two great divisions, "the Dhe and the Hele of the Doâb, or Pachhâde and Deswâle of Rohilkhand and Delhi. The former (the Dhe and Pachhâde) are a later swarm from that teeming hive of nations which has been winging its way from the North West from time immemorial."

The Maharaja of Bhartpûr is the most distinguished member of the Jât tribe in these Provinces.

The Jâts are very numerous in the Muzaffarnagar district, where they have a great many sub-divisions. Some have come thither from the Panjab at a comparatively recent period, while others have been there for a very long time. The Salaklain and Balain Jâts were reputed to have once held a *chaurâsi* of (or eighty-four) villages on the western side of the district. The Balains are a very extensive sub-division of the Jâts.

They are the most numerous of all the land-owning tribes in Meerut, and look upon Hariâna and Râjputâna as the countries whence their forefathers originally came. " They gained their first footing," says Mr. W. A. Forbes, the late Collector of Meerut," in the Chaprauli and Barot *pargannahs* of the Meerut district, pushing out before them the Taga occupants of the soil; and thence they spread themselves, though in less compact colonies, over the whole district. The Jâts, as a caste, are again sub-divided amongst themselves into distinct families or tribes, which, in many respects, particularly as regards marriage, hold aloof from each other. There are the Hela Jâts, the Dehta, the Sulkhan, and the Des or Desî Jâts, all distinct from each other, and recognizing some distinguishing customs. The latter, or Desî tribe, are found in the greatest numbers. As agriculturists they are the very best farmers and the most industrious of all the castes in these Provinces, patient and longsuffering as tax-payers, quiet and peace-loving generally as subjects, but, like their parent stock, the Rajpoots, easily roused to avenge a fancied wrong, or in obedience to their chieftain's call" (*a*).

The Jâts of Bulandshahr came from Hariâna, and first of all were cultivators of the soil, but afterwards, on Raja Suraj Mull acquiring possession of the Doâb, embraced the opportunity of seizing the villages which they now occupy. They have added the estate of Kocheswar. At the last Census they held as many as one hundred and ninety-five villages in that district alone (*b*).

In Aligarh the Jâts have several clans as follows:—

1. Thâkurailai. These have a temple at Karaolî. They are descended from Raja Suraj Mull, and his followers :
2. Thenwâ.
3. Agâ.
4. Sinsinwar.
5. Khandia.

(3–5: These three clans are from the same ancestor.)

6. Nau Nâga. These are said to have sprung from Rajpoots of the Lunar Race. They have been in the district for a very long period (*c*).

The Jâts were among the earliest known inhabitants of the district of Shâhjahânpûr. Nearly one half of the Hindu population of the Mathurâ district consists of members of this tribe. Formerly, they were divided here, as

(*a*) Report of the Census of the North-Western Provinces for 1865, App. B., Mr. W. A. Forbes' Memorandum, p. 12.

(*b*) *Ibid*, Mr. G. H. Lawrence's Memorandum, p. 21.

(*c*) Mr. Cline's Memorandum, p. 27.

elsewhere, into two branches, Deswâla and Pachâde, the latter having come into that part of the country at a comparatively recent period; but of late years they have blended together.

Most of the Jât clans, it is said, are represented in the district of Agra, and are most conspicuous in the *pargannahs* of Pharrab, Khandaulî, and Ferozabâd. They have been in those parts for several centuries, and are supposed to have come thither from Aligarh, Mathurâ, and Bhartpûr. A few are found in the district of Jhânsî, in Bundelkhand.

A clan of Jâts known by the term Aolâniya occupies about forty villages in Panipat Bângar, who are in reality Gatwâras. "Although Hindus, they claim the title of Malik, which, they say, was bestowed upon them by a certain king as a token of their superiority to their brethren." Another clan, termed Aûdî and Hûdî indiscriminately, holds twenty villages in the same place, and twenty more in Sonîpat Bângar (*a*).

The Bagrîs also, between Hariâna and the Ghâgrâ, are said to be Jâts; but there is considerable doubt respecting them. Some suppose that they are aborigines, an opinion held by Colonel Tod. The term Bagrî, however, is used as a designation of clans connected with various tribes (*b*). Bâgar, says Sir H. Elliot, is likewise the name of a considerable tract in Mâlwâ, the inhabitants of which are called Bagrî. This circumstance gives a clue, perhaps, to the origin of the entire family.

The Korîs are an extensive clan of Jâts in the country districts around Agra. The Dahiyas are in Rohtak, Kharkhanda, Mandauthî, Panipat, and Sonîpat Bangar. The Dalâls occupy villages also in Rohtak. The Jâglâîns are proprietors of a few villages in Panipat Bangar. The Jâkhars are a clan of the same tribe (*c*). The Jatrânîs are found in Rohilkhand and Delhi.

Gûjar.

This is a very numerous tribe in certain districts of the North-Western Provinces, and is chiefly addicted to agricultural pursuits. In the Muzaffarnagar district they have the tradition that their great ancestor on the father's side was a Rajpoot, but they are by no means certain of their ancestor on the mother's side. Some say that she was a Vaisya; others, that she was a Sudra;

(*a*) Elliot's Glossary, Vol. I., p. 8.

(*b*) *Ibid*, p. 9.

(*c*) *Ibid*, pp, 88, 130.

and others still, that she was even a Chamâr. The probability perhaps is that the Gûjars of those parts are the offspring of intermarriages between Rajpoots and women of their own and other tribes. The Kalsan Gûjars of the Shamlî Tahsil of that district state that they are descended from Kalsa, a Rajpoot chief, who settled at Kaivânâ nearly seven hundred years ago. Many of the clan have become Mahomedans.

The Supplemental Glossary has some interesting and valuable observations on this tribe. It states that they have given names not only to Gujerât in Western India, but also to Gujerât and Gujrânwâlâ in the Panjab. The writer seems to think that they are partly of Rajpoot blood, and partly of the blood of other castes. In the last century the present district of Sahâranpûr was called Gujerât, and the threefold division of that tract of those days is still usually adopted by the people. According to the enumeration of the Glossary, the tribe consisted of eighty-four clans; but this is well-known to be a conventional number amongst the natives of India. General Cunningham has some singular speculations concerning the Gûjars, whom he considers to be of Tartar origin (*a*).

In his Memorandum on the Castes of Meerut, Mr. W. A. Forbes gives his opinion that the Gûjars have sprung from the same root as the Jâts. "It is quite uncertain," he states, "when or in what manner they came into this part of the country. The prevalent idea is that they arrived before the Jâts. They are of unsettled habits, and much given to cattle-stealing and plunder, rarely proving themselves good farmers, but showing many of the instincts of a half civilized nomad tribe. We find them generally holding lands along the borders of the rivers Jumna, Ganges, and the Hindun, where the grass jungles, and rough uncultivated lands, offer attractions to them for grazing their herds of cattle. Their legends point to Gujerât as the land whence they first came" (*b*).

According to Mr. G. H. Lawrence, the Gûjars are divided into three clans, as follows:

1 Bhatti Gûjars.
2 Nâgar Gûjars.
3 Hindwânsa Gûjars.

The Bhatti Gûjars, he says, are descended from Rao Kosal, a Bhatti Rajpoot; the Nâgar Gûjars, from Raja Nâg, of the Tomara tribe; and the

(*a*) Elliot's Glossary, Vol. I., pp. 99, 101.

(*b*) Report of the Census of the North-Western Provinces for 1865, Memorandum on the Castes of Meerut by Mr. W. A. Forbes, pp. 13, 14.

Hindwânsa Gûjars, from an alliance between the Ponwar Rajpoots and the Nâgar Gûjars. Probably these three clans of Gûjars are restricted to the Bulandshahr district, of which Mr. Lawrence was the Collector and Magistrate. His opinion is, that the race came originally from Gujerât (*a*). The Bhatti Gûjars have a few families in Benares.

The Gûjars of Bijnour sometimes pretend to be degraded Rajpoots and sometimes Ahîrs. They came into that district from the Upper Doâb about one hundred years ago. This tribe seems to have been one of the earliest recorded races inhabiting the district of Shâhjahânpûr, with whom were associated Jâts and Ahirs. The Gûjars of Farakhabâd came thither from Gurmukteswar. The Jâttis, and Jhinjars, and Jinhars, are said to be clans of this tribe.

The tribe is found in the Etah district, and its principal families are Dhantolî, Hurduî, and Bâbai; but none are of any note, or are large land-holders. There are several thousands of Gûjars in Jhânsî, where they have been, according to their own traditions, for the last six hundred years, having come originally from the west. One of their chiefs, Bishan Singh, was the founder of the present small State of Sampthar.

The Bhûrtiyas of Mirzapûr are generally believed to be Gûjars, who have changed their name to that which they now bear.

A clan of this tribe, known by the name of Batâr, and supposed to occupy fifty-two villages, is found in Gangoh and Lakhnauti, in the district of Sahâranpûr, and also in Bijnour. The Chamâîn is another clan in the possession of twelve villages in Panipat Bangar (*b*). Mr. Beames states, on the authority of Dixon's Mairwâra, that a Chandela branch of the Gûjars inhabits the Mairwâra country (*c*).

(*a*) Report of the Census of the North-Western Provinces for 1865, Memorandum on the Castes of Bulandshahr, by Mr. G. H. Lawrence, pp. 21, 22.

(*b*) Supplemental Glossary, Vol. I., p. 71.

(*c*) *Ibid*, p. 76.

CHAPTER XIII.

THE DONWAR, LAUTAMIA, KAKAN, SUKALBANS, KULHAN, MAHROR, RAWAT, TEHA, CHAKWAIN, RORA, BAHERIYA, AND KHASIYA TRIBES.

Donwâr.

THIS tribe is found in considerable numbers in the districts of Mirzapûr, Azimgarh, and Jaunpûr: a few also reside in Gorakhpûr. Sir H. Elliot regards this clan as of mixed Brahman and Rajpoot descent, from the circumstance, apparently, that some of them are called Rajpoots, and others Bhûinhârs, as though the latter were necessarily a distinct race from the former, whereas Bhûinhârs may be Rajpoots, or may be Brahmans. He also says, that the Donwârs were once strong enough "to establish a principality on the Kosi in Western Tirhût; and there are several monuments still existing in that neighbourhood which attest the power of the Donwâr Raja, Karnâ Deo" (*a*).

Dr. W. Oldham discerns a marked difference between the Donwâr Rajpoots and the Donwâr Bhûinhârs of the Ghazipûr district. The former are of a dark complexion, and have not Aryan features, while the latter, it would seem, are both of Aryan complexion and feature. It is quite possible that the Rajpoots may have aboriginal blood in their veins; yet, if so, it is curious that they have retained no tradition on the subject.

The Donwâr Rajpoots occupy various places in the Ghazipûr district. In the Garhâ *pargannah*, they have five large villages; in Saidpûr, twelve villages; and are in considerable force in the Ghazipûr *pargannah;* while others still are found in the *pargannahs* of Cawnpûr, Bahariabâd, and Baliah. These last 'own all rights of fishery and of other spontaneous products of the great Surâhâ Lake' (*b*).

The tribe belongs to the Bhâraddwâj *gotra* or order.

(*a*) Elliot's Supplemental Glossary, Vol. I.; p. 86.
(*b*) Memoir of the Ghazipûr District, p. 65.

Lautamia.

This clan of Rajpoots was once in possession of the Doâbî *pargannah*, in the Ghazipûr district. Although they have, for the most part, lost the proprietorship of this tract, which has passed into the hands of the wealthy and influential Raja of Domraon, yet they continue to inhabit the soil in large numbers. They occupy many villages, which they have taken on lease from the Raja. As the land is peculiarly productive, not a few of the people are rich.

"They are," says Dr. Oldham, "a sturdy, independent race, and addicted to feuds and affrays of a serious character. Their origin is doubtful; and they are thought to rank very low amongst Rajpoots. Many of them are closely associated with the organized gangs of Dosâdh robbers, for whom this *pargannah* is famous. Not long since an immense amount of valuable Panjab and Cashmere cloths was recovered from the house of a Lautamia, of great apparent respectability, the nephew of a Subahdâr in the army. Beriah, the chief village of the Lautamias, contains a population of 6,766" (*a*).

Kâkan.

Some members of this small clan are settled in the Azimgarh district. They state that their ancestors were originally inhabitants of Gujerât. Others are found in the Shâdîabâd *pargannah*, of the Ghazipûr district, where they are numerous, although their existence seems not to have been known to the compilers of the Census Report of 1865. At the Permanent Settlement, fifty-eight estates were assigned to them. They have a tradition that, about fifteen generations back, Ratan Rai, the founder of the clan, "came from Mhowaldamau, expelled the Bhars, and took possession of the country which they now hold" (*b*).

The Kâkans of Azimgarh assert that Mor Bhatt, the founder of the clan in that district, first settled in the Nathûpûr *pargannah*. From his four wives are descended the four families now found in the district, of which the most numerous is the last. They are as follows (*c*):

1. Brahman Bayâsî.
2. Bais Kshatriya.
3. Lakhauncha.
4. Mall.

The Kâkans are of the Gaurî *gotra* or order.

(*a*) Memoir of the Ghazipûr District, p. 59.
(*b*) *Ibid*, Part I., p. 62.
(*c*) Census of the North-Western Provinces for 1865, Vol. I., Appendix B., p. 112.

Sûkalbans.

This clan of Rajpoots is found in the Ghazipûr district, in the heart of the Zamânîah *pargannah*, where it is in possession of three *taluqas* or large estates. Nawal, one of their principal villages, contains upwards of five thousand inhabitants. They are, however, fast being impoverished by Benares bankers and Ghazipûr lawyers (*a*).

Kulhan or Kulhans.

This clan of Rajpoots is found in Gorakhpûr. It originally came from the west, under the two chiefs Udai Râj Singh and Akhai Râj Singh, who received a grant of land in that district from the Emperor of Delhi. When Oudh became independent of the Delhi Emperors, Raja Jai Singh was at the head of the tribe; and Raja Jubraj Singh, the third in descent from him, was at its head when the country fell into the hands of the English Government. The Raja of Mastî is its present representative. The tribe is scattered over several *pargannahs*. In Rasulpûr Ghaus, they hold large estates, where the chiefs of the clan are styled Babus of Chaukhara, and are said to be descended from former Rajas of that territory. A considerable colony of Kulhans inhabits the Province of Oudh. They have the privilege of sending eight chiefs to the Governor-General's Durbar.

Mahror or Mahrawar.

This is said to be a spurious clan of Rajpoots of the district of Unao in Oudh. They were originally palanquin-bearers, called Kahâr or Mahra, in the service of Raja Tilakchand, the head of the Bais Rajpoots of Baiswâra. On occasion of his troops being suddenly seized with panic while fighting with the Malhiabâd Pathans, he himself was wounded, and would have fallen into the hands of the enemy, but for the intrepidity of his palanquin-bearers, who fought their way bravely until they conveyed him to a place of safety. The Raja, grateful for their gallant conduct, thereupon elevated them to the rank of Rajpoots, and bestowed upon them a dozen villages. They have since greatly increased, and have been able to add other villages to their estate. Moreover, their position as Rajpoots is recognized by other tribes, which intermarry freely with them (*b*). They are of the Kausik and Vatsa *gotras*, or orders, of Rajpoots.

(*a*) Dr. W. Oldham's Statistical Memoir of the Ghazipûr District, Part I., pp. 65, 66.

(*b*) Mr. C. A. Elliott's Chronicles of Oonao, p. 62.

The *Pargannahs* of Rasulâbâd and Asîwan, in the same district, are, says Mr. Elliott, " full of a caste called Gamhelas, who profess to be descended from the Mahrors, but to be illegitimate, an Ahîr woman having been their ancestor. The Mahrors, too, agree in this story ; but the Gamhelas are so enormously numerous, that it is difficult to conceive that they should have all descended in so short a time from a single pair. They are found in great numbers in Rohilkhand, and are considered the best cultivating class in these parts. They do not wear the sacred cord, or take the title of Singh ; and marry solely among each other" (*a*).

A few members of this tribe are settled in Benares, some of whom are zemindars, or proprietors of land, and others are engaged in trade. Small communities of Mahrors are met with in the widely separated districts of Azimgarh and Morâdabâd. They have a colony also in Gorakhpûr, where they are regarded as low-born Rajpoots.

The tribe is known by the terms Madawar and Mahrawar, as well as by that of Mahror.

Rawat.

This clan, like the Mahrors, belongs to the district of Unao, in Oudh. It is commonly believed that they are descended from an illegitimate progeny of Raja Tilakchand, of Baiswârâ. Other accounts, however, of their origin are given. Their own statement is, that they are genuine Baises. The conclusion arrived at by Mr. C. A. Elliott is, that they are illegitimate descendants of Tilakchand by an Ahîr woman.

It is said that Raja Tilakchand gave them the *Pargannah* of Harha, called also Ratânâ, or Rawatânâ, after them. They only possess now three out of the twelve portions into which the pargannah is divided. Their own account is, that they were robbed of their possessions by an aboriginal tribe of Sonârs, who rose so fiercely upon them that they almost destroyed their race. Full revenge was taken by a survivor, Binay Singh, who, by the aid of a force from Delhi, attacked the Sonârs at night while they were in a state of intoxication, and cut to pieces the whole clan. The sovereignty over the entire *Pargannah* of Harha was regained by Dalnârain Singh, about the year 1700, A. D., and embraced also a portion of the *Pargannah* of Unao, which they seized from the Sayads. But Dalnârain Singh, who received the title of Chîpî Khân, was not wise in his

(*a*) Mr. C. A. Elliott's Chronicles of Oonao, pp. 62, 63.

generation, for he divided his property equally between the children of his two wives. This caused a deadly quarrel, which ended in his being killed by his eldest son. On account of the confusion in the family, Safdar Jang, the Nawab of Oudh, determined to demand a considerable increase of revenue from the brothers, which being refused, they were besieged in their Fort at Bihtar for a long time. For forty years they were kept out of possession of their estates, and regained them only in the year 1780 (*a*).

The Rawats are also found in the district of Fathpûr. The head of the clan, a few years ago, was Thâkur Lâl Sâh of Baijânt.

Teha.

A colony of this tribe, numbering a hundred families, or between five and six hundred persons, is found in the Azimgarh district. I am not aware that it is met with elsewhere.

Chakrwâin.

An insignificant clan of Rajpoots, in the Ghazipûr district, where they seem to be confined to the Kopâchit *Pargannah.*

Rora.

This tribe seems to exist in only two districts of these Provinces, one Benares, the other Sahâranpûr. In the former, its numbers are small, amounting to a few hundred souls. In the latter, however, the tribe has eight hundred or a thousand families. The Roras are engaged in trade. It is doubtful whether their claim to be regarded as Kshatriyas is well-founded. They speak of themselves as such ; and also make use of the terms Rora-khatri and Khatrirora.

Baheriya.

A small community of Rajpoots found at Chunâr, in the Mirzapûr district, and also at Ghisua, in the district of Jaunpûr.

Khasiya.

This is an extensive tribe of Rajpoots inhabiting the hill country of Garhwâl, Kumaon, and Dehra Dûn. Their right to the rank of Rajpoots is questioned by some Hindus. The main reason for this, I imagine, is, first of all,

(*a*) Mr. C. A. Elliott's Chronicles of Oonao, pp. 63, 65.

the fact of their long residence in these regions, and, secondly, because they have no tribal connexions in the plains. Thus Hindu immigrants and visitors of high caste from the plains, finding it difficult to account for their origin, and not being able to trace their relationship to themselves, have been too ready to throw suspicion on the genuineness of their birth.

That the tribe is very old, is manifest from the word which designates them, which is the ancient appellation of Kumaon, formerly called Khas-des, or the country of the Khas people. The singular circumstance, that they do not wear the sacred cord, and personally engage in agricultural labour, in both respects being unlike Rajpoots of the plains, is not a proof, as has been supposed, of their not being Rajpoots, but of the great simplicity and antiquity of their usages. The natives of Kumaon look upon the Khasiyas as the oldest inhabitants of the province. Nearly one half of the entire population of Garhwâl consists of them.

It is said that Dehra Dûn was peopled by the Khasiyas from Garhwâl, sent thither by the Raja of that Province. They have the titles among them of Rawat, Bisht Negî, Karaolî, and Raulior.

PART III.

MIXED CASTES AND TRIBES—VAISYAS, SUDRAS, AND OTHERS.

CHAPTER I.

ON THE SOCIAL AND POLITICAL RELATIONS OF THE VAISYAS AND SUDRAS. CEREMONIES AMONG THE SUDRA CASTES.

The relation of the Vaisya and Sudra castes to the genuine Aryan tribes, which entered India in the pre-Vedic era, and gradually established themselves in various parts of the country, has proved a fertile subject of controversy. That the Vaisyas were formerly chiefly engaged in rural pursuits seems certain and incontestible. If this were so, who and what were the Sudras? Were they a helot race, partly aboriginal, and partly not so? It would be out of place for the writer to enter the lists of disputation on these subjects in the present work. As a fact, the Vaisyas are now scarcely at all an agricultural people, while the Sudras have stepped into the position which they once occupied in the cultivation of the soil. At the same time, in the social and political revolutions which have at times passed over the country, the two great races of Vaisyas and Sudras have become so intimately blended that it is hard to point with precision to any leading distinction between them. All indeed that, for the most part, can be said respecting them, amounts to the statement merely, that certain castes are purer Vaisyas or purer Sudras than certain others. Here and there a Vaisya caste may be found with an irreproachable lineage for many generations. Yet it is hardly to be expected that any Vaisya caste should furnish satisfactory proof of its own caste-purity in ancient times. Their traditions trace back their history in some cases a few hundred years; but almost every instance is confined within the limits of the period of the Mahomedan conquest of India. Absence of proof, however, is in itself after all no positive evidence against the antiquity of any caste. It is therefore not improbable that a small number of Vaisya castes of great strictness in the observance of the rules of their order, may be descended from primitive Vaisya tribes with little or no intermingling with other castes.

In ancient Hindu periods the middle and lower castes were of no political weight or authority, and were not deemed worthy of consultation, or even of consideration, by the higher castes. And this, in the main, was their condition likewise under their Mahomedan conquerors. Under British rule, however, the relation of the castes has been radically changed. Their presumed impurity of blood, and inherent inferiority, owing, as imagined, to the operation of divine laws in creation, were sufficient to prevent their ever rising to an equal social and political position with either the Brahman or the Rajpoot, so long as these were able to retain the government of the country in their own hands. As races subject to the Mahomedan invaders, they were evidently too much despised for their ignorance and superstition, to venture for an instant to supplant the higher castes, especially as they had nothing to commend them to the good opinion of their rulers.

What was impossible under former administrations, is possible under English law, the fundamental principle of which is, that all men are equal. It has taken a century for this fundamental principle to be understood by the natives of India, so absolutely were they under the dominion of caste prejudice and tyranny; and even now it is nowhere comprehended with that clearness and exactness of perception with which an Englishman regards it, while in many places it fails to exert any influence at all. In towns and cities, however, and over a considerable extent of country around them, the influence of English law is more or less strongly felt. It is aided by that spirit of our Indian rulers which prompts them to select the persons best fitted for the offices in their disposal, irrespective of caste, or rank, or anything else. It is sustained and strengthened by the sound education offered to the natives of every rank through the medium of colleges and schools. This influence is the vitalizing power of Englishmen themselves, is the element in which they live and breathe, is that subtle spirit which is seen in all their movements, and reflects itself from them upon the natives in every direction. Add to this the Christian faith which consciously or unconsciously forms the web and the woof of British legislation, whether in England or in India, and which strives to elevate the depressed, to abolish ignorance, and to generate the desire for freedom in every breast, and we have in these collective forces an energy of irresistible potency in moving and transforming the masses of India.

The result is a national revolution and reformation. The religious aspect of the change I pass over in this place. Its social and political import, however, in a work of this nature, demands some consideration. It is plain, to any person of reflection, that the old landmarks separating class from class by impassable barriers, and preserving all for ages in certain relative positions, no longer exist in their former intensity. The dominant Brahman and Rajpoot tribes have lost all their authority and much of their influence. The Sudra no longer thinks it a sin to read; on the contrary, he conceives it possible to become as wise as the Brahman, and does not hesitate to endeavour to surpass him. The Sudra and the Vaisya aim at the highest official posts, and find themselves elected often over the heads of high caste applicants, whom they are acute enough to perceive to be inferior to themselves. The Brahman looks on with amazement at the subversion of his order and the destruction of his interests.

The fairness of a system which makes all castes equal in the eye of the law, and gives them the same chance of success, is transparent. Yet in India it presents itself to the people as a new and strange idea, the meaning and bearing of which they are, as just remarked, unable fully to grasp. Even in England the upper classes are hardly accustomed to the abandonment of privilege, and look upon every attempt to curtail it with disfavour and suspicion. Caste prejudice in India may be said to be immeasurably stronger than the prejudice of rank among the aristocracy of England. Each of these classes watches over its special interests with a jealous eye. The two differ radically in this, that the English nobility are politically still very powerful, and therefore can defend their order when assailed. The higher castes of India, on the contrary, though even more tenacious of the rights of their order, which are associated in their minds with a divine sanction, are conscious at once of their utter powerlessness and political insignificance. For the loss they have thus sustained, nothing, in their judgment, counterbalances. Superior education, a just and equitable Government, the multiplication of the comforts of life, increased national prosperity, good roads and bridges, railroads, telegraphs, and so forth, are no sufficient compensation for this loss.

Nevertheless, the Hindus, gentle and pliable, have become reconciled to the change of system, and are endeavouring to make the best of their altered circumstances. The higher castes, too, in the main, submit themselves calmly to it. They are wise enough to perceive the manifold benefits which they secure from British rule; and they reflect also, that the same advantages were not possessed by their forefathers under Mahomedan sway.

This subject has also a special relation to the Mahomedan population of India. The elevation of the middle and lower classes has not merely been prejudicial to higher caste Hindus, but also to Mahomedans. If the higher castes have suffered much by the diminution of their authority during the last century of British administration, it is indisputable that the Mahomedans have suffered more, inasmuch as, while the former have been eager to reap the fruits of such administration, the latter have been, for the most part, inattentive to them. They have, moreover, felt their position all the more keenly, from the circumstance that they themselves were the immediate predecessors of the British in the government of the country. The fault lies chiefly with the Mahomedans, however, for they have pertinaciously resisted the friendly overtures of their rulers in many ways. At the same time, greater consideration might have been shown to them, whereby their good-will would have been more effectually courted, and perhaps secured, without in the least infringing on the evenhandedness of the British Government.

The phenomenon is striking, that British rule in India tends to elevate the masses, to depress the aristocracy, to make the middle class powerful, and to introduce uniformity into all grades of native society. This general action of the Government contrasts somewhat abruptly with the distribution of personal honours and distinctions to deserving persons, and with the special attention paid to natives of the upper ranks on great public occasions.

The Vaisyas and higher Sudras are to India much like what the middle class is to England. Public opinion, such as it is, is more moulded and influenced by them than by any of the other Hindu tribes. Add to them the Kayasths, or great Writer Caste, who occupy a position socially at the head of the Sudras, or between them and the Vaisyas, and are an exceedingly intelligent and enterprising people, and you have a middle class, eager, restless, persevering, self-willed, prosperous, and powerful. They are, on the whole, better educated even than the Brahmans, whose intellects, for the most part, only receive a one-sided training. They have broader, and consequently sounder views, on most questions of general interest than the twice-born, although they are far inferior to them in mental subtlety and keenness. In understanding and influence, they are considerably superior to the Kshatriya or Rajpoot caste, the members of which occupy a position undoubtedly of great social dignity, and naturally, I dare say, are as talented as the Vaisyas ; but they lack the vast opportunities for calling forth their ability, which the latter possess. The Rajpoot caste has supplied India with Rajas and warriors during many generations. The native soldiers of the Indian Government are still drawn largely from this tribe ; but the occupation of a soldier, although very honourable in India, much more so than in England, fails to impart to the caste that social and political power exerted by these other castes. And in regard to the Rajas, while it is still the fact that they are mostly Rajpoots or Kshatriyas, nevertheless they may be reckoned as scarcely more than ciphers in the great Hindu commonwealth. The truth is, having nothing to do, they lead an indolent, thoughtless life. Their wealth and rank inspire respect, which, combined with old family prestige, makes a Raja a little god in his own neighbourhood. But this is all. He has no authority, no occupation, no great interest at stake beyond the disposal of his fortune. He has no living voice wherewith to speak to the nation ; and he can do nothing of any importance without extensive consultation with his foreign rulers. Hence, with all his superfluity of quietness and ease, with his entire freedom from anxiety and care, he is scarcely satisfied. How should he be!

It is indisputable, that the policy pursued by the British Government in India has been to raise to unexampled prominence and importance the commercial or trading castes of the country, and to bring to the birth a great middle class, which could not possibly have had an existence under either Hindu or Mahomedan rule, and which has already thrown into the shade the sacred Brahman and the haughty noble, the ancient dispensers of honour and power, and of all the blessings supposed to constitute a people's happiness. As a nation of traders, we could not, perhaps, prevent our innate tendencies from manifesting themselves. Indeed, what other result was, in the nature of things, to have been anticipated? For the last hundred years India has been governed by the middle class of Great Britain—and has been governed grandly, and well. I pass no opinion on the subject, and only speak historically when I say, that the class ruling in India has raised up a class among the natives very similar to itself. The wisdom of such a course has hardly yet been ever properly tested. The test will have to be applied on any occasion of great political disturbance in the country, involving the social status and dignity of the castes.

In England, it should be remembered, the middle class is kept within bounds, and its utterances are freed from many crude and vain imaginings, by the classes both above and below it. Thus valuable checks are applied to its outspoken energy; and its practical sagacity is permitted to flow forth in benefits to the nation. But in India no such checks exist. The possessors and dispensers of power are foreigners, with no personal sympathy whatever for the people they govern. The sacerdotal class, formerly omnipotent, has lost all its prerogatives; the ancient nobility is a splendid phantom of the past, without life; the lower Sudras, and all beneath them, a vast multitude, are mere clods, ignorant and helpless. What remain, but the Vaisyas, and upper Sudra tribes ? In them is vitality, energy, enterprise. They have caught something of English inspiration — and are *par excellence* the progressive classes of India, at the present day. But they are without salutary checks, save those which come from the strong hand of the wise man. This is the class that is chiefly seeking the education of English schools and colleges, and by increasing its knowledge is augmenting its power.

Ceremonies among the Sudra Castes.

These ceremonies are, in many respects, like those observed by the Brahmans and Rajpoots ; but as there are important differences, I have deemed it best to give a separate account of them.

On the birth of a child among the Sudras, a Brahman is at once sent for, who announces the *nakshatra* or planet under which it has been born. A *chamain* or wife of a *chamâr* (a dealer in leather), is also summoned, for the purpose of taking charge of both mother and infant. She remains for six days, and then leaves, after receiving her *neg* or present of money, clothes, and other things. Her place is supplied by a nâûn, or wife of a barber, a person of more respectability, who continues her service for a month or upwards. On the sixth day the mother is allowed to bathe according to the time fixed by the Brahman ; and her friends visit her, bringing with them spices, clarified butter, and articles of clothing for the child. She also bathes on the twelfth day, and is considered to be ceremonially clean. Her friends now approach her person, which they are permitted to touch, offering their congratulations. During the whole of the first twelve days, the women of the neighbourhood gather themselves daily at the house, and sing songs, called Sohar, in honour of the occasion. If the infant is born in the *mûl nakshatra*, the woman remains impure for twenty-seven days, as amongst the Brahmans. But there are certain cases in which she may be compelled to continue apart from all other persons for a year, and in extreme cases for ten or even twelve years. On such occasions the father sees the face of his child for the first time reflected in clarified butter. Feasts are given to members of the caste both on the sixth and twelfth day.

When the child, if a boy, is six months old, and, if a girl, five months, the ceremony of Anaprâshanna is performed by the worship of fire; and the child is permitted to eat the food of Hindus for the first time. At the age of five or six years, the boy's head is shaved in the presence of some deity; after performing which ceremony he is put to learn the trade or occupation from which eventually he is to obtain his livelihood.

Marriage takes place when the boy is ten or twelve years old. A Brahman is first called, who, after stating the horoscope of the boy and girl, announces the lucky day on which the marriage ceremony may be performed. This being accomplished, the custom of *pânbîra* is observed, when *pawn* and money are given to the bridegroom. After this, presents of various kinds are sent from the house of the bride to that of the bridegroom. The way is now prepared for the ceremony of Mat-magra, at which women dig earth from the ground, and with it make the female figure, called *mâtrika*, which is afterwards worshipped. Oil is poured on the head of every woman who visits the house on that day. A Brahman is appointed to select the spot on which the marriage is to be performed, which is covered with plantain leaves spread over bamboo poles, and bears the designation of Marwa. The body of the bridegroom having been washed, it is rubbed all over with oil and *hardî*, a yellow powder, a ceremony termed Telhardî. The day before the marriage takes place, the eldest person of the bridegroom's family performs all the ceremonies required to satisfy the wishes of deceased ancestors. On the marriage day, called Bhatwân, the attending women engage in certain ceremonies, one of which is to prepare food for the bridegroom, a portion of which is taken away by him and buried. Women also fetch parched rice or *láwa* from the Bhûnja, or grain roaster, and putting it into the bridegroom's hand, both himself and his bride walk round the Marwa, otherwise termed Banrî. Before this ceremony, however, the bridegroom goes in procession to the house of the bride for the removal of the girl to the place where the marriage is to be celebrated. He is met by the bride's father a certain distance from the house, and Dwâr-pûja, or worship, is performed at the door of the house. The father applies the *tilak* or mark to the forehead of the bride, and assigns a house in which the marriage is to be celebrated. The ceremony is performed at night. A Brahman first reads *mantras*, or sacred texts, suitable to the occasion. After this the boy puts a crown made of flowers, called Maur, on his head, and goes to the place appointed for the marriage. On the second day he eats *khichari*, food made of condiments; after which the ceremony of Acharpakrai is performed, when the bride catches hold of the clothes of every woman present, and receives presents from them. During the night the bride's father is summoned. On coming he partakes of food, and performs certain ceremonies. On the third day the wedded pair proceed to his house, where, after a time, they worship Ganesh.

At the expiration of a year, or, in some cases, when the bride and bridegroom are very young, of three or four years, or even more, the second marriage or *gauna* is performed, which is somewhat similar to the first. After this they live together. Yet, should the husband die in the meantime, the wife is regarded as a widow, and, in many cases, is not permitted to marry again. The lower castes are, however, happily not so particular, and permit widows to re-marry.

The ceremonies observed on the death of a Sudra are very similar to those practised by the higher castes. On the first day the members of the family of the deceased are not permitted to eat anything. From the second day offerings begin to be made in the name of the departed one, with the view apparently of affording repose to his spirit. The near relative who has set fire to the funeral pile continues unclean till the tenth day, when his head is shaved, and he is regarded as ceremonially clean.

CHAPTER II.

SECTS OF DEVOTEES AND RELIGIOUS MENDICANTS.

Gosain, Dandî, Tridandî, Jogî, Sanyâsî, Bairâgî, Sri Vaishnao, Râdhâ Vallabhî, Bharthari, Kanphatha, Jangam, Digambar, Sanjogrâ, Nirmâlî, Sukh-pannî, Bâm-margî, Khâk, Baitâlî-Bhât, Sharbhange, Sakhîbhao, Abhyâgat, Kan-chahî, Pauhârî, Shivâchârî, Bramhachârî, Sewarâ, Jatî, Akâshmukhi, Urddhbâhû, Maunîdâsî, Abadhûta, Sadhanpanthi, Harischandî, Kartâbhajâ, Râmâvat, Râma-nandî, Charandain, Raidâspanthî, Kabîrpanthî, Dâdupanthî, Udâsî, Nânak-shâhî, Kûkapanthî, Akâlî, Suthra, Aghorî, Bahikatha, Kapâlî.

Gosain.

The term Gosain is so vaguely employed by Hindus generally, that it becomes necessary to explain its various significations, and also to show in what sense it furnishes the name to a distinct caste. Commonly, any devotee is called a Gosain, whether he lives a life of celibacy or not, whether he roams about the country collecting alms, or resides in a house like the rest of the people, whether he leads an idle existence, or employs himself in trade. The mark, however, that distinguishes all who bear this name is, that they are devoted to a religious life. Some besmear their bodies with ashes, wear their hair dishevelled and uncombed, and, in some instances, coiled round the head like a snake or rope. These formerly went naked, but being prohibited by the British Government to appear in this fashion in public, bid defiance to decency nevertheless by the scantiness of their apparel. They roam about the country in every direction, visiting especially spots of reputed sanctity, and as a class are the pests of society and incorrigible rogues. They mutter sacred texts or mantras, and are notably fond of uttering the names of certain favourite deities. Some of them can read, and a few may be learned; but for the most part they are stolidly ignorant. Others, of a much higher grade, reside in *maths* or monasteries, where they lead a life of contemplation and asceticism. Yet they quit their homes occasionally, and, like the first named, undertake tours for the purpose of begging, and also proceed on pilgrimage to remote places. Most of them wear a yellowish cloth, by which they make themselves conspicuous. Faqirs or devotees of both of these classes usually wear several garlands of beads suspended from their necks and hanging low down in front; and carry a short one in the hand, which by the action of a thumb and finger, they revolve perpetually, but slowly, keeping time with the low utterances proceeding from their lips. They also bear upon their foreheads, and frequently on other parts of their bodies, particularly the arms and chest, sacred marks or symbols, in honour of their gods.

In addition, there is a considerable number of Gosains, not however separated from the rest by any caste distinctions, who, although by profession belonging to this religious class, apply themselves, nevertheless, to commerce and trade. As merchants, bankers, tradesmen, they hold a very respectable position. Some carry on their transactions on a large scale. One of the principal bankers in the city of Mirzapore, is a Mahant or high-priest of Gosains—a celibate of great wealth and influence.

One of the chief peculiarities of this caste, is, that besides its natural increase from within, it is constantly adding to its numbers from without. Brahmans, Kshatriyas, Vaisyas, and Sudras, the two former especially, may, if they choose, become Gosains; but if they do so, and unite with the members of this fraternity in eating and drinking, holding full and free intercourse with them, they are cut off for ever from their own tribes. It is this circumstance which constitutes the Gosains a distinct and legitimate caste, and not merely a religious order.

The ceremony observed at the creation of a Gosain is as follows. The candidate is generally a boy, but may be an adult. At the Shivâ-râtrî festival (in honour of Shiva) water brought from a tank, in which an image of the god has been deposited, is applied to the head of the novitiate, which is thereupon shaved. The *guru*, or spiritual guide, whispers to the disciple a *mantra* or sacred text. In honour of the event all the Gosains in the neighbourhood assemble together, and give their new member their blessing; and a sweatmeat called *laddu*, made very large, is distributed amongst them. The novitiate is now regarded as a Gosain, but he does not become a perfect one until the Vijaiya Hom has been performed, at which a Gosain, famous for religion and learning, gives him the original *mantra* of Shiva. The ceremony generally occupies three days in Benares. On the first day, the Gosain is again shaved.

leaving a tuft on the top of the head called in Hindî Chundî, but in Sanskrit, Shikhâ. For that day he is considered to be a Brahman, and is obliged to beg at a few houses. On the second day, he is held to be a Bramhachârî, and wears coloured garments, and also the *janeo* or sacred cord. On the third day, the *janeo* is taken from him, and the Chundî is cut off. The *mantra* of Shiva is made known to him, and also the Rudri Gayatri (not the usual one daily pronounced by Brahmans). He is now a full Gosain or *wân-parast*, is removed from other persons, and abandons the secular world. Henceforth he is bound to observe all the tenets of the Gosains. The complete Gosains, who have performed the ceremony of Vijaya Hom, are celibates. It is customary therefore for men not to perform it until they are forty or fifty years of age, as it involves the abandonment of their wives and families. Gosains will eat food in the houses of Brahmans and Rajpoots only. At death their bodies are not burnt, but are either buried or thrown into the Ganges.

There are ten sub-divisions or clans of the Gosain caste or tribe, called Dasnâmî, as follows:

1. Gir.
2. Puri.
3. Bhârat.
4. Ban. (These wander in jungles, and never cut their hair).
5. Áran.
6. Bodlâ.
7. Jatî.
8. Sâgar.
9. Tîrth.
10. Ásram.

It is, however, difficult to give a correct list of the ten sub-divisions. In Wilson's Glossary, Bodlâ and Jatî are not stated, but Saraswatî and Pârvata are included in the list. Dr. Buchanan also mentions the names of Parbat, Saraswati, and Dândi. The last is certainly a mistake, as the Dândi is of a special class of devotees. All the branches associate together, and intermarry. In this part of India they worship Vishnu; though in some other parts they seem to be devoted to Shiva. Everywhere Sankara Achârya is regarded as their spiritual guide. Indeed, he is said to be the founder of the sect, and the ten sub-divisions are considered to have been established by his ten disciples, and to bear their names. Formerly, the number of *maths*, monasteries or conventual residences in Benares, was much larger than at the present day. A hundred years ago there were in the city, it is said, as many as fourteen hundred of these *maths*, while it is calculated that there are now not more than seven hundred. They are mostly to be found in the districts known as Lakshmi Kund, Sûraj Kund, Misr Pokhrû, Terhî Nîm, and Sâkhî Binaik. Many families of Gosains, at one time resident in Benares, have left for Hyderabad, where they are engaged in trade (*a*).

This entire chapter was completed before the author had seen the elaborate account of the religious sects of the Hindus, by the late distinguished Sanskrit scholar, Horace Hayman Wilson. It is altogether an independent statement, and being mainly concerned with the existing circumstances of the religious communities of which it treats, will be found in many points to supplement the more theoretical dissertation of that eminent man. A few brief extracts from Wilson's work have been occasionally added to the text.

Dandî.

The Dandîs are neither a caste nor a tribe of Hindus, but are an order of devotees. As they keep themselves very distinct from the rest of the community, they demand a separate notice. Their habits are peculiar. One of them has supplied an appellation for the entire class, derived from their habit of always carrying a staff in the hand. Hence the name Dandî, from *danda* a stick. They are Brahmans, and receive disciples only from the Brahmans.

The Dandîs do not touch fire, or metal, or vessels made of any sort of metal. It is impossible, therefore, for them to cook their own food like other Hindus. It is equally impossible also for them to handle money. They wear one long unsewn reddish cloth, thrown about the person. Although they are on principle penniless, yet they do not beg. Their dependance on the kindness and care of others is thus of the most absolute character. Yet they are not reduced to want, or even to distress: they are fed by the Brahmans, and the Gosains, another class of devotees, but of lax principles, and not restricted to any one caste. The Dandîs do not marry, and have no houses of their own. They have literally nothing they can call their own, except a diminutive mat to lie upon, a small pillow, the cloth they wear, a stick, and a *kamandal*, or hermit's pot for holding water. The stick they use at the age of fifty; previously to which, they are only disciples, and are not called Dandîs.

(*a*) Wilson's Glossary, p. 183.

Not a few of this religious order are learned men, and devote a large portion of their time to study and meditation. They are great readers of the Shâstras, such as the Mîmânsa, Nyâya, Manjûka, and others, and also of the Purânas. Many Brahmans, even Pandits, or learned Brahmans, come to them for instruction, which they impart freely, without the smallest recompense. All classes of the community pay them the greatest honour, even to worshipping them. They are addressed as Swâmî Jî, that is, Master, Lord, Spiritual Teacher. Although they are said to worship idols, yet they make no obeisance to them. They are singularly independent in all their actions, and make no *salam* or sign of respect to any object, human or divine.

Tridandi.

A species of Gosains. Originally they bore a trident as their emblem; hence the name which they assume. This practice, however, has ceased to be observed. They are Shaivas, or worshippers of Shiva, and in habits are like Gosains. The Tridandîs do not marry. Their bodies after death are buried, not burnt.

Jogi.

This class, or order, is of many kinds. Some are prognosticators of future events; others lead about animals of monstrous formation in order to excite religious wonder and curiosity; others have their ears split and wear in them a kind of ear-ring for sacred purposes. Persons of all castes can, in these latter days, enter the order; but this was not the rule originally. Jogîs are not particular on the subject of marriage, and some of them take to themselves wives. At death, their bodies are buried; and their tombs, termed *Samâdh*, are held in sacred estimation, and are often visited by pilgrims for idolatrous purposes.

The term Jogî or Yogî is properly applicable, says Mr. Wilson, "to the followers of the Yoga or Pâtanjala School of Philosophy, which, amongst other tenets, maintained the practicability of acquiring, even in life, entire command over elementary matter by means of certain ascetic practices" (a).

Sanyâsi.

The Sanyâsîs, like the Gosains, ascribe their origin to Sankara Achârya. The *mantra*, or religious text, and the *gayatri*, or daily ceremonial prayer, are

(a) Religious Sects of the Hindus, Vol. I., p. 206.

the same as those used by Gosains. They have similar customs likewise in respect to some of their social habits, as, for instance, they will partake of food only in the houses of Brahmans and Kshatriyas, and not in the houses of lower castes. But Sanyâsîs are never created from young boys, as Gosains for the most part are, and always from elderly men. After the Vijaiya Hom has been celebrated, they never touch metal of any kind, never ride in carriages of any description, never cook food for themselves, and never touch the bodies of persons except of those connected with their own order. At the ceremony of induction, they receive a stick or *lakut*, and a *kamandal*, or vessel for holding water. Should the *kamandal* be broken by any misadventure, a *sanskâr* or ceremony is performed like that observed on the death of a man.

At death, a horrible custom is observed, the origin of which I am unacquainted with. A cocoa-nut is broken on the head of the deceased by a person specially appointed for the purpose, until it is smashed to pieces. The body is then wrapped in *gerua-vastra*, or reddish cloth, and is thrown into the Ganges.

Bairâgî.

Pure Bairâgî devotees are professedly followers of Râmanand, the founder of a famous Hindu sect, and his celebrated disciple, Râmanuj. They are mostly taken from the Sudra castes. The ceremony of induction is very similar to that observed among the Gosains. At death, their bodies are burnt like those of other Hindus. Bairâgîs are numerous in Benares, and are inordinate beggars. They do not marry.

The word Bairâgî is very commonly applied as a generic term to many sects of devotees.

Sri Vaishnava.

These are devotees worshipping Vishnu in the form of the four-handed Lakshminarain, holding the *sankha*, shell, the *chakra*, discus, *gada*, club, and a lotus-flower, in the four hands. Their *tilak* on the forehead is in the form of a trident. It is likewise borne on the arms, breast, and abdomen. They are akin to the Râmanujis and Râmanandis, and are called by the common name of Bairâgî. Disciples are taken from the Brahmanical caste. These devotees wear clothes of *pewar*, a kind of yellow colour, have a *kanthi*, or sacred garland around the neck, and also a rosary of *tulsi* wood. They never touch, or pay homage to, Shiva; nor do they put on *rudraksh*, or garland of Eleocarpus berries.

The Sri Vaishnavas are disciples of Vishnu Swâmi, one of the four *sampradayas* or sects of Vaishnavas among the Bairâgîs. These are 1, the Râmanandis; 2, the Nimânujis; 3, the Mâdhu Achâryas; and, 4, the Sri Vaishnavas. Some add one more, namely, the Râdhâ Vallabhas; while others substitute it in place of the fourth. The *tilak*, or mark on the forehead, of the Nimânuj sect, is of this form | and is made of sandal-wood or of a red pigment. The *tilak* of the Mâdhu Acharyas is a black mark extending from the eye-brow up the forehead to the hair. These four sects, it is affirmed, have developed and separated into fifty-two divisions or minor sects.

Râdhâ Vallabhi.

A name applied to certain devotees who worship Krishna and his wife Râdhâ, and take great interest in all the *lîlas* or sports of Krishna with his numerous wives and concubines. Nevertheless, they profess a high degree of ceremonial purity, and do not eat fish or flesh, or drink spirits. They worship Krishna very early in the morning, and, in addition, many times in the course of the day. The founder of the sect was Vallabha Swâmi.

In the worship rendered to Krishna, the god is represented in various forms and characters. Each form and character is only sustained for a few minutes, and then changed for a new one. They are termed Jhankis. The Râḍhâballabhî devotees are very jealous of the worshippers both of Shiva and of Râm. They observe, however, most of the ceremonies of the Bairâgîs. At death, their bodies are burnt.

The Baniyas, or tradespeople, and mahâjans, or bankers, of Benares, are, to a large extent, worshippers of Krishna in one form or another. They worship him under such names as Gopâl, Ranchhaur, Râdh, Vallabh, Râdhâraman, and so forth. They exhibit a *tilak* on the forehead, of *chandan* and *roli* (*a*) in the form of a note of admiration, or in the form of a loop the round portion below meeting near the eyebrows. The former *tilak* is always of *roli*, the latter of *chandan*.

Bharthari.

A sect of devotees who regard Raja Bhart as their founder and head. They are reckoned as Jogîs, because Raja Bhart, it is asserted, was a disciple of a Jogî. They carry a musical instrument in their hands, on which they play, while they sing the exploits of Raja Bhart. Their abode in Benares is principally at Raori

(*a*) A mixture of rice, turmeric, alum, and acid.

Talao. There are many of the sect in the city. They walk about wearing the *gerua-vastra*, or reddish cloth, worn commonly by devotees. At death, they are buried.

Kanphatha.

This name is derived from the custom observed by this class of devotees of slitting their ears and wearing a small cylindrical object in the incision. The Kanphathas eat flesh, drink spirits, and partake of food in houses of all castes. They are found only in the temples of Bhairo, yet they use the *mantras*, or sacred texts, both of Shiva and Bhairo. In the temple of Kâl Bhairo in Benares are some ten or a dozen members of this order.

The Kanphathas profess to be followers of Gorakhnâth. The slitting of the ear is practised during the ceremony of induction. They wear *gerua-vastra* or reddish cloth, and a head-dress of black ribbons, like the Sutharasains, a sect of Nânak-shâhîs. The novitiate is kept closely confined in a house for forty days, when he is brought out, and is made a perfect disciple. The Kanphathas carry in their hands a *han morchhal*, or fan made of peacock's feathers, with which they make passes over the credulous, for the purpose of exorcising evil spirits with which they may be possessed, and of keeping imps and goblins at a distance.

There are many Kanphathas in Benares, some of whom are very rich. They are the priests of Kâl Bhairo temple. They are sometimes termed Jogîs. At death, the Kanphathas are buried in their own houses.

Jangam.

The Jangam sings the exploits and adventures of the god Shiva. He carries with him a little bell, which he rings before commencing his songs. There are only a few of this order in Benares ; and they reside in the quarter of the city known as Raori Talao. The Jangams commonly do not marry. At death, their bodies are either buried or thrown into the Ganges.

Digambar.

A name applied to a class of devotees who live absolutely separated from society and from all family connexions. The word is derived from *dik*, a quarter of the globe, and *ambar*, apparel, and indicates one who has the world or universe for his covering.

"The Jains," says Professor Wilson, "are divided into two principal divisions, Digambaras and Soetambaras, the former of which appears to have the best pretensions to antiquity. The discriminating difference is implied in these terms, the former meaning the sky-clad, that is naked, and the latter the white-robed, the teachers being so dressed. All the Dakhini Jains appear to belong to the Digambara division. So it is said do the majority of the Jains in Western India" (*a*).

Sanjogrâ.

This sect consists of those Bairâgis only who have wives or concubines, and their descendants. These latter, however, may be either married persons, or celibates. The Sanjogrâs are found at Assi Ghât, at the southern extremity of the city.

Nirmâli.

A sect of Vaishnavas who devote all their time to the one purpose of keeping themselves clean. They bathe many times, and wash their hands one hundred and eight times, daily. While they do not separate themselves from their families, they refrain from touching even their children, lest they should be defiled. They are very careful not to take the life of any creature. Women as well as men may belong to this sect.

Sukhpanni.

Applied to certain followers of Krishna who pay great attention to personal cleanliness, and wash themselves many times in the day, using various purifying substances. They live apart from society, and have no disciples. The Sukhpannis are of both sexes; and their bodies are burnt after death.

Bâm-Margi.

These are not strictly devotees. They marry, drink wine, lead a sensual life, and profess to follow the teachings of a Bâmâ, or woman.

Khâki.

A kind of Bairâgi, whose ceremonies they observe. They are called Khâki, or ashy, because they besmear their bodies with ashes. "The reputed founder," says Wilson, "is Kîl, the disciple of Krishnadâs, whom some accounts make the disciple of Râmanand; but the history of the Khâki sect is not known, and seems to be of modern origin" (*b*).

(*a*) Religous Sects of the Hindus, Vol. I., p. 339.
(*b*) *Ibid*, Vol. II., p. 98.

Baitâli Bhât.

A name given to the descendants of Baital, who was a famous Râj Bhât at the court of Vikramaditya. Having quarrelled with the Raja, he abandoned both him and his creed, and united himself with the Gosains, in whose praise he made verses, a practice followed by his descendants. These devotees marry, and live like Gosains, on whose bounty they are dependant. They are acquainted with a curious kind of alphabet called *Baitâli akshar.* One of their peculiar habits is, that, although they live by charity, yet they refuse to take alms except from the Gosains, to whom they act the important part of family registrars and genealogists by inserting their pedigrees in books kept for the purpose. This sect lives at Lakshmi Kund, in Benares. On the death of one of its members, his body is buried.

Sharbhange.

These profess the tenets of Sharbhanga, who flourished in the days of Râm, and is alluded to in the Râmâyana. They are Vaishnavas, or worshippers of Vishnu, yet live commonly as Bairâgîs.

Sakhibhao.

A sect of Hindu devotees paying special attention to the qualities of female deities. They live like women, and wear their dress. They do not indulge in marriage.

Abhyâgat.

A sect of devotees who live alone, and subsist by begging. They dwell in monasteries.

Kanchani.

A sect among the Gosains who gain their livelihood by dancing and singing. They wear the red cloth as devotees, and observe most of the ceremonies of the Gosains. They marry. At death, their bodies are either buried or thrown into a river.

Pauhâri.

These are a sect of Gosains or Bairâgîs who eat neither grain, nor vegetables, nor any herbs, and subsist on cow's milk only. The name is derived from *pay*, the Sanskrit for milk, and *ahâr*, food.

Shivâchâri.

The Shivâchâris come from Coorg, in the Bombay Presidency, and reside at Jangambâri and Kidâr Ghât in Benares. They are worshippers of Shiva, wear *rudrâksh*, or a garland made of berries of the Eleocarpus, and have a small image of the god Shiva suspended in a box round their necks, which they do not suffer any one to touch. They besmear their bodies with ashes, especially their foreheads. The members of this sect are not exclusively devotees: some of them are married, and reside with their families. They live for the most part as Gosains, and are treated as such.

Bramhachârî.

This name is given to a sect of Brahman ascetics. They wear red cloth and the *rudrâksh*, let their hair and beard grow, and besmear their bodies with ashes. They are worshippers of Shiva. The Bramhachârîs live as recluses apart from their families, and at death their bodies are burnt.

The word Bramhachârî is also applied to a religious student, to persons learned in the Vedas, and in various other ways.

Sewarâ.

The Sewarâs aspire to the character of very holy persons. They let their beards grow long like the Bairâgîs, besmear their bodies with ashes, and wear *gerua-vastra* or reddish cloth. They are not particular in eating food with Hindus of various castes, or even with Mahomedans, and are addicted to drinking spirits. They beg alms from door to door, and do not hesitate, if occasion offers, to rob simpletons, both men and women, by their tricks. Their religion appears to be a form of Shaivism. There is reason for supposing the Sewarâs to be of Buddhist origin. Some of them are celibates, but not all. They have their disciples like many other devotees, yet not in all cases. When they die, their bodies are buried in the ground.

There is another sect of Sewarâs, called Jatî, connected, it is affirmed, with the Buddhists. These practise celibacy and pretend to great sanctity. They walk about with head and feet bare, holding a red stick in the hand. They also carry with them a kind of brush made of peacocks' feathers, with which they sweep the ground before sitting down, lest they should injure a worm or insect. These persons do not disclose their tenets to strangers. They make disciples like the Gosains, and live in monasteries.

Jatî.

There are three sects of devotees bearing this designation. The first consists of those Gosains, Bairâgîs, and Udâsis, who practise celibacy. The second is akin to the Jogî devotees. The third professes to be of Buddhist origin, and is also called Sewarâ, as described already. The two latter sects have their bands of disciples. The second at death are burnt; but the third are either buried or thrown into a river.

Akâshmukhi.

An appellation derived from *âkâsh*, the firmament or sky, and *mukh*, the face, and applied to a sect of devotees whose habit is to raise their faces upwards to the sky, and to keep them in that position until the muscles of the neck become rigid, and the head becomes fixed in that position.

Urddhbâhû.

These are Bairâgîs who keep one or both hands in an erect position for a number of years until they become shrivelled, and the finger-nails grow to several inches in length, occasionally penetrating through the hand and protruding beyond. By this inhuman practice they acquire a character for great sanctity.

Maunîdâsî.

Devotees under a vow of silence, generally for a term of years, of whom there are said to be many in the city of Benares. They are regarded as possessing extreme sanctity, and are even worshipped by other Hindus.

Abadhûta.

There is properly no sect of devotees of this name; but Gosains who lead the life of a *nâgâ*, or naked devotee, are called Abadhûta. The word means *discarded*, *shaken*, and is applied to this class of people, under the idea that they have shaken the world away from them or separated themselves from it, and have no further interest in its affairs.

Sadhanpanthî.

There are no devotees of this appellation, but the name is applied to the followers of Sadhan. This Sadhan was a common butcher of Benares about two centuries ago, and was a great *bhagat*, that is, was very fervent in the observances of Hinduism. He is reputed to have had only one weight for weighing his meat. This was a sacred stone called *Sâligrâm*. With this he could weigh, it is said, the smallest as well as the greatest, the lightest as well as the heaviest, quantities. He is believed not to have died, but to have ascended living to the heavenly regions, like the prophet Elijah.

Harischandî.

Followers of Harischand, a Raja who lived in ancient times, and became famous for his self-denial and devotion. He is said to have abdicated his regal functions, and to have practised asceticism, living like a common devotee. "The Harischandîs," says Wilson, "are Doms, or sweepers, in the Western Provinces."

Kartâbhajâ.

A class of Bairâgîs, who believe in the unity of God.

Râmâvat.

These are disciples of Râmanuj and Mâdhu Achârya, and worshippers of Vishnu and Râm. Their bodies are marked with the *sankha* or shell, *gada*, or club, *chakra*, or discus, and the lotus-flower, symbols of Vishnu. These marks are generally made at Dwârkâ; yet it is customary for a new disciple to receive them wherever he may be initiated, for the sect admits no fresh member unless he has first been marked upon his body with the symbols. The *tilak*, or special distinctive mark applied to the forehead, is of this form ⌊|⌋, the strokes on the sides being made with *chandan* or powdered sandal-wood, the middle stroke with *roli*, a pigment already described. The Râmâvats are of all castes.

Râmanandî.

Ascetic disciples of Râmanand, the founder of a Hindu sect. Brahmans and Kshatriyas, but no other castes, are permitted to enter this order of devotees.

Râmanandîs and Râmanujis differ only in the *tilak*, or sacred mark, applied to the forehead. Their tenets are the same.

Charandain.

Disciples of Charan who lived in the days of Râmanuj. Their ceremonies and habits are similar to those of Vaishnavas, Bairâgîs, and Kabîrpanthis.

Raidâspanthî.

This word is derived from Raidâs, a Chamâr, or leather-seller, famous in his day for religious fervour. He was a disciple of Râmanuj. The Chamâr caste regarding him as a great *bhagat*, or religious person, claim relationship to him, and speak of themselves as Raidâsis, or disciples of Raidâs. The appellation, therefore, of Raidâspanthî rather designates a sect than a class of devotees.

Kabîrpanthi.

Disciples of Kabîr, who founded a sect, of which many members are met with in Benares, and in other parts of the North Western Provinces. Their chief place in Benares is at Kabîr-Chaura. They eschew marriage. Disciples from all castes are admitted into the fraternity. At death, their bodies are burnt, not buried. Kabîr was the most famous of the twelve disciples of Râmanand.

Dâdupanthi.

The Dâdupanthîs are disciples of Kabîr, the founder of a Hindu sect, and therefore are properly Kabîrpanthîs; but they derive their origin from Dâdu, a follower of Kabîr, and a founder of a sect. These people are distinguished personally by their pointed cap and flowing robe. They live much like Bairâgîs, and do not marry.

Udâsî.

The Udâsî devotees profess the tenets of Nânak Shâh, and are, among Sikhs, similar to Sanyâsîs, among Hindus. They reside in monasteries, and eat what is cooked by other persons. They worship the Granth or sacred book of Nânak Shâh.

The Udâsîs are derived from all castes. The ceremony of discipleship is similar to that existing among Gosains. Instead of *laddu*, they distribute a sweetmeat, called *halua*, at the creation of a new Udâsî. The members of this sect will eat food in the houses of Hindus of all castes. Like Bairâgîs and Gosains, they have five *akhâras* or places of assembly in Benares, known as, Niranjani, Nirbâni, Gûdar, Sûkhar, and Rûkhar. Like them also, some of their number are termed Nâgâ (from *nanga*, naked,) because they go naked.

Nânak-Shâhi.

These are also followers of Nânak Shâh. They differ from Udâsîs in that the latter live in a peculiar ascetic manner not practised by the Nânak-Shâhîs. The members of this religious order, on becoming devotees, do not marry; they wear the *gerua-vastra*, or red cloth. They have no *Nâgâs*, or naked ascetics, like the Udâsîs, and will partake of food in the houses of all Hindus. They do not worship idols, but the Granth or sacred book of Nânak.

Kûkapanthî.

Like the Nânak Shâhîs, only more rigid. They wear a peculiar uniform. The term is derived from the loud tone in which they utter their *mantra*, or sacred text, compared to the *kûk* or loud note of the *kaku* or *kokila.* The Kûkapanthîs intensely detest all other sects.

Akâlî.

These are Sikh devotees, who wear a blue turban on their heads girdled with an iron circlet. Occasionally they decorate their heads with several of such circlets. In their hands they carry a small rod. The Akâlîs are rigid followers of Nânak.

Suthra.

A name given to a class of devotees who are the disciples of Nânak. They beg alms, going from house to house, singing the exploits of some famous Hindu chief, and striking together a couple of cylinders which they carry in their hands. Their heads are covered with a turban made of black ribands. The Suthras do not marry. They are found in the monastery of Nâgar Sen, a famous Suthra, in a district of Benares known as Aurangabâd, where they have a company of disciples. Their bodies at death are either buried or burnt.

Aghorî.

This is the name of a flagrantly indecent and abominable set of beggars. who have rendered themselves notorious for the disgusting vileness of their habits. Prowling about in the pursuit of their miserable calling, which, however, is one of the most successful in India, they will take no denial. In case of the refusal of alms they will besmear themselves with filth, and eat the most loathsome garbage, in the presence of the persons who withhold their money from them. They are a pest to native society.

The Aghorîs deduce their origin from Kinâ Râm and Kâlu Râm (the *guru* or spiritual guide of Kinâ Râm), who are supposed to have lived in Benares about one hundred years ago. Hindus of all castes may enter the order. On induction their bodies are first shaved, and they are sent to Asht-bhuja, the shrine of a famous goddess six miles from Mirzapûr, where they practice incantations until they imagine they have acquired the power of the goddess Aghor-mukhi, whom they worship, and whose tenets they observe.

The Aghorîs eat all kinds of food, including the carcases of jackals, cats, and other animals, which die of themselves.

Bahikathâ.

This is another class of beggars as notorious and as much feared and shunned as the Aghorîs. On presenting themselves before a house, and asking for aid, should their importunity not be attended to, they begin to cut themselves about the head and body, inflicting deep gashes and stabs: this they continue, until, in sheer horror and consternation, the family thus addressed gives him everything he demands.

Kapâlî.

A class of devotees who adopt the *mantra*, or sacred text, of the female deity Kâlî. They are somewhat similar in their habits to the Aghorîs, but not so shameless and abominable. They eat flesh and drink spirits ; but refrain from eating dead carcases.

CHAPTER III.

BARDS, MUSICIANS, SINGERS, DANCERS, BUFFOONS, &c.

BHAT, KATHAK, RAMJANA, DHARHI, KALAVANT, MIRASI, GAUNHARIN, BHAND, PAWARIYA, BHAIRIYA, BHAGATIYA, BAHURUPIYA.

Bhât.

A TRIBE of bards more distinguished in ancient than in modern times. Formerly, they cultivated the art of making poetry on the spur of the moment, at marriage festivals and on other great occasions. Either the stimulus has been wanting, or the spirit of poetry has diminished in the tribe, for they rarely now-a-days exhibit any pretension to such a gift. Still, they are in considerable request for the exercise of their talents and skill in the recitation of poetry. All families of respectability send for them on days of special importance and interest to themselves, when, in the presence of all assembled, they give in pompous language a genealogical history of the families that have summoned them, or repeat the chronicles of the neighbourhood, or unfold the historical records of some great and well-known house, or recite passages from the Râmâyana, Mahâbhârata, or other national poems.

The Bhât is also called Dasaundhî and Bhârata. Although he continues a distinct tribe, yet his profession as a bard and chronicler is shared by Mahomedans. Not a few of the tribe occupy a respectable position in native society. The women of the Mahomedan Bhâts, on certain occasions, sing in public, but they and the wives of the Kathaks are the only women of reputation who do so. The wives and daughters of Hindu Bhâts, however, do not sing in public.

The Bhâts are said to be divided into three branches, as follows:

1. Birm-Bhât, also called Brahma-Bhât.
2. Jâga-Bhât.
3. Charan-Bhât.

Sir Henry Elliot has some interesting observations on the distinction between the Bhâts and the Jâgas. "By some tribes," he says, "the Bhât and Jâga are considered synonymous; but those who pretend to greater accuracy distinguish them by calling the former Birm-Bhât or Badî, and the latter Jâga-Bhât. The former recite the deeds of ancestors at weddings and other festive occasions : the latter keep the family records, particularly of Rajpoots, and are entitled by right of succession to retain the office; whereas, the Birm-Bhâts are hired and paid for the particular occasion. Jâga-Bhâts pay visits to their constituents every two or three years, and receive the perquisites to which they are entitled. After recording all the births which have taken place since their last tour, they are remunerated with rupees, cattle, or clothes, according to the ability of the registering party. 'Those of the North-Western Rajpoots generally reside between the borders of Rajpootana and the Dehli territory.' Many also live at Dâranagar on the Ganges, and travel to the remote East in order to collect their fees. Whereas, the Birm-Bhâts are resident in towns and kasbas, and do not emigrate periodically" (*a*). Wilson states that, in the West of India, the Bhât is identified with the Charan, and "his personal security is held sufficient for the payment of a debt, or fulfilment of an engagement;" but that, should it not be performed, the Bhât, or some one of his family, destroys himself, the guilty party, however, being held responsible for the same (*b*). The Charan-Bhâts are peculiar to Rajpootana, where they have 'long retained their character as the surest guarantees of agreements of independent chiefs or private individuals.'

In Rajpootana, the Charans and other Bhâts exercise a vast influence over the people. They rank, says Malcolm, "as the genealogists of proud and ignorant chiefs; and favoured individuals often combine with that office the station of counsellors, and establish an ascendancy over the minds of their superior, which is stronger from being grounded upon a mysterious feeling of awe. It is to them that the proudest Rajpoot looks for solace in adversity, and for increased joy and exultation in prosperity" (*c*).

The Bhâts are notorious for their rapacity as beggars, and are much dreaded by their employers on account of the power they have of distorting family history at public recitations, if they choose to do so, and of subjecting any member to general ridicule. This tribe is said to have sprung from the union

(*a*) Elliot's Supplemental Glossary, Vol. I., p. 18.

(*b*) Wilson's Glossary, p. 79.

(*c*) Sir John Malcolm's Central India, Vol. I., pp. 131, 132.

of a Kshatriya with a Vaisya woman; but another account is, that its common ancestors were a Kshatriya father and a Brahman widow (*a*); while, by a third tradition, the Bhâts are said to be the progeny of a Brahman father and a Sudra mother. It is evident, therefore, that no reliance can be placed on tradition at at all in the matter. Elliot gives the following sub-divisions of the tribe, namely, Atsela, Mahâpâtr, Kailea, Mainpûrîwâlâ, Jangira, Bhatara, and Dasaundhî. To these, he adds, Sîkatpûrea, Nagauri, Chaurâsi, Gajbhim, Chûngele, Gûjriwâlâ, and Baruâ (*b*). The Dasaundhîs or Dasaundhans are in the lower Doâb and to the east of Oudh.

The tribe is known in many parts of the country. In the Morâdabâd district they have existed at Bilârî, Amroha, and Hassanpûr from time immemorial. They are well known in Mathurâ, where they wear the sacred cord; but this custom, I believe, is also practised by the tribe elsewhere.

Kathak.

The Kathaks are professional musicians. They are 'to the manner born,' and form a distinct tribe and caste. The gift or inspiration of music is hereditary in this tribe, just as that of catching birds is hereditary among the Baheliyas, or that of buying and selling among the Agarwâlâs. The Kathaks, however, are only one of several tribes of Hindus devoted to music, dancing and singing; and must not by any means be confounded with the Khatiks, who are poulterers. They affect to be of high caste, equal in fact to the Rajpoots, and nearly equal to the Brahmans; and wear the *janeo*, or sacred cord, which none but men of good caste are allowed to wear. Further west, the Kathaks do not make a *salam* in saluting any one, as natives of India commonly do, but give their *âshîrbâd*, or blessing, like the Brahmans. Their women are not usually seen in public, but live in the retirement of the zenana, an additional testimony to the respectability of the tribe. An exception to this rule, however, is permitted at marriages, at which women of the tribe, as well as men, are present. The former play on two kinds of instruments, one called a dhol, or small drum, the other called majîra, consisting of two metallic cups, which are used for keeping time by being struck together, and so producing a sharp jingling sound. The latter play on various instruments, and also sing and dance. They do not suffer their wives to appear on any other occasions; yet

(*a*) Sir John Malcolm's Central India, Vol. I., p. 78.
(*b*) Elliot's Supplemental Glossary, Vol. I., p. 19.

women commonly accompany them to all musical festivals. Such women, who belong to many castes, come to the Kathaks' houses for instruction in the art of singing and dancing. They are always and everywhere women of loose character. In India all professional singing and dancing, when performed by women, with very few exceptions, is performed by prostitutes. Indeed, a prostitute and a professional dancer or singer are, in the common speech of the people, correlative terms. The Kathaks receive one-half of the earnings of these women, in payment for the instruction they have given. They are very frequently hired together, the Kathaks to play on instruments, the women to dance and sing.

The customs of Hindus are peculiar in regard to music and dancing. While it is common for men to perform on instruments, and that too in great variety, women do so comparatively to a very small extent, and only use a few and, for the most part, simple instruments. Singing is practised by both sexes, but chiefly by the gentler sex. Women at work in the fields, or going to their homes when their work is done, sing plaintive strains of a very pleasing character, frequently with a refrain, in which a part only join at a time. But as to dancing, it is eschewed by every decent and honourable woman, and a woman would instantly lose her character were she once to indulge in it. It is on this account that Hindus have been unable to comprehend the propriety of English ladies amusing themselves in this manner ; yet many, however, at last, are beginning to understand it.

Râmjanâ, or Râmjani.

This is another Hindu tribe of professional musicians. They wear the sacred cord, and call themselves Kshatriyas ; but in social position there is a great difference between them and the Kathaks. This arises from the fact that, except at marriage festivals, the latter keep their wives and daughters rigidly secluded in the zenana, whereas the Râmjanâs, on the contrary, are commonly accompanied by their wives wherever they go. They also, like the Kathaks, give instruction in singing and dancing to women intending to be professional performers. The caste is devoted to prostitution. The female children born in the caste are brought up to immorality and vice ; the sons, however, are trained as musicians, and sometimes engage in trade or other occupations, and have a chance, therefore, which their sisters never have, of leading an honorable life. The Râmjanâ is a distinct and acknowledged caste, yet it differs from others in admitting women from various castes into the order.

Dhârhi.

A class of Mahomedan players. Both men and women perform on musical instruments, or sing, or dance, wherever they can obtain employment. When they have no engagements they wander about the country visiting villages and towns, or performing in private houses, and in this manner earn a livelihood.

Kalâvant.

These are Mahomedan performers, but are much higher in rank than the Dhârhîs ; are regarded, indeed, as persons of reputation and respectability.

Mirâsi.

This is a class of Mahomedans, who teach girls singing and dancing. The women not only sing and dance, but are also employed as jesters in the presence of native ladies, in zenanas, or female apartments, of large houses. The men are said to be highly respected by Mahomedans, though for what especial reason I have been unable to learn.

Gaunhârin.

These are *natch* girls, or dancing women. They form a very numerous class in all towns and cities in India. They are not a distinct caste, but are more or less attached to all the castes. Although notoriously immoral, yet they are sent for by all classes of the community, even the most respectable and virtuous, on occasion of a great family festivity. So necessary, in a social point of view, is the presence of these and other professional singers and performers at a marriage, or at the birth of a son, or when any other important event occurs, that a man of wealth and station would suffer in reputation, and would be held as slighting his friends, and even his caste, did he not employ them.

The Gaunhârins not only dance and sing, but also play on the Sâringî and Tablâ. The Sâringî is, in appearance, somewhat like a violin, and is played with a bow ; the Tablâ is a small drum with only one opening, which is covered with a thin skin, the part opposite to this being round, and made of wood. The drum rests upon the ground, the covered opening being uppermost, and is struck rapidly and sharply by the fingers. Sometimes two such drums are played by the right and left hands together. The dancing of these women is, for the most part, very quiet ; indeed, when compared with many who are addicted to this amusement, it may be considered tame and lifeless. Their singing is mostly plaintive, but they seldom give the full tension to their voices, or allow them to ring out clearly and satisfactorily, on account of their foolish and inveterate habit of chewing pawn, which, strange to say, many of them do not altogether desist from even at the time and in the act of singing.

Bhând or Bhânr.

This is the name given to mimics, buffoons, and jesters. Formerly, Hindus as well as Mussalmans devoted themselves to this calling, but the former have, for the most part, retired from it. They are present at all joyous festivals, such as a marriage, or the birth of a son, and contribute their jokes just as the Gaunhârins contribute their dancing and song.

Respecting the Bhânds of Oudh, Mr. P. Carnegy says that they are divided into seven or more clans. "The Bhând," he remarks, "is a genealogist and bard. The Birm-Bhând, or Bodi, recites the deeds of ancestors at occasional festive gatherings. The Joga-Bhând periodically records all domestic events among the Rajpoot families" (*a*). But he seems to confound the Bhânds with the Bhâts.

Pâwariya.

A class of dancers at public festivals. They are found in the districts east of Oudh (*b*).

Bhairiya.

A dissolute and disorderly caste. They wander about in the company of dancing women, and are notorious thieves and scoundrels. They form but a small community, yet are found in many of the districts of these Provinces (*c*). There are several hundred families in Cawnpûr. The caste is also styled Bedia.

Bhagatiya.

A caste consisting of loose people who pass their time in buffoonery, singing and dancing. They are found in Agra, Etawah, Cawnpûr, and as far east as Ghazipûr, where they number more than a hundred families.

Bahurûpiya.

The Bahurûpiyas are a class of people found in small numbers in many places of these provinces. They assume a multitude of disguises, in the characters both of men and women, and attend public and private festivals in the train of mimics, musicians, dancers, and others. They are taken from all classes of native society, and are neither connected with the Bhânds nor Bhâts.

(*a*) Mr. P. Carnegy's Races of Oudh, p. 83.
(*b*) Mr. E. A. Reade's Inferior Castes of the North-Western Provinces, p. 44.
(*c*) *Ibid*, p. 37.

CHAPTER IV.

CASTES OF BANKERS, MERCHANTS, AND TRADERS.

KHATRI. RAI SANKTA PRASAD. RORA, PURWAL, PALLIWAL, UNAYE, AND RAUNIAR.

Khatrî.

THIS Hindu tribe is an ethnological puzzle. In some respects, they resemble the great Kshatriya or Rajpoot race; in others, they differ from it. Instead of being addicted to government, and delighting in war, they are exclusively devoted to trade; and, consequently, are naturally placed among the commercial classes. Judged by their own traditions and social habits, they are as high in rank as Rajpoots. Indeed, in Benares they lay claim to a closer observance of the ancient customs of Rajpoots than that which is practised by modern Rajpoot tribes. This claim, as stated to me by a native gentleman of the Khatrî tribe, of high respectability in Benares, is as follows.

The sacred cord is worn by Kshatriyas and Khatrîs as well as by Brahmans; but while formerly Kshatriya boys were invested with it at the age of eight, like Brahman boys, they are not invested with it now until their marriage; yet Khatrîs have preserved the old custom, and their male children receive the cord on reaching eight years of age. Moreover, Khatrî boys at the same age begin to study the Vedas, to repeat the *gayatri*, or sacred text, spoken by all Brahmans at their daily devotions, and to perform other religious duties. Not so the Kshatriyas, who do not study the Vedas at all nor repeat the *gayatrî*, and who commence their religious exercises at no fixed age. Again, in ancient times, as is stated in the Mahâbhârata and other Hindu writings, Brahmans would eat food (*kachha khânâ*) cooked by Kshatriyas; but they will not do so now, yet they have no objection to partake of such food when cooked by Khatrîs. In regard to the family priest also, formerly he was of the same *gotra* or general order as the Kshatriya, in whose house he dwelt; but this is not the custom now, yet it is so in the case of the Khatrî family.

The Khatrîs came originally from the Panjab, where, it seems, no difference appears in the pronunciation of the two names Khatrî and Kshatriya. Mr. George Campbell gives his opinion on the claim of the Khatrîs to be the descendants of the old Kshatriyas: 'I am inclined,' he says, 'to think that they really have the best claim to that honour.' 'The old Sanskrit books,' he adds, 'make the Brahmans and Kshatriyas to have remotely sprung from a common origin. May it not be that in early Aryan days the Brahmans of Kashmere may first have become literary and civilized, and ruled on the Saraswatî by peaceful arts, after the fashion of the earliest Egyptians before the art of war was invented; and that later a cognate tribe of Khatrîs, of the Cabul country, rougher and more warlike, may have come down upon them like the shepherd kings, and assumed the rule of the military caste of early Hindu history?' (*a*).

When a marriage takes place among Khatrîs, it is performed quietly, without dancing, singing, and the noise and tumult customary among most other castes. On occasion of a banquet given by a Khatrî, there is a stringent rule that only those persons are to be present who have been invited. Other castes are very lax on this point, for when a feast is prepared by any of them, not only the invited guests are present, but also many of their friends and relations.

The account of this tribe furnished by Mr. Campbell, in his 'Ethnology of India,' is, in my judgment, one of the most useful portions of that work. The following extract is too important to be curtailed. "Trade," he says, "is their main occupation; but in fact they have broader and more distinguishing features. Besides monopolising the trade of the Panjab and the greater part of Afghanistan, and doing a good deal beyond those limits, they are in the Panjab the chief civil administrators, and have almost all literate work in their hands. So far as the Sikhs have a priesthood, they are, moreover, the priests or *gurus* of the Sikhs. Both Nânak and Govind were, and the Sodîs and Bedîs of the present day are, Khatrîs. Thus, then, they are in fact in the Panjab, so far as a more energetic race will permit them, all that Mahratta Brahmans are in the Mahratta country, besides engrossing the trade which the Mahratta Brahmans have not. They are not usually military in their character, but are quite capable of using the sword when necessary. Dewan Sawan Mull, Governor of Mooltan, and his notorious successor Mûlrâj, and very many of Runjeet Singh's chief functionaries, were Khatrîs. Even under Mahomedan

(*a*) Ethnology of India, pp. 112, 113.

rulers in the west, they have risen to high administrative posts. There is a record of a Khatrî Dewan of Badakshan or Kûndûz; and, I believe, of a Khatrî Governor of Peshawar under the Afghans. The emperor Akbar's famous minister, Todar Mull, was a Khatrî; and a relative of that man of undoubted energy, the great Commissioner Contractor of Agra, Jotee Parshad, lately informed me that he also is a Khatrî. Altogether, there can be no doubt that these Khatrîs are one of the most acute, energetic, and remarkable races in India, though in fact, except locally in the Panjab, they are not much known to Europeans. The Khatrîs are staunch Hindus; and it is somewhat singular that, while giving a religion and priests to the Sikhs, they themselves are comparatively seldom Sikhs. The Khatrîs are a very fine, fair, handsome race. And, as may be gathered from what I have already said, they are very generally educated.

"There is a large subordinate class of Khatrîs, somewhat lower, but of equal mercantile energy, called Rors, or Roras. The proper Khatrîs of higher grade will often deny all connexion with them, or at least only admit that they have some sort of bastard kindred with Khatrîs; but I think there can be no doubt that they are ethnologically the same, and they are certainly mixed up with Khatrîs in their avocations. I shall treat the whole kindred as generically Khatrîs.

"Speaking of the Khatrîs, then, thus broadly, they have, as I have said, the whole trade of the Panjab and of most of Afghanistan. No village can get on without the Khatrî who keeps the accounts, does the banking business, and buys and sells the grain. They seem, too, to get on with the people better than most traders and usurers of this kind. In Afghanistan, among a rough and alien people, the Khatrîs are, as a rule, confined to the position of humble dealers, shop-keepers, and money-lenders; but in that capacity the Pathans seem to look at them as a kind of valuable animal; and a Pathan will steal another man's Khatrî, not only for the sake of ransom, as is frequently done on the Peshawar and Hazârah frontier, but also as he might steal a milch-cow, or as Jews might, I dare say, be carried off in the Middle Ages with a view to render them profitable.

"I do not know the exact limits of Khatrî occupation to the west, but certainly in all eastern Afghanistan they seem to be just as much a part of the established community as they are in the Panjab. They find their way far into Central Asia, but the farther they get the more depressed and humiliating is their position. In Turkistan, Vambery speaks of them with great contempt, as yellow-faced Hindus of a cowardly and sneaking character. Under Turcoman rule they could hardly be otherwise. They are the only Hindus known in Central Asia. In the Panjab they are so numerous that they cannot all be rich and mercantile; and many of them hold land, cultivate, take service, and follow various avocations.

"The Khatrîs are altogether excluded from Brahman Kashmere. In the hills, however, the 'Kakkas,' on the east bank of the Jhelum, are said to have been originally Khatrîs (they are a curiously handsome race); and in the interior of the Kangra hills there is an interesting race of fine patriarchal-looking shepherds called 'Gaddîs,' most of whom are Khatrîs. Khatrî traders are numerous in Dehli; are found in Agra, Lucknow, and Patna; and are well known in the Barâ Bazar of Calcutta, though there they are principally connected with Panjab firms.

"The Khatrîs do not seem, as a rule, to reach the western coast: in the Bombay market, I cannot find that they have any considerable place. In Scinde, however, I find in Captain Burton's book an acount of a race of pretended Kshatriyas who are really Banians of the Nânak-Shâhi (Sikh) faith,' and who trade, and have a large share of public offices. These are evidently Khatrîs. Loodianah is a large and thriving town of mercantile Khatrîs, with a numerous colony of Kashmeree shawl-weavers" (*a*).

The Khatrîs are divided into two great branches:

I. Purbiya, or eastern Khatrîs.

II. Pachhainya, or western Khatrîs.

The Purbiyas are said to have come long ago from the Panjab, and to have settled in the eastern provinces of India. They have gradually forgotten the names of the towns and villages of the Panjab whence they originally emigrated, as well also the families from which they sprang. This is not the case, however, with the Pachhainyas.

The Pachhainyas of Benares are sub-divided into six sub-tribes, each of which embraces a number of clans.

Pachhainya Khatrîs of Benares.

First sub-tribe—Arhai Ghar, or Chauzâtî.

Four Clans.

Clan.	*Gotra.*	*Clan.*	*Gotra.*
1. Khanna.	Kaunsil.	3. Kapûr.	Kaunsil.
2. Set.	Vatsa.	4. Mehrâ.	Kaunsil.

(*a*) Mr. George Campbell's Ethnology of India, pp. 108—112.

This sub-tribes tands at the head of the Pachhainya Khatrîs. They are particular on the subject of marriage, and will not give their daughters in marriage to any of the remaining sub-tribes. They will, however, marry their sons into the families of the four next sub-tribes, although they will not permit Chhazâtî men to intermarry with Chauzâtî women.

This sub-tribe apparently originally consisted of Arhai Ghar, or two-and-a-half families; which were subsequently increased to four, thence designated Chauzâtî, or four castes.

Many of the Kapûr clan, it is said, have become Mahomedans.

Second Sub-tribe—Chhazâtî.

SIX CLANS.

1. Bahel.
2. Dhanwan.
3. Beri.
4. Vij.
5. Saigal.
6. Chopra.

Third Sub-tribe—Panjzâtî.

Fourth Sub-tribe—Bahrî.

TWELVE CLANS.

1. Upal.
2. Dugal.
3. Puri.
4. Kochar.
5. Nande.
6. Mahpe.
7. Hânde.
8. Bhalle.
9. Mangal.
10. Badahre.
11. Sowâtî.
12. Kulhar.

All these clans intermarry. They also marry their daughters into the three preceding sub-tribes; but cannot receive their women in marriage.

Fifth Sub-tribe—Bâwanjâhî.

FIFTY-TWO CLANS.

All these clans intermarry. The Bahrî clans will receive their women in marriage; but will not give their own in return.

Sixth Sub-tribe—Kukrân.

Nine Clans.

1. Kohalî.
2. Anad.
3. Bhasîrn.
4. Chûadhâ.
5. Sabrwâl.
6. Sûrî.
7. Sâhanî.
8. Ghei.
9. Sethî.

These nine clans intermarry. The Kukrâns keep themselves distinct from the other sub-tribes, and do not intermarry with any of them.

Rai Sankta Prasad, the native gentleman of Benares through whom I have obtained most of the information respecting the Khatrîs of that city, belongs to the Sâhanî clan of the Kukrân sub-tribe of Pachhainya Khatrîs. He speaks English, takes interest in the education and well-being of the people, and is one of the disciples of Hindu progress, of whom, happily, many are now-a-days to be found in Benares and other Indian cities, and whose number is yearly increasing.

There is a clan of Khatrîs in the Bareilly district, bearing the name of Bara-ghar, which, according to tradition, was established in the time of Aurungzebe. It is said, that, during the Ajmere campaign, a large number of Khatrîs were killed. On this being reported to the emperor, he called a meeting of Khatrîs, with the object of prevailing upon them to give husbands to the widows. Some of them consenting, a new clan was formed called Bara-ghar (great house or family); while those dissenting were called Châr-ghar (four families); and those who induced the emperor to abandon his purpose, were called Adhi-ghar (half a family) (*a*). Whether there is any truth in this tradition, I am unable to say.

In Behar, says Dr. Buchanan, one half of the Khatrîs are goldsmiths.

In the Province of Oudh, Raja Bihârî Lâl of Morâwan is a Khatrî, as are likewise three other Taluqdârs. The Raja's family has been in the Province about one hundred and fifty years (*b*).

This tribe settled in Etawah about four hundred years ago. Some came from Jalaun, at the head of whom was the famous Mota Mull, who erected a splendid house for himself, the ruins of which are still visible. "He built the old 'Bisranth,' and bathing ghâts of the Jumna's banks; and left a name for munificence and pious works unsurpassed in our annals." The origin of the

(*a*) Report of the Census of the North-Western Provinces, for 1865, Vol I., Appendix B., p. 59.

(*b*) Mr. P. Carnegy's Races of Oudh, p. 60.

others is not known. They became wealthy bankers, whose fame extended far and wide. The present Etawah bankers are descended from them (*a*).

Rora.

This Vaisya clan professes to be connected with the Khatrî tribe, on the ground of the great similarity in the customs of the two tribes. I am not aware, however, that any close social intercourse, such as intermarriage, and partaking of cooked food together (a very important matter among Hindus), subsists between them. The Khatrîs do not include the Roras in their own tribe; and therefore, practically, they are distinct from one another. In Benares the Roras are mostly brokers, yet in other places they are tradesmen. They have three divisions, as follows:

1. Khatrî.
2. Lahorî.
3. Rora.

The third of these divisions, the Rora, is considered to be of purer lineage than the other two.

Purwâl or Purwâr.

This is not so numerous as some other Vaisya clans. It numbers upwards of twelve thousand persons in Mainpûrî. There are some families in Benares; and even as far south as Lallatpûr a considerable number of Purwâls are to be found.

The term Purwâl is said to be derived from *pûrî*, a sacred place. The Purwâls live in large houses in Benares, and are persons of consequence. Their number, however, is small.

The caste is divided into twenty branches. Its members are partly Vaishnavas, and partly Jainîs. They are engaged in trade.

Pallîwâll.

This clan came originally from Palli, in Marwâr. It is said, though with what truth I am unable to affirm, that the Pallîwâls are not pure Vaisyas, and

(*a*) Mr. A. O. Hume's Memorandum on Castes, Census Report, Vol. II., App. B., p. 87.

that they have Birbûjar blood in their veins. They migrated eastward in the age of Alla-ud-dîn Ghorî. Families of them have settled in several *pargannahs* of the Agra district. The caste is also found at Hamîrpûr. Some of its members are adherents of the Jain religion.

Unaya.

The Kanoujiya Brahmans have placed this clan among the Kayasths, though with no sufficient reason. The ground of their doing so evidently is that they eat meat, drink spirits, and engage in trade. They are in fact Baniyas or traders. Yet their habits are not unlike those of the Kayasths.

The caste is said to have twenty sub-divisions, all which are engaged in trade.

Rauniâr.

A class of tradespeople, found in various parts of the North-Western Provinces. In Benares they may number about one hundred families. They form a distinct caste. The tribe originally came from the west. It is sometimes called Niâr; but this is evidently a corruption or shortening of Rauniâr.

The caste is very numerous in Gorakhpûr, and is in considerable force also in Mirzapûr

CHAPTER V.

CASTES OF TRADERS.—(Continued.)

Agarwâlâ.

THIS is by far the most important family of the Vaisya Tribes throughout a large portion of Northern, North-Western, and Central India. Proud of their wealth and distinction, they affect to speak of themselves as the only true Vaisyas ; and some pandits are weak enough to support their pretensions. They have a tradition, which the Chaudhri, or headman of the clan in Benares, communicated to me, that they came originally from the banks of the Godavery, and that their common ancestor was Dhan Pâl. This man had a daughter named Muktâ, who married one Yâgyavalkya, by whom she had eight sons: Sivâ, Anilâ, Nâlâ, Nandâ, Kundâ, Ballobhâ, Sekhârâ, and Kumûd. The descendants of these men became scattered over the country, even as far as Gujerât; and gradually forsaking the customs of their caste mingled with the Sudras. One only remained faithful, Agar Sen, or, as he is otherwise called, Agar Nâth, or simply Agar ; from whom all Agarwâlâs have sprung *(a)*. The only value of this family tradition is, that it points to the ancestors of this caste previous to the birth of its acknowledged founder, Agar Sen.

This patriarch lived with his wife Madharû at Agroha, now a small town on the confines of Hariâna. Here the family prospered, became wealthy, and powerful. During the struggle between the Buddhists and Hindus, thousands of Agarwâlâs are said to have been killed, and many more, to save themselves, apostatized to Buddhism. After the great war when, the Agarwâlâ annals affirm, the prolonged contest between these two religious sects terminated in favour of the Hindu faith, the condition of the Agarwâlâs, who had been meanwhile scattered about the country, was much improved, so that they became once more opulent and flourishing *(b)*. This statement is somewhat

(*a*) M. S. on the Agarwâlâs, by Babu Haris Chandra, Chaudhri, or head-man, of the clan in Benares.

(*b*) *Ibid.* This tradition respecting the wars between the Buddhists and Hindus is exceedingly important as well as interesting.

opposed to the account given by Sir Henry Elliot, in his Supplemental Glossary, that the Agarwâlâs emigrated from Agroha to all parts of India, "after the capture of that place by Shahâb-ud-dîn Ghorî (a)." It is, however, so far corroborated by the traditions of the tribe in Benares, that it is indisputable that a heavy blow was inflicted by this monarch on their ancestors in Agroha, which caused the dispersion here alluded to. Yet, as already stated, many had left Agroha, and located themselves in various parts of the country, long before this. The Agarwâlâs speak of this conflict with the Mahomedans as peculiarly disastrous to their tribe, not only in destroying their integral character, and in separating them into numerous sub-divisions, but also in the great slaughter which the enemy effected, on account of which multitudes of women immolated themselves as Suttees on the funeral pile of their husbands (b). The Agarwâlâs of Chunâr and Mârwâr date their arrival in these places from this period. They are now among the most distinguished of the tribe.

Throughout the whole of the earlier epoch of Mahomedan rule in India the Agarwâlâs were in a very depressed condition, forming in fact a perfect contrast to their condition under British rule. It is not easy to account for this, unless it be that the Mahomedans, proud of their military prowess, and of their capacity to govern, looked with contempt on a class devoted exclusively to trade. With the accession of the Mogul emperors, however, the circumstances of the tribe began to improve, and gradually the Agarwâlâs made their way to posts of honour.

Agar Sen, the Agroha ancestor of the tribe, is said to have had seventeen sons, from whom the seventeen gotras, sects or clans, of the Agarwâlas, are descended (c). These are as follows:

Gotras or Clans of Agarwâlâs (d).

1. Garga.	5. Kasila.
2. Gobhila.	6. Sinhala.
3. Garwâlâ.	7. Mangala.
4. Batsila.	8. Bhâdala.

(a) Elliot's Supplemental Glossary, Vol. I., p. 2.
(b) M. S. on the Agarwâlâs, by Babu Haris Chandra.
(c) *Ibid.* Also Elphinstone's History of India, Vol. II., p. 241.
(d) *Ibid.*

9. Tingala.
10. Erana.
11. Tâyal.
12. Terana.
13. Thingala.
14. Tittila.
15. Nîtal.
16. Tundala.
17. Goila and Goina.
17½. Bindala.

The last, or Bindala, is only half a clan, but is always reckoned in Benares as supernumerary to the seventeen. These are not all found in the city: some, as Terana, and Kasila, have no representatives there. The most numerous clan in the city is the Goila. In addition to the above, other clans are mentioned which are not brought into this category, such as:

1. Dasâ.
2. Birâdarî-Râja.

The Dasâs are illegitimate descendants from an Agarwâlâ named Basû, and therefore are excluded from intercourse with the other sub-castes. The Birâdarî-râja clan are said to be descended from an Agarwâlâ named Ratan Chand, who was made a Raja by the emperor Farokhsir in the former part of the last century. By some persons, however, this clan is regarded as the same as the Dasâs.

The Purbiya, or eastern Agarwâlâs, form one large branch, in contradistinction to the Pachhainya, or western branch. The former are regarded as of older date in Benares than the latter. The two divisions may eat together, but cannot intermarry. Formerly, they intermarried, but in consequence of a quarrel, became disunited, and remained so for a number of years. Steps have been taken of late to effect a reconciliation, with some measure of success. The Agarwâlâs are particular in observing caste rules: they are said not to eat meat: and their widows do not marry again. A large number, probably one half, of the entire tribe, are attached to the Jain religion. Indeed, in the eastern districts of these provinces, they intermarry with the Sarâogîs, a well-known Jain sect.

The Agarwâlâs are found in every village and town in the Bulandshahr district. Those of Mainpûrî profess the Jain religion. A family of the tribe made its way from Gorakhpûr to Etawah about the close of the sixteenth century. "One Lâl Bihâra," says Mr. A. O. Hume, "was the head of the house, and was one of the royal treasurers. He spent some time at Kora Jahânâbâd, but died in Etawah, where his son, Baijnâth, built the palace, and his grandson, Jai Chand, the Kattra, now owned and occupied by his multitudinous descendants, many of whom are still wealthy merchants and considerable land-holders. Of the humble traders, or Baniyas, scattered everywhere about the district, a large proportion are Agarwâlâs (*a*)." Zemindars of this tribe are located in the Havali Chunâr *pargannah* of the Mirzapûr district, having come originally from Delhi. There are some also in the Karwat *pargannah* of the same district.

It has been remarked already that the Chaudhri, or headman of the Agarwâlâ tribe in Benares, is Babu Haris Chandra. He is of the Sinhala *gotra* or clan. In the attack on Agroha by Shahâb-ud-dîn, many persons belonging to this clan were slain. Their widows, who immolated themselves, are still worshipped as Suttees in the family house in the city. Two of these were wives of his direct ancestors. They are represented by certain figures or images. On quitting Agroha the family resided for many years at Lakhnautî, a village near Delhi; but it was not until the reign of Bahâdur Shâh, son of Aurungzebe, that any of its members rose to distinction. Under this ruler some of them occupied a high position in the State, and attained to the rank of Raja. Going back thirteen generations from the present time, the lineal ancestor was Bâlkrishna. One of his sons was sent as an ambassador to the Nawab of Murshidâbâd, with whom he so much ingratiated himself that, as a token of good-will and confidence, His Highness presented him with an estate in Râjmahâl, which still in part remains with the family. One of his descendants married the daughter of Sahu Râm Chandra, a banker of great reputation in Benares, a hundred years ago, in the time of the famous Balwant Sing, Raja of Benares. At his death he bequeathed his property to his son-in-law, Anu Chandra, who had two brothers and ten sons, besides many daughters. One of the brothers became a *fakir* or devotee, and founded a *math* or monastic house at Bhâgulpûr, which is still in existence. So great, however, have been since then the changes of fortune in the family, that its only surviving representatives are Babu Haris Chandra and his brother.

(*a*) Census Report for 1865. Mr. A. O. Hume's Memorandum, Appendix B., p. 89.

CHAPTER VI.

CASTES OF TRADERS—(*Continued.*)

OSWAL, BABU SIVA PRASAD, C S. I., RASTOGI, AGRAHRI, DHUSAR, BANDARWAR, DHANUK, MAHESHWARI, SONI, VISHNUI, PATHEL, SRI MAL, SRI SRI MAL, SRI MAL PATTAN, BARANWAR, MAHOBIA, LOHIYA, JATI, JAISWAL, BARHSENI, BAUDDH-MATI, KHARELIWAL, KASARWANI, UMMAR, KASAUNDHAN, KUSHTA, MAHRU, AND BANJARA.

Oswâl.

THE Oswâls are a wealthy class of Baniyas found in Benares and in many other parts of these provinces. Their original country is Gujerât and Marwâr, where they reside in large numbers. Many of them are attached to the Jain religion, and are known as Sarâogîs. The word Sarâogî is, says Wilson, a corruption of 'srâvok,' a lay worshipper of Buddha, or a Jaina, that is a follower of the Jain religion.

It is a singular circumstance, in connexion with the trading castes, that many of their members are devoted to the Jain religion, or to some other modification of the Buddhist faith. In Benares the following tribes and clans are more or less illustrations of these remarks :—

1. Oswâl.
2. Srî Mâl.
3. Srî Srî Mâl.
4. Srîmâlî Pattan.
5. Purwâl.
6. Kharelwâl.
7. Pallîwâl.
8. Agarwâlâ.
9. Lohiya.
10. Jaiswâl.
11. Bauddh-mattî.
12. Jattî.

Babu Siva Prasâd, C. S. I.

A distinguished member of this caste in Benares is Babu Siva Prasâd, C. S. I., Inspector of Schools. This gentleman has for many years occupied a

x 1

foremost place in the city, and in these provinces generally, for the intelligence and zeal he has displayed in promoting the education of the people. He has not only written and compiled a large number of useful books in the Hindî and Urdu languages, for the use of schools, but has also by his personal intercourse with multitudes of people in all parts of the country imparted a great stimulus to the cause of education among them. This is acknowledged, not only by the Government, but likewise by all classes of the community: so that he has come to be justly regarded as an enlightened reformer, who, instead of inventing baseless theories and impracticable schemes of national improvement, like so many of his fellow-countrymen, is heartily and effectively laboring, by the adoption of wise and beneficial plans, for their welfare. On several occasions the Government have shown their high appreciation of the Babu's public spirit and ability. He has received a grant of land, has been created a Commander of the Star of India, and latterly has been appointed to the post of Inspector of Schools, in succession to R. Griffith, Esq., Principal of Queen's College, Benares, with whom he was previously associated for several years as Joint Inspector. The high position of full Inspector is one never before attained by a native of India. On conferring the title of Commander of the Star of India upon the Babu, at a Durbar held in Benares, Sir William Muir, Lieutenant-Governor of the North-Western Provinces, stated his great satisfaction that a native of the country had been found so well qualified in every way to hold this important office, and expressed the hope that others, emulating his spirit and example, and possessed of his conspicuous qualifications, might come to the front, and be selected for similar posts.

Babu Siva Prasâd has furnished me with an account of his family history. The following outline will be read with interest.

The family is descended from Srestha Dhândhal, of the Parmâr caste, who in the year 1001 Sambat, or A. D. 945, erected a Jain temple in the Jaipûr territory. His posterity seems to have remained in that country until the eleventh generation, when on account of the attack of the emperor Alâuddîn Khilji on the fort of Ranthambhaur, its representative, Bhânâ, with his son, quitted the land in company with the Raja in 1335 Sambat, or A. D. 1279, and came to Champâner. Bhânâ's descendant, in the fifth generation, was Gorâ who in 1485 Sambat, or A. D. 1429, left Champaner, and settled in Ahmadabâd. Ten generations from Gorâ, that is 1684 Sambat, or A. D. 1628, Padmasî quitted Ahmadabâd and came to Khambhât. He was contemporary with Kaliyân Sâgar Sûr, the Jain high priest.

Amardat, grandson of Padmasî, presented a valuable diamond to the emperor Shâh Jahân, who in return conferred on him the title of Rai. He had two sons, Rai Uday Chand and Keṣarî Singh. Rai Uday Chand had four sons, namely, Rai Mitra Sen, Subhâg Chand, Fath Chand, and Rai Singh. Subhâg Chand had a son named Amar Chand, who had two sons, Rai Muhkam Singh and Raja Dâl Chand.

Fath Chand was adopted by his maternal uncle, Mânik Chand, and acquired the title of Jagat Seth from the emperor Muhammad Shâh for cheapening grain in Delhi. His grandson, Jagat Seth Mahtab Rai and his cousin, Srûp Chand, were killed by the Nawab Kâsim Ali Khân, of Murshidâbâd, for taking the side of the East India Company. It appears that, at the massacre perpetrated in Delhi by Nâdir Shâh, several members of the family were put to death, but Raja Dâl Chand, Jagat Seth, Mahtab Rai, and Srûp Chand, escaped to Murshidâbâd. On occasion of the arrest of Raja Dâl Chand by the Nawab of that city, the other two voluntarily accompanied him to prison, where they allowed him to escape, and bore the punishment of death to which the Nawab in revenge sentenced them. Jagat Seth was esteemed the wealthiest man of his time. Clive said of him, that, next to God, if the East India Company was obliged to any one man in the world for its possessions in India, that man was Jagat Seth.

Raja Dâl Chand effected his escape into the kingdom of Oudh. He was a man of great virtue, and was regarded with much esteem and veneration by his contemporaries. His son, Raja Uttam Chand, died in his life-time ; but he had adopted his sister's son, Babu Gopi Chand.

It should be remarked that, from the time of Rai Amardat down to the period of Rai Mahkam Singh, the family enjoyed the hereditary post of jewellers to the emperor of Delhi. Besides which, the younger branches of the family held, at various times, many important posts in the public service, as Mansabdars, or feudal knights, contractors, and so forth.

During the minority of Babu Gopi Chand, the family lost much of its property. His only son was Babu Siva Prasâd, who, at the death of his father, was twelve years of age. On leaving College the Babu, at the age of sixteen, entered the service of the Maharaja of Bhartpûr as Wakeel. Being dissatisfied, not to say, disgusted with the irregular practices of the native Durbar, he threw up his situation, and accepted the post of Naib Munshi in the Secretariat of the Foreign Department during the First Sikh War. After this he was Mîr Munshi in the Simla Agency for the period of eight years. Some time afterwards he became Joint Inspector of Schools in the Benares Province, and, as already observed, has been recently created Inspector of Schools. He has two sons, Satchit and Anand.

Rastogi.

This is a numerous tribe of Vaisyas engaged extensively in trade, and having its roots in many districts of these provinces. They are much addicted to banking, and are a wealthy and industrious people. Mr. P. Carnegy notices a peculiarity respecting them, that their women will not eat food cooked by their husbands. They are said to have come originally from Amethî. The tribe is divided into three clans, as follows:

1. Amethî.
2. Indrapati.
3. Mauhariya.

These clans are separate from one another, and do not intermarry.

Large numbers of the tribe are found in Benares, who pursue many kinds of trade. Some of its members are persons of wealth and position. The principal of them, who are, at the same time, Chaudhris or head-men of the tribe in that city, are Hingû Sâhû, and Gol Sâhû.

The caste is met with in all districts east of Cawnpûr. There are also families in Agra; and a considerable colony is settled in Bijnour.

Agrahri.

This clan has the tradition of being descended partly from a Vaisya and partly from a Brahmanical ancestor. It is, however, regarded as of the Vaisya tribe, and, like other Baniyas, is engaged in trade. The members of the clan wear the sacred cord; but this also is the practice of many other clans of this great tribe. Polygamy is indulged in by the Agrahrîs; on which account, it is said, they have lost the high position which they formerly held. Yet why this should have been the case, is not apparent, seeing that Brahmans and Rajpoots, who are much superior to them in social rank, are not dishonoured by their polygamist habits.

The Agrahrîs are divided into several classes, some of which are as follows:

1. Uttaraha.
2. Pachhawân.
3. Banârasî.
4. Tânchara.
5. Dâlâman.
6. Mahuliya.
7. Ajudhiyabasî (from Ajudhiya).
8. Chhîanwe (from ninety-six *pargannahs*).

Most of these clans are found in Benares: and the first three of them intermarry. The Agrahrîs form a very numerous class of tradesmen in that city, many of whom are of slender means.

Dhûsar.

This tribe of Vaisyas came originally, it is said, from Delhi. In that city they are distinguished for their talents as singers. They cultivate a peculiar strain or measure, in which they are unsurpassed. The Dhûsars are rigid in the maintenance of the purity of their order, and in the performance of Hindu ceremonies and duties; and neither eat meat nor drink any kind of spirit. In religion they are mostly worshippers of Vishnu rather than of Shiva. Their occupation, like that of the majority of Vaisyas, is trade and commerce; some take to the profession of soldiers. Under Mahomedan rule the caste was in a flourishing condition (*a*). There is a hill to the south called Dhûsî, at which is a sacred tank and also a Hindu monastery. Thither the Dhûsars from all parts of the country proceed on pilgrimage. It is a spot specially venerated by the tribe. They have a tradition that this is their primitive home, from which their ancestors issued, before occupying the province around Delhi, and thence scattering themselves over the country at large.

The Dhûsars are an intelligent and energetic race. Under the Mahomedan emperors they occasionally filled high posts. They are found in Allahabad, Agra, Mathurâ, Bulandshahr, and more or less in most towns of the North-Western Provinces. Those in the Alaigarh district are descended from Rao Sûjan Singh and his followers, who came from Koel to Mathurâ about one hundred and thirty years ago.

It is said that no Sarâogîs are found among the Dhûsars.

Bandarwâr.

The Bandarwârs are a very numerous tribe of Baniyas, having no fewer than thirty-six separate clans, some of the chief of which are the following:

1. Sonariya.
2. Sethiawar.
3. Chandhariya.
4. Sonparûya.
5. Rupiya.
6. Mâdhan.
7. Badhua Jî.

The clans seem to intermarry freely with each other. There are very few members of the tribe in Benares, not more in fact than some half dozen families.

(*a*) M. S. on Caste, by Kishori Lâl.

Dhânuk.

A caste of Baniyas. It has very few families in Benares.

Maheshwarî.

This large tribe of Baniyas or traders has seventy-two sub-divisions. As it is represented by only three or four families in Benares, these separate clans are to be sought for elsewhere. The common home of the tribe is at Bikanîr, in Rajpooṭana, where its members are bankers, merchants, and shop-keepers.

The Maheshwarîs, like the Dhûsars, are very attentive to their religious ceremonies. Most of them are Vaishnavas, or followers of Vishnu, although some are devòted to the Jain religion.

In the North-Western Provinces the caste is found in Jaunpûr, Mirzapûr, Ghazipûr, Bijnaur, Muzaffarnagar, as well as in Benares.

Sonî.

This tribe came originally from Gujerât. It numbers about thirty families in Benares, which are engaged in trade. Its separate clans intermarry.

Vishnûî.

The great trading Vaisya classes are in these Provinces more addicted to the worship of Vishnu than other Hindus, yet, for the most part, they worship other divinities likewise. Not a few of them, such as some of the Oswâls and Agarwâlâs, are attached to the Jain religion. One clan of the Vaisyas, however, is exclusively devoted to Vishnu, the second member of the Hindu Triad, and is known by the name of Vishnûî.

The Vishnûîs, strange to say, do not appear to be held in great esteem by Hindus generally, who consider the food and water touched by a Vishnûî as polluted. The Vishnûîs, however, exhibit the same sensitiveness, for they will not eat food or drink water which has been touched by other Hindus. The founder of this sect was one Jhâma Jî. There are several thousands of the sect in the district of Bijnaur.

The Vishnûîs read the Qurân, and fast and pray like Mahomedans; and also observe the Ekâdasî fast of the eleventh day after the new moon and full moon, like strict Hindus. Mahomedans may be initiated into this caste, which seems to have borrowed from them the custom of burying its dead, instead of burning them, according to the almost universal practice among Hindus.

This caste has been settled in various parts of the Morâdabâd district for the last three hundred years and upwards.

Sir H. Elliot says that the "tribe is of growing importance in Rehar, Sherkot, and some of the neighbouring *pargannahs* of Rohilkhand. They are found in great numbers in Bikanîr, Nagor, and Hissar; and small communities of them are also found in the Upper Doab." Respecting their customs, he adds, "they worship according to the Hindu ceremonial three times a day, and pray after the Musalman fashion five times a day. They keep twenty-eight holidays during the year, and observe the fast of Ramzân. They read both the Qurân and Hindu Pothîs" (*a*).

This tribe is divided into twenty branches.

Pathel.

This is properly a division of the great agricultural tribe of Kumbhîs. In Gujerât the Pathels till the soil, and perform various kinds of menial duties; but their representatives in Benares are exclusively devoted to trade, and therefore rank as Vaisyas. There are about twenty families of them in that city. The chief men among them are Gopâl Dâs and Munnî Dâs, who are wealthy merchants residing in Chaukhambha, a principal street of the city. The Pathels are divided into two clans as follows:—

1. Barhua.
2. Pathel.

These clans intermarry.

Srî Mâl.

A Baniya caste of Benares. Some of its members are attached to the Jain religion.

Srî Srî Mâl.

A caste of traders in Benares distinct from Srî Mâl and Srîmâlî Pattan. Some of its members are of the Jain faith.

Srî Mâl Pattan.

A caste of Baniyas or traders, of whom a small community exists in Benares. They came originally from Bithur near Cawnpûr. The *gotra* of those in Benares is called Kanchûlî. Some of the caste are attached to the Jain religion.

(*a*) Elliot's Supplemental Glossary, Vol. I., p. 43.

Baranwâr.

Communities of this trading caste are settled in Ghazipûr, Jaunpûr, Azimgarh, Gorakhpûr, and Morâdabâd. It is divided into twenty branches.

Mahobia.

These Baniyas are from Mahoba. There are many of the caste in Benares who are employed as shop-keepers. Their common *gotra* is Matal. The caste is also found in Cawnpûr.

Lohiya.

The Lohiyas are a numerous class of shop-keepers in Benares. They profess that their ancestors came from Allahabad, which they regard as the home of the caste. The Lohiyas of Benares are of the Kâsyap *gotra.* Some adhere to the Jain religion. The caste is also met with in Agra, in small numbers.

Jâti.

A small community of shop-keepers in Benares. According to their traditions, they have come from Jodhpûr. Their common *gotra* is called Tael. Some of them are of the Jain faith.

Jaiswâl.

A numerous Vaisya caste of Benares, sprung from Ujain. Some of them are Jainis in religion. The caste is also found in Mathurâ and Agra : in the latter district it numbers several hundred families. Those in Benares are of the Singhal *gotra.*

Barhsent.

The Barhsenîs in Benares are bankers, and are a considerable community. They state that their original home was Agroha. In Benares they are of the Garg *gotra.* Numerous families of the caste are found both in Mathurâ and Morâdabâd.

Bauddh-Matt.

A numerous caste in Benares engaged in all kinds of trade. They profess to have sprung from Mainpûrî. They belong to the Burhel *gotra.* It might have been fairly conjectured that the members of this caste were all attached to the Buddhist religion, as such is the proper meaning of the name they have chosen for themselves. Yet such does not seem to be the case. Some of them, however, I cannot say how many, are of the Jain faith, a perversion of Buddhism.

Khareliwâl.

A trading caste from Jaipûr settled in Benares. They are few in number in that city, and all belong to the Amerîa *gotra.* Some of them are of the Jain religion.

Kasarwânî.

Upwards of thirty thousand members of this tribe are located in the Banda district alone. Benares, Mirzapûr, Jaunpûr, and Fathpûr also contain many families. In the city of Benares the tribe is wealthy and numerous. Some of its members are great merchants, while others are only small tradesmen.

The Kasarwânîs are divided into three clans.

1. Kashmîrî.
2. Purbiya.
3. Allahabâdî.

The Kashmîrî Kasarwânîs came from Kari Manikpûr. They number about sixty families in Benares. The Purbiyas are very numerous in the city, and are stated to amount to twelve hundred families. Originally there were only two clans; but not long since a serious quarrel arose, which caused the formation of a third. The three, however, intermarry. Râm Kishan and Râm Charan are two Chaudhrîs or head-men of this caste in Benares.

Ummar.

A numerous and influential tribe of Baniyas, who are found as far as Agra to the west, Lallatpûr to the south, Gorakhpûr to the north, and Benares and Azimgarh to the east. They hold a very respectable position among the Vaisya tribes. Their widows unfortunately are not allowed to marry again. The Ummars are very few in number in Benares. The tribe has three divisions, as follows:

1. Til-Ummar.
2. Dirh-Ummar.
3. Dusre.

These are again sub-divided into twenty branches. The Til-Ummars are the highest in rank ; the next are the Dirh-Ummars.

Kasaundhan.

This tribe is said by Kishorî Lâl to have come originally from Lucknow, but unfortunately he neglects to give his authority for the statement. More than twenty thousand persons of this clan reside in Hamîrpûr. They are numerous also in Benares, Fathpûr, and other places. Their widows do not marry again. They are, for the most part, worshippers of Vishnu. They are general traders, both wholesale and retail ; some are bankers. They are divided into two clans, as follows:

1. Purbiya.
2. Pachhaiyan.

Kushtâ.

The Kushtâs are reckoned among the Baniyas. They are, for the most part, engaged in silk manufactures. The following clans are found in Benares, but in small numbers.

1. Patwâ.
2. Dakhinî.
3. Banarasî.

These clans are totally distinct, and do not intermarry. The Kushtâ Patwâs are different from the Patwâ tribe already described.

Mahru.

The chief seat of this caste is in Agra, where, by the last Census, it had a community of nearly ten thousand persons. The Mahrus are engaged in various departments of trade.

Banjâra.

A mixed race of wandering merchants, consisting, to a large extent, of accretions from a multitude of castes. They are found in all directions in these

Provinces. There seems to be an original Banjâra tribe inhabiting the lowlands beneath the mountain range from Gorakhpûr to Hardwâr. They were once a very turbulent race, but have at last been brought into order. In their wanderings they generally take with them their wives and children, and are to be found, I imagine, more or less, throughout India.

For a full account of this heterogenous race, see Wilson's Glossary, p. 60, and Sir H. Elliot's Supplemental Glossary, Vol. I., pp. 52-56.

The Naiks are a class of Banjâras, who have settled down in the Benares and Allahabad districts, and are engaged in agricultural pursuits.

CHAPTER VII.

SMALL TRADERS—CONFECTIONERS, OILMEN, HAWKERS, DRUG AND PERFUME-SELLERS, SPIRIT-SELLERS, AND GRAIN-ROASTERS.

HALWAI, TELI, BISATI, GANDHI, KALWAR, BHUNJA OR BHAR-BHUNJA.

Halwai.

THE Confectioner Caste. Although persons of many castes, especially Vaisyas, including even Brahmans, are employed in the manufacture and sale of sweetmeats, nevertheless, in the province of Benares, and in the Lower Doâb, there is a separate tribe engaged in this occupation. Hindus are passionately fond of sweetmeats, and, if they can afford it, will eat them to an enormous extent. Some almost live upon them. As there is a large proportion of *ghi* or clarified butter commonly used in their manufacture, those who eat largely of this kind of food are apt to become inordinately fat. Hindus, especially Bengalis, are very skilful as confectioners, and produce many varieties of sweetmeats never seen in England or France.

The Halwâîs are often confounded with the Bhûnjâs, or grain-roasters, arising from the fact that the one frequently pursues the business of the other. Yet they are distinct castes, and have no marriage connexion with one another. The Halwaîs have seven sub-divisions:

1. Kanoujea.
2. Pachpiria.
3. Bauniwâlâ.
4. Gaunr.
5. Madhesia.
6. Tîhara.
7. Lakhnawa.

Intermarriages to some slight extent are occasionally permitted between some of these clans; but as a rule they keep apart. All the clans are found in

Benares, but the most numerous are the Pachpirias and Madhesias. The former worship five *deotas* or deities. They also worship the *jhanda*, or flag erected by Mahomedans in honour of Gâzî Mîân, a Moslem saint; and also the *taziya*, a small model representation of the tomb of Hasan and Hassain, carried by the Mahomedan sect of Shiahs at the festival of the Muharram. They likewise go on pilgrimage with members of this sect to Bahraich in Oudh, where the saint was killed and buried. But they are Hindus, notwithstanding. Some of the Kanoujeas intermarry with the Madhesias.

The word Halwâî is derived from Halua, a kind of sweetmeat.

This caste is chiefly found in the eastern districts of these provinces. According to the last Census, there were more than seventeen thousand members of the caste in Mirzapûr alone.

Telî.

These are sellers of oil (tel). They occupy a respectable position among the lower castes; nevertheless, the higher castes will not permit them to touch their food. Most of them manufacture oil, as well as sell it. In Benares they have a considerable number of sub-divisions or clans, which, for the most part, do not intermarry or eat together. I have collected the following:

1. Bîâhut Bans.
2. Jaunpûrî.
3. Kanoujia.
4. Turkiya-telî.
5. Châchara.
6. Banarasiya.
7. Gulhariya.
8. Gulhânî.
9. Sri Bâstak.
10. Jaiswâra.
11. Lâhorî.

The Bîâhût Bansis are considered far above the rest, from the circumstance that they do not suffer their widows to re-marry. All the remaining sub-castes permit this liberty to their widows. The Jaunpûrî-telîs are not sellers of oil at all; but sell *dâl*, a sort of pea, extensively eaten by the inhabitants of the North Western Provinces. The Jaunpûrîs, Kanoujias, Lâhorîs, and Banarasiyas, as their names denote, belong specially to Jaunpûr, Kanauj, Lahore, and Benares. The Turkiya-telîs are Mahomedans. I heard of another clan of this tribe in Mirzapûr, called Khara.

The Gulhânis of Mirzapûr are the lowest in rank of all the sub-divisions of this caste.

Bisâti.

Properly one who hawks his goods about from place to place, and keeps no shop for the exhibition of his wares. He is commonly found seated on the ground with his goods spread out for sale on a mat before him.

Gandhi.

Seller of drugs and perfumes. The word is derived from *gandha,* smell, perfume, any fragrant substance. In the Karnatic it is used for sandal-wood (*a*). In Benares upwards of a hundred families are engaged in this trade.

Kalwâr.

Spirit-sellers form a distinct caste and clan among Hindus. In Benares, and this part of India generally, they are called Kalwârs. Toddy or spirit is in these Provinces chiefly made either from the flowers of the Mahûâ tree, or from very coarse sugar called *gur*. The Kalwârs have shops licensed for its sale. No other persons besides them engage in the traffic. Although ranking among the Vaisyas they are not regarded as very reputable members of the community. Drunkenness and immorality are more or less associated with them and their trade. As a race Hindus are not much addicted to intoxication from drinking fiery spirits. Nevertheless, the habit of smoking opium and *gânja*, a preparation of hemp, and also of chewing, smoking, and drinking an infusion of *bhâng*, another preparation of the same plant, is very common. Bhâng is said, by Dr. O' Shâughnessy, to consist of the large leaves and capsules of the hemp plant; and *gânja*, of the remaining parts dried (*b*). Brahmans, although they never smoke at all, are largely given to the use of Bhâng which, like the other two narcotics, imparts a fearful stimulus to the system, and has a maddening effect upon the brain.

The Kalwârs have the following sub-divisions.

1. Bîâhût.
2. Jaiswârâ.
3. Rangkî.
4. Raikalâr.
5. Surhî, or Sirdhî
6. Bhuj-kalaura.
7. Bhojphuria.
8. Gurer.
9. Tânk.

(*a*) Wilson's Glossary, p. 164.
(*b*) *Ibid*, p. 76.

The Bîâhûts are in position and reputation far superior to the rest. They neither sell nor drink spirits ; nor do they eat flesh. They are tradesmen and bankers. The Jaiswârâs may have as many wives as they please. The Rangkîs are Mahomedans. In their place, therefore, should be inserted, I imagine, the Gurers, another sub-caste, of which I have received information. The Surhîs, or as I have heard them also called, Sunrîs, are lowest in the list. They eat swine's flesh, a fact which sinks them very low in the Hindu social scale. The Bhuj-kalauras are a mixed people, formed from the union of the Bhunjas (who roast grain) with the Kalwârs. These are said not to be found in Benares ; they are met with in Mirzapûr. The Jaiswârâs are numerous in the sacred city. None of these sub-divisional castes intermarry. Their widows are not permitted to marry again.

Bhunjâ, or Bhar–Bhunjâ.

A caste employed in roasting or parching grain. The word is derived from *bhunnâ* to parch. Rice, peas, *gram* (a kind of pea), and other kinds of grain, are parched, and sold in the bazars. During the hot season it is common to feed horses with roasted grain. Some of the Bhunjâs are sweetmeat-sellers, especially the Kându clan, and many members of the two castes of Bhunjâs and Halwâîs confound them together. But the distinction is easily ascertained by putting the simple question, whether they eat together and intermarry.

The Bhunjâs are divided into seven sub-castes, some of which are the following:

1. Kanoujea.
2. Kûndu.
3. Madhesia.
4. Jaiswârâ.
5. Sakhsena.
6. Utarrâhâ.

These clans do not intermarry. The Kanoujeas and Madhesias of this caste are quite distinct from the clans of these names belonging to the Halwâî tribe, and have no connexion with them in the way of marriage. Both the Kanoujeas and Kândus sell sweetmeats as well as parch grain. The Kândus also sow and reap the *Singhârâ*.

There is a close connexion between the Bhunjâs and Kahârs, and I have found it impossible to obtain a complete list of the seven sub-divisions of the one which does not contain one or more of the sub-divisional names of the other, and yet they are two distinct castes, and do not intermarry. The chief cause of the difficulty lies in this, that the various clans care so little about one another that few persons trouble themselves to inquire which are the proper clans of their tribe. The Bhar Bhunjâs are said to spring from a Kahâr father, and Sudra mother (*a*).

The caste is very numerous, and is found in nearly all the districts of these Provinces. It is variously styled Bhunjâ, Bhar-Bhunjâ, Bhûrjî, Bhar-Bhûja, Bhad-Bhûja, Bar-Bhunjâ, Bhujârî, and Bhunjârî.

(*a*) Wilson's Glossary, p. 78.

CHAPTER VIII.

THE KAYASTH OR WRITER CASTE—THE KAYASTHS OF BENGAL—BABU GURU DAS MITRA.

KAYASTH.

The Writer Caste comes somewhere at the head of the Sudras, or between them and the Vaisyas. Nothing is known decisively respecting its origin; and although disputation on the subject seems to have been unbounded, no satisfactory result has been arrived at. The Kayasths themselves affirm that their common ancestor, on the father's side, was a Brahman; and therefore lay claim to a high position among Indian castes. But the Brahmans repudiate the connexion, and deny their right to the claim, giving them the rank of Sudras merely. Wilson, in his Glossary, states that they sprang from a Kshatriya father and a Vaisya mother, but gives no authority for the assertion. According to the Padam Purânâ, they derive their origin, like the superior castes, from Brahmâ, the first deity of the Hindu Triad. The Brahmans assent to this; but add, that it was from the feet of Brahmâ, the least honorable part, from which they imagine all the Sudra castes have proceeded. The Kayasths as a body trace their descent from one Chitrgupt, though none can show who he was, or in what epoch he existed. They regard him as a species of divinity, who after this life will summon them before him, and dispense justice upon them according to their actions; sending the good to heaven, and the wicked to hell. The Jâtimâlâ says that the Kayasths are true Sudras. Manu, however, (x, 6) states that they are the offspring of a Brahman father and a Sudra mother. With so many different authorities, it is impossible to affirm which is correct.

In point of education, intelligence, and enterprise, this caste occupies deservedly a high position. A large number of Government officials in Indian Courts of Law, and of *waqils*, or barristers, belong to it; and in fact it supplies writers and accountants to all classes of the community, official and non-official

Thus it comes to pass that the influence and importance of the Kayasths are felt in every direction, and are hardly equalled in proportion to their numbers by any other caste, not excepting even the Brahmanical. As revenue officers, expounders of law, keepers of registers of property, and so forth, they are extensively employed; indeed, they regard such duties as theirs by special birthright, while other persons who may discharge them are, in their estimation, interlopers. These views are rudely dealt with by the liberal Government of India, which shows no respect to persons or castes, and selects for its servants the best qualified individuals. Nevertheless, the Kayasths adhere to the notion in spite of the difficulty of defending it.

The proportion of men able to read and write in this caste is, I believe, greater than in any other, excepting the Brahmans. They are eager in the pursuit of knowledge, and send their sons in large numbers, both to the Government and Missionary Colleges and Schools in all parts of the country. I understand that a considerable number of the women of this tribe can read; and that it is esteemed a shame for any man of the caste not to be able to do so. In regard to their position in Bengal, Mr. Campbell, in his "Ethnology of India," makes the following observations :—"In Bengal," he says, "the Kaits seem to rank next, or nearly next, to the Brahmins, and form an aristocratic class. They have extensive proprietary rights in the land, and also, I believe, cultivate a good deal. Of the ministerial places in the public offices, they have the larger share. In the educational institutions and higher professions of Calcutta, they are, I believe, quite equal to the Brahmins, all qualities taken together; though some detailed information of different classes, as shown by the educational tests, would be very interesting. Among the Native Pleaders of the High Court, most of the ablest men are either Brahmins or Kaits; perhaps the ablest of all, at this moment (1866), is a Kait" (*a*). Speaking of the Kayasths in Hindustan Proper, in contradistinction to Bengal and other parts of India, his remarks are of value. "Somehow there has sprung up this special Writer class, which among Hindus has not only rivalled the Brahmins, but in Hindustan may be said to have almost wholly ousted them from secular literate work, and under our Government is rapidly ousting the Mahomedans also. Very sharp and clever these Kaits certainly are" (*b*).

The Kayasths are notorious for their drinking and gambling propensities. On special occasions many of them devote day and night to these vices, by reason

(*a*) Mr. Campbell's "Ethnology of India," p. 119.
(*b*) *Ibid*, p. 118.

of which the caste loses much of that respectability which its talent and education would otherwise secure. These terrible evils well illustrate, however, the bondage of caste. Whatever any caste sanctions, whether it be right or wrong, its members are in honor bound to carry out. This accounts for the prevalence of these two pernicious habits among the Kayasths. The caste upholds and sanctions them, so that I believe he would be regarded as a renegàde who should not, on great occasions, indulge in them. Yet a few persons are to be found here and there in the caste, who altogether spurn such habits ; and to keep themselves quite pure, as they imagine, from pollution, neither drink sprits, nor gamble, nor eat flesh. They are termed *bhagats*, or religious persons, and wear the sacred thread, and the *kanthi* or small necklace of beads. Should they, at any time, fall into temptation, these sacred objects are taken from them.

There is one other evil to which this tribe is addicted, which indeed is not peculiar to the Kayasth caste, but is cherished, more or less, by all the castes of every degree. This is the inordinate expense incurred at marriage festivals. Some members of the Kayasth caste, the Sri Bâstabs, in particular, indulge in such expenses to a most extravagant and ruinous extent. Men, with an income of ten rupees a month, will spend three hundred, and even five hundred, at the marriage of their daughters, which they have borrowed at the enormous interest of twenty-four per cent per annum, or more, and under the burden of which they lie for many years, and at their death hand down, perhaps, to their children. Great and most laudable efforts have been made of late in Benares, Allahabad, and other cities in the North-Western Provinces, to bring, not only the Kayasths, but all the principal castes, to agree to a great diminution of marriage expenses. This, it is hoped, will facilitate marriages ; lessen, if not wipe out, the crime of infanticide so prevalent among certain castes; and give to Hindu girls, not only a better chance to live, but also a more honorable, because less expensive, position in native society.

The Kayasths are called Devî-putr, or sons of *devi*, a term used to express a female divinity in general. In other words, they pay more homage to female deities than to male ; though why, I am unable to say. They hold Brahmans in great respect, more so, perhaps, than other castes ; although every caste, from the highest to the lowest, reverences the Brahmans, even to worshipping them.

This tribe is divided into twelve sub-castes, which are really independent of one another, as, with the exception of the Mâthurs, the first on the list, they do not intermarry, nor eat cooked food together. They may smoke together, however, from the same cocoa-nut hookah,—a condition of considerable liberty

They may all likewise drink spirits with one another indiscriminately. For some unexplained reason, it is the privilege of all the sub-castes below the first to intermarry with it, although they are not permitted to intermarry with one another. The sub-castes are descended, tradition affirms, from one father, Chitrgupt, and two mothers ; one the daughter of Sûraj Rishi, the other the daughter of Surma Rishi. From the first marriage four sub-castes have, it is said, proceeded ; and the remainder from the second. There is also half a caste call Unai, commonly appended to these twelve, sprung, it is asserted, from a concubine of Chitrgupt. But the Kayasths proper do not associate with its members. Yet they are always spoken of as Kayasths. So that, in public Hindu estimation, there are twelve and a half castes of Kayasths. It should be stated, however, that the impure Unai sub-caste of Kayasths is devoted to trade, and does not pursue the special occupation of the Writer caste. The twelve sub-castes are as follows :—

1. Mâthur (from Mathurâ.)
2. Bhaṭnâgar (from Bhatnair or Bhatnagar.)
3. Saksenâ (from Farakhabâd.)
4. Srî Bâstab.
5. Kul Sarisht.
6. Amasht (Ambastha.)
7. Sûraj Dhuj.
8. Karan.
9. Bâlmîk.
10. Ashtânâ.
11. Nigam.
12. Gaur (from Bengal.)

12½. Unai.

Owing to the privilege of intermarriage with the other sub-castes, the Mâthurs are diminishing continually as a separate sub-caste, and may in time be entirely intermingled with the rest. There are but few families of them in Benares. The custom of the Bhatnâgars in regard to marriage is the same as that of the Agarwâlas and Khatrîs. They agree with the Mâthurs in eating cooked rice and *dâl* (a kind of pea) with all their clothes on, in which respect they differ from other Hindus, who always remove their outer garments in partaking of cooked food, in which is no *ghi* or clarified butter. This is called *kachâ khânâ*, in opposition to *pakkâ khânâ*, dry food, or food cooked *with ghi*, which is eaten by all classes properly clothed (*a*). The Bhatnâgars of the

(*a*) The distinction between *kachâ khânâ* and *pakkâ khânâ* is very curious, and, in the social life of Hindus, of incalculable importance. The former consists of cooked food, such as, rice and *dâl*, and of a coarse thick flat cake, baked. Before partaking of this food, all Hindus, as a rule, wash hands and feet, and remove their garments from their persons, including the turban and skull-cap, leaving only a cloth round the loins. The castes are exceedingly particular in eating this *kachâ khânâ* apart. A Brahman and a Rajpoot, for instance,

West eat fowls and meat, luxuries eschewed by their brethren of the East. The Saksenâs have three divisions :—

1. Asl.
2. Dûsre.
3. Khare.

These do not intermarry. The Srî Bâstabs are perhaps the most important of all the Kayasth sub-castes ; and although enumerated ordinarily as fourth in the list, should properly be at its head. They are said to have come originally from Ajudhiya. Most of the Kayasths in Benares belong to this sub-caste. They are also numerous in Mirzapûr and Allahabad. There are two divisions commonly made of the Srî Bâstabs :—

1. Khare.
2. Dûsre.

These also do not intermarry. Two other clans of this sub-caste descended, it is said, from one mother, are spread over Jhûsî, Fathpûr, Nawâbganj, Arail, and places in their vicinity. These are :—

1. Niple Shabân.
2. Buddhi Shabân.

In Gorakhpûr certain honorary titles are attached to the Srî Bâstabs, such as :—

Pânde.
Amodhâ.
Qânûngo.
Muhtavi.
Bhouni.

The Kayasths of the district of Muzaffarnagar are mostly of the Bhatnâgar clan. Those of Kayrâna state that they originally came from Barh when Rajpoots were ruling in Delhi, a period long ago assuredly (*a.*)

The Gaurs are divided into two clans :—

1. Gaur.
2. Shimâlî Gaur.

These can eat and drink together; but, as to marriage, a Gaur boy can marry a Shimâlî Gaur girl, not a Shimâlî Gaur boy a Gaur girl. Should

eating it together, would both be expelled from their several castes. The *pakkâ khânâ*, which embraces sweatmeats, most kinds of food, though not all, cooked with *ghi*, and all dry food, is eaten by Hindus together indiscriminately, and, if they choose, with all their clothes on, and also without a previous laving of feet as well as of hands.

(*a*) Report of the Census of the North-Western Provinces, 1865, Appendix B, p. 8.

the two latter break through their caste rules of propriety, and marry, their children rank not with the Gaurs, but with the Shimâlî Gaurs. This sub-caste originally came from Bengal. In the neighbourhood of Delhi some of the Gaurs have formed alliances with Bhatnâgar families : their children are called Shimâlî Gaurs. The Karans are found in numbers in Tirhût, where they are employed as *pâtwâris* or village accountants. The habits and customs of the Sûraj Dhuj Kayasths are in many respects like those of Brahmans. Indeed, they presume to call themselves Brahmans. They are numerous in Delhi, where a division of the city is called by their name.

In the district of Meerut, the Kayasths have secured for themselves a position as landed proprietors.(*a*). It is said that this tribe was the first among the Hindu races of India to acquire a knowledge of the Persian language under the Mahomedan emperors, and hence the importance to which they attained.

The Amasht, Srî Bâstab, and Karan clans, are numerous in Behar. There are some families also of the Bhatnâgar, Mâthur, and Saksenâ clans. The Srî Bâstabs are said to have come originally from Tirhût.

Kayasths are proprietors of many villages in the Cawnpûr district. Not long since they held no fewer than forty-eight in the *pargannah* of Ghâtampûr ; and at one time they were the chief landed proprietors in the *pargannah* of Bhognîpûr Musanagar.

Landed proprietors of this tribe have possessions in various parts of the district of Fathpûr. A short time ago they held twenty-seven separate estates in the *pargannah* of Ekdillah alone. They had also seventeen in the Kotlah *pargannah*.

"Numerous members of the caste," says Mr. P. Carnegy, "rose to high places and honors under the kings of Oudh." He gives a list of the names of fifteen Rajas of the Kayasth tribe, who, he states, were the best known of those who rose to distinction. "The title of Raja," he adds, "which these men acquired, seems to have been for life only ; and the life-title has been recognized by the British Government in favor of Tej Krishan, the son of Raja Bâl Krishan, the late Finance Minister of the ex-king. There is no Kayasth Taluqdâr with the title of Raja in the Viceroy's Durbar list, although there are seven others mentioned of less degree" (*b*).

In most of the *pargannahs* of the Ghazipûr district there are a few villages

(*a*) Plowden's Census of the North-Western Provinces, Appendix B., p. 14.

(*b*) Mr. P. Carnegy's Races of Oudh, p. 59.

" belonging to communities of Kayasths, or Lâlas, of the families of the hereditary Qânûngoes, or superintendents of village records and accounts" (*a*).

Mr. A. O. Hume gives a singular instance of long proprietorship among the Kayasths of Etawah :—" Of the Kayasths, Chaudhrî Ganga Parshâd, of Bûrhîdanna and Umrî, Taluqdâr and Honorary Magistrate, still (with branches of his family) holds nearly the same villages they obtained in grant some six hundred and fifty years ago" (*b*).

The Kayasths are numerous in Etawah. The Ayara family, belonging to the Saksena clan, occupies a conspicuous position among them. This family has been in Etawah from the death of Jai Chand, of Kanouj, and entered the service of Samersa, on his taking possession of Etawah. "Pokhar Dâs and Nirmal Dâs, his sons," says Mr. Hume, " obtained from Samersa, or his son, the office of Chaudhrî, and with it, as usual, a grant of several villages, many of which their descendants still hold. The office of Qânûngo of Etawah is hereditary in this family ; and has always been held from Samersa's era up to the present time by some member of it." "Besides these," he adds, " there are the Chakwa and Parasna Kayasths, to whose family belonged the famous Raja Nawal Rai, whom the Nawab Bangash killed. These are Saksena Kharrai. Again, there are the Ek-dil Kayasths, Saksena, Dûsera, and others, whose ancestors were one and all followers or servants of the Chauhân Rajas, to whom they owed their estates still held by their descendants, as well as many others that have now passed into other hands" (*c*).

In the Etah district several Kayasth families have landed possessions. The Saksena, Srî Bâstab, and Kul Sarisht clans, are all found in the district.

The wealthiest landholders throughout the whole of the Fathpûr district belong to this tribe. They originally came from Hatgaon.

The Kayasths are numerous in the Allahabad district. " They seem," says Mr. Ricketts, " to have been the marked recipients of favor from the Mahomedan emperors."

" The Qânûngo-ships of several *pargannahs*, and other possessions, were given to several families of Delhi Kayasths. There is one family of Kayasths in Karrah, who are apostates to Mahomedanism. This was either to obtain or retain a Qânûngo-ship. The Qânûngo-ship is gone ; but they are still Mahomedans,

(*a*) Memoirs of the Ghazipûr District, p. 45.

(*b*) Census of the North-Western Provinces for 1865; Mr. A. O. Hume's Memorandum, p. 82.

(*c*) Mr. A. O. Hume's Memorandum on the Castes of Etawah, p. 87.

though they retain the Kayasth customs as far as is compatible with their new religion" (*a*). Landed proprietors of this tribe are located in the Mirzapûr district.

The Kayasths of Bengal.

From the manuscript on Hindu Castes by Babu Kishorî Lâl, a native of the North-Western Provinces, I learn that there are four separate clans of Kayasths in Bengal, the names of which are as follows :—

1. Kewas.
2. Newas.
3. Sirdatt.
4. Abnî.

For the correctness of this list, I am unable to vouch. It certainly does not agree with one which I have received from a respectable Bengali Kayasth of Benares. He states that the Bengali Kayasths are divided into eleven clans, three of which are Kulîn, and are of higher rank than the rest.

1. Ghose, } Kulîns.
2. Bhose, } Kulîns.
3. Mitr, } Kulîns.
4. De.
5. Datt.
6. Kor.
7. Pâlit.
8. Sen.
9. Singh.
10. Dâs.
11. Guha.

All these different clans, including even the Kulîns, intermarry; and in that respect set a praiseworthy example to the Kayasth clans of the North-Western Provinces. Many Bengali Kayasths are found in Benares, of whom a considerable number are Government officials retired on their pensions.

Babu Guru Dâs Mitra.

The Bengali community in Benares is very large, amounting to not fewer than twenty thousand persons. At the head of it stands the Babu, whose name is given above. He is a Kayasth of Calcutta, and is a son of the late Babu Rajendra Mitra, formerly a leader of native society in Benares. The family dates its connection with the British in India as far back as about the year 1686, when one of its ancestors, Govind Râm Mitra, received an appointment from

(*a*) Census of the North-Western Provinces for 1865; Mr. Ricketts' Memorandum on the Tribes of Allahabad, Vol. II., Appendix B., p. 130.

Mr. Job Charnock, the governor of the English factory at Calcutta, and settled in a district near the present fort called from that time to the present after him, Govindpûr. It is evident, from the records of the East India Company of the last century, that Govind Râm was for a long period a faithful and influential servant of the Company. When in 1756 the Nawab Sirâja Daulah plundered the English factory in Calcutta, Govind Râm showed his loyalty by fighting against him, and, on occasion of the English residents being thrust into the Black Hole, Govind Râm was seized and placed in confinement. After the battle of Plassey, in the next year, Govind Râm was appointed by the Company as Deputy Superintendent of the Police of Calcutta (*a*).

Babu Rajendra Mitra, father of the present Babu, received a *khilat*, or robe of honor, from the Government in 1852, for the liberality and public spirit displayed by him ; and the Honorable Court of Directors specially noticed him in a Despatch of the 1st December of that year. Babu Guru Dâs Mitra worthily maintains the honour of his house by his patriotism and loyalty. In the mutiny he nobly co-operated with the Government, in conjunction with the late Raja Sir Deo Narain Singh Bahadur, in endeavouring to quell the spirit of disaffection in Benares, and in affording substantial aid to the authorities. The Commissioner of Benares and Governor-General's Agent, thus wrote of him to the Government of India :—" I have much satisfaction in stating that Babu Guru Dâs Mitra, son of the good Rajendra Mitra, has done all in his power during the mutiny to assist Government. He attended in person at the Mint on the night of the mutiny. He, during the following days, gave supplies for the troops ; he furnished six or seven horses, a *palki-garry* (or coach), a number of carts, wheels—and, in short, as far as his ability extended, did all that he could to identify himself with the cause of Government" (*b*). On several occasions the Babu has made valuable benefactions to the city. His family belongs to the Gaur clan of Kayasths.

(*a*) An Account of the late Govind Râm Mitra and his Descendants, pp. 1—7 (printed for private circulation).

(*b*) *Ibid*, p. 26.

CHAPTER IX.

GOLDSMITHS AND JEWELLERS—ARTIZANS AND MANUFACTURERS—POTTERS, ROPE MAKERS—BRAZIERS, IRON SMELTERS, &c.

SONAR, NIARIYA, BARHAI, KHARADI, LOHAR, QALAIGAR, SANDHARA OR BARHIYA, LAHERA, KUMHAR, KAMANGAR AND TIRGAR, HAWAIGAR, DABGAR, PATWA OR PATAHRA, BANBATTA, CHURIHAR, KASERA, THATHERA, BHARIYA, AND ODHIYA.

Sonâr.

THE Sonârs are goldsmiths, silversmiths, and jewellers. In Benares they profess to derive their origin from the Kshatriyas. Some persons speak of them, however, as standing in a high position among the Sudra family. The Mahratta Sonâr caste regards itself as allied to the Brahmans, and the sub-castes style themselves Upa-Brahmanas, or minor Brahmans (*a*). Whatever may have been the origin of the Sonârs, they are not now socially of higher rank than the Vaisyas, to which great family, as manufacturers and traders, they properly belong. They are said to have a peculiar language or dialect of their own. This statement, however, I have not had the opportunity to verify.

The Sonârs of Benares are divided into three tribes :—

I. Bârah Mûl or twelve Roots.
II. Bâwan Mûl or fifty-two Roots.
III. Bâîs Mûl or twenty-two Roots.

I shall only give a detailed account of the first, or Bârah Mûl tribe. This is divided into twelve clans, as follows :—

1. Râmtullî of Râmtullî Ganj.
2. Thâkur of Thâkur Ganj.

(*a*) Wilson's Glossary of Indian Terms, p. 488.

3. Naugrahia of Naugrah.
4. Phûl of Phûlwari.
5. Aldemana of Aldeman.
7. Râjghatiâ of Râjghât.
8. Anguria of Anguri.
9. Tâte of Tâte Ganj.
10. Phaphe of Phaphe Ganj.
11. Nautakia of Nautake Ganj.
12. Tandora of Tânde.

The last, namely the Tandora clan, is again sub-divided into thirteen minor clans :—

1. Singh Tandora of Singhpûr.
2. Amlohiyâ of Amlo.
3. Jhanjhiya of Jhânjhî Tolâ.
4. Sugvahair of Sugvâri.
5. Naktu, Naik of Naktu Ganj.
6. Alona of Agra.
7. Nujariya of Agra.
8. Tahakhiya of Agra.
9. Ghosivâl of Ghosia.
10. Khâspûrî of Khâspûr.
11. Purhia of Puraniya.
12. Ghatkiya of Andhrî.
13. Purbî of Phâphâ.

Niâriya.

This clan is connected with the Sonârs. Its occupation is peculiar. The refuse collected in the shops of goldsmiths and silversmiths, consisting of small particles of gold and silver, intermingled with dust and all sorts of rubbish, is purchased and carried away by the Niâriya, who, with great care and diligence, separates the precious from the vile. This occupation is sufficiently remunerative to give employment to a distinct caste of Hindus.

Barhai.

The Carpenter Caste, called also Kokâs. Although carpenters are frequently employed as blacksmiths, yet they form distinct castes, quite independent of one another. Both have the character of being hard-working, enterprising, and intelligent; and are undoubtedly superior in many respects to most Hindus of their own rank in native society. As artizans, they exhibit little or no inventive power; but in imitating the workmanship of others, they are, perhaps, unsurpassed in the whole world. They are equally clever in working from designs and models.

The Barhai caste is said to be divided into seven clans; but in reality it has many more. In Benares and its neighbourhood, there are the following:—

1. Janeodhârî.
2. Khâtî.
3. Maghaiya.
4. Kokâs.
5. Setbândâ Râmeshwar.
6. Kanoujea.
7. Pargangiya.

The Janeodhârîs eat no meat, wear the sacred cord (janeo), and regard themselves as far superior to all the rest. They are said to come from the Doâb. The Khâtîs simply manufacture wheels. The Kokâs are from Delhi, and make chairs and tables. Those designated Setbândâ Râmeshwar are manufacturers of puppets or dolls, with which they perform in public. They also have a character for begging. They are therefore not a reputable branch of the caste. The clans neither eat together, nor smoke together, nor intermarry. Mahomedans also work as carpenters, as well as Hindus.

Sir Henry Elliot has given in his Glossary the names of other clans not found in this list, as Kûka, Mahûr, Tânk, Uprautiya, Baman-Barhai or Mathuria, Ojha Gaur, and Chamâr Barhai (*a*). Kûka is, I suspect, intended for Kokâs; the Baman-Barhais and Ojha Gaurs are, probably, Brahmans employed as carpenters; and the Chamâr-Barhais are undoubtedly Chamârs.

Widows are permitted to re-marry in this caste.

Kharâdî.

The Kharâdî is a turner. The Hindustani word for *to turn* (by the lathe) is *kharâdnâ.* In addition to his usual occupation as a turner, which is shared, to some extent, by the Barhai or carpenter, he enjoys a monopoly in the manufacture of wooden toys. The caste is not numerous. The Kharâdîs are a very industrious and respectable class of artizans. They also bear the names of Kanair, Kundera, and Kundaira.

(*a*) Elliot's Supplemental Glossary, Vol. I., p. 56.

Lohâr.

The Blacksmith Caste. Some of the members of the caste not only work in iron, but also labor as carpenters. Hindu blacksmiths are clever artizans, and in intelligence are far superior to most other tribes holding socially an equal rank with them. They are divided into seven clans as follows :—

1. Kanoujea.
2. Mahouliya.
3. Srî Bâstak.
4. Mallik.
5. Banarasiya.
6. Chaurashâ.
7. Purbiya.

All these are found in Benares. None of them intermarry. I have also heard of other clans, such as—

1. Maghaiya.
2. Sînar.
3. Mathuriya.

The Lohârs are popularly said to be descended from the Rishi or ancient sage, Viskarma, and are consequently supposed to belong to this *gotra.*

Qalaigar.

The Qalaigar is properly one who tins copper cooking utensils, by which process they are rendered safe and suitable for culinary purposes. But he also occasionally pursues the profession of a gilder. Both Hindus and Mahomedans follow the occupation of tin-men. It is a separate caste among the Hindus.

Sandhara or Barhiya.

The Sandhara sharpens and cleans swords, knives, and all kinds of implements of iron and steel. He is also a polisher and furbisher. The clan professes to have come originally from Marwâr, and to be related to the Rajpoots. Mahomedans who pursue the same avocation are called Sikligars, or more properly Saiqalgars. Indeed, occasionally, Hindus themselves are likewise so styled. The caste also bears the designation of Barhîya.

Lahera.

These are properly earthenware-varnishers. But as this occupation is, I suppose, insufficient for their maintenance, they unite to it that of carrying bricks on asses for erecting houses and walls. They are, consequently, in both respects intimately connected with the Kumhâr or Potter tribe.

Kumhâr.

The Potter Caste. They manufacture all kinds of earthen vessels, whether for domestic or general use. These are made by the hand, and often display considerable ingenuity. Many of them, especially those that are of complicated construction, are made as follows. A large wheel is placed in an horizontal position on a small and well-lubricated pivot fixed strongly into the ground. On the centre of the wheel above the pivot, a quantity of prepared clay is deposited; then by means of a stick the wheel is made to revolve very rapidly, and sufficient impetus is imparted to it to keep it in motion for several minutes. Seating himself down on the ground before the wheel, and stretching his arms over, the Kumhâr manipulates the revolving clay into the shape intended, and, having done so, separates it by means of a thin cord from the rest of the clay, and re-commences the same operation, there being enough clay on the wheel for the manufacture of a dozen vessels or more. When the wheel slackens in speed, he places the stick in a hole near one of the spokes, and revolving it a few times forcibly, sends it on again with its original speed. The vessels when made are burnt in a kiln. In addition to this employment, he also makes bricks and tiles.

The word Kumhâr is derived from the sanskrit *Kumbhakârâ*, *kumbha* meaning a water-jar. The caste has seven sub-divisions:—

1. Kanoujea.
2. Hatheliya.
3. Swariya.
4. Bardhiya.
5. Godaihiya.
6. Kasgar or Kastora.
7. Chauhânia Misr.

The first three sub-castes are chiefly employed in making tiles and bricks. The Bardhiyas convey clay and earth on the backs of bullocks. The Godaihiyas perform the same operation, but on donkeys. The Kasgars occupy themselves mostly in making dishes and plates on which food is eaten. They are sometimes called Kastora. The Chauhânia Misrs claim to have been once Brahmans. Their compound name is partly of a Rajpoot, and partly of a Brahman origin, the Chauhâns being a well-known tribe of Rajpoots, and the Misrs being Brahmans of a certain rank. Whether the claim of this clan is sound, is hard to say.

This is one of the most numerous castes inhabiting the North-Western Provinces. It is computed that nearly half a million of Kumhârs are scattered over its various districts, of whom upwards of sixty thousand are in Gorakhpûr alone. They are, for the most part, an industrious and well-conducted people.

Kamangar and Tîrgar.

Manufacturers of bows and arrows. Some of them practise the surgical art in the setting of fractured and dislocated limbs. They are found in several districts, but are a small community.

Hawaigar.

The Hawaigars sell gunpowder and fireworks which they manufacture. They are very skilful in their art, so far as their knowledge extends, yet they bear no comparison with the firework-manufacturers of England. Many, perhaps most, of the clan are Mahomedans.

The natives of India are passionately fond of fireworks of every description, and exhibit a strong predilection for those which produce a great and stunning report. At marriages and other important festivals, they chiefly gratify their taste in such matters. On occasion of a marriage in a family of position, the loud reports of the *bam* may be heard throughout the night, while fire-balloons are sent up, and fireworks are discharged at intervals. The *bam* produces a sound not unlike that of a cannon. It is a notorious fact that in the mutiny the first panic which occurred in one of the stations of the North-Western Provinces arose solely from the distant reports of the harmless *bam* at a marriage festival in a neighbouring village.

Dabgar.

The Dabgars are a low caste employed in the manufacture of large leathern vessels for holding *ghi*, or clarified butter, and of vessels in which *atta* and glue are deposited. They eat the flesh of goats. They are said to have no divisions in their caste. The Dabgars form a considerable colony in Cawnpûr, and are found in small numbers in several other districts.

Patwa or Patahra.

A tribe engaged in the manufacture and sale of ornaments, made of zinc and tin, and other inferior metals, worn by men and women, but chiefly by the latter. They also make trinkets of silk and silk cloth, edged with gold. More expensive ornaments of silver, gold, and jewels, do not fall within their province. Nevertheless, those they manufacture are of manifold kinds but cheap, and suited to the wants of the lower classes of the people. When it is borne in mind that every Hindu woman and girl, unless a widow, wears several ornaments, and commonly a great many, and that boys, and not a few men likewise, indulge in the same taste, it will be readily understood that the trade in these wares is immense. The clan has five sub-divisions, as follows :—

1. Kharewâl, or Khandiwâl.
2. Kharâ or Khare.
3. Deobansî.
4. Laherâ.
5. Jogi Patwâ.

These are quite distinct from one another, and do not intermarry.

The Patwas knit silken cords ; and in Behar, where silk is produced, many families are employed in weaving silk cloth, or silk and cotton mixed, or cotton alone.

The caste is found in most of the districts of these provinces, but generally in small numbers. There are upwards of a thousand in Benares.

Banbatta.

A caste of rope-makers. They also interlace charpoys, or native beds, with twine or fine rope. They belong to the districts of the Upper Doab (*a*).

Chûrîhâr.

Chûrî is a bracelet made of *lac* or sealing-wax, and worn round the arm by Hindu women. They wear usually many at a time painted with various colours. A custom prevails amongst them of decorating themselves with these ornaments at a certain season of the year. The *chûrî* is very brittle, and easily breaks.

The Chûrîhâr is a manufacturer of *chûrîs*, and of all other articles made of *lac*. The principal manufacturer in Benares is exceedingly wealthy, and resides in a mansion known as Chûrîhâr-kî-kothî, situated near the Mân Mandil Observatory. He is very charitable, and gives what is called *sadâbart*, or daily alms, consisting of rice and grain, to all beggars who apply, and distributes copper money on the eleventh day of the moon.

(*a*) Mr. E. A. Reade's Inferior Castes of the North-Western Provinces, p. 26.

Kasera.

The Kaseras are workers in kasa, a compound metal, and also in brass and copper, and in most other kinds of metal, including gold and silver, but excluding iron and tin. They manufacture utensils for domestic use, which in India, for the most part, are made of either copper or brass. They also, to some extent, manufacture ornaments to be worn on the person, many of which are either made entirely of one or other of these two metals, or of several metals compounded together. Women âre exceedingly fond of wearing ornaments made of a beautifully white compound metal, white as silver, yet much cheaper.

As artizans and traders, the Kasera caste occupies a high position. They are said to be above the Vaisya, or Commercial caste, and to hold a place between this and the Kshatriya caste. The reasons assigned for this opinion are, that the tribe in all its sub-divisions is more punctilious on many matters considered to be of importance by Hindus than the Vaisya or Sudra castes usually are, and that they all wear the sacred thread. This, however, is no sufficient reason for elevating them above the Vaisyas, to which family they naturally belong. They are divided into seven clans :—

1. Purbiya.
2. Pachhawân.
3. Gorakhpûrî.
4. Tank.
5. Tâncharâ.
6. Bharîyâ.
7. Golar.

None of these intermarry or eat together. The four first sub-divisions are names given to such Kaseras as have emigrated from those parts of the country to which they refer. The Purbiyas are from the east, the Pachhawâns from the west; the Gorakhpûrîs from the district of Gorakhpûr; and the Tanks, most probably, from the principality of Tonk.

This tribe is very numerous in the city of Mirzapûr, where a considerable trade is carried on in brass wares. The Kaseras manufacture all kinds of brass utensils, which are sent to distant parts of the country for sale.

Thathera.

The Thatheras are distinct from the Kaseras, although, to some extent, they labor in the same metals. Yet their work is of a heavier and rougher cast, and embraces iron, tin, and zinc, as well as brass, copper, and kasa. They also carve the vessels manufactured by the Kaseras. It is very difficult to draw an exact line between the two castes ; for in some respects they pursue the same calling. Nevertheless, they keep themselves entirely apart, and do not permit family alliances with one another.

Bhariyâ.

The workers in brass, iron, and other metals, in some cases, but not in all, make moulds and cast their own vessels. The Bhariya caste is specially engaged in the occupation of preparing moulds, of various shapes and kinds, for casting vessels. The Bhariyas, although connected by their avocation with the Thatheras and Kaseras, are, nevertheless, a distinct caste, and do not intermarry with either.

Odhiya.

A caste of iron smelters and workers in iron. They are looked down upon and despised by many castes, for what reason, I am unable to say. The caste embraces a small community, and inhabits the Allahabad province and the country to the south (*a*).

(*a*) Mr. E. A. Reade's Inferior Castes of the North-Western Provinces, p. 32.

CHAPTER X.

AGRICULTURAL CASTES.

KUMBHI, KOERI, KACHHI, KUKANI, KUTWAR, BHURTIYA, MALI, GANDHRI, KUNJRA, RANGAR, DHAIL-PHORA, BARAYI, AND TAMBOLI.

Kumbhi.

THE great agricultural class of India is known by various designations appertaining to different localities. One of the most extensive tribes of cultivators is the Kumbhi, otherwise called Ḳumbhî, Kunbi, and Kurmî, which is found over a large portion of Hindustan proper, and in Central India. To the west, however, its numbers greatly diminish.

As tillers of the soil the Kumbhis are industrious and plodding. They have neither the energy nor ability for hard labour exhibited by husbandmen in England. Nevertheless, they have great powers of endurance, and are of indomitable perseverance. As a class they are, I am inclined to think, higher in the social scale, as compared with the rest of the community, than the corresponding class in England. Not that they are better educated, or indeed so well educated, or more intelligent ; but they certainly command higher respect and consideration from other people than the labouring classes of England. Again, while the cultivator in India receives much smaller wages than the cultivator in England (*a*), yet he is really as well off. His wants are few, and food is cheap. There is, I believe, less of grinding poverty among this class in India than is seen in the same class at home. Of course, should the rains fail, and famine, or even scarcity, appear—and one or other is, alas, but too frequent—not only fearful and widespread want, but also appalling mortality, are the result.

(*a*) The ordinary wages of a husbandman in India are about two rupees and a half, or five shillings, per month. A few may receive three rupees, but more receive only two. Many labourers are paid in kind, and rarely handle money at all.

The Kumbhis are distinguished from the Koerîs, as the latter are frequently gardeners as well as husbandmen. Socially, they are on an equality, which is hardly the case with similar classes in England. They are, however, totally distinct, and have no more intercourse with one another, though living side by side, than Frenchmen and Englishmen. But it is almost needless to make an observation of this nature, seeing that the same spirit of separation and exclusiveness holds good with all the castes, and of a multitude of sub-castes likewise, which are virtually distinct nationalities. In the cultivation of the fields, and in tending cattle, the women work as hard as their husbands. I have never seen them ploughing, but they perform all other kinds of field labour.

The sub-divisions of this caste are numerous. Seven is the standard number, however; but the details are not the same in any two places. In Benares there are the following :—

1. Athariya.
2. Ghorcharhâ.
3. Jaiswârâ.
4. Gujerâtî.
5. Patarghichâ.
6. Patariya.
7. Channan-nâû.

These do not intermarry or eat together. In Mirzapûr I heard of two others :—

1. Mahtau.
2. Manwâr.

These are said to intermarry with the Channan-nâû clan. Sir H. Elliot has given additional information concerning this caste. He speaks of the Jhûnaiya clan, to the west of the Upper Jumna, and of other divisions of the tribe : " as the Singraur and Chaparya of the Lower Doâb ; the Jharî of Nagpûr, the Ghameta, Samsawar, Kachisa, and Chandani of Behar ; the Saithawar, Putanawar, Atharya, Chunanaun, and Akharwar, of Gorakhpûr and Benares ; the Rawat, Jadon, Bhartî, Kattiar, and Gangwarî of Rohilkhand. These also have no communion of food or marriage." He adds, " there are several Kurmîs, or Kumbis, among the Marattas ; and the Gwalior, as well as the Satara, families are of that stock "(a). He is, I think, in error in placing the Kewats among the sub-divisions of this caste.

(a) Elliot's Supplemental Glossary, Vol. I., pp 156,7.

This tribe occupies clusters of villages in the Budaon district ; but they are not found there in great numbers

In the province of Behar, there are, on the authority of Buchanan, the following clans, Magahi, forming one half of the whole, Ghameta, Ayudhiya, Samsawar, Yasawar (or Jaiswâra), Kachisa, Chandani, and Desi, which last is a spurious race.

In some parts of the country members of this caste have large possessions in land. In the year 1848, out of thirty-eight estates of which the *pargannah* of Dhâtâ in the Fathpûr district was composed, no fewer than twenty-seven were in the hands of the Kumbhis, there called Kûrmîs ; which circumstance, it was rightly conjectured, was the chief cause of the thriving condition of that *pargannah*. In the Jalaun district they are a very useful people, engaged in agriculture, but hold no influential position. They are very old inhabitants of some parts of Gorakhpûr.

The Kumbhis are found in great numbers in the country about Chunâr. They came from Jainagar and other places, to the east. A few are landholders, but most are cultivators.

Koerî.

This tribe is also called Mûrâo, but it is most commonly spoken of in this neighbourhood by the term Koerî. These and the Kumbhis are the great agricultural classes of these provinces. Many other castes, more or less, are employed in the cultivation of the soil. Indeed, every Hindu, however humble his station, likes to have his plot of ground, which himself or his wife and children, or other relations, or in default of them, some of his friends, may cultivate. Property in land is considered by the people generally, of every rank and caste, to be the safest and most satisfactory mode of investing money, little or much, notwithstanding the heavy tax upon the soil. The Koerîs and Kumbhis are agriculturists by profession, and, perhaps, least of all the castes, have suffered themselves to be diverted from their own proper occupation.

Both these classes are very laborious in their habits; on which account, and also for their general peaceableness, they have secured the respect of all the other castes. While both are engaged in the cultivation of the land, the main distinction between them—for they are quite separate as tribes—is, that a considerable number of the Koerîs are vegetable gardeners. They have immense gardens in the vicinity of cities and towns, which are supplied by them with various kinds of vegetables.

The Koerîs are the principal growers of poppy, and producers of opium, both in Benares and Behar. At Hindu marriages a custom universally prevails of placing a high crown, called *maur*, made partly of leaves and flowers, on the head of the bridegroom, and a smaller one called *maurî*, on the head of the bride. It is said that no wedding can take place without these crowns. They are made by the gardeners, who receive a considerable price for them, according to the circumstances of the parties.

This tribe has seven sub-divisions, which are not the same everywhere. Indeed, were all that exist to be numbered up, they would, it is likely, amount to as many as twenty, or even thirty. The seven known in Benares are as follows :—

1. Kanoujea.
2. Hardiya.
3. Illahâbâdî.
4. Brijbâsî.
5. Korî.
6. Purbihâ.
7. Dakhinahâ.

All these are found in Benares except the Korîs. These sub-castes do not intermarry or eat together. In Mirzapûr I heard of others :

1. Nârâîgana.
2. Banârasiyà.
3. Kachwâhâ.

The second class, as their name denotes, are evidently immigrants from Benares. Others are given by Sir H. Elliot in his Supplemental Glossary. In Ghazipûr, in addition to some of the above are these clans:

1. Torikoriya.
2. Bardwâr.

The Koerîs, Buchanan says, are of four clans, Kanoujea, Jarahar, Chiramait, and Bharu.

The Koerîs are numerous in the district of Jhânsî, where they pursue the occupation of weaving. Their tradition is, that they came from Benares about seven hundred years ago. They manufacture *khârua* and other cotton goods.

Kâchhî.

The Kâchhîs are, like the Kumbhis, cultivators. The pursuits of both, so far as I have been able to ascertain, are much the same, and yet perhaps the

Kâchhîs are more frequently employed as gardeners than the other class. They are a peaceable and industrious people. Some of them are artizans.

The Kâchhîs state that they have seven clans; but in reality they have more than this number. Sir H. Elliot enumerates the following: Kanoujiya, Hardîha, Singrauriya, Jaunpuriya, Bamhaniya or Magahya, Jarelha, Kachhwâhâ, Dhakolya, Sakhsena, and Sachan (*a*). These clans do not associate together or intermarry. In Behar the Kâchhîs are largely engaged in the cultivation of the poppy. This tribe is found in many of the districts of these provinces, and is very numerous.

The Kâchhîs of Lallatpûr are divided into four clans, as follows: 1 Kachhwâhâ; 2 Saloriya; 3 Hardiya; 4 Amwar.

The Kâchhîs of Jhânsî claim to be descended from the Kachhwâhâ Rajpoots; and affirm that their ancestors came from Narwar a thousand years ago.

Kukanî.

An agricultural caste, many members of which reside in the Bhadohî *pargannah* of the Mirzapûr district. There are a few also in Benares.

Kutwâr.

A class of cultivators found in small numbers in various districts, especially to the north of the Jumna. They are also employed as watchmen (*b*).

Bhûrtiya.

A small agricultural caste found chiefly in Tuppeh Upraudh of the Mirzapûr district, where they are reputed to have sprung from the Gujars of Gujerât. They are also met with on the banks of the Jumna. A few inhabit the district of Gorakhpûr.

Mâlî.

Although many Koerîs are employed as gardeners, yet they are more especially what are termed in England market-gardeners, while the Mâlî is the general gardener. He lays out gardens, plants fruit-trees, sows flower-seed, and, in fact, performs the various duties of a garden containing fruits, flowers, and vegetables. The word is derived from the Sanskrit *mâl*, a wreath.

(*a*) Supplemental Glossary, Vol. I., p. 145.
(*b*) Mr. E. A. Reade's Inferior Castes, &c., p. 30.

In laying out a flower garden, and in arranging beds, the Mâlî is exceedingly expert. His powers in this respect are hardly surpassed by gardeners in England. He lacks of course the excellent botanical knowledge of many English gardeners, and also the peculiar skill displayed by them in grafting and crossing, and in watching the habits of plants. Yet in manipulative labour, especially when superintended by a European, he is, though much slower in execution, almost, if not quite, equal to gardeners at home.

According to Buchanan, the Mâlîs are divided into the following clans:

1. Magahi.
2. Sirmaur.
3. Banarasiya.
4. Kanoujiya.
5. Baghel.
6. Kahauliya.
7. Desi.

The tribe permits the re-marriage of widows. "One Arjun, a man of this caste," says Mr. P. Carnegy, "rose to the honorary distinction of Raja under the kings of Oudh, and thereafter added Singh to his name (*a*).."

In the Bijnour district the Sanî caste is said to be the same as the Mâlî caste. The Sanî is spoken of as a first-rate gardener, florist, and vegetable grower. Mâlîs are found in many parts of the North-Western Provinces. They have been known to be in the Morâdabâd district for several hundred years past. Some of them are reputed to have come originally from Ajudhiya and Lucknow.

In some places Mâlîs are employed as vaccinators, and prescribe medicine to persons attacked with small-pox. Such Mâlîs are called Darshaniyas.

Gandhrî.

The Gandhrîs and the Mâlîs were formerly one clan, but they have become gradually distinct classes, so that now there is no intermarriage between them, and they are really separate clans. The Gandhrî no longer devotes himself to the general duties of a gardener, but is exclusively engaged in the preparation of perfumes from flowers. These he extracts by various processes. The manufacture of the Otto of Roses calls forth his highest powers. It is, however, very remunerative, and well re-pays his utmost skill.

(*a*) Mr. P.. Carnegy's Races of Oudh, p. 92.

Kunjrâ.

A small and humble caste of cultivators principally engaged in the growth and sale of vegetables. They are hard-working and industrious. The caste is found in the districts to the east of Oudh (*a*).

Rângar.

The Rângars are, to some extent, an agricultural class. Some of them have been employed as sepoys. They are numerous in Shekawatî and the Bhattî territory. Colonies of the caste are found in the Upper Doab and Rohilkhand (*b*). They have, as a class, the reputation of being turbulent and disorderly. Some of them have embraced the Mahomedan faith.

Dhailphora.

A low caste of cultivators. They are also employed as servants. The caste is found to the east of Oudh (*c*).

Barayî.

This is a very numerous and wealthy tribe in Benares, exclusively devoted to the sale of *pawn*, a condiment eaten by natives of all classes, Hindu and Mahomedan. Pawn is an aromatic plant cultivated on an extensive scale in various parts of the country. It is a creeper, and grows much like the vine, needing poles for its support. Its leaves are gathered while fresh and green, and are in this condition brought to the shops for sale. No other portion of the plant is eaten. But the leaves are never eaten alone. The Barayî, or pawn-seller, puts in each leaf a little catechu, part of a betel-nut, and a small quantity of moistened chalk. The leaf is then folded neatly into the shape of an equilateral triangle, and kept firm by the insertion of a clove into the overlapping edges. Half-a-dozen of such folded leaves are sold for one pice (a fraction over a third of a penny) in the open bazars of Benares. Sometimes cardamums, dried cocoa-nut, and other ingredients, are added to impart delicacy to the flavour, while at the same time some of those just mentioned are diminished. The leaf with its contents, just as sold, is chewed by the natives, and it is surprising how passionately fond they all are of it. If they can afford

(*a*) Mr. E. A. Reade's Inferior Castes of the North-Western Provinces, p. 30.
(*b*) *Ibid*, p. 21.
(*c*) *Ibid*, p. 27.

to do so, they will eat it from morning to night ; even young children will eat it with great apparent relish. Europeans, for the most part, abhor it ; and it is difficult to understand how the natives so universally enjoy its strong aromatic and astringent flavour, for the taste for such a compound is certainly not natural to any one. Pawn is undoubtedly an excellent stomachic, and imparts a considerable stimulus to the digestive organs. Yet the inordinate degree in which it is indulged must be injurious to the system. The strain upon the salivary glands of those who are constantly chewing it cannot but be prejudicial to those organs. The gums of the jaws in appearance are powerfully affected, and being dyed a yellowish red by the mixture in the mouth, are somewhat disgusting to look upon.

This tribe has many sub-divisions.

1. Chaurasiya.
2. Jaiswâra.
3. Srî Bâstak.
4. Bherihârâ.
5. Tamoulî.
6. Magaihiya.
7. Nasalkânî.
8. Phuhîhârâ.
9. Dhanwariya.

All these are in Benares: none of them intermarry or eat together. The Tamoulis are few in number on the Benares side of the Ganges; but are very numerous on the opposite side. The pawn-sellers are scattered all over the city and suburbs. They are, however, chiefly found in the Aurungâbâd, Sûrajkund, and Misrpokra districts, where some of them reside in large and splendid mansions. They have a bazar, called Darîbâ, near Sûrajkund, specially devoted to the sale of pawn.

Tambolî.

This clan is also engaged in the manufacture and sale of *pawn*, yet has no family connexion or intercourse with the Barayî clan, but keeps itself entirely distinct from it. The Tambolî sells betel-nut as well as pâwn; and appears to be more of a wholesale trader than the Barayî. Some of the Tambolîs have extensive gardens for the production of the *pawn-leaf.* It is singular that the *Barayîs* and Tambolîs should be so distinct as castes, and yet should be so closely connected in their trade and occupation.

It is questionable whether there is any real difference in the occupation of the Tambolî and Barayî castes. Mr. E. A. Reade, in his "Inferior Castes of the North-Western Provinces," says that the Barayîs are growers, and the Tambolîs sellers of *pawn*. But this is certainly not a correct statement respecting the two castes in Benares, as both in that city are manufacturers and sellers.

In the North-Western Provinces no fewer than one hundred and thirteen thousand persons are engaged in the trade in pawn (*a*). Upwards of forty thousand of these are in the district of Gorakhpûr.

(*a*) Report of the Census of the North-Western Provinces for 1865, Vol. II., p. 26.

CHAPTER XI.

CASTES OF HERDSMEN, SHEPHERDS, &C.

AHIR, AHAR, GARARIYA, AND RIWARI.

Ahîr.

THIS is a very extensive tribe of herdsmen scattered over a large portion of India. In Benares and its neighbourhood it is chiefly confined to two clans, Gwâl Bans and Dharor, which are restricted to rearing cattle. Whether such a restriction exists in other parts of India, I am unable to say; but there is reason to believe that, in earlier times, when the Ahîrs were held in greater consideration than they are at the present day, the tribe was as much a race of shepherds as of keepers of cattle.

The word Ahîr is contracted from Abhîra. Now if this be the caste referred to by Manu, in his Institutes, it follows that the Ahîr is three-fourths a Brahman, and one-fourth a Vaisya (*a*). The Ahîrs practise the custom of some other castes in regard to the marriage of younger brothers with the widows of elder brothers.

Formerly, the *pargannah* or barony of Ahrorâ, in the Mirzapûr district, was called Ahîrwâra, or the country of the Ahîrs; and it is probable that it was, to a large extent, if not exclusively, in the hands of this tribe. The Ahîrs are found "in great numbers," says Sir Henry Elliot, "in the southern parts of the Dehli territory, from Rewârî, on the borders of Mewât, to the Bikanîr frontier, in a tract of country known under the name of Bîghoto. A dense population of Ahîrs (Tîklewala) will also be found in a line extending from the Kâla Nadî, in the neighbourhood of Marehrah, to near Bîbameyu on the Jumna; and from Salîmpûr Majhaulî in Gorakhpûr to Singraulî in

(*a*) Manu, X, 8, 15.

Mirzapûr" (*a*). The investigations conducted by Sir Henry into the distribution of this tribe were very extensive. Respecting their origin, he remarks, "The Ahîrs of these Provinces all trace their origin to Mathurâ, or places a little to the west of it. There appear to be three grand divisions amongst them: the Nandbans, the Jadubans, and Gwâlbans, which acknowledge no connexion, except that of being all Ahîrs. Those of the Central Doâb usually style themselves Nandbans; those to the west of the Jumna and the Upper Doâb, Jadubans; and those in the Lower Doâb and Benares, Gwâlbans. The latter seem to have no sub-divisions, or Gots. The principal Gots of the Nandbans are, Samarphallâ, Kishnaut, Bhagtâ, Bilehnia, Diswâr, Nagowa, Kanaudha, Dûnr, Râwat, Tengûrea, Kor, Kamaria, Barausia, Mûjwâr, Dahima, Nirban, Kharkarî, Dirhor, Sîtolia, Jarwaria, Barothî, Gonda, and Phâtak; amounting in all to eighty-four. In Bîghoto, besides many of these, there are the Molak, Sântoria, Khosia, Khallia, Lonîwal, Aphariya or Aphiriya, Mailâ, Mhailâ, Khoro, Sesotia, Gandwâl, Gird, Bhâmsarâ, Jânjaria, Kânkauria, and Nigânia; amounting in all to sixty-four (*b*)." He adds, that the first in rank among these are the Khoros, a position, however, which is disputed by the Aphiriyas. Of the last two clans, many, it seems, are Mahomedans.

Respecting the history of the tribe, the same accurate and careful writer states the following. "This pastoral tribe, of the Yadubansî stock, was formerly of much greater consideration in India than it is at present. In the Râmayana and Mahâbhârat the Abhîras in the West are spoken of; and in the Puranic Geography, the country on the western coast of India, from the Taptî to Devagarh, is called Abhira, or the region of Cowherds. When the Kâttîs arrived in Gujerât, in the eighth century, they found the greater part of the country in possession of the Ahîrs. The name of Asîrgarh, which Ferishta and the "Khazâna Amira" say is derived from Asa Ahîr, shows that the tribe was of some importance in the Dekkan also; and there is no doubt that we have trace of the name in the Abira of Ptolemy, which he places above Patalene. Ahîrs were also at one time Rajas of Nepal, at the beginning of our era; and they are perhaps connected with the Pâla, or shepherd dynasty, which ruled in Bengal from the ninth to the latter part of the eleventh century, and which, if we may put trust in monumental inscriptions, were for some time the universal monarchs of India" (*c*).

(*a*) Elliot's Supplemental Glossary, Vol. I., p. 3.
(*b*) *Ibid*, Vol. I., pp. 3, 4.
(*c*) *Ibid*, Vol. I., pp. 2, 3.

In Benares and its neighbourhood the names of only a few clans have reached me, such as:

1. Gwâl Bans.
2. Channan-nâû.
3. Dharor.
4. Dhengar.
5. Gaddî.
6. Ghosî.
7. Krishanot.
8. Majrot.
9. Churiya.

None of these intermarry or eat together. The Ghosîs are chiefly, and the Gaddîs are partly, Mahomedans. From the Gwâl Bans clan all will drink water. The Ahîrs not only rear cattle, but also make butter and curds, which they sell together with milk. Some of them are tradesmen ; and some are field-labourers.

The Ahîrs of Meerut are supposed to be an intermediate tribe between the Jâts and the Gûjars. The three smoke and drink together. They are said to have come thither from Riwârî as far as Gurgaon and the hill country of the Dekhan. The famous Fort of Asirgarh (fort of Asîr) is believed to have originally belonged to 'Asîr,' a chief of the clan ; hence the term Asîr or Ahîr. The Ahîrs follow the same occupation of herdsmen as the Gûjars, but differ from them in being more industrious and less troublesome and turbulent *(a)*.

Commonly, the Ahîrs are regarded as Sudras. In the Bhagwat Purâna, Nand Ahîr is spoken of as a Vaisya. The tribe has been in the Bijnour district for a very long time. In the Budaon district this clan has acquired considerable influence and wealth by reason of its enterprise and energy. It has extensive landed possessions in the *pargannahs* of Râjpûrah and Asadpûr. They came from Hânsî and Hissar, whence they were driven out some seven hundred years ago.

The district of Bareilly was formerly a dense jungle inhabited by a race of Ahîrs or herdsmen, and hence called Tappa Ahîran. In the time of Timûr, the Ahîrs becoming turbulent and disorderly, two Hindu chiefs, Raja Kharak Singh and Rai Hari Singh, of Tirhût, were despatched by the emperor to reduce them to order. In this they succeeded so well, and so satisfactorily to

(a) Plowden's Report of the Census of the North-Western Provinces for 1865, Appendix B., Mr. Forbes' paper on the Castes of Meerut, p. 14.

themselves, that they not only quelled the rebellion of the Ahîrs, and routed their forces, but took possession of the country, as far as Chaupala, now called Morâdabâd, on the one side, and Powain and Kharal, in what is now the district of Shâhjahânpûr, on the other, where some of their descendants are still found (*a*).

Dr. Buchanan says of the Ahîrs of Gorakhpûr, "that they possess the exclusive right of milking the cow; so that, on all occasions, for this purpose an Ahîr must be hired, even by the low tribes. All people, however, may prepare the cow's milk, and may milk the buffalo. The Ahîrs are also much employed to show game, as they are well acquainted with the forests. Many are employed as carters, in bringing timber from the woods; a few are engaged in trade. On the day of the Diwâli (a festival in honour of Lakshmi, the goddess of wealth), they eat tame pork; and on all occasions, such as are not of the sect of Vishnu, eat the wild hog" (*b*). In most places only the very lowest castes will eat the domestic pig. In the Aurangabâd Nagar *pargannah* of this district, the Ahîrs and Gautam Rajpoots are the prevailing castes.

A wealthy family of Ahîrs has possession of a *jaghire* or large estate in Hassanpûr Maghar of the Gorakhpûr district, originally given to it on condition that it should keep the adjacent forests free from depredators.

The flourishing town of Balah, in the Ghazipûr district, and several villages in its neighbourhood, are in the hands of a clan of this tribe. Some of their ancestors, in the time of the Mahomedan emperors, embraced Islamism. Their descendants disavow their Hindu origin, and style themselves Shaikhs (*c*). In this district Ahîrs are chiefly found in the centre and west, and also to the south of the Ganges. They are mostly Gwâl-Bansîs and Dharors. For generations past they have been notorious as cattle-stealers.

Ahîrs together with Gûjars and Jâts were among the earliest known settlers in the district of Shâhjahânpûr. The traditions of those occupying the Agra district show that they originally came from Hariâna. They have been in that part of the country for several hundred years. Some of the Ahîr landowners of Pargannah Fyzabâd claim to be descended from an Ahîr Raja of Berat. Another account is, that they were settled there by Raja Chandra Sen.

(*a*) Census of the North-Western Provinces, for 1865, Vol. I., Appendix B., p. 48.

(*b*) Statistical Memoirs of the Ghazipur District, p. 45.

(*c*) Report of the Census of the North-Western Provinces for 1865, Appendix B., Memorandum by Mr. F. S. Growse, p. 75.

This is a numerous tribe in the Mainpûrî district, where some are proprietors of considerable estates. They are chiefly found in the two *pargannahs* of Shikoabâd and Mustafabâd. The following is a list of their clans :

1. Phâtak.
2. Nigâna.
3. Jiwariya or Jarwariya.
4. Dhumar.
5. Dunr.
6. Kamariya.
7. Karaiya.
8. Sondalî.
9. Râût.
10. Lahugaya.
11. Angûrî.
12. Bhrâgadî.
13. Mâlgoraya.
14. Gaindua or Gadua.
15. Bâdosiya.
16. Ghosî.

With the exception of the Phâtaks, all the rest are of the Nandbansî division of Ahîrs (*a*). The Kamariyas occupy fifty-seven villages in two *pargannahs* of the district. One of these, Painhat, is famous for a festival held there in honor of two heroes, a Brahman and an Ahîr.

The Phâtak Ahîrs possess twenty-one villages in Shikoabâd. Mr. Growse gives the following account of their origin derived from themselves : "There was a Raja of Chittore of the Sisodiya line of Rajpoots, commonly designated the Kateri Rana. His capital was attacked by the King of Delhi ; and of the twelve gates of the city, one only held out. Therefore, when the invading army had retired, the Raja decreed that the guard of the twelfth gate and their descendants should ever thereafter be distinguished by the name of Phâtak. They profess to be actually descended from this Rana by a marriage with the daughter of Digpâl, Raja of Mahaban, an Ahîr ; and they are accordingly reckoned among the Ahîrs" (*a*).

According to the last Census, there were in 1865 upwards of sixty thousand Ahîrs scattered about the district of Etah. The tribe has been there for many centuries, yet came originally, it is said, from Mathurâ, or the country further west. The families are chiefly of the Nandbansî and Yadubansî races.

Ahîrs are numerous in some parts of the Gorakhpûr district, where they settled on account of the excellent herbage which the land supplied.

According to the last Census there are upwards of two millions of Ahîrs in these Provinces alone (*b*).

(*a*) Report of the Census of the North-Western Provinces for 1865, Vol. I., Memorandum by Mr. F. S. Growse, p. 78.

(*b*) *Ibid*, Vol. II., p. 25.

The Abhars of Agra and Etawah are most probably the same as the Ahîrs of other districts. The two words have evidently the same root. The Abhars are courageous and athletic, and are said to be good cultivators (*a*).

The Ahîrs of the Agorî *pargannah* of the Mirzapûr district are termed Mahtus.

Ahar.

This tribe is most probably connected with the Ahîrs already noticed, although they will by no means acknowledge any relationship to them. Whatever may have been their origin, there is no question that now they are a separate caste. Yet their claim to be descended from the Yadubansîs is the same as that put forward by the Ahîrs. The latter contend that they are the posterity of Krishna himself, and state that the Ahars are only the children of the cowherds of Krishna (*b*).

The caste is very numerous in the district of Morâdâbâd, where it has existed from time immemorial. There is a tract of country to the west of the Râmgangâ called Aharât, extending into a portion of Rohilkhand. According to Sir H. Elliot, the clans designated as Bhattî, Nagâwat, Naugorî, Rûkar, Bâsian, Ora, Bukiâin, Diswâr, Bhûsiâîn, and Birraria, belong to this tribe (*c*).

Garariya.

The Shepherd Tribe. They rear sheep and goats, but not cattle, which are in the hands of the Ahîrs, another tribe. There is a striking difference subsisting between Hindu and English shepherds in their treatment of sheep. The latter are rough and harsh as compared with the former, and allow their flocks to be frightened and distressed by the furious barking of their watch-dogs. The Hindu, on the contrary, is a model of gentleness in attending to his charge, but, nevertheless, trains them to docility just as effectively. Without noise, or bluster, or angry dog, he keeps them under perfect control; and in removing them from one field to another, he goes before, and they follow.

The custom of a younger brother marrying the widow of an elder brother prevails in this tribe. But it is by no means peculiar to it. The Jâts, Gûjars, Khatiks, Chamârs, Dhûsias, Ahîrs, Bhars, Julâhirs, and Dhunias, all practise

(*a*) Inferior Castes of the North-Western Provinces, by Mr. E. A. Reade, p. 13.

(*b*) Elliot's Glossary, Vol. I., p. 6.

(*c*) *Ibid*, p. 7.

it. The elder brother is not, I understand, permitted to marry the widow of a younger brother.

The Garariyas are professedly divided into seven clans, but acknowledge several others. In Benares the seven are as follows:

1. Dhengar.
2. Nîkhar.
3. Jaunpûrî.
4. Illahabâdî.
5. Bakarkasau.
6. Namdâwâle.
7. Chikwâ.

None of these intermarry. The first four clans keep sheep and goats, not so the remaining three. They also manufacture blankets. The Bakarkasau and Namdâwâle clans do so likewise. The Chikwâs are Mahomedans. I have also heard of two other clans of Garariyas in this neighbourhood, namely :—

1. Bharariya.
2. Baikatâ.

Bharariya is evidently derived from *bher*, a sheep. Nevertheless, this clan is not employed in tending sheep, but in other kinds of labour. The Baikatas are the lowest in rank among the Garariyas. They live by begging scraps of hair from the other clans that keep flocks, and selling the proceeds. This is their sole occupation. A few only of this class reside in Benares; they are, for the most part, found in country districts. In addition to these sub-castes, others are mentioned by Sir Henry Elliot, as Tasselha or Pachhade, Chak, Bareiya, Paihwar, and Bhaiyatar (*a*).

This tribe is spread over the whole of these Provinces, but seems to be most numerous in the country between Allahabad and Farakhabâd. In some places they have resided from time immemorial. In the Agra district their subdivisions are manifold, and keep themselves distinct from one another.

There are upwards of twenty thousand members of this tribe in the district of Etah, where they are divided into the following clans:

1. Nîkhar.
2. Tasahla.
3. Pachâdî.
4. Chak Dhênjarî.
5. Barya.
6. Bhiatar Kâlar.

Riwârî.

A tribe engaged in rearing and training camels.

(*a*) Elliot's Supplemental Glossary, Vol. I., p. 120.

CHAPTER XII.

CASTES OF PERSONAL ATTENDANTS AND SERVANTS.

KAHAR, KANHAR, GOAIYAD, DIRZI, NAU OR HAJAM, DHOBI, PARWANIYA, JALWA OR JALALIYA, DHANKAR, BARGAHI, AND KAMKAR.

Kahâr.

THIS tribe is partly employed in agriculture ; but its chief occupation throughout a great portion of these Provinces is that of carrying palankeens. Indeed, the word Kahâr is said to be a contraction of Kandhâr, from *Kandha*, a shoulder. The Kahâr is properly a palankeen-bearer, both amongst natives and Europeans. In many places, it is impossible to obtain other persons for the purpose. On which account, as the caste holds a monopoly of this kind of employment, it is apt to be very exacting in the rate charged for carrying people. But the Government has fixed an uniform rate for all palankeen-bearers whom it may employ, which is observed also by the public generally. Kahârs are likewise employed as house-servants, in the capacity of *Bearers*. They are the highest caste of Hindus that can usually be obtained for such service. Other Hindus so employed are, for the most part, of a lower grade, not recognized at all as Sudras ; whereas Kahârs are considered to occupy a fair position in the great Sudra family.

This caste, I understand, bears the name of Kamkar in Patna and throughout the country in that direction. It numbers professedly seven clans ; but the accounts are very conflicting, and it will appear from the following list that more than a dozen exist.

1. Jaiswârâ.
2. Gonr or Gond.
3. Dhuria.
4. Kharwârâ.
5. Batmâ.
6. Rawânî.
7. Turhâ.
8. Dhîmar.
9. Gonrîâ.
10. Murîârî.
11. Jetans.
12. Kanoujiya.
13. Baradiya (from Fyzabad).
14. Tonha.

The Gonriâ is not to be confounded with the Gonr, although they are in name so much alike. The Gonrs are employed in roasting grain for the market; and also in breaking stones. They are likewise palankeen-bearers. Their name is also spelt Gond, the d and r in Hindí being the same letter. Whether they are connected in any way with the great aboriginal tribe of Gonds extending for hundreds of miles through Central India, is hard to say. The name is the same, and it is by no means impossible that the Hinduized Gonds of Benares and elsewhere may, at some remote period of Indian history, have separated themselves from the aboriginal stock. Further investigation might throw light on the subject.

The Dhurias are fishermen : they likewise, when in season, pick the Singhârâ, an aquatic plant yielding a bulbous vegetable, which grows in prolific abundance in ponds and tanks in Northern India. It is of a sweetish flavour, and when pealed is white and crisp. It is eaten both raw and cooked. As an article of diet it is, I imagine, not very nutritious. It is however extremely cheap, and all classes of the natives are fond of it. The Balmâs and Turhâs are not found in these parts. The former are said to be in the districts to the south ; and the latter in the country to the east. Only a few of the Rawânî clan are in this neighbourhood ; but it is more abundant farther eastward. They are palankeen-bearers and also field-labourers. The widows of Kahârs may marry again. Some Kahârs feed on pork.

The Dhîmars carry palankeens, catch fish for the market, make nets, and are employed as porters and labourers. The Tonhâs are very numerous to the east of Ghazipûr. The Gonriâs manufacture nets, work in fields, and carry water.

The Kahâr tribe or caste, in all its clans, numbers in these Provinces nearly seven hundred thousands persons (*a*). It is one of the most useful and laborious of the industrial classes.

Kanhar.

The chief employment of this caste is to supply water both to Hindu and Mahomedan families. Some of its members also act as servants in respectable Hindu families.

Goaiyad.

A small caste somewhat similar to Kahârs, employed as cultivators and bearers. Some are also boatmen. They are found both in Benares and Allahabad.

(*a*) Report of the Census of the North-Western Provinces for 1865, Vol. I., p. 26.

Dirzî.

The occupation of a tailor is held in much greater estimation in India than in England. It is common for a family to keep its own Dirzî or tailor, who ranks equal to any servant of the house. Many Mahomedans are employed in this way, who, in testimony to the honourable position they occupy, receive commonly from all natives, Hindu and Mussalman, the appellation of Khalîfas or Caliphs. The skill displayed by these Khalîfas in the manufacture of garments worn by Europeans of both sexes, is sometimes very astonishing. They have no power of invention—not the smallest—but in imitative ability, they are prodigies. Yet they are provokingly slow in execution. This, however, is a characteristic of the races of India generally. The Hindu is slow in all his movements. In addition to the Mahomedans engaged in this calling, there is a considerable number of Hindus, of an inferior caste, who pursue it likewise. They are a separate tribe, and are divided into seven sub-castes or clans, as follows:—

1. Srî Bâstak.
2. Nâm Deo.
3. Tânchâra.
4. Dhanesh.
5. Panjâbî.
6. Gaur.
7. Kantak.

All these sub-castes are found in Benares. They are distinct and separate from one another in their social habits and life, and do not intermarry. The list given above no doubt differs somewhat from the list of clans in other places; and even in Benares the list is not uniform, for the name of another clan, the Saksenî, making the eighth, has been brought to my notice.

Nâû.

The Barber Caste, called also Hajâm. The occupation of a barber in India is far wider in its operations than in England. He shaves the head as well as the face, pares the nails both of hands and feet, cleans the ears, bleeds and cups. In addition, he is a very important personage in Hindu families, on certain public occasions. At a marriage feast, and also at other festivals, the Nâû is commissioned to visit the persons who are to be invited, and to solicit their attendance. When all are assembled the Nâû is present to hand the guests water, or pawn, or the hookah, as they may desire. He also partakes of the food either with the guests, or retired to a short distance from them, in the intervals of his service. And when the feast is over, the Nâû removes the food that remains, and distributes it among the Doms, one of the lowest of Hindu tribes.

The Nâû is also sometimes employed as a go-between in making arrangements for marriages between parties, and in seeking out for a youth a suitable girl to be his bride. In many social ceremonies, his position ranks only next to that of the Brahman himself. On occasion of a funeral, he shaves the head of the living and of the dead; and invites friends and relatives to the funeral.

The wife of the Nâû, called Nainî or Naunia, is of equal importance, as a useful and necessary public servant, with her husband. At the birth of a child in Hindu families, for the first six days, a Chamain, or wife of a Chamâr, a man of the leather caste, attends both upon the child and its mother; after which they are both committed to the care of a Nainî.

In Benares there are three divisions of this caste:

1. Srî Bâstak.
2. Kanoujea.
3. Bhojpuria.

The tribe is spread about the country in many directions. In the Muzaffarnagar district they have the tradition that they settled there as long ago as the time of Prithi Raj.

Dhobî.

The Washerman Caste. Hindus, even the poorest, and of the lowest castes, do not wash their own clothes. Although the garments worn by many are both scanty and simple, yet the thought never occurs to them that, for the sake of economy, it would be advisable for themselves or their wives to devote an hour or two occasionally to this operation. That it is contrary to their habit, and to the custom of the country, is a sufficient reason with them to pay a Dhobî for doing that which they could so easily do themselves. It is common, when they bathe, for Hindus to shake and rinse the clothes which they have removed from their persons, and to hang them out to dry. This much they will do; but the thorough wash they cannot bring themselves to undertake. This must be accomplished by those whose caste and business are to wash.

Dhobîs are very clever at their trade. Before beginning the operation of washing, the clothes are gathered together in a bundle, and steamed, that is, they are hung for a time over a cauldron of boiling water. After this they are taken to a stream or pond, where they are thoroughly washed with the aid of fuller's earth. The Dhobî steps nearly knee-deep into the water, and taking a quantity of clothes by one end in his two hands he raises them aloft in the air and brings them heavily down upon a huge stone slab, grooved, at his feet. This threshing operation he repeats until the clothes are perfectly clean. They are not, however, quite so strong as when he commenced. Yet when dried they are beautifully white.

The branches of this tribe are numerous:

1. Kanoujea.
2. Magahiya.
3. Belwâr.
4. Pagahiya.
5. Bâtham.
6. Marwârî.
7. Shaikh.
8. Pachpiriya.
9. Kâlika Devî.
10. Palihâr.
11. Ammâ.

Nearly all of these are found in Benares; the most numerous clans are the Kanoujeas and Shaikhs, the last of whom are Mahomedans. The sub-castes are very exclusive in their dealings with one another, and do not intermarry, or eat and drink together. Sir Henry Elliot is wrong, I think, in supposing that there is any real distinction between the Bâthams and Srî Bâthams (*a*). He refers to another clan of Dhobîs called Bharkâ, which, he says, is found from Mainpûrî and Etawah onwards to the far west. A large proportion of the Bharkâs, however, have been converted to the Mahomedan religion.

Parwaniya.

This tribe has only one special occupation in Benares; yet is, nevertheless, a numerous body. Ten or twelve days after the birth of a son in the family of a Hindu, two members of this caste come to the house, where they spend some time in singing songs of gratulation and joy, keeping time by the beating of a drum. In return, they receive grain, money, and clothes, frequently those which have been already worn, and sometimes cloth. The last article they sell, in case they do not require it for their own use. They also sing at weddings. On these occasions, they also play on a peculiar kind of musical instrument. This is their proper employment and calling. In addition, they manufacture fans and umbrellas of palm leaves, yet they find it difficult to kill time, and are reported to be a lazy, ignorant, and worthless race. Some of them manufacture *pankhas* or fans.

(*a*) Elliot's Supplemental Glossary, p. 81.

Jalwá or Jalâliyâ.

A few days after the birth of a child in a Hindu family persons of this tribe come to the house and cry out for some time, making a great noise. This is accounted a preservative from ghosts, imps, and hobgoblins, who are supposed to be frightened away from the infant by the shouts and shrieks which are made. Cats are kept at a distance, lest they should bring with them an evil spirit to the molestation of the child. The Jalwâs having performed their part in a full measure of shouting, receive their fee, and take their departure.

Dhankar.

A small caste of carriers or porters. They are a strong, able-bodied class of men, with a commendable reputation for fidelity. They are found to the east of Allahabad *(a)*.

Bargâhi.

A caste engaged, for the most part, as servants to the upper classes of Hindus. They have the character of being faithful and intrepid. They are found mostly on the right bank of the Jumna (*b*). Upwards of a thousand individuals of the caste are in Mirzapûr, and a smaller community is met with in the Gorakhpûr district.

Kamkar.

A caste of servants employed chiefly by Hindus. They are found in Benares, Allahabad, Azimgarh, and Gorakhpûr. In the last named district they numbered, at the Census of 1865, upwards of fourteen thousand persons.

(a) Mr. E. A. Reade's Inferior Castes of the North-Western Provinces, p. 27.
(b) *Ibid*, p. 15.

CHAPTER XIII.

CASTES OF WEAVERS, THREAD-SPINNERS, DYERS, BOATMEN, SALT-MANUFACTURERS, AND OTHERS.

KATERA OR DHUNIYA, KOLI OR KORI, TANTI, TANTRA, KATOH, RANGREZ, CHHIPI, MALLAH, NUNIYA OR LUNIYA, BELDAR, BHATIGARA, BHARTHI, AND PALLIDAR.

Katera or Dhuniya.

A CASTE employed in carding or combing cotton. They are also called Dhuniyas. Many Mahomedans as well as Hindus pursue this occupation. The instrument by which the combing and cleaning are performed, is simply a bow. Squatting on the ground before a quantity of fresh cotton, which is ordinarily full of dirt, seeds, bits of stick, and so forth, the bow being in his left hand, and a wooden mallet in his right, the Katera strikes the string of the bow, and brings it quivering to the surface of the cotton, portions of which adhering to it in light fibres are at once caught up by the string. The striking being repeated continuously without interruption, all the cotton is by degrees beautifully combed, and at the same time its foul particles, becoming separated from the fibres, and being weighty, fall away of themselves.

The caste is found in Benares, and also in the Doâb, and districts east of Oudh.

Kolî or Korî.

A Caste of Weavers. Their wives are also employed as wet-nurses. The community is small, and is found in Agra, and in other western districts in these Provinces (*a*). The Kolîs are reputed to be partly of a Bais Rajpoot origin.

(*a*) Mr. E. A. Reade's Inferior Castes of the North-Western Provinces, p. 29.

Tanti.

A Caste of Weavers, whose occupation is to make edging of silk and of various kinds of metal. They also manufacture *kim khâb (kin kob)* or cloth richly inwoven with gold and silver, and also dresses embroidered with the same costly materials. They are said to have come originally from Gujerat. In Benares there is only one family of this tribe, which is wealthy, and lives in a spacious house in the city.

Tantra.

The Tantras are a separate clan employed in the manufacture of silken threads and stuffs. They are said to have come originally from the south. They are considered to be of a low caste, as Brahmans will never eat food in their houses.

Katoh.

A small and respectable Caste of Thread-spinners found in the districts to the east of Oudh (*a*).

Rangrez.

A Caste of Dyers. The word is derived from *rang*, colour, and *rez*, a worker. The caste is found in most districts of these Provinces.

Chhîpî, or Chhîpî-gar.

A Caste of Cloth-printers. Their especial occupation is to stamp chintz and other cotton cloths. They are not a numerous class, and yet are found in most districts of these Provinces. In Benares they form a distinct caste.

The Chhîpîs claim to be Râthor Rajpoots, on the ground of some connexion which the caste is supposed to have once had with that tribe.

Mallâh.

All boatmen are called Mallâhs, no matter what caste they may belong to. Yet there is a special tribe of Mallâhs, divided into several clans. These are the following :

1. Mallâh.
2. Muria, or Murîârî.
3. Pandûbî.
4. Bathawâ, or Badhariya.
5. Chainî, Chain, or Chai.
6. Surâyâ.
7. Guriyâ.
8. Tîar.
9. Kulwant, or Kulwat.
10. Kewat.

(*a*) Mr. E. A. Reade's Inferior Castes of the North-Western Provinces, p. 31.

These are sailors and fishermen. They also manufacture fishing nets. The Mallâhs have a tradition, that at one time the sub-castes intermarried, a custom which they have ceased to observe. Hindus of several other castes pursue the occupation of a Mallâh. By many persons the Kewats and Mallâhs are regarded as belonging to the same tribe, and therefore I have included the former in the latter. Yet they are not merely boatmen and fishermen, but are also basket-makers. The Murîârîs are fishermen. The Guriyâs are stone-masons. The Chains are steersmen. There is a tradition among the members of the caste that while all are descended from a common father, by name Nikhad, yet that only the Kewats are descended from the married wife, and the rest are the offspring of an irregular marriage.

The Kewats are of the Kâsyap *gotra* or order. This clan does not intermarry with the others. A widow is permitted to re-marry.

This caste numbers from eighteen hundred to two thousand persons in Benares.

The Mallâhs of Benares affirm that Râm being pleased with the head of the caste, gave him a horse, on which he placed a bridle, not on the head, but, in his ignorance, on the tail. Hence, the custom, it is stated, of having the helm at the stern of a boat instead of in front.

Nuniya or Luniya.

The word Nuniya or Luniya is derived from *non* or *lon* salt ; and consequently the name Nuniya designates the original occupation of the caste, that of manufacturing salt. But this occupation has given place to others, and now, in some parts of the country, as Benares and Mirzapûr, the members of this caste are obliged to abandon entirely their proper employment, or they would starve. The Government of India, having a monopoly of salt, does not permit it to be made by the people except in certain districts, even though it may be present in the soil in considerable abundance. For instance, the land in various portions of the Benares Province is largely impregnated with saltpetre, which affects the growth of cereals and other plants. Houses made of mud or sun-dried bricks frequently exhibit, on becoming damp, a thin coating of saltpetre on their surface ; and indeed it is by no means an uncommon occurrence for houses built even of red bricks burnt in a kiln to be seriously damaged by the exudation of moisture surcharged with saltpetre. It would be an easy matter, therefore, for salt to be manufactured in those districts. The Nuniya, however, finding no scope for his business, has wisely taken in hand other species of labour. He digs water-courses, ponds, wells and tanks. He also makes bricks and tiles.

The Nuniyas in these parts are said by themselves to have come from Sambhal. They have seven sub-divisions in their tribe, for the most part distinct from one another. I have obtained two lists, both which, as they differ considerably from each other, I will give. One is from Benares, the other from Mirzapûr.

Sub-divisions of the Nuniyâ tribe in Benares.

1. Chauhân.
2. Oudhiya. (These are from Oudh, and are manufacturers of saltpetre.)
3. Musahar. (Palanquin-bearers.)
4. Bind. (Servants.)
5. Bhûînhâr. (Occupiers of land.)
6. Lodha. (Field-labourers.)
7. Paramtârî. (None of this caste in Benares. They are found in the country farther west.)

In addition to this list the two undermentioned clans are also regarded as Nuniyas in Benares :

1. Dasaundhiya.
2. Bûjar.

Sub-divisions of the Nuniyâ tribe in Mirzapûr.

1. Bach Gotra Chauhân (Wear the janeo or sacred cord. Their permanent place of residence is Sambhal.
2. Bach Gotra Chauhân (Do not wear the janeo or sacred cord.)
3. Bhûînhâr.
4. Bin.
5. Pachkoutâ.
6. Lodh.
7. Musahar.

It is manifest that there is great similarity in these lists. Prominence is given in both to the Chauhân Nuniyas. The Chauhâns are a well-known tribe of Rajpoots, descended, it is supposed, from a common ancestor Bach or Vatsa (*a*).

(*a*) Elliot's Supplemental Glossary, Vol. I., pp. 63, 68.

Hence they are all said to belong to the Vatsa *gotra*. The nature of the relationship, if any, originally subsisting between so high and distinguished a people as the Chauhâns with a race so much inferior in social position and natural endowments, is unsusceptible, in all likelihood, of satisfactory explanation. The former have a tradition that they came from the neighbourhood of Sambhar and Ajmere. The Nuniyas trace their origin to Sambhal, which most probably should be Sambhar. Judging from the history of other inferior castes, the Chauhân Nuniyas, at the least, may have sprung either from outcast Chauhân Rajpoots or from Chauhân Rajpoot fathers and Sudra mothers.

Just as the Chauhân Nuniyâs seem to be connected with the Chauhân Rajpoots, in the same manner do the Bhûînhâr Nuniyas appear connected with the Bhûînhâr Brahmans, though what its nature is, besides the mere name, is not so manifest.

In addition to the division mentioned above, the Nuniyas are also separated into two great classes, Purbiya, and Pachhainya, or Eastern and Western.

Notwithstanding the presence in both lists of the Musahars as a sub-division of Nuniyas, my conviction is that they are a separate and distinct tribe of themselves. I have not thought it right, however, to eliminate them from the lists, preferring to adopt the opinions of the natives on this matter even when they run counter to my own judgment. The Musahars are a very peculiar race. Their occupation is properly to collect wood, leaves, herbs, and medicines, in the jungles, and to bring them to the towns and villages for sale. They are also sellers of birds and honey. Their food consists of snakes, frogs, iguanas, jackals, foxes, and the like. They will also eat the relics of a feast. In addition to the occupation just stated, they also labour for hire as palanquin-bearers. As a class they are noted for their truthfulness and honesty; and, it is said, are never found in prison.

The Lodh clan, like the Musahar, is, in my judgment, an independent tribe. It is of very ancient date, and is referred to in early chronicles and traditions. The Lodh is supposed to have been primitively a seller of the bark of the *lodh* tree, the *symplocos racemosa*, used as a dye, and for medical purposes. The Lodhs are now, however, an extensive class of agriculturists. In parts of the Morâdabâd district, they seem to have resided from time immemorial. Mr. C. A. Elliott, in his Chronicles of Oonao in Oudh, speaks of the Lodhs as one of the low caste tribes which inhabited that district in ancient times. They have been in the Agra district for several hundred years, and are reputed to have come from Mathurâ and Bhartpûr.

The Lodhs number nearly sixty thousand persons in the Etah district alone. They are not only cultivators of the soil, but, in some instances, are landholders also. They have six divisions or sub-clans, as follows:

1. Pataria.
2. Mathuria.
3. Sankalajaria.
4. Lakhia.
5. Kharia.
6. Pania.

The Lodhs are very old inhabitants of this district. The most numerous sub-clan in the Etah *pargannah* is the Pataria. They are found also in the Lallatpûr and Jhânsî districts, where they have been for a long period.

These Nuniya clans do not, for the most part, intermarry, or eat together. In the second list, the Bach Gotra Chauhân, of the second grade, will give his daughter in marriage to the son of a Bhûînhâr ; but not his son to a daughter of the same. The Lodh and Musahar will eat together, yet do not intermarry. The Bach Gotra Chauhân of the first grade regards himself as much purer and of far higher caste than his brother of the same name of the second grade. He will not allow the widows of his sub-caste to marry again, whereas the widows of the second grade of Bach Gotra Chauhâns are permitted to do so. Hence the members of the first grade despise and sneer at those of the second, and will hold no social intercourse with them, being as much distinct from them as though they belonged to a totally different tribe.

The low social position of the Nuniyas is supposed to have arisen from two circumstances, first, that they have taken to an occupation which brings them in contact with the earth, and secondly, that they have acquired the habit of eating field-mice. These are reasons assigned by natives, but which perhaps should rather be received as results than as causes.

Beldâr.

The occupation of the Beldûr is to dig, to construct mud walls, and the like. The word comes from *bel*, in Persian a spade, or digging implement, and *dâr*, one who handles or uses it.

The Beldârs are found in various parts of these Provinces. They do not restrict themselves to their proper calling, but in towns and cities are largely employed in carrying heavy packages by means of stout poles resting on the shoulders of two or more.

The designation of Beldâr is common to many classes of ordinary labourers employed in heavy manual work. Entire colonies of Beldârs are found in some places as wood-cutters.

Bharthi.

A caste of wood-splitters. They buy wood, cut it into small pieces, and sell it. There are only a few members of the caste in Benares ; but a great many in the district of Mirzapûr.

Bhatiyârâ.

These are properly keepers of Serais, or native inns. They are found in all districts. They seem to be unsuited to engage in any other occupation.

Pallidâr.

A class of carriers, such as of grain, sugar, and salt. They are found in various districts of the Doâb, and as far east as Gorakhpûr.

CHAPTER XIV.

HUNTERS AND FOWLERS.

BAHELIYA OR BADHAK, KAROUL, AND ARAKH.

Baheliya, or Badhak.

THE members of this tribe are by profession hunters, gamekeepers, and bird-catchers. They are exceedingly expert in the art of catching birds, and great practice has given them wonderful powers of manipulation. A man is seated on the ground with a long pole in his hand, at one end of which is a sharp spike. He slowly introduces the pole among a number of birds carelessly hopping about picking up grain, giving it a zig-zag direction and imitating as much as possible the movement of a snake. Having brought the point near one of the birds, which is fascinated by its stealthy approach, he suddenly jerks it into its breast, and then, drawing it to him, releases the poor palpitating creature, putting it away in his bag, and recommences the same operation. The Baheliya also catches birds with a kind of lime taken from the Maddâr tree, by means of a long pole, as in the former instance. The viscous substance at the end of the pole, on touching the bird, sticks to it, and it is caught. The Baheliya is employed likewise in making ropes, and also as a watchman, and in other kinds of service.

Mr. P. Carnegy is wrong in supposing that this clàn is peculiar to the eastern division of Oudh. It is met with in the Doâb, in Benares, and indeed in nearly all the districts of the North Western Provinces. Mr. Reade remarks upon the Baheliyas, that they are 'hardy, active, and generally of good character. A stigma has been attached to this class in the Mainpûrî district as thieves and highway robbers ; but this appears to have arisen from confounding them with the Borias' (*a*).

(*a*) Mr. Reade's Inferior Castes of the North-Western Provinces, p. 14.

Karoul.

A tribe devoted to the pursuit of game, which they bring to the market for sale. There are none of the tribe in Benares ; but some fifty families reside at the village of Jâdûpûr, four miles distant. The tribe, it is said, contains the prescriptive number of seven clans, several of which on enumeration I found to consist of Mahomedans. The Hindu clans are as follows :

1. Hajârî.
2. Uttariya.
3. Purbiya.
4. Koireriya.

These do not intermarry. Of the Mahomedan clans, one is called Turkiya, possibly an Afghan race, or descendants of the early Moslem invaders of India. The Karouls of Jâdûpûr are employed largely in the capacity of sepoys, or soldiers, in the families of the native nobility and gentry of Benares. They are a manly race. Although only Sudras they indulge the habit of affixing 'Singh' to their names as though they were Rajpoots.

Arakh.

A caste devoted to hunting and sport. They are a hardy, enthusiastic, and dirty race. Some are employed as watchmen. The caste is chiefly found in Bundelkhand, Mirzapûr, and the southern districts of the Rewah principality (*a*). Several thousands likewise inhabit the districts of Gorakhpûr, Allahabad, Fathpûr, Shâhjahânpûr, and Benares.

Other castes addicted to hunting and field sports will be described in the next part.

(*a*) Mr. E. A. Reade's Inferior Castes of the North-Western Provinces, p. 14.

PART IV.

ABORIGINAL TRIBES AND INFERIOR CASTES.

CHAPTER I.

THE BHAR TRIBE.

THIS race, variously known by the terms Râjbhar, Bharat, Bharpatwa, and Bhar, once inhabited a wide tract of country extending from Gorakhpûr, in Northern India, to Saugor, in Central India. Other tribes, such as the Cherûs, the Majhwârs, and the Kols, were, in places, associated with them; but there is good reason to believe that the Bhars greatly outnumbered them all. They were very powerful in Oudh; and the country lying between Benares and Allahabad, on either side of the Ganges, a tract of about seventy miles in length, was almost exclusively in their possession. The entire district of Allahabad also was originally in their hands; and traces of them are still to be seen in every *pargannah*, more especially in the *pargannahs* situated across the Ganges and Jumna. Their forts there, called Bhar-dîh, some of which are of vast size, are very numerous; and they have the credit of having excavated all the deep tanks which now exist. The *pargannah* of Khairagarh bears very abundant traces of their toil and enterprise. The stone fort of that name, of immense proportions, is said to have been their work (*a*).

In the district of Banda, on its eastern side, are extensive hill forts, which Dr. Wilton Oldham, formerly Assistant Magistrate of that district, informs me are of cyclopæan dimensions, and are attributed to the Bhars. In particular, he mentions Lukwa situated in the Chîbû *pargannah*.

Vestiges of this race are found in many places in the districts of Mirzapûr, Jaunpûr, Azimgarh, Ghazipûr, Gorakhpûr, and in the province of Oudh, where numerous embankments, tanks, subterraneous caverns, and stone forts, still testify to their energy and skill. The present inhabitants of Azimgarh have a tradition that their country, in the time of Râm, with whose kingdom of Ajudhiya it was formerly connected, was occupied by Râjbhars and Asûrs. The Bhars have left behind them large mud forts, of which specimens may be seen

(*a*) Report of Revenue Settlement, Allahabad Vol. II., Part I.

at Harbanspûr and Unchgaon, near the town of Azimgarh, and also at Ghosi. The Kunwâr and Manghai rivers of the district seem to have been connected by a trench called Asûrain, the work, it is said, of its primitive inhabitants. The Hari Bândh or dam at Amîn-nagar, in the Nizâmâbâd *pargannah*, is an embankment generally ascribed to them (*a*).

The Bhars once possessed the northern portion of the present district of Ghazipûr, now divided into the *pargannahs* of Shâdîâbad, Pachotar, Zuhûrâbâd, and Laknesar. One Bhar chief lived at Zuhûrâbâd, while another occupied the fort of Laknesar-dîh, the deserted village of Laknesar (*b*). Yet the race, in association with other aboriginal tribes, was not confined to this limited tract, but was once spread abroad in various directions in that part of the country. " The Hindu land-owning tribes," says Dr. Oldham, " all agree in stating that, at the time of the first immigration of their forefathers, the entire country, except a few tracts held by Brahmans, so far as the forests had been cleared, was occupied by aborigines not of the Aryan race, who were in the habit of eating the flesh of swine, and using intoxicating drinks, and were called Seorees, Bhars, and Cherûs" (*c*). This tradition is current, says the same writer, throughout the Benares Province, Oudh, and Behar.

How far the extensive district of Gorakhpûr was occupied by the Bhars, is uncertain. We know that the Kausik tribe of Rajpoots ousted them from a portion of their territory, and retain possession of it to the present day.

Respecting the Bhars of Oudh, Mr. P. Carnegy, Deputy Commissioner of Fyzabâd, remarks, that " the ruins of their former masonry forts are to be traced by scores in our districts; and the name of their former capital, where they were finally overthrown by the Mahomedans, after being, according to popular tradition, artfully plied with spirits, was Kasbhawanpûr, the modern town of Sultânpûr, destroyed by us after the re-occupation of the Province" (*d*). The Bhar *raj* or dominion included the whole of eastern Oudh. Every great natural work or ancient relic there, is attributed, says Mr. C. A. Elliott, in his Chronicles of Oonao, either to the devil or the Bhars. He states, moreover, that " almost every town whose name does not end in *pûr*, or *âbâd*, or *mow*, or is not distinctly derivable from a proper name, is claimed by tradition, in the east of Oudh, as a Bhar town. The district of Bharaich is (if we may trust its

(*a*) Settlement Report of the Azimgarh District, Vol. I., Sections 23, 24.

(*b*) Dr. Oldham's Memoir of the Ghazipûr District, Part I., p. 46.

(*c*) *Ibid.*

(*d*) Mr. P. Carnegy's Races of Oudh, p. 22.

traditions) their oldest abode, and the name of the town of Bharaich is said to be derived from them. From thence they spread southwards through the districts of Fyzabâd and Sultânpûr; and it is in the latter district that they maintained themselves latest, being only finally extirpated in the reign of Alamgîr. It is said that some of their number may be found there even now, living a wild gipsy life in the jungles" (*a*).

The district of Mirzapûr exhibits traces and remains of this people to a greater extent than of any other tribe. The *pargannah* of Bhadohî, or, more properly, "Bhardohî," is called after them. Mr. Duthoit, late Deputy Superintendent of the Family Domains of the Maharaja of Benares, in his recent elaborate report on this *pargannah*, says, that traces of the Bhars abound on all sides, in the form of old tanks and village forts. "One cannot go for three miles in any direction without coming upon some of the latter." Their tanks are Suraj-bedi, that is, longer from east to west than from north to south; and thereby distinguishable from modern tanks, which are Chandr-bedi, and lie north and south. The bricks found in the Bhar-dîhs or forts, are of enormous dimensions, and frequently measure nineteen inches in length, eleven in breadth, and two and a quarter in thickness. In quality and size they are similar to bricks often seen in ancient Buddhist buildings (*b*).

This *pargannah* stretches along the north bank of the Ganges; yet on the south side of that river, likewise, Bhar forts and towns are met with. One of their principal cities was situated about five miles to the west of the modern city of Mirzapûr, and was evidently of great extent. Its brick and stone *debris* lies scattered over the fields for several miles. This old city is called Pampâpûrâ by the people now living in the neighbourhood. It is probable that the original name has been lost, and that this name was given to it by the Rajpoots who took the country from the Bhars. From its size and the substantial nature of the buildings, which, judging from the relics, it contained, the city must have been of sufficient importance to be the capital of the country. It included within its circuit the ancient town of Vindhyâchal, famous in the Purânas, and still celebrated throughout a great part of India for its shrine of the goddess Vindhyesvarî, which many thousands of pilgrims from every quarter visit yearly. To the east of the town are the remains of the fort, from which spot, in a westerly direction, *debris* is found in great abundance.

(*a*) Chronicles of Oonao, p. 26.

(*b*) Report of the Bhadohee pargannah, p. 2.

Tradition says that the city once possessed one hundred and fifty temples, all which were destroyed by that indomitable enemy of idolatry, the emperor Aurungzebe. This is perhaps an exaggeration ; yet that there were formerly magnificent temples on this spot, is indisputable. Below the Ashtbhûjî bungalow, a sanatarium erected on a spur of the ridge immediately above the site of the ancient city by a public-spirited native gentleman of Mirzapûr, for the special benefit of its European residents, is a massive square building having the appearance of a fort. It is, however, a Hindu monastery, with a temple on its summit, reputed to be of some sanctity. This edifice has in its walls, breastworks, and foundations, a multitude of carved stones and figures, while many more cover the ground in its vicinity. The sculptures found here and elsewhere in many places among the outlying fields, for a great distance, are not of modern Hindu style—indeed, in point of design and skilfulness of execution, are far superior to the productions of Hindus of later times. Some of the figures are of that curious type described, hesitatingly, by Mr. Fergusson, in his "Tree and Serpent Worship in India," as Dasyas, or aborigines, in contradistinction to the immigrant tribes of Hindus. They are readily distinguishable by their peculiar head-dress and long-pointed beards. They constitute, however, but a small portion of the figures, which are, for the most part, representations of Hindu men and women, with most elaborate turbans and head-dresses, while exceedingly few apparently are of a sacred character. It is probable that nearly all these relics point to a later period of Bhar history, when Hindus had come and settled among them. The contrast between the long-bearded figures and the Hindu figures, is very striking. It is questionable whether, at the date of most of these sculptures, the Bhars were still in possession of the country ; indeed, I am inclined to the supposition that it had, in part or in whole, already passed from them into the hands of the Rajpoots, who are known to have been the rulers over this tract for a period of five hundred years. At the same time, the position and attitude of the Bhar figures on these sculptures indicate that, at the time of their execution, the Bhars were still a people of importance. It is right to add, however, that a few of the sculptures, yet only a few, represent the Bhars as the superior race, and attached to the Buddhist or Jain religion.

My friend, C. J. Sibold, Esq., of Mirzapûr, has made an excellent collection of sculptures from the numerous remains at Pampâpûrâ, from which a few, admirably drawn by a native artist, have been selected for description. I have chiefly chosen those which exhibit the bearded figures. Some of these are

10½ inches from lower edge of chin to middle of forehead.
1 foot 5 inches from inner point of one ear, across the bridge of the nose, to inner part of the other ear.
1 foot 3½ inches from lower part of head-dress to the apex.
2 feet 2 inches from lower edge of chin to the apex of the head-dress.

THACKER, SPINK & Co CALCUTTA

BEARDED BHAR FIGURES

1 2 4 3

THACKER, SPINK & Cº CALCUTTA

5

6

7

8

THACKER, SPINK & Cº CALCUTTA

BEARDED BHAR FIGURES

9

THACKER SPINK & C° CALCUTTA

10

THACKER, SPINK & Co CALCUTTA

evidently sacred objects. It will be observed that the cast of countenance of all the bearded figures is of a peculiar type, differing considerably from the Hindu countenances with which, in some instances, they are associated, and also from Hindu faces of the present day.

The figures 1 and 2 are probably Bhar Rajas. The same may be said of the bearded figure 3, the other countenances being of a Hindu cast. Moreover, while the Bhar, is seated, and occupies an honorable position, the Hindu to the left is standing, and is probably an attendant. The sharply pointed beards of the Bhars, in most of these sketches, are very curious, being altogether unlike anything seen among the natives of India of modern times. Their head-dresses too are singular. The lower part of that of figure 1 looks like a crown.

The bearded figure 4, judging from his elaborate turban and long ear-rings, is a person of some distinction. His short beard has the appearance of a necker-chief. The artist has, I suspect, hardly caught its true expression. The Hindu attendant is presenting something kneeling. In the compartment to the left, the figure with a Hindu countenance, is seated cross-legged. It is four-armed, and therefore a deity, perhaps the household god of the Bhar chief. If this be so, it shows that the sketch represents a period when the Bhars worshipped Hindu idols.

Figure 5 seems to be at his devotions. He has one hand partly clasping the other. Figure 6 is in contemplation. He is not a devotee, as some might perhaps be inclined to imagine, for he has several bracelets and armlets on his wrist and arm ; nevertheless, it is probable that he is religiously engaged. Figures 7 and 8 display a considerable difference of head-dress. Their physiog-nomies are not of a Hindu type. The head of 7 is remarkable for the size of its ear-rings.

The central figure in the next Plate, compared with the remaining figures, is of colossal proportions. Being headless, it is impossible to speak about it with precision. The stumps of its four arms indicate that it was a divinity—but of what religion ? The elephant and deer were sacred animals with the Buddhists, and are very frequently found on their sculptures. The four arms, however, seem to point to a Hindu deity. Of the thirteen subordinate human figures, the three upper ones are beardless, and most likely represent Hindus. Two of these are worshipping the central figure. The ten lower figures have all pointed beards, and present a great similarity of physiognomy. Those in an erect posture are perhaps intended to represent priests, or, it may be, men of rank in attendance on the god. One of them holds in his hand a flag, another grasps a kind of club. All have on their heads a high conical cap or turban. The four bearded personages seated below display a very different style of head-dress, and seem to be of a humbler position in life. It is remarkable that the erect figures, and the divinity also, are adorned with what has the appearance of the sacred thread, while the sitting figures above and below are destitute of it. The Bhar figures, 1 and 4, have the thread also, but 2 and 3 are without it. I am at a loss to explain this very singular circumstance. My own impression is that the Bhars learnt the custom of wearing the thread from the Rajpoots, who came amongst them. But this must have been done before the Bhars were subdued, and while the Rajpoots were mere servants to them; for it is hardly likely that the Rajpoots, after they had subjugated the Bhars, would have suffered them to wear a sacred badge, which only Hindus of good caste were permitted to assume. Figure 10 is a four-armed divinity ; yet exhibits the Bhar type of countenance seen in Nos. 7 and 8. The conical cap and pointed beard are much like those observed in the erect figures of No. 9. The figure is four feet four inches in height.

It will be readily perceived that the beautiful figure No. 11, represented in the last Plate, displays a very different countenance from any of the Bhar figures described above. I believe it to be a likeness of a Gaharwâr Rajpoot, probably of a chief of the family that took possession of the Bhar territory of Kantit. The conical head-dress is of the same description as that worn by the Bhar chiefs in the sketches already noticed, but is more ornamented and magnificent. The figure is a divinity, as is manifest from the third eye set in the middle of the forehead ; and represents, very probably, Shiva as Trilochan, or the three-eyed. As a specimen of art, the relic is worthy of study. It is of colossal size, and originally belonged to a statue some ten or twelve feet in height.

Mr. Woodburn, Settlement Officer in Oudh, in his Report on the Mangalsi pargannah of the Fyzabâd district, has some interesting, though somewhat fanciful, observations on the nature and use of the Bhar forts in that part of Oudh. "Bhar forts, as they are called, are common in the *pargannah*. They are in general simple rounded mounds, more or less lofty, strewn with broken brick. The mounds appear to be, in the main, artificial ; and their area is never large. If the dwellings of the Bhars were confined to the mound, the population of that day must have been very scanty. This is hardly consistent with the revenue returns of Akbar's reign for the neighbourhood; and yet, according to the corroborative accounts of the Rajpoot tribes, the Bhars were dominant till Akbar's time. Impressed, however, with that idea, and feeling it hard to believe that a small population, living on an exuberant soil, could have lived in a state of constant strife, I conceived that the mounds were possibly constructed as a sanitary precaution against the malaria of a region of marshes and forests. The theory is scarcely justified by the position of some of the mounds with which I became acquainted. But however this may be, there can be no doubt a great change has taken place in the habits of the people since the days of the mound makers. Brick strongholds have been succeeded by clay huts ; and, as in the case of Kalâparpûr (where there is a Bhar fort,) the people have formed the notion that evil and misfortune haunt the dwelling-places of their forerunners. It is strange how the name of the Bhars should have adhered to places that now know them no more."

That the Bhars were not a barbarous race, but were partially civilized, is sufficiently proved by the numerous works of skill which they have left. Their massive forts, found throughout the country which they once inhabited, testify to their warlike propensities, yet they were probably erected chiefly as means of defence, and as places of refuge ; for, in their later history, it is certain they were exposed to fierce attacks from their Rajpoot neighbours. The same energy and talent which they exhibited in defending themselves against their enemies, they also displayed in more peaceful pursuits. Whence this people obtained their civilization, which placed them much above the condition of many other aboriginal tribes, it is hard to say, unless we suppose that it had its origin in themselves. I know not why we should be so ready always to ascribe all the ancient civilization of India to successive troops of Hindu immigrants. The more I investigate the matter, the stronger do my convictions become, that the Hindu tribes have learnt much from the aboriginal races, but that, in the course of ages, these races have been so completely subdued, and have been so ground down by oppression, and treated with such extreme rigour and scorn, that, in the present condition of abject debasement in which we find them, we have no adequate means of judging of their original genius and power. Mr. Thomason, late Lieutenant-Governor of the North-Western Provinces, in his Report on the Ceded Portion of the District of Azimgarh, says of the Bhars and the tribes associated with them :—" The inhabitants of the country, by whatever name they are distinguished, were a powerful and industrious people, as is evident by the large works they have left behind them" (*a*).

(*a*) Mr. Thomason's Report of the Ceded Portion of the District of Azimgarh, p. 13.

How long, prior to the Rajpoot invasions, the Bhars had occupied this tract of country, cannot be ascertained ; yet the prosperity to which they had attained, and the civilization which they had acquired, are sound reasons for thinking that they had held possession of it for a protracted period. Six, or, at the most, seven hundred years ago, the whole of the Benares Province, a large portion of the Province of Oudh, and perhaps a considerable portion of outlying territories, were, beyond all dispute, chiefly in the hands of the Bhars and other aboriginal non-Aryan tribes. The fall of Kanouj and Delhi, at the end of the twelfth century, set free the great Rajpoot families, and sent them wandering all over the country in quest of new homes. These came in contact with the aboriginal tribes, and either subdued them at once, or, as was probably more frequently the case, obtained employment and lands from them, in the first instance, and afterwards, as opportunity served, by degrees seized their possessions, overthrew their owners, and expelled them. This process was a long or short one, according to circumstances. In some instances, several hundred years elapsed before the end was gained. Yet finally the same conclusion was attained everywhere.

The traditions of all the land-owning tribes of the tracts referred to accord with these statements, bearing united testimony to the fact, that, a few hundred years ago, the middle Ganges' valley was occupied by non-Aryan aboriginal races. The history of the period preceding the Rajpoot immigrations, is partly historical, and partly conjectural. During the prevalence of Buddhism in Northern India, the Aryan races appear to have been everywhere dominant. Some of the aboriginal tribes blended with them, though to what extent, is uncertain. As Hinduism began to re-assert its authority and claims, on the decay of Buddhism, a fierce struggle seems to have arisen between the two religious factions. Yet how far the Aryans had cultivated the soil, and spread themselves out into villages and towns, is, strictly speaking, unknown. Whether, indeed, the country was well, or only scantily, populated, is equally uncertain. Most probably the latter supposition is the correct one. This, however, is tolerably clear, that the aboriginal tribes were in a subject condition. We have trustworthy information respecting the kingdom of Benares, and a portion of that country of which Ajudhiya was the capital. They were governed by Hindus. Both were originally chief seats of Hinduism. Afterwards, in both places, Buddhism was very powerful. And, lastly, in both kingdoms, Hinduism became once more in the ascendant. Nevertheless, the Aryan race, in its tremendous efforts to shake off the Buddhist creed, greatly enfeebled itself, and was consequently unable to cope with the aboriginal tribes, which, taking advantage of the religious and political strife which was destroying the life of the Hindu nation, endeavored to regain their ancient lands, from which ages before they had been driven away into the forests and mountains.

The remarks of Dr. Oldham respecting the district known by the modern name of Ghazipûr, is equally applicable to the whole of the Benares Province:—"On the downfal of Buddhism in this part of India, the distinction between the Aryans and the aborigines became as marked as ever. The former, weakened by their internecine war, were unable to hold the country; the latter, removed from the civilizing influences to which they had been subjected, relapsed wholly or partially into barbarism. And hence it was that this district, which, thirteen hundred years ago, formed an important part of a civilized Aryan monarchy, eight hundred years ago was under the sway of a number of petty semi-barbarous aboriginal chiefs, and had a very small Aryan population; while, on the other hand, the upper valley of the Ganges was filled with a teeming population of Hindus, who were in a position to send out colonies even before the coming of the Mussulmans, but who, on their coming, were compelled to do so" (*a*). In this passage Dr. Oldham, I think, somewhat under-rates the civilization of the aboriginal tribes, which, as before remarked, judging from existing remains, was considerable.

To the same purport are the observations of Mr. C. A. Elliott, respecting the changes in the distribution of the races of Oudh. The two periods in the history of that country, namely Aryan and post-Aryan, he describes as follows:—"When the Aryan race," he says, "invaded the Gangetic valley, and the Sûrajbansîs settled in Ajudhiya, the natural resource for the aborigines would be to fly to the hills, and find refuge in their impenetrable fastnesses, girded about with the deathly Terai. When the curtain rises again, we find Ajudhiya destroyed, the Sûrajbansîs utterly vanished, and a great extent of country ruled over by aborigines call Cherûs in the far east, Bhars in the centre, and Rajpusîs in the west. This great revolution seems to be satisfactorily explained by the conjecture that the Bhars, Cherûs, &c., were the aborigines whom the Aryans had driven to the hills, and who, swarming down from thence not long after the beginning of our era, overwhelmed the Aryan civilization, not only in Sahetan and the other northern towns, but in Ajudhiya itself, drove the Sûrajbansîs under Kanak Sen to emigrate into distant Gujerât, and spread over all

(*a*) Dr. Oldham's Statistical Memoir of the Ghazipûr District, p. 49.

the plain between the Himalayas and that spur of the Vindhyan Range which passes through the south of Mirzapûr" (*a*).

These aboriginal races having once re-entered the tracts of country which they had wrested from the Aryan tribes, settled upon them, and remained comparatively unmolested for a long period extending over hundreds of years. All this is plain when it is considered how firm was the hold which they had on the country when the wave of Rajpoot immigration began to flow in upon them. Their cities and towns, their industrial arts, their huge earthworks, their canals and trenches connecting rivers, and so forth, are irrefragable proofs of their permanence and prosperity.

Yet it must not be imagined that the land was cleared and cultivated to the extent in which we now see it. On the contrary, it is likely that, not only during this period of non-Aryan occupation of this portion of India, but also during the preceding period of Aryan occupation, the country had not been largely brought under cultivation, and that immense forests abounded extending over many miles. My own conviction is, that only in comparatively recent times, especially since the reign of Akbar, have the vast plains of Northern India been subjected to the plough and the harrow. The emperor Baber, grandfather of Akbar, in his Memoirs, says, that, while at Chunar, a lion, a rhinoceros, and a wild buffalo, were seen close on the edge of his camp, and that many elephants roamed in the jungle around Chunar, and, apparently, even as far as, and beyond, Benares. Elephants are known to have frequented the jungle between Chunar and Allahabad, in the sixteenth century, and the hills to the south of the Ganges must at that time have been almost unapproachable.

It is certain, therefore, that, at the time when the Bhars and other industrious aboriginal races planted their villages, and cultivated the lands around them, vast tracts, infested by wild beasts, remained uncleared. They inhabited, in short, an illimitable forest, which they cleared in places, and cultivated, subduing the untamed land, providing against dearth by digging splendid tanks, banking up morasses, utilizing water-courses, and thus laying the foundations of social happiness and comfort. "All inquiry," says Mr. G. Ricketts, "shows that the civilization of this district (namely Allahabad), and its reclamation from the primitive jungle, was of comparatively recent date, that is, within four hundred and fifty years. Very few of the Mahomedans claim descent from the followers of Shahâb-ud-dîn; but few Hindus date back beyond the reign of Jai

(*a*) Mr. C. A. Elliott's Chronicles of Oonao, p. 27.

Chand of Kanouj, whose followers, when defeated by Shahâb-ud-dîn, populated a portion of this district—but almost all state that their ancestors took possession of those jungle tracts, which form their present estates, within this period." If our own remarks respecting the social condition of the Bhars be correct, the estimate Mr. Ricketts forms of the civilization of this tribe, and of others in their neighbourhood, is altogether unsatisfactory *(a)*.

Sir Henry Elliot considers it strange that so little notice is taken of the Bhars in the Purânas. The fact may be accounted for in two ways. In the first place, Brahmanical writers generally speak of the Dasyas, Asuryas, and all other non-Hindu races, with superciliousness and contempt; and, consequently, rarely exhibit a particle of interest in their welfare. In the second place, the abandonment of a considerable tract of country on the part of the Aryans who occupied them, or their expulsion therefrom by aboriginal races, was an act of such little honor, that it was only natural, not only that the circumstance should not be referred to in records devoted to the purposes of the Hindu tribes, but also that the aborigines themselves, who had profited by it, should be unnoticed. Sir H. Elliot conjectures, however, that an obscure reference to the Bhars is to be found in the Brahma Purâna, where, it is said:—" Among the descendants of Jayadhwaja are the Bhâratas, who, it is added, are not commonly specified *from their great number*. So also the 'Harivansa' says of the Bhâratas, I, p. 157, 'they form an immense family, whose numbers it is impossible to mention.' Or they may perhaps be the Bhargas, of the 'Mahâbhârata,' subdued by Bhim Sen, on his eastern expedition" *(b)*.

With all their industry and capacity the Bhars were destined to perish. The chief cause of their destruction was, doubtless, as already stated, the success of the Mahomedan invasions of India, whereby the great Rajpoot rulers of Kanouj and Delhi were overthrown, and the Rajpoot tribes generally of Upper India, coming into collision with a foe stronger than themselves, were compelled to surrender their old possessions, and to seek out new homes. Being driven from their own countries they fled into the more secure regions of the east, where, coming in contact with aboriginal tribes, they gradually subdued them.

In the Ghazipûr and Azimgarh districts, a fierce and prolonged contest was carried on between the Bhars and the Sengarh Rajpoots from Phaphund, in

(a) Census Report of the North-Western Provinces for 1865, Vol. I., Appendix B; Mr. G. Rickett's Paper on the Castes and Tribes of Allahabad, p. 127.

(b) Elliot's Supplemental Glossary, p. 83.

the district of Etawah. These latter first entered the northern part of Ghazipûr in the employment of the Bhar Raja, who resided there. After a time, receiving some provocation from the Raja, they killed him, and endeavored to seize his territory. The Bhars, however, bravely defended their lands ; but the superior military skill of their enemies was more than a match for their courage and numbers, and they were obliged to submit to the yoke of the conqueror. The Sengarhs had two chiefs, Hari Thâkur and Bîr Thâkur. The descendants of the former occupy the Laknesar pargannah, while those of the latter are found partly in the Zuhurabâd pargannah, of the Ghazipûr district, and partly in a portion of Sikandarpûr, in the Azimgarh district. They reckon fifteen generations since their arrival in these parts, which shows that the Bhar rule lasted until a comparatively recent period (*a*).

The extensive *pargannah* of Kantit, in the Mirzapûr district, derives its name, according to tradition, from the famous Raja Karn, who, it is said, came on a *tirth* or pilgrimage to the island of Râm Gyah, in the Ganges, near Vindhyâchal. Karn-tirth has been contracted into Kantit. Formerly, this tract was in the possession of the Bhars; but was wrested from them by the Gaharwâr Rajpoots, under their chief, Gûdhan Deo, of the family of Raja Jai Chand of Kanouj, who massacred the Bhar ruler together with his relations and attendants. The capital of the Bhar kingdom in these parts was, I conjecture, the extensive city of Pampâpûrâ, from which the sculptures were brought, which have already been described. Gûdhan Deo built forts on his domains, portions of which are still standing.

This chief also took from the Bhars the lands of Khairagarh, now a *pargannah* in the Allahabad district, which afterwards fell to one of his sons. The number *chaurâsi*, or eighty-four, was applied to so many villages. Hence there is a Tuppeh Chaurâsî, or sub-division, consisting of eighty-four villages, both in the *pargannah* of Kantit and of Khairagarh. This family became very powerful, and spread over a wide extent of country, occupying large tracts in the districts of Allahabad, Mirzapûr, Jaunpûr, and Benares. The present Raja of Mânda, one of Gûdhan Deo's descendants, possesses a small portion only of this territory; yet it consists of six hundred and seventy-five square miles (*b*). It has been said that the Gaharwâr Rajpoots once ruled from old Kanouj to Allahabad and Mirzapûr; but this perhaps is only conjecture.

(*a*) Dr. Oldham's Statistical Memoir of the Ghazipûr District, Chap. III, Sec. 9.

(*b*) Mr. C. Raikes' Settlement Records of the Kantit Pargannah, Sec. 4; Report of Revenue Settlement, Allahabad, Vol. II., Part I, Sec. 29.

To the north of the Ganges, in what is the now the Bhadohî *pargannah*, the Bhar principality was destroyed by the Monas Rajpoots, who came from Amber, or old Jaipûr, where the elder branch of the clan still exists. The tradition of the circumstance, universally believed in the neighbourhood, is as follows. Five persons of the Mon race undertook to perform a pilgrimage from their own country to Benares. Passing through the Bhar territory they were attracted by its advantages, and determined to remain there, and to settle among its inhabitants. They were joined by other members of their tribe, whom they invited over. As they increased in numbers and importance, the Bhars sought to make alliances with them; but their overtures being discountenanced, disputes at length arose on the subject of intermarriage, which increased to blows. This seems to have been the signal for a general attack upon the Bhars; and, in the struggle which ensued, the Monas people were so successful that they not only completely subjugated the aborigines, but utterly destroyed them. At the present day, scarcely a Bhar is to be found from one extremity of the *pargannah* to the other, so absolute and entire has been their extermination.

Fortune, however, is a fickle goddess, and the fate of the Monas Rajpoots of Bhadohî, and also of the Gaharwâr Rajpoots of Kantit, affords notable instances of her inconstancy. The former calling in the aid of Pirthîpat Singh, Raja of Partâbgarh, to settle their family disputes, fell into his power; and, in the year 1751, the *pargannah* passed from his hands into those of Balwant Singh, Raja of Benares, with whose descendants it still remains. This powerful and ambitious chieftain also obtained possession of the Kantit lands, driving out the Gaharwâr, Raja Vikramajît, who with his attendants sought safety in flight. For nearly five hundred years the Raja and his predecessors had occupied the country. On the rebellion of Raja Cheit Singh of Benares, Warren Hastings sent for Raja Gobindjît, son of Vikramajît, from his hiding-place, for the purpose of restoring to him his patrimonial estate of Kantit. The new Raja of Benares, however, had sufficient influence with the British Government to hinder its restoration; and he only received a tenth part of the original receipts. His successors now reside in the old Gaharwâr fort of Bijaigarh, the domains of which were afterwards given in commutation of the tenth. The prestige of the ancient Gaharwâr family, in the flourishing commercial city of Mirzapûr, is very great; and when the mutiny was at its height, the Government wisely availed themselves of it in preserving order among the people (*a*).

(*a*) Report of the Bhadohî Pargannah, pp. 4, 5, 8; Mr. C. Raikes' Settlement Records of the Kantit Pargannah, Sec. 6.

It is greatly to the credit of Balwant Singh, the first Raja of Benares, that, during the time of his occupancy of the Kantit estate, he exerted himself most energetically in promoting the prosperity of the new and rising city of Mirzapûr. He sent over traders of various kinds from Benares; and a detachment of horse and foot was stationed there for the security of its inhabitants. The trade of the city rapidly increased; and it is not too much to say that its present important position, as one of the chief centres of trade in these Provinces, is mainly the result of the Raja's enterprise *(a)*.

In the district of Allahabad, several tribes of Rajpoots, at various times, ejected the Bhars. For instance, the Bais Rajpoots are found in Jhansa *pargannah;* the Monas Rajpoots in Kawai; the Sonak in Meh; the Tissyâl in Sikandra; and the Nanwak in Nawâb Ganj. The Bisen Rajpoots have settled in Karra, and Atharban, in the Doâb (*b*).

The Bais Rajpoots of Oudh were very ruthless in their treatment of these industrious aborigines. Mr. Patrick Carnegy, in his "Historical Sketch of Fyzabâd," gives a particular account of the successful raids made by members of the Bais tribe into that part of Oudh now known as the district of Fyzabâd. The Bais of Malethu overthrew and dispossessed the Bhars only two hundred years ago. The Bais of Sohwal and Rûrû aided in the suppression of the Bhars four hundred years ago. The Bais of Uchhâpali did the same about the same period. The Bais of Râmpûr Bhagun Tikrî fought the Bhars in the time of the emperor Jehângîr. The Bais of Gonda took service under the Bhar chief some three hundred years back, embraced the opportunity of killing him, and seized his estates. The great Bais families holding lands in the *pargannah* of Mangalsi, expelled the Bhars from two to three hundred years ago. The Mahomedans residing there state that Mangal Sen, from whose name the word Mangalsi is derived, was a Bhar.

I have already referred to the territory in the Gorakhpûr district, now occupied by the Kausik Rajpoots, and formerly occupied by the Bhars, who were driven out from their lands, or destroyed, like the rest of their race.

The Rajpoot tribes, although the principal, were not the only enemies of the Bhars. The Mahomedans also, at various times, settled in many places on their lands. In the Allahabad district the *pargannahs* of Chail and Karâlî are

(*a*) Report of the Bhadohî Pargannah, pp. 4, 5, 8; Mr. C. Raike's Settlement Records of the Kantit Pargannah, Sec. 6.

(*b*) Report of Revenue Settlement, Allahabad, Vol. II., Part I, Sec. 45; Settlement Report of the Azimgarh District, Vol. I., Sec. 24.

almost entirely in the occupation of Mahomedan proprietors. Being near the city itself in which the Nâzim, or chief local officer, and his underlings, resided, it is not remarkable that these *pargannahs* should have fallen a prey to their cupidity. When the kingdom of Jaunpûr was established, in the fourteenth century, all this part of the country formed a portion of the king of Jaunpûr's dominions ; and remained so until the downfall of the last king, Hussain Khan, towards the end of the fifteenth century.

If the dates given above be correct, it is plain that the Bhars, not a great while ago, were the lords of the soil over a considerable portion of the Benares Province and the Province of Oudh. It does not appear that, at any time, they possessed sovereign power. It is probable that they peacefully acknowledged the supremacy of the reigning monarch in these Provinces for the time being, first of the kings of Kanouj, then of the first Mahomedan emperors, then of the kings of Jaunpûr, and lastly of the Mogul emperors. Whether in the dark middle ages of Indian history, prior to the invasions of Mahmûd of Ghazni and his hosts, and after the fall and expulsion of the Buddhists, the Bhars were ever independent rulers, is a problem which cannot be solved.

Yet what has become of the old Bhar race ? Their fate has been most disastrous, inasmuch as, they have not only been robbed of their lands and of all authority incident to wealth and rank, but their conquerors have plunged them in the lowest depths of humiliation. Their present condition proves conclusively that they were ever regarded by their oppressors as fair game, to be hunted down and destroyed. Not content with doing their utmost to exterminate the Bhars during long centuries of grinding tyranny, they have degraded the survivors of the race to the most abject condition in the social scale. Here and there, in many places, as will presently be shown, Bhars are still found ; but, with few exceptions, their state is one of great social ignominy. They are largely employed to tend swine, an office which in India only the most despised and disreputable classes will undertake. Perhaps this office is a remnant of the old habits of the Bhars, and indicates, as is indeed almost certain, that their ancestors ate pork and the flesh of other animals. By some persons, the Bhars are included in the caste of Pâsîs, one of the most ignoble of the non-Hindu castes.

It would be interesting to learn the history of the degradation of a race of people, of enterprise and skill, of originality and singular practical ability, which it is evident once characterized them in no ordinary degree. Their supplanters, whether Rajpoots, Brahmans, or Mahomedans, though more civilized and refined, are not to be compared with the humbler aborigines, whom they have ruined in regard to the great works of public utility which have been produced in the land. In default of such historical information—which indeed there is little probability of our ever acquiring—the only explanation of the circumstance that I can give is, that their present miserable condition is the result of the pride and intolerance of their conquerors. As a non-Aryan tribe, they were considered impure, and altogether unfit to be the companions of the twice-born and their associates. Their industry, their natural gifts, their energy and perseverence, constituted, in the judgment of these high-caste intolerants, no claim to their consideration; on the contrary, may have furnished a reason, in addition to their religious uncleanness, for depressing them as low as possible. The mental superiority of the Aryan races over the Bhars, and other similar aboriginal tribes, admits of no dispute; and it is equally certain that, in industry and practical sagacity, they were barely equal to them. This is proved by the fact, patent to all residing in those parts of India to which special reference has been made in this chapter, that there are more numerous remains of their mechanical ability and skill in that tract than of all the Rajpoot and other Aryan tribes that succeeded them. In the view of the author, special measures should be adopted by philanthropists for the social and political regeneration of the Bhar, the Seorî, which has suffered a like degradation, and other aboriginal tribes. Well-informed and generous Hindus, who are deriving incalculable benefit from British rule in India, aspirants for political distinctions and favors, men animated, or professing to be animated, with noble desires for the enlightenment of their fellow countrymen, may fairly be called upon to render efficient aid in this enterprise. Nor should the Government withhold a helping hand. It has paid little practical attention to these despised classes hitherto. This is a grave, though unintentional, error. Why should not the Bhar, and the Seorî, have a chance to recover their lost social position? The Government has it in its power to afford them this chance. Has it yet the will?

A few of the Bhar tribe, although they may not have saved themselves from social contempt, are still in possession of property and comparative independence. While not a single Bhar landed-proprietor exists in the Bhadohî *pargannah* of the Mirzapûr district, there are two Bhar landlords, or were not long since, in the neighbouring *pargannah* of Kantit, in the same district. But these men, disloyal to their tribe, though wise in their generation, feeling the grievous burden of their social position, affect a Rajpoot title, notwithstanding that it is well known they are descended directly from the Bhars. The extensive tract in the Vindhya Hills, known as the Talluqa of Koindîh, belongs to a Bhar clan.

In the Allahabad district this unfortunate race seems to have been well nigh extinguished. There are, however, three Bhar villages in the Khairagarh *pargannah*, namely Majera, Kaliyânpûr, and Omraicha, the families of which are said to have right to six others, although in reality only occupying these three. It is probable that the Bhars, driven away from more civilized regions, retreated into the wild jungle of Khairagarh, and remained there long after multitudes of their race in other places had been destroyed. But they were finally expelled by the present Raja of Mânda, to whom reference has been already made. The Arail and Barrah *pargannahs* have also Bhars residing in them. They are likewise met with in every village of *pargannah* Salîmpûr Majholî, in the Gorakhpûr district. In Shâhâbâd they still held a portion of the extensive domains formerly in the possession of the tribe. A *pargannah* of Chota Nagpûr is called Bharwa.

In fact, the Bhars still cling with pertinacity to the country in which their more fortunate ancestors flourished for so many generations. In most of the cities and towns, and in not a few of the villages likewise, scattered members of the tribe are found. They exhibit little tribal cohesiveness or *esprit de corps*, and are utterly destitute of spirit and enterprise. In the Ghazipûr district alone, there are fifty-six thousand Bhars; in Gorakhpûr, sixty-three thousand; in Azimgarh, sixty-nine thousand; in Benares, thirty-three thousand; and many more in other places. Bhars are commonly employed as village policemen, and also as ploughmen. It is said that there are properly two divisions of them, the Bhars and the Râjbhars, the latter differing from the former in not eating swine's flesh, and being regarded, consequently, as more honorable than they. It is not improbable that they may be descended from the old Bhar nobility. Rajpoots are in the habit of purchasing female children from the Râjbhars, and marrying them to their sons: this arises from the habit of infanticide which has existed for so long among some of the Rajpoot tribes.

In spite of the pertinacity with which, if tradition is correct, the higher castes kept aloof from Bhar alliances, they were not always successful in doing so. In the Allahabad district, for instance, three examples are found of unions with Bhar families. Mr. G. Ricketts, in his Memorandum, states that "three influential castes or clans claim an admixture of Bhar blood. These are the Bharors, Garhors, and Tikaits. The two former are not numerous. They are landed proprietors in the southern portions of this (Allahabad) district; and appear to be a connecting link between the higher castes, who are generally landed proprietors, and those inferior castes whose lot is servitude. The Tikaits are numerous, and possess much influence. A Chauhân leader carried off his Bhar chief's daughter. The descendants are still proprietors of a portion of that Bhar chief's possessions" *(a)*.

Mr. P. Carnegy, in his Notes on the Races of Oudh, indulges the strange notion, that the Bhars are of Rajpoot origin, and the Cherûs also, "and such like." And yet he acknowledges that the "weight of opinion seems to be in favor of the belief that the Bhars may have been the so-called aborigines of Eastern Oudh, which formerly included Azimgarh and Gorakhpûr." This view he dissents from, holding that, if they were "not the aborigines of Eastern Oudh, they were, at any rate, Rajpoots in Râma's time, or long before the Christian era" *(b)*.

Whether the Bhars were originally connected with the Cherûs, Seorîs, and other ancient races of Northern India, is a question of considerable ethnological interest. The Cherûs are sometimes spoken of as a branch of the Bhars; and as to the Seorîs, it was the opinion of Sir H. Elliot, that there was great reason to suppose that the Cherûs and Seorîs were formerly one and the same; yet he says it is very difficult to trace the connexion between these tribes. It is certainly remarkable that the *pargannah* of Barhar in the Mirzapûr district, which I have no doubt should be "Bharhar," the second syllable "har" being the reduplication of the "har" of the first syllable, is, at the present time, partly inhabited by a race of Seorîs.

My own belief is, that many of the aboriginal tribes of India were originally blended together. All investigation into the races of India goes to prove, that, at various epochs, separate tribes have spread over the land, one pushing forward another, the weaker and less civilized retreating to the jungles and hilly fastnesses, and the stronger, in their turn, giving place to fresh and more vigorous clans. It may be impossible to prove, therefore, what is nevertheless highly probable, that, in very ancient times, most of these tribes were exceedingly few in number, for it is a singular circumstance, opposed indeed, when regarded superficially, to the assumption I am making, that the races of India, whether Aryan or non-Aryan, for a long succession of ages, have largely maintained their distinctive individuality, notwithstanding the fluctuations in their respective histories. Still, to some extent, they have united with one another; and it is indisputable that a large number of the low castes of India have sprung from unions between the races. In many instances a careful scrutiny can detect

(a) Mr. Ricketts' Report, p. 128.
(b) Mr. P. Carnegy's Races of Oudh, p. 19.

in these castes, not only their special differences, but also the very names by which the clans they represent were primarily designated.

This scattering of tribes over the country has produced a result which perhaps is not found on the same scale in any other part of the world, namely that every district in India has its peculiar clans, with their own traditions and annals; and has, in addition, a host of fragmentary and isolated remnants of lost or vanquished tribes, like the Bhars, of which, in some cases, scarcely more than their bare names can now be traced.

But the subject of the history of the aboriginal races of India, is one which, although material is being gradually collected for its elucidation, is nevertheless so intricate and involved, that it will require long and patient research before satisfactory conclusions are attained. The unravelling of the tangled skein of Indian history, is necessarily a work of time, and of great difficulty. Yet something has been already accomplished by earnest, conscientious, and painstaking laborers. Exceedingly harassing as the task undoubtedly is, still knot after knot of the disordered thread is being gradually unloosened. The enterprise is one demanding perseverance and industry, which will achieve in this, as in most pursuits, far greater and more brilliant results than the sudden efforts of an intense and fitful enthusiasm.

In addition to my own independent investigations on the subject of this chapter, I have received considerable assistance in its preparation from the following works :—Mr. Plowden's General Report of the Census of the North-Western Provinces for 1865; Mr. G. Ricketts' Memorandum on the Castes of Allahabad, in the General Report; Report on the Bhadohee Pargannah of the Family Domains of the Maharaja of Benares, by Mr. Duthoit, Deputy Superintendent; Settlement Records of the Kantit Pargannah, Mirzapûr, by Mr. C. Raikes; Revenue Settlement Reports of Gorakhpûr, Allahabad, and Azimgarh ; Benares Magazine, Vol. II; Dr. Wilton Oldham's Report on the Ghazipûr District; Sir H. Elliot's Supplemental Glossary; Memoirs of the Emperor Baber; Mr. C. A. Elliott's Chronicles of Oonao, a District in Oudh; and Mr. P. Carnegy's Races, Tribes, and Castes of the Province of Oudh.

CHAPTER II.

THE CHERU, THARU, SEORI, KOL, KHARWAR OR KHAIRWAR, AND BAWARYA TRIBES.

Cherû.

PROBABLY, the Bhars, Seorîs, and Cherûs, together with other aboriginal tribes which have not been so successful in maintaining their identity, were in a remote period of antiquity only one race. This is a conjecture which, from the absence of historical records and other trustworthy data, hardly admits of proof. It was the opinion of Sir H. Elliot that the Seorîs and Cherûs belonged to one family; but Buchanan thinks they were originally two distinct tribes. It is certain that in the historical period, commencing six or seven hundred years ago, in which the Bhars, Seorîs, and Cherûs flourished, they were separate and independent, or quasi-independent, tribes of great industry and enterprise. The period is related to a prior one, of longer or shorter duration, when these races were manifestly in existence, though little of a definite character is revealed respecting them.

It is a singular circumstance, the proofs of which are in such abundance, and are so diversified, that there is no resisting their weight, that the province of Benares, and the province of Oudh, besides portions of other provinces contiguous to them, should, in the post-Buddhist age of India, have been chiefly in the hands and under the jurisdiction of these and kindred aboriginal tribes, subsequent to an epoch when it is equally certain that they were for many centuries subject to genuine Hindu races.

The tradition of the Cherûs is that they belong to the great Serpent Race, whose traces and descendants are found in various parts of India. It is not improbable, therefore, that they are related to the Nâga tribes in the Assam hills, to the aborigines of Nâgpûr, to the Nâgbansî Rajpoots, and to the wandering Nâga devotees. The Cherû has distinctive features, but this is true likewise of most of the aboriginal tribes, and also more or less of the lower castes of Hindus, which are a mixture of Hindu and aboriginal blood. In the Shahâbâd district, and perhaps elsewhere, the Cherûs have a peculiar custom, noticed by Buchanan, of appointing a Raja for every five or six families, who is created in the Rajpoot fashion by the application of a mark or *thîka* to the forehead. He makes a strong statement respecting them, that they were once lords of the Gangetic provinces, and probably possessed paramount authority in India (*a*).

Although this opinion of Buchanan cannot in its entirety be supported by proofs, yet it is incontestible that the Cherûs were formerly a powerful race. They occupied tracts of country from Behar to Gorakhpûr, in the north, as far as the banks of the Soane in the Mirzapûr district, to the south. All the east of Ghazipûr, says Dr. W. Oldham, "was the country of the Cherûs. Very extensive remains of brick and debris, covering between twenty and thirty acres, are to be seen at Pakka Kot, on the Sarjû, in Kopâchit; and remains of earthen embankments, still larger, are at Wyna, in Pargannah Balliah. With regard to these places, no prevailing tradition, as far as I can ascertain, has survived; but the people of the country say that, from the Kot of Bîrpûr, on the Ganges, a great Cherû Raja, Tîkam Deo, ruled over the Mahomedabâd *pargannah* when their ancestors first came. Mahîpa Cherû, who had his strong-hold at the deserted village of Deorî, north of the Sûrâha Lake, was, on the advent of the Hindus, the lord of the delta between the Ghogra and the Ganges" (*b*). There is a tradition floating among the people that this Lake was excavated by the Cherûs under Raja Sûrat, though probably it is an old reach of the Ganges. It is remarkable that in the Ghazipûr district the race has been so completely exterminated that not an individual remains. Yet in the Bahîa *pargannah* of the neighbouring district of Shahâbâd, the Cherûs are found in considerable numbers. Indeed, until lately this district and others in Behar, were, to a large extent, the property of the tribe. The Hayobans Rajpoots of Haldî have family documents, showing that, while they were in Bahîa, they waged perpetual warfare with the Cherûs during a period of several hundred years, and at last were completely victorious. But even as recently as the reign of Shîr Shâh, the Cherûs were a formidable enemy (*c*).

The extensive tract of forest land to the south of the district of Mirzapûr was at one time completely in the hands of aboriginal tribes, such as the Cherûs, Bhars, and Kharwârs, which, after a severe and prolonged struggle, were eventually subdued by the Chandel Rajpoots. The Cherûs are still found scattered

(*a*) Buchanan's Eastern India, Vol. I., p. 494.

(*b*) Statistical Memoir of the Ghazipûr District, Part I., p. 46.

(*c*) *Ibid*, p. 51.

among the Khymore hills. The Raja of Palamau, although affecting a Rajpoot origin, is stated to be in reality a Cherû. 'For years,' says Dr. Oldham, 'two Cherû robbers, named Norah and Korah, infested the Soane valley under the great peak of Mangesar, and, armed with bows and arrows, committed many daring robberies and some murders. Their arrest could not be effected, as after each of their crimes they ascended the steep cliffs of Mangesar, and were harboured by the rude villagers living on the summit.' They were afterwards captured by the villagers, at the instigation of the Magistrate, and were brought to him 'tied down on string beds.' Dr. Oldham suggests that the Cherand *pargannah* and Cherand Island, in the Sâran district, received their names from this tribe (*a*).

Traces of the Cherûs are met with over a wide extent of country. Remains of buildings imputed to them still exist at Sasserâm, Râmgarh, and Buddha Gya. For several hundred miles to the west, as far as the Central Doâb, tradition points here and there to them as original lords of the soil (*b*). The ancient monuments of the district of Shahâbâd are chiefly attributed to the Cherûs. The race was subdued in that district by the Seorîs, another aboriginal tribe, who, in their turn, were destroyed by the Rajpoots.

Thâru.

The Thârus are one of the aboriginal races of India now in a depressed and abject condition, yet formerly of considerable influence and power. In the Gorakhpûr district the ruins in the villages of Ratkas and Deoganj, near Lâlganj, are traditionally regarded by the people as having been the residences of Thârus in ancient times. The Tilpûr *pargannah* near the *Tarai* was once in the possession of this tribe, who were expelled therefrom by Tilvîkrâm Sen by the help of the Banjâras. He gave his name to the *pargannah*, and his family held it until they were overthrown by the Nawab Kâsim Ali Khân. It was ceded to the British by the Nepalese in the year 1815. The jungle of Bûrîdî in Tuppeh Sehra was assigned to a colony of Thârus from the Nepal territory, and by them brought under cultivation.

A clan of Thârus, called Barwâik, a race of Tibetan origin, occupies villages, says Mr. Beames, in the plains of northern Gorakhpûr and Champâran. I suspect, however, that these Barwâiks are not a clan of Thârus, but rather hereditary office-bearers among the Thârus (*c*).

(*a*) Statistical Memoir of the Ghazipûr District, Part I., p. 51.

(*b*) Elliot's Supplemental Glossary, Vol. I., pp. 60, 61.

(*c*) Report of the Census of the North-Western Provinces for 1865; Appendix B., p. 62.

In his short essay on the Tarai pargannahs, Mr. E. Colvin, formerly superintendent of the pargannahs, remarks that "the Thâru traditions state that they come from Chittore, and refer to Jaimal and Pattah. They state that they were driven from their home and settled here. The reference would seem to indicate the third sack of Chittore, that is, by Akbar, about 1560 A. D. They claim to have been originally Rajpoots; and state that their ancestors lost their caste by taking to intoxicating liquors and rearing fowls. I have never heard from them any allusion to a Goorkha or hill origin, an idea which their type of feature itself suggests. The Thârus, as the Bhuksas, are divided into *gotras;* and interspersed with them are other tribes, who are generally called Thârus, but who are quite distinct" (*a*). The claim to be Rajpoots put forward by this and other aboriginal tribes, must be regarded with great suspicion. In every case, I believe, it arises simply from the low social position to which all these tribes have sunk, and the natural desire to be regarded as of honorable origin.

Mr. Colvin has an important remark on the derivation of the word Thâru. "A Thâru, it is true, will say, 'we came to live in the Tarai, and became Thârus;' but if the commonly accepted derivation of Tarai, that is, *tarâ hûâ*, to be wet or damp, is the true one, the initial *th* of the Thâru is unaccounted for. The word Tarua, however, by which they are commonly known, has no sound of the *h*." This tribe, says Mr. Colvin, has no acknowledged leaders, but an office called *barwâik* is hereditary in certain families. The Thârus live in houses made of posts driven into the ground, with beams resting on them. "The walls are made of reeds, locally termed *tant*, tied with grass, and generally smeared over with mud and cowdung, with a thatched roof. The Thârus keep their residences scrupulously clean. For wells, which they only use for drinking purposes, and never for irrigation, a hollowed tree is sunk into the ground" (*b*).

Seori.

This tribe of aborigines existed side by side with the Bhars, Cherûs, Kols, Kharwârs, and other indigenous races, having branches or clans in various directions. They were settled in the Mirzapûr district probably before the Mahomedan period in India commenced. There is reason to believe that, when Bhola Sirwa, a Rajpoot Chief of Hastinâpûr, about the eleventh century of

(*a*) Report of the Census of the North-Western Provinces for 1865; Appendix B., p. 60.

(*b*) *Ibid*, pp. 61, 62.

the Christian era, settled in the tract, afterwards designated Bhola *pargannah* from his own name, he came in contact with the Seorîs. These people were finally ejected from their estates by the Qiladar, or commandant of the Fort of Chunâr, to make way for his Mussalman followers, at the close of the twelfth century (*a*).

From traditions current in the Shahâbâd district, we know that the Cherûs and the Seorîs came into violent collision, which terminated in the triumph of the latter, and in the ejection of the former from their ancient home. The Seorîs, however, had to give place, like other aboriginal tribes, to colonies of Rajpoots and Brahmans, not only in Shahâbâd, but also in all the tracts in which they were settled. They were once strong in Ghazipûr, but they have entirely abandoned it. The plains of the Ganges, the old haunts of the tribe in the times of its prosperity, are annually visited by a race of Seorîs from Central India. These much resemble the gipsies of Europe. "Their women wear a tartan dress, and often have a kind of horn projecting from the forehead as an ornament. They live in light and easily-moved booths made of grass and reeds; are fond of intoxicating drinks; and eat the flesh of swine and oxen. They procure wives for their young men by kidnapping female children; and live principally by jugglery, coining false money, and theft. During the hot season they often attack by night the *banjâras* or travelling merchants, when halting at the camping grounds amid the hills and forests of Sirgûja, and drive off their pack bullocks, which, during the rainy season, they pasture in the jungle, and, early in November, bring for sale into the Mirzapûr district." One woman of the tribe whom Dr. Oldham, the narrator, saw, had with her a sack containing the bones of her deceased husband, who had died during the annual migration southwards. 'She had carried his remains about with her for hundreds of miles, in order that she might throw them into the sacred waters of the Ganges. This fact seems to indicate that the Ganges' valley was once the home of the tribe, as it is only people residing within a moderate distance of the river who are in the habit of committing to its waters the remains of their dead' (*b*).

Traces of this race are still found in the district of Ghazipûr, and are an evidence at once both of their power and skill. About four miles west of the city of this name is a lofty mound, called a fort by the natives, who ascribe its erection to the Seorîs. Sculptured stones, bricks, and a great abundance

(*a*) Mr. Wynyard's Pargannah Report.

(*b*) Memoirs of the Ghazipûr District, p. 50.

of debris, are scattered upon it. The fort is situated near the junction of the Gangî with the Ganges. According to tradition it was formerly occupied by a Seorî Chief. The country to the south of the Ganges, bordered by the Gangî, and also by the present *pargannah* of Zamâniah, was once in the hands of this tribe (*a*).

Kol.

A low caste or tribe employed in cutting down jungle from year to year, and in conveying the wood to Benares and other places for sale. The Kols are also water-carriers and fishermen. In all probability they are connected with the aboriginal tribes of Kols found in Chhotâ Nâgpûr, Mirzapûr, and other parts of the country. The word Kûli, Anglicized *cooly*, is derived from these people. This is not the place for a disquisition on the Kols, or I might attempt to show, what I believe is not difficult of proof, that representatives of the Kol family may be traced over a large portion, not only of the Benares province, but also of the neighbouring provinces. The Bhars, the Kols, the Cherûs, the Seorîs, and others, were indisputably former occupants of all this part of India throughout a circuit of many miles, and had their own princes, if not their own government. They have long since lost their power and importance, and wherever they are discovered living among the Hindus, like the Kols of Benares, are in a very servile condition, and are as hewers of wood and drawers of water to the rest of the community. Respecting the Kol tribes of Chhotâ Nâgpûr, much interesting information may be gathered from Colonel Dalton's Essay in the Journal of the Asiatic Society of Bengal for 1866, Part II. (*b*).

One division of the Kantit *pargannah*, in the Mirzapûr district, namely that now styled the *tuppeh* or sub-division of Saktîsgarh, was, in ancient times, occupied by the Kols, and seems never to have been in the possession of the Bhars. The Kols continued to hold it long after the Rajpoots had established themselves in their neighbourhood, the chief reason of this being, that neither their lands, nor their chattels, nor their own persons, furnished a bait sufficiently tempting. They were a people living in swamps in the dense jungle, their favourite dwellings being stone caverns surrounded by deep pools of water. Here they lived in comparative independence and security. They were, however, eventually subdued, though in what era does not appear ; but in the

(*a*) Memoirs of the Ghazipûr District, p. 46.

(*b*) The Essay is in a Special Number of the Journal, devoted to the Ethnology of India, and is entitled "The Kols of Chhotâ Nâgpûr," by Lieut.-Col. Dalton, Commissioner of Chhotâ Nâgpûr.

reign of Akbar a small tax was imposed upon them. When Sakat Singh, a descendant of Gûdhan Deo, was Raja of Kantit, he seized the country occupied by the Kols for non-payment of the tax, and, apparently with the permission of the emperor, annexed it to his own estate. On the site of their stronghold he erected a fort, which is still known as the Saktîsgarh fort. In its neighbourhood the jungles continue to be infested with tigers and other wild animals; and for tiger-shooting perhaps no region in India surpasses it. The Kols have not been utterly exterminated, but are yet found in some places, and are mostly employed in agriculture. The *tuppeh* was formerly called Kolâna, a term even now occasionally applied to it (*a*). The Kol king seems to have had his residence at Golhanpûr (or Golharpûr) after Sakat Singh's seizure of the country (*b*).

Kharwâr or Kairwâr.

An aboriginal tribe inhabiting the *pargannahs* of Barhar, Agorî, Bijaigarh, Singraulî, and other places to the south of the Mirzapûr district. The Baland Rajas of this tribe, who flourished about seven hundred years ago, held possession of a considerable portion of this territory, from which they were expelled by a colony of Chandel Rajpoots in the beginning of the thirteenth century (*c*).

The Kharwârs state that their original seat was Khaira Garh; yet their name is said to be derived from their occupation of extracting *katha* or catechu from the khair or catechu tree, an occupation, however, which many of them affect now to despise. It is significant that a sub-division of the tribe are called Khairaha Kharwârs. Although Khaira Garh is spoken of as the ancient home of the race, yet the members of the tribe are unable to state explicitly its exact situation. There is a *pargannah* of this name in the Allahabad district, which is probably the territory in question. One reason, in addition to its name, leading to this supposition, is, that the *pargannah* is inhabited by an aboriginal tribe of hillmen, called Ben Bans, an appellation though not restricted to the Kharwârs yet chiefly applied to them. The present Raja of Singraulî is a Kharwâr, but styles himself Ben Bans (*d*).

Judging from the extensive ruins and debris scattered over the country between the Nawa Nûth stream of Chaura as far as Gothânî on the Bijal, it is manifest that the site was once occupied by a considerable city, which,

(*a*) Mr. C. Raikes' Settlement Records of the Kantit Pargannah, Sect. 4.

(*b*) *Ibid*, Note by W. R.

(*c*) Pargannah Reports of the Mirzapûr District, by Mr. Roberts, Vol. V., pp. 83—85.

(*d*) *Ibid.*

according to local tradition, was as large as Benares. A few structural buildings only now remain. There are several temples at Gothânî, and in the fort of Agorî. Ruins also are found on most of the neighbouring hills. The fort was for ages the abode of the Baland Rajas, whose memory still lingers among the hills and valleys. All the great architectural works found in those tracts are ascribed to the Balands, who are believed to have ruled over an enterprising and industrious people. It is remarkable that they are said to have erected their buildings by the labours of Asûrya architects, whom they retained in their employ. The forts of Bijaigarh and Bardî, and the large tanks at Pûr and Korâdî, are fruits of their skill.

The struggle between the Mahomedan invaders and Prithî Râj caused the dispersion of many Rajpoot clans over large tracts of these provinces; yet this was not the only influence contributing to such a result. The two rival Rajpoot houses of Delhi and Kanouj, weakening one another, and so preparing the way for their final destruction, in the shock administered to the great families by whose instrumentality they had maintained their position and preserved their strength, were still further enfeebled by the flight of numbers of their followers, who abandoning the conflict sought rest and quietness in other regions. In the successes gained by Prithî Râj the Chandel Rajas of Mahoba suffered greatly. Two princes of the family, Barî Mal and Parî Mal, flying before the victorious arms of Prithî Râj, sought refuge with Raja Maddan, the Baland ruler of the Kharwârs, and entered into his service. Being skilled in war, and possessing greater aptitude for posts of importance than the aborigines who held them, the Chandels so ingratiated themselves with the Raja that they became his personal attendants, and gained both honors and authority. They were placed over his army and revenue, and thus acquired immense influence. Their opportunity for action and for the display of their real character and object at length arrived, and they played the game of treachery so often played by Rajpoot emigrants with the simple aboriginal rulers in those earlier times, and always successfully. The death of Raja Maddan was approaching. It was reckoned unlucky to die on the southern bank of the Soane, and he was consequently removed to the northern bank, where he remained awaiting his end. Feeling it drawing near, he called for his son that he might give him his last counsels and instructions, having first ordered the removal of all his attendants. Dim of sight, his strength failing, he was deluded into the belief that his son had obeyed his commands, and was the only person within hearing of his voice. The son, however, had not been summoned, and an indistinct murmur from the lips of a Chandel represented the utterance of his mouth. The dying man was deceived like Isaac, and without suspicion unburdening his heart and gave the important and eagerly desired information of the place in which the family treasure was deposited. On the death of the Raja the Chandels seized the fort and estates, and became the rulers over the principality. The son was at the time hunting in the forest, and hearing of the circumstance was able to escape to the hills with a few attendants (*a*).

The remainder of the tale I will give in the words of Mr. Roberts:—"On arriving at manhood the grandsons of the Baland Raja, Ghâtam and others, with their adherents, defeated the Chandels and got possession of the fort, putting to death all the members of the reigning Raja. One Ranee, who was far gone in pregnancy, made her escape into the territory of Kantit (now one of the *pargannahs* of the Mirzapûr district), with a single female attendant. On the road the Ranee was delivered of a male child; and died soon after giving him birth. The nurse took the child, and placing it in a tray *(oran)*, pursued her road until she came to the house of a Seorî (one of the aboriginal races) zemindâr (or land-owner), a man of great consideration, where she sought and obtained refuge. The child was brought up in the zemindâr's family, and was named Oran, to commemorate the incident of his having been placed in a tray *(oran)* after his birth.

"As he grew up he excelled in feats of arms and horsemanship, and was remarkable for his fine person. He was designed by the zemindâr to be the husband of his daughter ; but his accomplishments and manly beauty having attracted the notice of the Ghaharwâr Raja of Bijaipûr (Kantit), the Raja caused inquiries to be made concerning the youth. When it was made known to the Raja that the young man was the son of one of the Ranees of the family of the Chandel Rajas of Agorî, the Raja caused him to be taken from the house of the Seorî, and to become an inmate of the royal house of Bijaipûr. The Raja gave him his daughter in marriage, and ultimately assembling a large force drove Raja Ghâtam from Agorî, and restored Oran Deo (after having administered the *tilak*, or mark, applied to the forehead, conferring on him the title of Raja) to the Rajaship of Agorî, Barhar, Bijaigarh, and Bardî" (*b*). And thus the iron heel of the Rajpoot, as in many other instances, stamped out for ever the political life of the aboriginal race.

(*a*) Pargannah Reports of the Mirzapûr District, by Mr. Roberts, formerly Magistrate and Collector of Mirzapûr, and lately one of the Judges of the High Court, Allahabad, Vol. V.

(*b*) Mirzapûr Pargannah Reports, by Mr. Roberts, Vol. V.

Although Oran Deo was united in marriage to a Gaharwâr Râjpûtanî, yet he did not cast off the Seorî's daughter, by whom he had several children, whose descendants are scattered about the Barhar *pargannah*, and although called Chandels by courtesy, are known to have tainted blood.

For five hundred years the family of Oran Deo continued in the undisputed occupation of the territory ; yet ruin came upon it at last, about the middle of the last century, when Raja Sambhu Sah succumbed to the power of Balwant Singh, the famous Raja of Benares, by whom he was ejected from his ancestral possessions ; but the family was subsequently restored by the British Government to a portion of its former estates. The present Raja of Barhar is a descendant of Oran Deo and his Gaharwâr wife.

It is not improbable that the Baland Rajas, and after them the Chandel Rajas, for several generations, were really independent princes; yet it is well known that the later Chandel Rajas acknowledged the supremacy of the Mahomedan emperors, and paid land revenue into the treasury of the Nazim at Chunâr, in skins of elephants and deer, bamboos, timber, and other forest productions, to the value of eight thousand rupees yearly.

The descendants of the original Baland Rajas reside in the territory of the Maharaja of Rewa, where they are proprietors of the Marwas *pargannah*. They still cherish the hope of one day regaining their ancient possessions, and are said to have made a vow that they will not bind the turban on their heads until they are once more established in the fort of Agorî, the seat of their ancestors.

According to tradition thirty Baland Kharwâr Rajas were in succession rulers of Agorî, and twenty-two Chandel Rajas. Further information respecting the latter will be found in the chapter concerning the Chandel Rajpoots (*a*).

Bawâryâ.

In the jungles to the south of the Mirzapûr district is a very rude tribe, of primitive habits, and leading a precarious life. Their practice in raising crops is peculiar. Before the rainy season commences, timber is cut down in the forest, burnt, and reduced to ashes. When the seed is sown, the ashes are scattered over the ground together with it. This method of cultivation is called *bawanra*, from which word the tribe appears to have received its designation.

(*a*) Mirzapûr Pargannah Reports, by Mr. Roberts, Vol. V.

The harvest of grain which is reaped maintains the tribe only for a few months. For the rest of the time they are dependant on the flesh of animals and the roots of trees. The Bawậryâs are apparently few in number, and are found scattered about the hills (*a*).

It should be added that the *bawanra* method of cultivation is pursued by some of the aboriginal Cherûs and Kharwârs, as well as by the tribe already mentioned.

(*a*) Mirzapûr Pargannah Reports, by Mr. Roberts, Vol. V., p. 192.

CHAPTER III.

GIPSIES, JUGGLERS, ROPE-DANCERS, SNAKE-CHARMERS, THIMBLE-RIGGERS, AND ROBBERS.

NAT, KANJAR, MADARI, CHAI, AND BADHAK.

Nat.

THIS and the Kanjar tribe, in their normal condition, lead a vagrant life, avoiding houses, and preferring the shade of trees, or light temporary habitations,. to a fixed and permanent home. Their old habits, however, are being gradually broken down, for the steady and· onward progress of civilization in India is influencing for good even the most untamed and vagabond tribes.

These two races, although their modes of life are so much alike, are nevertheless quite distinct in India. It is commonly believed that the Gipsies of Europe have sprung from them. It would be deeply interesting to know in what respects the Gipsies of Spain differ from those of England, France, and other western countries, and also from one another ; and likewise whether the points of unlikeness are traceable in the clans of the two Indian tribes to which they are supposed to be related.

Wilson says that the Nats are "a tribe of vagrants, who live by feats of dexterity, sleight of hand, fortune-telling, and the like, and correspond in their habits with the Gipsies of Europe" (*a*). Yet all the members of the tribe have not the same occupation. It professes to have seven clans, which are, for the most part, separated from one another by their occupations.. These are the following:—

1. Kshatriya.
2. Snake-exhibitors.
3. Bear-exhibitors.
4. Jugglers.
5. Dancers.
6. Rope-dancers.
7. Monkey-exhibitors.

(*a*) Wilson's Glossary of Indian Terms, p. 369.

I have not learnt what is the connexion between the first or Kshatriya clan with the great Kshatriya or Rajpoot tribes. The distinctive professions which the clans follow, are perpetuated from father to son.

The Rope-dancers are expert gymnasts, and perform various clever antics with long bamboos. They make use of only one musical instrument, the drum.

The Nats will eat all kinds of flesh, except beef. They do not drink spirits and other intoxicating liquors. I am not aware that any Nat families are to be found residing in Benares, although they are constantly seen in the streets and suburbs of the city pursuing their peculiar avocations. There are a few families living in the town of Gangâpûr, eight miles off.

In the Bhâgalpûr district the Nats are divided into the northern and southern; the former being designated Chet, and the latter, Mâl. The Mâls are separated into three clans, *viz.*

1. Kamarpâli.
2. Dangarpâli.
3. Mârpâli.

The Nats, inhabiting the mountains to the north, are called by their southern brethren, Samarpâli. All the clans are most probably of the same origin (*a*).

In Oudh the Nats, according to Mr. P. Carnegy, have the following eight sub-divisions:—

1. Gwâliârî.
   1. Kapûrî.
   2. Bhâtu.
   3. Sarwânî.
2. Sanwat.
3. Brijbâsî.
4. Bachgotî.
5. Bijaniah.
6. Bareah.
7. Mahâwat.
8. Bâzîgar.

The Gwâliârîs are dealers in cattle; their women bleed, and extract teeth. The Sanwats pursue the same trade. These and the two last, namely the Mahawats and Bâzîgars, are Mahomedans converted from Hinduism. The Brijbâsîs perform in public by walking on stilts. They bury their dead. The Bachgotîs are wrestlers, and contend with the single stick. These also bury their dead. The Bijaniahs dance on the tight rope. Their dead are buried in an upright posture. The Bareahs are not public performers. They are fond of attending feasts uninvited. Their dead are buried. The Mahâwats trade in

(*a*) Buchanan's Eastern India, Vol. II, p. 126.

cattle. The Bâzîgars are conjurors. They also bury their dead. All the Nats are prone to drink to excess. They are, for the most part, of unclean habits. Many of them practise as doctors, and are expert in the use of herbs (*a*).

Dr. Wilton Oldham gives the following list of clans of the Nat tribe in the Ghazipûr district:—

1. Rârî.
2. Bhantû.
3. Gwâl.
4. Lodhra.
5. Magaiyah.
6. Jûgilah.
7. Jhassîth.

Kanjar.

The Kanjar and Nat tribes are supposed to be the same as the Gipsy tribes of Spain, England, and other parts of Europe.

In Benares the Kanjar is a maker of ropes and reed-matting. He also twists cotton and hemp into threads, which he sells ; and manufactures large brushes for the cleaning of cotton yarn. At the commencement of the hot season, he takes the sweet-scented *kaskas* grass and works it into a light bamboo frame. In Benares and the North-Western Provinces generally, where a hot wind prevails more or less for several months, this frame is inserted in the door-ways of bungalows, to the west, the direction in which it invariably blows. Being kept well saturated with water thrown upon it from the outside, the hot air, as it blows through, becomes suddenly cooled and damped, and enters the room to the exhilaration of all within.

The Kanjar tribe is divided into seven clans :—

1. Maraiya.
2. Sankat.
3. Bhains.
4. Sodâ.
5. Lakarhâr.
6. Goher.
7. Dhobî-bans.

The first six of these clans eat together, and inter-marry, but hold themselves entirely aloof from the last. Only the four first clans are found in Benares ; the remaining three inhabit the country further west. The Kanjars will not eat beef, but will eat everything else. Some of them are bird-catchers, and use a spiked rod for piercing little birds.

The Nats regard the Kanjars as unclean in comparison with themselves The latter, says Mr. P. Carnegy, are known also in the North-Western and

(*a*) Mr. P. Carnegy's Notes on the Races of Oudh, pp. 16, 17.

Central Provinces, as Sansîs and Syorâs, and frequently pass themselves off as Banjâras (*a*).

Madâri.

A tribe of snake-charmers and jugglers. They rear both snakes and scorpions, which they carry about the country for exhibition. In decoying snakes from holes, or from any places in which they may have secreted themselves, they are marvellously clever. They seem to accomplish the feat mainly by playing plaintive strains on a musical instrument. In tricks of jugglery they appear to be equally accomplished. The musical instrument on which they perform in public is called *tumbi* or *tomri*, and is made from the dried gourd of the bitter kaddu plant. It emits a sound like that produced by bagpipes.

Châi.

A class of jugglers, thimble-riggers, and adventurers, who attend fairs and other festivals like men of the same profession in England. They are notorious for all kinds of artifices for making money. They are found in Oudh and in the districts to the east. Gorakhpûr alone is said to possess upwards of thirteen thousand (*b*).

Badhak.

From *badha*, striking, killing, slaughter. A caste of professional robbers and assassins. Formerly, they committed great havoc in the country in association with Thugs, another class of murderers ; but of late years they have been much broken up, and have been compelled to resort to gentler avocations. Their chief haunts were in the border country of Oudh, where they lived with impunity under the lax government of the Oudh kings. It is impossible, however, for such persons to indulge in such pursuits while the administration is in the firm hands of British rulers. The Badhaks, therefore, have mostly taken to other modes of life, and have mingled with the masses. In some districts they are called Khors or Siyâr Marwas, on account of their habits of eating the flesh of the jackal (*c*).

(*a*) Mr. P. Carnegy's Notes on the Races of Oudh, p. 18.

(*b*) Census Report for 1865, Vol. II., p. 36.

(*c*) Mr. E. A. Reade's Inferior Castes of the North-Western Provinces, p. 38.

CHAPTER IV.

WORKERS IN LEATHER, LABOURERS, SERVANTS, WORKERS IN CANE AND PALM-LEAVES, SCAVENGERS.

CHAMAR, DOSADH, DHARKAR, MIHTAR OR BHANGI.

Chamâr.

THIS is one of the most numerous of the inferior castes. Many of its members are menial servants, especially those of the first or Jaiswârâ subdivision. They are willing, obedient, patient, and capable of great endurance; yet are apt to be light-fingered and deceitful. It is a singular phenomenon, and hard to be explained, that, although they come so much in contact with foreign residents in India, they should, nevertheless, have been so little improved by such intercourse. I believe that of all the Hindus who have been brought extensively under European influence, they have profited the least. This may partly be accounted for, but not wholly, by the degraded condition which they have held for many generations, whereby the caste intellect has become permanently blunted and enfeebled. This inability to assimilate new ideas and to advance beyond the old deteriorated mental standard of the caste, is apparent not merely among the Chamârs, but also among the inferior castes generally. There is a marked difference of intellectal power between them and all the superior castes, especially the Brahmanical. The *vis inertiæ* of the former is immeasurably greater than of the latter; and after the most persistent efforts to educate him, the low caste man seldom or never rises to even the mediocrity of ability exhibited by the better castes.

The higher castes look contemptuously on the Chamârs, and regard them as an unclean race. This is owing chiefly, perhaps, to the fact that they are traders in leather, an impure substance, in the estimation of Hindus. A Brahman or other Hindu of any strictness will touch nothing made of leather.

Hence, books bound with this material, are very obnoxious to such a man. This feeling, though still very strong in some parts of the country, is becoming much enfeebled among Hindus, of all castes, who associate with Europeans, or receive instruction in their schools. The word Chamâr comes from Châm, leather; and the members of the caste are tanners, leather-sellers, leather-cutters, leather-dyers, shoemakers, shoemenders, curriers, and harness-makers. There is, however, another reason for this supercilious disdain on the part of the better castes towards the Chamârs. It is commonly thought that they do not belong to the Hindu race, except by a very remote relationship; that, in short, they are properly out-castes, and have no right to be regarded as Hindus.

Who the Chamârs and other inferior castes originally were, has been for some time a puzzling question to ethnologists. From their appearance, complexion, and social position, it has been concluded, that some of them partially, and others entirely, are descended from aboriginal tribes. In this view, in the main, I concur. Yet that there has been a great intermingling of races in India, is indisputable. This is manifest from the countenances alone of many members of the lower castes. Some of these, especially the children, are of great beauty; and have thin lips, a well-moulded face, and an expression of intelligence equal, and even superior to, multitudes of Brahmans. An exemplification of this observation is sometimes strikingly seen in the caste under review.

In regard to the origin of the Chamâr caste, we are not left to mere assumptions. Manu states it authoritatively. The Kârâvara, or worker in leather, he says, is descended from a Nishâda father and Vaidiha mother (*a*). Now the Nishâda, on the same authority, is the offspring of a Brahman husband and Sudra wife (*b*); and the Vaidiha, of a Vaisya husband and Brahman wife (*c*). Consequently, the Kârâvara was one-half of Brahmanical, one-fourth of Vaisya, and one-fourth of Sudra descent. If the workers in leather of the present day are lineal descendants of the workers in leather of Manu's time, the Chamârs may fairly consider themselves of no mean degree, and may hold up their heads boldly in the presence of the superior castes. The rigidity and exclusiveness of caste prejudices among the Chamârs, are highly favorable to this supposition, as much so as, for the same reason, modern Brahmans may be held to be the posterity of Brahman ancestors who lived two thousand five hundred years ago.

(*a*) Manu, Chap. X, p. 36; see Introduction.

(*b*) *Ibid*, p. 8.

(*c*) *Ibid*, p. 17.

There is a tradition common among the Chamârs, from which, if true, we may gather that, in former times, Brahmans and Chamârs associated together in friendly intercourse, a thing impossible in the existing age. In the Sat Jug two men, one a Brahman, the other a Chamâr, it is said, were accustomed to bathe together in the Ganges. One day the Chamâr, not being able to perform his ablutions as usual, requested the Brahman to make obeisance to the river in his name. The Brahman complied with his request, and while in the act of doing so, Gangâ, the goddess of the sacred stream, appeared, and receiving the offering with both her hands, removed from her wrist a valuable *kangan* or bracelet, and gave it to the Brahman for presentation to the Chamâr. But the Brahman kept it to himself; on which account he was cursed by the goddess, who declared that thenceforward he should beg for his subsistence. From that time, it is added, Brahmans have been beggars.

The Chamârs speak of themselves as having sprung from a common ancestor, Nonâ Chamâr, whose name they invoke in times of sorrow and trouble, or when visited by sickness, or bitten by snakes, or stung by scorpions, or generally in any season of calamity. The Nonâ Chamain (female of Chamâr) is regarded by Hindu families as a witch, whose invisible presence and agency are to be avoided by the performance of certain ceremonies and incantations. Hindu children are bidden to beware of Nonâ Chamain, and have their imaginations excited by dread of her, in the same way as English children are frightened at the mention of ghosts and goblins. The caste has seven sub-divisions in Benares, which are somewhat different in other places.

1. Jaiswârâ. The principal sub-caste. Many Jaiswârâs are servants.
2. Dhûsia or Jhûsia. Shoe-makers and harness-makers.
3. Kori. Weavers, grooms, field-laborers.
4. Dosâdh. Weavers, grooms, field-laborers.
5. Kuril. Workers in leather.
6. Rangiya. Leather-dyers.
7. Jâtûâ. Labourers.

The Jaiswârâs do not carry burdens on their shoulders, but on their heads. Should they, at any time, neglect this ancient custom of their order, they would be liable to ejection from their caste. Next to them, in the above list, should properly be inserted the Chamâr Mangatiwas, who are really as distinct a subdivision as any of the rest. These people are professional beggars, and subsist on the generosity of the Jaiswârâs. Once a year they visit all the families of this minor caste, and have a recognized prescriptive right to a *pice* (a small copper coin, in value between a farthing and a half-penny) and a round flat cake, called *roti*, from every house. This much they can claim; but they occasionally receive other small favors, in addition. The same families of Chamâr Mangatiwas, or their descendants, beg of the same families of Jaiswârâs, or their descendants, from generation to generation. This is their only source of livelihood, and only occupation.

The Dhûsias properly belong to Ghazipûr and other districts further East, where they may intermarry with the Jaiswârâs, though in Benares they keep aloof from them. All these sub-divisional castes in Benares are separate from one another, including the Chamâr Mangatiwas,—who form in reality an eighth sub-caste,—and do not intermarry or eat cooked food together. The Koris come from Oudh; the Kurils from the Central and Lower Doâb; the Jâtûâs from the Western Provinces (*a*). In the supplemental Glossary of Sir Henry Elliot, edited by Mr. Beames, the latter states in a note that Jhûsia is a mere local name, from Jhûsi, near Allahabad. That the Dhûsias or Jhûsias may have originally proceeded from a village or town named Dhûsi or Jhûsi, is probable; but in regard to this clan of Chamârs, the tribe generally assigns to them the country eastward of Saidpûr, in the Ghazipûr district, as is so accurately stated in the text by Sir Henry Elliot, and not that of Allahabad and its neighbourhood. From enquiry I understand that there are none of this sub-division at Jhûsi, near Allahabad.

The Dosâdhs are very numerous in Shahâbâd, and in the districts of Gorakhpûr and Ghazipûr. In each of the two latter districts, they number upwards of twenty thousand persons. There are also many in Benares, Azimgarh, Mirzapûr, and the Lower Doâb. In some places they are addicted to agriculture; but in others, as Ghazipûr, they are notorious thieves and scoundrels. Mr. E. A. Reade states that many Dosâdhs were amongst the native troops who fought under Clive at the battle of Plassey; and adds that 'they are strong, take service readily, and are generally trustworthy' (*b*). The clan is sometimes employed in very menial occupations, for instance, as executioners, and to remove dead bodies.

Two other clans in Benares have come under my notice:—

1. Katua. Leather-cutters.
2. Tantua. These manufacture strips or strings of leather, called *tânt*.

(*a*) Elliot's Supplemental Glossary, Vol. I., p. 70.

(*b*) Mr. E. A. Reade's Inferior Castes of the North-Western Provinces, p. 16.

The Chamârs form one of the most numerous tribes in these Provinces, where, according to the Census of 1865, they exceed three millions and a half. They are found largely in every district, except on the hills, where their numbers are small. They are a hard-working, plodding, though down-trodden and degraded people. It would be worthy of the enterprising and progressive Government of these Provinces to pay special attention to the elevation of this and other similarly laborious and debased tribes.

In various parts of these Provinces, the Chamârs have clans differing from those given above. The Jatlots are in Rohilkhand; the Aharwârs, Sakarwârs, and Dohârs, in the Central Doâb; the Garaiyas, Magahyas, Dakshiniyas, and Kanaujiyas, in Behar (a).

Dharkâr.

A very low caste, much lower, for instance, than the Chamârs, or workers in leather, yet considerably above the Doms. The members are permitted to come near a high caste Hindu, and are therefore not treated with absolute contempt. They are workers in reeds and canes, and manufacture cane stools and chairs, palm-leaf fans, matting for floors, and the like. Some of them are employed as porters. The caste has seven sub-divisions, as follows:—

The Dharkâr caste of Benares.	*The Dharkâr caste of Mirzapûr.*
1. Ben-bansî.	1. Ben-bansi.
2. Turia.	2. Barûâ.
3. Ajudhia-bâsî.	3. Basor.
4. Baskhor or Bansphor.	4. Dakhaniya.
5. Litkahâ.	5. Barjîhâ.
6. Basor.	6. Ghâtiya.
7. Thop.	7. Dom.

There is a considerable discrepancy in these two lists. This, however, to one accustomed to the ignorance of the inferior castes, is no matter for astonishment. I believe that a dozen lists taken in the same number of towns would be all different, not only in regard to this caste, but also in regard to most of the lower castes.

These sub-divisional castes are really distinct castes, and do not intermarry or eat together. The Ben-bansîs are the most respectable, and, in social

(a) Supplemental Glossary, Vol. I., p. 71.

position, are held to be superior to the rest. The Dom included in the Mirzapûr list is a mistake. In comparison with him a Dharkâr is a clean and honorable man. Some of the Doms are workers in cane and make baskets, like the Dharkârs, which circumstance may account for their being erroneously ranked by many natives amongst the Dharkâr sub-castes. Yet Dharkârs occasionally say that the Doms belong to their tribe, and Doms sometimes say the same. See the section on the Doms.

The Dharkârs are found chiefly in the districts to the east of the Jumna, where they are numerous. In Gorakhpûr they number upwards of ten thousand persons, and in Mirzapûr they are more than five thousand.

Mihtar, *Bhangî*, *Halâlkhor*, or *Chûhrâ*.

The Sweeper or Scavenger caste, a very unclean and despicable tribe, in the opinion of Hindus. It has seven sub-divisions, which vary in different places. In Benares they are as follows:—

1. Shaikh.
2. Hela.
3. Lâlbegî.
4. Ghazipûrî Râût.
5. Dînâpûrî Râût.
6. Hârî.
7. Bânsphor (Bamboo-cutters.)

The Shaikhs are Mahomedans. The Helas are distinguished from the rest by not touching dogs, an important distinction, in the eyes of the caste, because the cleaning and feeding of dogs is one of the usual duties that it performs. Many gentlemen keep Mihtars solely for this purpose. Moreover, the Helas will not eat food left by all people, only that left by Hindus (*a*). The Lâlbegîs and Ghazipûrî Râûts, on the contrary, will eat food left at the tables of Europeans, as well as the leavings of Hindus. There are many members of the first four sub-divisions in Benares. The Dînâpûrî Râûts agree in taste with the Helas, in rejecting the food of Europeans ; and therefore keep themselves quite apart from the Ghazipûrî Râûts. There are no families of Hârîs in Benares ; but here and there one may be found engaged in some menial calling. The Bânsphors are not properly sweepers at all, for they gain a livelihood by the manufacture of baskets.

In Mirzapûr I heard of another sub-caste of Mihtars, called Gadahla. These people rear donkeys, and use them for removing refuse from the city.

(*a*) Elliot's Supplemental Glossary, Vol. I., p. 32.

All these sub-castes are perfectly distinct from one another, and do not intermarry. Mr. P. Carnegy states that in Oudh, however, the various clans do intermarry. Most of them in some other districts of India will eat the flesh of animals that die of disease or old age ; but not in Benares. It is optional with the caste to bury or burn their dead. The Shaikhs of course follow the Mahomedan custom of burial. The Lâlbegîs once a year erect a long pole covered with flags, colored cloth, and other things, including cocoa-nuts, in honor of Pîr Zahr or Lâl Guru, as he is otherwise called ; to which they render worship as to a god. In this they are like the low Mahomedans, who worship a similarly decorated pole, erected to Gâzî Mîân, a *pîr* or saint.

Sir H. Elliot gives the following list of the sub-divisions of the Mihtars: Banîwâl, Bîlparwâr, Tâk, Gahlot, Kholî, Gâgrâ, Sardhî, Chandâlia, Sirsâwâl, and Siriyâr ; and says that they differ from the Helas and Râûts. In Benares, however, as I have observed above, the two last clans are included in the tribe, although it is possible they may be excluded elsewhere.

In villages the Mihtar is commonly called Chûhrâ, although the other designations are also in use.

Mr. E. A. Reade remarks respecting the Bhangîs, that 'they are known to be brave, and to aspire to military service. Runjeet Singh had one or more Bhangî corps. But they cannot be assorted with other classes without much prejudice' (*a*).

(*a*) Mr. E. A. Reade's Inferior Castes of the North-Western Provinces, p. 25.

CHAPTER V.

VILLAGE WATCHMEN, POULTERERS, BURNERS OF THE DEAD.

PASI, KHATIK, DOM, ACHARJ.

Pâsî.

THIS is one of the lowest of the castes. It is not regarded by Hindus proper as allied in any way to themselves. There is reason for believing that the Pâsîs are an aboriginal race. My own conviction is, that they are also of a non-Aryan type. They have, however, sunk so low socially, and have been so long despised and shunned by the conquering tribes, as to have lost all traces of former independence and honour. Their own tradition is, that they sprang from the famous Parasrâm, not in the order of nature, but from the perspiration that flowed from his forehead, by which five Pâsîs were produced, from whom the entire race has descended. This interesting event is said to have taken place at Anantâl in Oudh.

In villages Pâsîs are commonly employed as watchmen to catch thieves ; in return for which they receive either a plot of land or some other consideration. Should they fail in producing the thief who has stolen any property, they have to make good the loss. In addition, Pâsîs tend pigs, and labour in fields and gardens. Some of the Pâsî men are said to be of fair complexion. They are divided into several sub-castes, or clans, as follows:—

1. Jaiswârâ.
2. Kaînswât, or Kaithwân.
3. Gûjar.
4. Tirsuliya.
5. Pasîwân.
6. Chiriyamâr.
7. Biadîh.
8. Bihârî.
9. Bhar (?).

I have also heard the Belkhars spoken of as Pâsîs. The Pâsîs reckon the Khatiks as one of the clans of their caste, although the Khatiks have seven clans of their own, one of which, however, embraces the Pâsîs. The Bhars are sometimes classed among the Pâsîs. They have a tradition that in ancient times they were one and the same race, which is indeed very probable. A separate treatise on the Bhars is given in this work, to which the reader is referred for further information respecting this interesting but unfortunate people. Their custom at marriage festivals is noticed in the section on the Khatiks. As these inferior tribes evidently coalesce with one another now, it is, I conceive, exceedingly probable that in ancient times they were associated together.

The Pâsîs were once very powerful in Oudh. "In the Kheri (Mahomadi) district," says Mr. P. Carnegy, "the Pâsîs, Rajpâsîs, Aruks, Motîs, and Khatiks, are looked upon as kindred classes. The Rajpâsîs of that part of Oudh say that they are descended from Ratan Datt Singh, a Thâkur of Pataungâh near Nimkhâr, and a Pâsî woman who bore him several children. These at his death are said to have inherited their father's estate; and, in time, from them a powerful clan has descended. They are alleged to have usurped, and to have held, for some generations, the great Matholi estate, their chief assuming the title of Raja; and they attribute their loss of that property to the treachery of the head of the Ahban clan of Rajpoots, between whose daughter and the son of the Rajpâsî chief a marriage was being arranged." This Rajpoot, he adds, put to death most of the Rajpâsîs whom he had invited to the wedding, and seized their lands. Those who escaped settled in other parts of the country.

Mr. Carnegy gives the following sub-divisions of the Pâsîs in the Sîtâpûr district: Rajpâsî, Aruk, Bachar, Mohni, Khatik. "It is affirmed," he says, "by some that they are a branch of the Kerât tribe of Dwârkâ. An heroic Pâsî named Sen of Barniya, figures prominently in the poetical accounts of the celebrated battles of Alâ and Udal; and this gives colour to their asserted connexion with ancient Kanouj, where those heroes flourished. It seems to be admitted in the Sîtâpûr district, that the Pâsîs were once entire masters of Khairâbâd. The Aruks of Khairâbâd state that their ancestors formerly ruled in Chittore, and that members of their tribe abound in other trans-Gangetic districts. Others of the Araks say that they are descended from Ratan Dich, who lived in the days of the Mahâbhârat war. There is a considerable Aruk colony in *Pargannah* Atrolâ, of the Gondâh district, the members of which say that their ancestor came from Sândila in Hardui" (*a*).

(*a*) Mr. P. Carnegy's Races of Oudh, pp. 61, 62.

Khatik.

THE lower castes, to some extent, run into one another. For instance, the Pâsî caste enumerates several clans, such as the Khatik and Gûjar, as belonging to themselves, which are properly distinct tribes. The reason of this is generally to be found in the similarity of their employment, although they take care not to intermarry or to eat together. In this way the Khatiks also include the Pâsîs among the clans of their castes. These are seven, as follows :—

1. Bakar Kâ Sâo.
2. Chalan Mahrâo.
3. Ghor Charâo.
4. Ajudhiya-bâsî.
5. Sunkhar.
6. Baurea.
7. Pâsî.

The first clan, Bakar Kâ Sâo, sells and slaughters goats. The Chalan Mahrâos are workers in leather, especially in using it for covering or lining. The Ghor Charâos are grooms. The Ajudhiya-bâsîs came originally from Ajudhiya in Oudh. They sell fruit and vegetables, and do general work for hire. The Sunkhars are poulterers and fruit-sellers. All these sub-castes feed swine, and consequently are regarded with abomination by the upper castes. None of them intermarry, or eat together. At one time the Sunkhars and Pâsîs smoked the same hookah, but the former have so sunk in the estimation of the latter from the time that they commenced to trade in poultry, that this act of mutual esteem and confidence has been discontinued. Some of the Khatiks extract the *tari* or *arrack* from the palm tree. Others are butchers, and stonecutters; but as a class they rear poultry and pigs.

At the marriage festivals of Khatiks, including Pâsîs, boys dress themselves in women's clothes and dance in public; but the Bhars, who are sometimes classed among the Pâsîs, do not observe this custom, and make use of the drum and other instruments of music on such occasions, which the others do not.

The Khatiks are a numerous caste, and are found in almost every district of these Provinces.

Dom.

The Dom is generally considered by Hindus to be the type and representative of all uncleanness. In their opinion humanity finds its extremest degradation in him. If they regard him at all, it is from a distance; but any near approach would awaken in their breasts the utmost abhorrence. He is loathed and avoided as scum and filth; in short, no language can properly designate the social degradation of his position.

The occupation of the Dom is, in some respects, the same as that of the Dharkâr caste, namely to make cane chairs and stools, and palm-leaf fans. He also manufactures various articles from the bark of the bamboo. He eats the flesh of diseased animals, and of such as die of their own accord. He is usually very poor, and is dressed in tattered garments. But this is not always the case; for in Benares there are two or three families of this caste living in good houses, and possessing considerable wealth. In the same city Doms are commonly employed as street-sweepers.

In Benares, and perhaps in other cities of India likewise, the burning of the dead cannot be performed without the assistance of the Dom. On the arrival of the dead body at the place of cremation, which in that city is at the base of one of the steep stairs or *ghats*, called the Burning Ghât, leading down from the streets above to the bed of the river Ganges, the Dom supplies five logs of wood, which he lays in order upon the ground, the rest of the wood being given by the family of the deceased. When the pile is ready for burning, a handful of lighted straw is brought by the Dom, and is taken from him and applied by one of the chief members of the family to the wood. The Dom is the only person who can furnish the light for the purpose ; and if from any circumstance the services of one cannot be obtained, great delay and inconvenience are apt to arise. The Dom exacts his fee for three things, namely first for the five logs, secondly, for the bunch of straw, and, thirdly, for the light.

Some persons have thought, and with great reason, that the members of this caste, if indeed it can be called such, are descendants of an aboriginal tribe. Dark complexioned, low of stature, and somewhat repulsive in appearance, they are readily distinguishable from all the better castes of Hindus. From their aspect they seem to have sprung originally from the jungles rather than from civilized regions. Yet there is reason for supposing that in early times they were a people of some power and importance. There is a tradition that they formerly occupied the country beyond the Gogra river, and were neighbours of the Bhars, another aboriginal race. Remains of ancient forts still bear their name (*a*). Their degradation may be accounted for in the same manner as that of the Bhars, namely by being conquered and subjected by Hindus, who instead of introducing them into their own castes, a course never adopted with

(*a*) Elliot's Supplemental Glossary, Vol. I., p. 84.

the aborigines of the land throughout all the ages of Hinduism, behaved towards them in the true spirit of caste prejudice and pride, and treated them at length with all the contempt of which they were capable, so that they gradually sank to the present position of extremest abjectness which they at present occupy.

In the Province of Kumaon, the Doms are a much more respectable class of people than those bearing the same name in Benares and the eastern districts generally. They are in fact the artizan class, and are employed as carpenters, masons, and the like.

Respecting this race, Sir H. Elliot remarks, that "tradition fixes their residence to the north of the Gogra, touching the Bhars on the east, in the vicinity of Rohini. Several old forts testify to their former importance, and still retain the names of their founders; as, for instance, Domdiha and Domangarh. Râmgarh and Sahankot, on the Rohini, are also Dom forts" (*a*).

Achârj or Achârya.

The term Achârj is used variously. It is applied to a religious teacher, and also to the head of a Hindu monastery, and to the chief priest of a temple. Wilson says that it designates those Brahmans who are employed among the Marathas as cooks. It is a title, moreover, he affirms, of Tamil carpenters and other artisans (*b*). In certain parts of the North-Western Provinces, a very low class of persons are called Achârj. These receive the clothing of persons after their death.

(*a*) Elliot's Supplemental Glossary, Vol. I., p. 84.
(*b*) Wilson's Glossary, p. 3.

CHAPTER VI.

INFERIOR CASTES LIVING CHIEFLY ON THE BORDERS OF TOWNS AND VILLAGES, OR IN THE JUNGLE.

DHANGAR, BARI, VED, DHANUKH, AHELIYA OR AHERIYA.

Dhângar.

A TRIBE chiefly employed in felling the jungle. They are an industrious and active people. 'They put their hands to any service, and are able-bodied and well-conducted' (*a*). Wilson remarks that the Dhângars are 'a tribe of people inhabiting the hill country in Râmgarh and Chhotâ Nâgpûr. Some of them come periodically to the plains for employment, and are enjoyed as labourers and scavengers' (*b*). These Dhângars appear to be different from the shepherds and wool-weavers of this name in Southern India, although they may be the same as the Dhângar cultivators of Telingâna; yet I suppose, these are much higher in social rank than the Dhângars of Northern India.

The Dhângars are found chiefly in Gorakhpûr and Behar; but they are met with, to some extent, both in Benares and Mirzapûr.

Bâri.

A caste consisting of only one clan. Their special and peculiar occupation is to stitch together large leaves by the insertion of small wooden pegs. They make a kind of cup for shop-keepers in the bazar, in which they wrap their wares when sold. On occasion of great dinners given by private families, or at caste banquets, which are very numerous, and to which all the castes are addicted, they make broad platters of leaves, for holding the food intended for the guests. In addition, they are employed as torch-bearers, and also as barbers. Formerly, it is said, they proved themselves excellent soldiers in the king of Oudh's service; and some of them even became Rajas (*c*). Their widows

(*a*) Mr. E. A. Reade's Inferior Castes of the North-Western Provinces, pp. 15, 16.

(*b*) Wilson's Glossary, p. 135.

(*c*) Elliot's Supplemental Glossary, Vol. I., p. 49; Wilson's Glossary of Indian Terms, p. 64.

remarry. As the Bârîs of necessity spend much of their time in the jungle in collecting leaves, they are not only employed in their special occupation of stitching them together, but also in cutting down the trees of the forest. They have the reputation of great fidelity to their employers. Hindus have a proverb, 'the Bârî dies fighting for his master (*a*).'

Ved.

A low tribe living chiefly in the jungles, where they collect together broad leaves, and manufacture tiny skewers of wood intended for stitching leaves into various shapes, such as, plates or cups, for eating food from, or for holding sweatmeats, rice, and other things. They bring the leaves in great bundles, and the skewers also, into the city for sale. This tribe is I think the same as that described by Wilson as Beda, the members of which are considered to be out-castes, or Chandâls, and live by the chase as hunters and fowlers (*b*).

Dhânukh.

This word is the same as 'dhânukh,' a bow. The members of the tribe or caste are fowlers and archers. They are also employed as watchmen, and in various menial occupations. The women of this caste are in great request in towns and cities as midwives.

The Dhânukhs have descended, according to the Padma Purânâ, says Sir H. Elliot, from a Châmar husband and a Chandâl wife. 'From Dhânukhs have proceeded the Aheriyas, who are also occupied as fowlers. Aheriyas are said not to consume dead carcases as the Dhânukhs do.' This caste has no objection to the flesh of pigs. The seven sub-divisions of this caste, are, on the same authority, as follows :—

1. Longbasta.
2. Mathuriya.
3. Kathariya.
4. Jaiswârâ.
5. Magahya.
6. Dojwâr.
7. Chhilatya.

These clans hold no social intercourse with one another either in the way of marriage, or of eating, drinking, or smoking.

In some districts the caste is very numerous. In Shâjahânpûr, Bareilly, Farakhabâd, Mainpûrî, Etawah, and Cawnpûr, it numbers many thousands. Smaller communities are found in other places.

(*a*) Mr. Reade's Inferior Races of the North-Western Provinces, p. 14.
(*b*) Wilson's Glossary, p. 70.

Aheliya or Aheriya.

A tribe of wild and uncivilized people, exceedingly poor, and almost destitute of clothing. They catch snakes, roast, and eat them. This in fact is the chief employment of some of them. In various parts of the country they are brought under better influences than those to which they were formerly exposed; so that there is reason to hope for their improvement. Indeed, in some places, as in the Aligarh district, they are beginning to cultivate land, and are becoming more civilized every day. Even there, however, they are still notoriously bad characters.

The Aheliyas are, to some extent, fowlers. Elliot says they sprang from the Dhânukhs.